Harold Robbins

BY THE SAME AUTHOR

Beautiful Shadow: A Life of Patricia Highsmith
The Lying Tongue, a novel

Harold Robbins

The Man Who Invented Sex

Andrew Wilson

BLOOMSBURY

Published by Bloomsbury USA, New York
Distributed to the trade by Holtzbrinck Publishers

All papers used by Bloomsbury USA are natural, recyclable
products made from wood grown in well-managed
forests. The manufacturing processes conform to the
environmental regulations of the country of origin.

LIBRARY OF CONGRESS CATALOGING-IN-PUBLICATION DATA

Wilson, Andrew, 1967 June 6–
Harold Robbins: the man who invented sex / Andrew Wilson.—1st U.S. ed.
p. cm.
ISBN-10 1–59691–008–9
ISBN-13 978–1–59691–008–9
1. Robbins, Harold, 1916–1997. 2. Novelists, American—20th century—Biography.
I. Title.

PS3568.O224Z95 2007
813'.54—dc22
[B]
2007009067

First U.S. Edition 2007

1 3 5 7 9 10 8 6 4 2

Typeset by Hewer Text UK Ltd, Edinburgh
Printed in the United States of America by Quebecor World Fairfield

INTRODUCTION

ON SUNDAY, 25 APRIL 1982, sixty-five-year-old best-selling novelist Harold Robbins was sitting at the bar in his Beverly Hills mansion sipping a scotch on the rocks. As he took a swig of his drink, he smiled to himself. After all, he had a lot to be pleased about—he had just completed his seventeenth novel, *Spellbinder*, while his previous book, *Goodbye, Janette*, which had had the largest advance first printing of any novel in the world when it was published in the summer of 1981, occupied the number-seven slot on that day's *New York Times* paperback best-seller list.

A few hours earlier he had hosted a party at his Phyllis Morris–designed house on Tower Grove Drive, overlooking Los Angeles, to celebrate the marriage of his twenty-six-year-old daughter, Caryn, to her boyfriend, Michael Press. As befits a man labeled the "godfather of the airport novel" and the "Onassis of supermarket literature," the party was a lavish one: guests drank jeroboams of the best champagne and feasted on great dollops of caviar. At the end of the reception a family friend walked over to Robbins and pointed to a picture of a glamorous-looking brunette on the wall. "A very interesting painting," the guest asked. "Who's it of?" Robbins, who, despite his satyrical image, prided himself on his sharp, calculating mind, blinked and, for once, was lost for words. "I don't know," he mumbled. "I don't know."[1] The subject of the portrait was in fact his wife, Grace, a petite, beautiful younger woman to whom he had been married for seventeen years.

Grace, who had overheard the conversation, thought initially that her husband must have been joking, but when she realized he really didn't recognize her image, she called the emergency services and he was rushed to hospital. There the author was diagnosed as having had a minor stroke that affected his brain in a particularly cruel manner: he was left suffering from aphasia, a condition that meant he often forgot his words while trying to speak. The impact on his writing was even more severe. Something he had once described as easy—next to masturbation, it's the most fun thing you can do by yourself, he said—was now painfully difficult. Whereas he had been able to bash out five thousand words a day and finish a novel within the space of three months—he was known as "the man with the smoking typewriter"—now his sentences had been reduced to something resembling alphabet soup, a messy scramble of inverted phrases and garbled grammar.

Had this fact been reported in the press, the less kind might have felt tempted to make a joke about the author's ill-flowing sentences; as his style had always been awkward and clumsy and sometimes so basic it often approached the infantile, nobody would notice the difference between Robbins's writing pre- and poststroke. But the novelist was the first to admit that he wasn't so much a writer per se as a storyteller, a producer of accelerated narratives that, during the last half of the twentieth century, gripped the popular imagination. He dismissed the finer points of stylistics as irrelevant, a mere distraction from the unstoppable stampede of the story.

His 1961 novel *The Carpetbaggers*—which was made into a film starring George Peppard, Alan Ladd, and Carroll Baker—was estimated to be the fourth most read title in history, while at one point he was said to be selling forty thousand copies of his books a day. "There are individual books by other authors that come up and do as well as a particular book of mine," he said, "but I do it every time."[2]

Contemporary Authors stated that, during Robbins's lifetime, he had shifted an astonishing 750 million copies of his books worldwide. "Do I think of myself as a literary man?" he said, answering a journalist's question. "Hell, no. I'm a story-teller. Literature follows the story-tellers. Just look how Dumas and Dickens are still being read today . . . What I write about sex and violence reflects contemporary America. You know, if there was no such thing as the written word I would be telling stories at street corners."[3]

In the process of becoming a best-selling author, he transformed himself into a brand, describing himself as "the Coca-Cola of the publishing industry."[4] Indeed, Robbins's fame has been such that he has been mentioned in an episode of *Fawlty Towers*, the 1988 film

D.O.A. starring Dennis Quaid, and more recently in a song by the band Sleeper. Paul Gitlin, the attorney and agent who negotiated increasingly large advances and whose name Harold managed to slip into many of his books, said, at the height of his client's success, that the author was a "singular role model for writers . . . the standard by which everyone else compares their success. He has never had anything but best-sellers."[5]

He was one of the first authors to realize that publicizing a novel was just as important as writing it, and in the late 1960s and early 1970s he toured America on a "blitzkrieg promotion."[6] "Harold is the P.T. Barnum of the book business," said Joseph E. Levine, who produced four films based on Robbins's books. "He eats up this circus life. Some writers won't lift a finger to help the book, the picture or themselves, but not Harold. I've never asked him to cross a tightrope over Times Square, but he'd do just about anything else I ask."[7]

When readers picked up one of the twenty novels that Robbins wrote during his lifetime, they knew what they were getting: a heady mix of sex and sentimentalism, poverty and power, glamour and glitz. Although he often told interviewers that he was a "people writer"—constructing his novels not according to a carefully planned plot but around certain strong personalities—his characters are, ironically, oddly flat creatures. And despite his favored device of intertwining first-person narrative with third person, we seldom get a sense of a character's interior life.

Yet it could be argued that there was no need to get under the skin of his protagonists, as his readers felt they were already familiar with his characters, which were, typically, thinly veiled portraits of iconic figures such as Howard Hughes and Jean Harlow (*The Carpetbaggers*), playboy Porfirio Rubirosa (*The Adventurers*), and Lana Turner (*Where Love Has Gone*). "With Harold's books we'd play the guessing game and there's nothing more fun than the guessing game," says best-selling author Jackie Collins. "Who is that mogul, who is that actress, who is this sexually available babe?"[8] His fans transferred whatever they knew, or thought they knew, about such pop cultural personalities onto the characters in his novels in much the same way as moviegoers project their own fantasies and desires onto a film star on the silver screen.

As one of the pioneers of the "Hollywood novel," Robbins cast himself in the role of a movie mogul. "Hemingway once asked me what my literary ambitions were," Robbins said. "I told him, 'Wealth.' And I got it."[9] With his homes in Los Angeles, the South of France, and Acapulco, a luxury boat—he often boasted he was "the only goddam author with his own yacht"—together with his fleet of fourteen cars, his loud clothes, his string of beautiful women, his orgies, and his drugs, he constructed himself as a larger-than-life, almost filmic personality.

Similarly, his books are, perhaps, the nearest literary equivalent to the cinematic experience, documents of pure narrative, populated by characters as thin as celluloid itself. During the 1960s and 1970s his work was so popular with film and television executives that one commentator observed that even "if he wrote a note to the milkman three film studios would bid for it."[10] Another critic explained his appeal: "Robbins knows the great Hollywood art, he keeps his story moving, shifting expertly from tears to laughter and from desperation to triumph."[11]

It's fitting, then, that Robbins—who won no distinguished literary prizes when he was alive—was awarded the "distinction" of having a star named after him on Hollywood Boulevard. Today the Walk of Fame, with its souvenir shops, fast-food outlets, and gaudy tourist traps is, like Robbins himself, a celebration of everything that is vulgar and tacky. Trainer-clad tourists shuffle up and down the street, heads bent, as they scan the pavement for the names of their favorite celebrities. Robbins's star is located in a particularly apposite position—near the twin attractions of *The Guinness Book of Records* and *Ripley's Believe It or Not* (he adored breaking publishing records, and like Ripley, the newspaper columnist who traveled the world in search of the outlandish and the bizarre, he often pushed truth to its outer limits) and right outside the former Erotic Museum—at 6741 Hollywood Boulevard. The property also once housed a business belonging to Shirley Maxwell, famous for fashioning padded brassieres, nicknamed "who can tells"; Paramount Studios was one of her biggest customers. At the end of the 1930s the building was purchased by Louis Epstein, whose Pickwick Books became something of a landmark on the strip.

If Robbins were alive today—he died in 1997, age eighty-one—he would no doubt appreciate the fact that his star is located outside a building associated with both sex and books. After all, he was arguably the first author to write about sex in popular, mass-market novels. For many readers of mainstream commercial fiction in the second half of the twentieth century, he was undoubtedly the man who invented sex. "Harold was the first person to brand himself as a trademark for a particular kind of sexy novel," says Michael Korda, his editor at Simon & Schuster, "so that all over the world it represented the forbidden."[12] Camille Paglia believes that Robbins's novels—which she says generated a kind of "sizzle" around publication, "a sense of taboo, a sense of transgression"—represented "the huge amoral energies, the tornadoes, that are loose in industrial capitalism . . . Harold Robbins was a prophet of sensibility that used to be scorned. 'This is America! This is the voice of America!' "[13]

In 1948 Robbins's first novel, *Never Love a Stranger*, was one of the books the Philadelphia vice squad seized from a number of stores and prosecuted on grounds of "immorality and obscenity." A year later Robbins and his New York publisher, Knopf, successfully fought the test case and in due course cleared the ground for greater freedoms of sexual expression.

Robbins—whose twin obsessions of money and sex enabled him to live out his own version of the American dream, metamorphosing himself into the world's first playboy writer—himself later took advantage of another famous ruling: Grove's and Penguin's 1960 victory against the outlawing of D. H. Lawrence's unexpurgated *Lady Chatterley's Lover*. "The *Lady Chatterley* victories meant that you could have all these classics at last, but it also meant that there were new freedoms to be had," says academic and author John Sutherland. "And Robbins was quick off the mark."[14]

In today's sex-saturated society it's difficult to imagine the effect that Robbins's books had on the popular consciousness, but he was, adds Sutherland, a "pioneer in the field."[15] Jann Robbins, the author's widow, remembers her grandmother reading *The Carpetbaggers* in bed by flashlight. If she had to take it out in public, she would cover it in a brown paper bag, and afterward she took a match to the pages of the novel and burned it.

Robbins loved telling stories about his life and passing them off as fact. Typical is the anecdote he told about having married a Chinese dancer named Muriel Ling, his first wife, who was bitten by a parrot, a gift from her father on her wedding day; the injury, he said, led to an attack of psittacosis, and she died six months later. Although this story was frequently reported in newspaper and magazine profiles of the author—it even made its way into his obituaries—it was nothing more than a fiction. Harold was the consummate teller of tall tales, both in his novels and, even more intriguingly, in his life. He was a master of self-invention and reinvention, constantly elaborating the narrative of his own existence.

Interestingly, Robbins chose to tell these anecdotes not only to journalists but also to friends and family, even to his wives and lovers, who blindly accepted his version of the truth. As a result, even those closest to him did not know the real Harold Robbins. With each telling of these stories Robbins came to believe in the exotic alternative narrative he had fashioned for himself until, toward the end of his life, it's questionable whether he was able to separate the outlandish fiction he had created for himself from the reality.

The stroke that threatened to destroy whatever writing ability he had left, on the day of his daughter's wedding in 1982, was perhaps a sign that his capacity for self-fictionalization was reaching a crisis point. If he could no longer write—no longer tell stories—what identity did he have left? Toward the end of his life he looked back at his career and at some of the critically appraised early novels that he had written before the success of *The Carpetbaggers* catapulted him into superstar status and, some believe, was responsible for his undoing. Could he have achieved more? Had he really sold out as some people thought? Did he end up despising his readers—and himself? And what were the psychological effects of transforming oneself into a fictional creation?

This book is an attempt to try to understand Harold Robbins, both as a cultural phenomenon and as a man. Although he left no diaries or journals and precious few letters—he believed that if you were going to write, you'd damn well better get paid for it—I have consulted the archives of his agents, publishers, and film producers and spoken to those who knew him, his editors, friends, enemies, and some of his many, many lovers. "A man is a thousand parts," Robbins wrote in his 1969 novel *The Inheritors*. "All of them other people."[16]

1

"Of all the people I knew, I knew myself least of all."
—*Never Love a Stranger*

THE TIRED-LOOKING woman clutched the bundle of rags closer to her breast. Weak and exhausted, she steadied herself on the railings outside the orphanage, before sitting down on the step. Although it was dark, she looked around to check that no one was near before peeling back the swaddling to reveal the face of her newborn baby. As she traced her fingers over his skin, she felt the tears that she had tried to suppress form in her eyes and fall onto her little boy's cheek. Biting her lip, she willed the tears to stop, but they kept flowing, waking the child from his sleep. Knowing that she did not have long, she raised the boy upward toward the sky and asked God's forgiveness for what she was about to do. She said a silent prayer to herself, placed an envelope inside the rags, kissed him on the forehead, and then placed him on the step. Almost instantly the baby cried out, and although every cell in her body ached for the child, she knew she dared not pick him up. As she walked away into the night, she told herself that the monks who ran the orphanage would look after her boy better than she could ever do. She had done the right thing.

Harold Robbins's beginnings were as dramatic as anything found in his fiction. Born to unknown parents in 1916, he was abandoned on the steps of an orphanage run by the Paulist Fathers, a Catholic missionary group, on West 59th Street and Tenth Avenue, in the notorious Hell's Kitchen area of New York. "I was apparently delivered there fully blown and circumcised at the age of eight days, which is odd because it was a Catholic orphanage—I spent eleven years there," he said.[1] "The orphanage assigned me the name Francis Kane on my birth certificate, I don't know where it came from," he added.[2]

After waking in the dormitory, he would have breakfast and then play in the yard, romping and running with his friends, but at the sound of the eight o'clock bell he would get into line and march into school, up the winding staircase to the classroom. The school day would begin with a prayer, followed by lessons that seemed to last forever. He would amuse himself by shooting spitballs at his friends in the class, and whenever the oppressive summer heat descended on Manhattan, he would escape to the nearby docks on West 54th Street, where he would sunbathe and swim in the Hudson. As he grew older, he felt stifled by the narrow rules and regulations of the orphanage. "I'm nothing but a prisoner here," he would think. "People in jail have as much freedom as me. And I didn't do nothin' to deserve it—nothin' to be in jail for—nothin' to be locked away at night for."[3]

The experience was a tough one. In a 1971 television interview with Alan Whicker, Robbins said that "of the sixteen boys that were in this, I guess you'd call it a dormitory, only about four or five of us are still alive. Three of them have been electrocuted [by the electric chair], four are in jail, the others are all more or less respectable citizens—except myself."[4]

He had an independent, rebellious nature and soon started to play hookey from school. "I was in trouble all the time," he said. When he was eight, he remembers waiting in the street to have his tonsils "yanked out," but he was so scared, he ran off, only to be caught and held down for the "instant surgery."[5]

After being rejected by dozens of potential foster couples—he would have to endure the humiliation of standing in line with other boys and being scrutinized by discerning would-be parents—when he was eleven he was finally adopted by a middle-class Jewish family from Brooklyn, who renamed him Harold Rubin. Despite the love they showered on him, the young boy did not feel at home. "They were nice people in their way, but we just couldn't make it together," he said. "As much as I hated the Catholic dogma, it was difficult having to suddenly adjust to a

Jewish family. They called me the 'goy.' My friends from the orphanage started calling me 'Jew bastard' and 'kike.' "[6]

Feeling unwanted and out of place, he started work running errands for a local bookie, and the experience of memorizing long lines of numbers become useful later, when he started work at Universal Pictures as a statistician. It was, he said, "great for memory training, as I had to remember all the bets; I didn't dare write anything down."[7] Soon he began to mix with the low life of Manhattan, fetching cigars for mobster Lucky Luciano, doing odd jobs for Frank Costello, and acting as a drug courier for a Jamaican bootlegger.

"It seemed to me the greatest job in the world," he said. "I'd get a dollar a time for delivering dope and there was always a little left so I would see what it was like."[8] He started to smoke grass at eight and sniffed cocaine when he was eleven or twelve, the same year he lost his virginity to a prostitute.

Sometimes men would come up to him on the streets of New York and proposition him. Did he want an ice cream cone? they would ask. And he would jerk them off for a quarter or a dime. "I thought that was normal," he said. "I didn't think there was anything wrong with it."[9] He progressed to dropping by the matinees held at the Apollo Theater in Harlem to make a little extra cash. "You'd see two movies, and then the burlesque would start and the old men would come in," he told Ian Parker of *The New Yorker*. "And I would get a quarter to jerk them off. I didn't think it was a wild thing. You know, I made a dollar, a dollar and a half, and I had enough money for the day. The only trouble, now I think about it, was they didn't have Kleenex in those days. I had to go to F.W. Woolworth and buy a package of handkerchiefs."[10]

When his adoptive parents told him they were going to leave Brooklyn for Florida, the fifteen-year-old boy decided not to accompany them, opting for a life in the military instead. He ran away, forged his parents' signature of consent, and joined the navy, stationed in Pensacola. One day his submarine was hit by a torpedo, but he swam to the surface, the only survivor.

This, like all these stories he told about his birth and upbringing, was not true. Over the course of nearly fifty years Robbins spun an intricate web of lies that served to obscure his real origins. He invented, sensationalized, exaggerated, and elaborated, massaging the truth, shaping it into more and more outlandish forms, until it bore little resemblance to the reality of his existence. Few bothered to question his version of events, and so with each passing year the mythology that Robbins created for himself took on the patina of truth. With a professionalism and intelligence that have to be ad-mired—Robbins had nothing if not chutzpah—he marketed his un-truths with all the energy of a world-class advertiser. He reveled in the playfulness of the game, stretching his stories into ever more excessive and bizarre forms, tailoring his lies according to his audience.

For instance, knowing that the readers of the gay magazine *The Advocate* would appreciate hearing about his homosexual experi-ences, he told the journalist that he regularly had sex with other men while serving in the navy. "I was on a submarine, and if you're on a submarine for 22 days you want sex," he said. "We were either jacking each other off or sucking each other off. Everybody knew that everybody else was doing it. If you were able to handle it, you could get fucked in the ass, but I couldn't handle it that well. We jerked off too, but you get bored with that. You'd jerk off so you could relax and sleep. You'd start jerking off, and some guy would come over and say, 'I'm gonna blow you.' So we did it, it was fun, and it was over."[11]

Toward the end of his life Robbins's already vivid capacity for self-reinvention reached near pathological proportions when he told George Christy of *The Hollywood Reporter* that he thought he might be the illegitimate child of Czar Nicholas of Russia, "who came to New York in 1916 to raise money to fight the Bolsheviks, and I like to think he banged the chambermaid at the Waldorf and I'm their son. I'm often very very czar-ish."[12]

One of the themes that snakes its way through all of Robbins's work is the quest for identity. His books are littered with the corpses of dead parents, a common trope that expressed the writer's sense of disloca-tion and unease. The opening chapter of *Never Love a Stranger* details the death of a woman, Frances Cain, during childbirth; her surviving son, Francis Kane, grows up in an orphanage and feels unsettled by the absence of a personal history: "He was a ghost, a wraith, a name without a body."[13] Similarly, at the beginning of *The Pirate*—a tale of excess wealth, heady sex, and copious amounts of drug-taking set against the exotic backdrop of the Middle East—a woman dies during childbirth, a plotline that Robbins created in order to interrogate the identity of the hero, the handsome and powerful Baydr Al Fay.

In *The Dream Merchants* Robbins's study of the pioneers of early Hollywood, the book's central character, Johnny Edge, loses his parents in an accident at a carnival when he is ten, while in *The Inheritors*, about the television industry, protagonist Stephen Gaunt is orphaned at sixteen when his mother and father die in a car crash. In *The Carpetbaggers* nearly every main character—Jonas Cord, Nevada Smith, and Jennie Denton—loses one or both parents when they are still children. The character of Rina Marlowe, whom Robbins roughly modeled on the movie actress Jean Harlow, is forced to endure the death of her father in a shipwreck, the death of her mother from illness, and then the loss of her adoptive brother and mother in a boating accident off Cape Cod.

Plotlines like this may sound both absurd and melodramatic, but they reflect Robbins's own insecurities surrounding his birth. "My heroes are usually restless characters ready for a change of scenery, looking for something without quite knowing what it is," he said. "I'm that way. What am I looking for? As an orphan, I never had the sense of identity one gets out of being special to one or more family-like persons. Perhaps I'm on a reconnaissance mission, trying to discover experiences that are already a normal part of living for others."[14]

Robbins articulated these feelings of rejection and abandonment in a series of intimate conversations with friends. However, his confessions were far from true ones. "He told me that *Never Love a Stranger* was completely autobiographical," says Diana Jervis-Read, Robbins's personal assistant and one of his closest friends. "He told me that he had used his real name in that book, the name of Francis Kane, which was given to him in the orphanage."[15] The actress Sylvia Miles, a friend from the early 1950s who starred in a staged version of his novel *A Stone for Danny Fisher*, distinctly remembers him telling her that he was an orphan. "He told me he didn't have a mother or a father and that he was deprived as a kid," she says. "He sounded like a 'street' person and he came from nothing."[16]

Ini Asmann, whom Harold employed to take his author photographs and who later became a lover, believed she knew everything about him. "He told me that yes, he was an orphan and that he had been found abandoned on the steps of the church," she says. "I didn't question him, I believed him."[17]

His friend and writing partner Caryn Matchinga, who had a brief affair with Harold, remembers him telling her that his original name was Francis Kane and that he had been brought up in a Catholic orphanage. "He told me that he didn't realize he was Jewish until someone found a necklace with a Star of David motif on it beyond a bureau in the room where he was born," she says. "It belonged to the woman who had given birth to him. That's how he realized that he was Jewish, not Catholic as he had assumed. But I suspect he didn't really know the truth, he was always searching for it. He was a sad, lonely man who didn't believe anybody loved him, including his wife and children. There was always an emptiness in him."[18]

So what was the truth about Harold Robbins? "All I know about Harold's childhood is what is in the books," says Michael Korda. "But, out of instinct, I'm inclined to believe it was not as rough as he made out. While it is perfectly plausible that Harold had such a childhood, it is something of a standard growing-up story, especially for those who moved from New York to Hollywood—the poor Jewish boy learning to fight his way out, the father who doesn't make any money, the black or Irish kids who beat the shit out of you. It's a cliché."[19]

Harold's close friend, the writer Steve Shagan, was also deeply suspicious of the version of his life Robbins chose to present to the world. "All that business of him being an orphan and being discovered on the steps of the orphanage—all that was an invented yarn," he says. "He made things up in every interview he gave, and yet everyone bought it. He was the master of selling himself."[20] "He certainly liked spinning stories," says Ken Minns, captain of Robbins's yacht. "There was a Walter Mitty element to him."[21]

Not only did the author, in publicity blurbs, publish two different birth dates—1916 (his true one) and 1912—but he had three different names: his writing name, Harold Robbins; Harold Rubin, the one he said had been given to him by his adoptive parents; and the one he maintained had been assigned to him by the Paulist-run orphanage, Francis Kane. However, although the Paulist Fathers, an organization created in the nineteenth century for the "pursuit of the holy missions, in the conversion of souls and in the dissemination of Christian doctrine," ran a day school, St. Paul the Apostle, they had nothing to do with running a New York orphanage.[22]

The writer had always maintained that he never knew the true circumstances of his origins, and his death certificate certainly seems to support this claim: in the space given to record the names of the mother and father of the deceased, the entry reads "UNK" or unknown. However, Robbins told friends that he suspected that his adoptive father, Charles Rubin, was in fact his real father, but he believed that his adoptive mother, Blanche, was not his biological mother. "His father was Jewish, his mother wasn't," Paul Gitlin, Harold's agent and confidant, told *The New Yorker*. "His father remarried, and the woman [Blanche] had children of her own, so he was a stray, so to speak, and the new wife didn't particularly want him around."[23]

During his lifetime, Robbins said, he spent thousands of dollars trying to trace the identities of his parents, but apparently he failed to turn up anything of substance. Diana Jervis-Read remembers a conversation in which he outlined his frustrations. "He told me that he thought Charles was his real father, but the wife [Blanche] was not his mother," she says. "Harold asked Charles to tell him the truth, but for some reason he wouldn't. He asked him when Charles was approaching death, but he wouldn't be drawn on it. That really upset Harold, the fact that Charles wouldn't tell him even when it didn't matter anymore. Harold wouldn't have shouted—that wasn't his style—but I can imagine that he might have asked in a slightly aggressive manner in order to cover up the fact that he was so upset. I can hear him saying, 'Why don't you f—ing well tell me?' It was his one great regret, the fact that he never knew."[24]

Recently released public records such as census returns make it possible for us to piece together a picture of Robbins's past. In 1930 forty-four-year-old Charles, who ran a drugstore, and Blanche, who was thirty-three, were living in Brooklyn, at 1184 Schenectady Avenue, with four children: Herbert, four, Doris, ten, Ruth, eleven, and

Harold, thirteen. While all the children had been born in New York, both Charles and Blanche had immigrated from Odessa, Russia. These documents contain nothing to suggest that the Rubins were anything but a conventional Jewish family. The couple presented themselves to the world as a perfectly respectable and middle-class unit, who had married in 1915 and had subsequently reared four healthy children.

After Harold's death his sister, Ruth Narod, maintained this position when she told an American television journalist that the Rubins were just an ordinary family like any other. Harold's search for his real parentage, she suggested, was nothing more than an extension of his active imagination. "I guess it was after his [Harold's] first two or three books came out, I happened to see him on TV being interviewed, and they asked him at that point was this his life story being brought up in a Catholic home and being adopted by a Jewish family," she said. "He says he was adopted by the Rubin family and the father was a pharmacist. Well, this was our family, and he wasn't adopted."[25]

Ruth presented a number of photographs to establish her case. Here was Harold as a baby, with his bright, intelligent eyes. Another picture showed him aged around five and Ruth about three, sitting with their father, Charles, who in his late thirties had already started to go bald. Other photographs present snapshots of a seemingly idyllic happy family: Harold, Ruth, Doris, and Herbert sitting on a donkey; the four children at play in fancy dress, with Harold wearing a pretend crown.

Whether Ruth was aware of the true circumstances surrounding her brother's birth is not known; she died in 2001, at age eighty-two, while her siblings, Doris and Herbert, have also passed away. Although Ruth was right that Harold was neither an orphan nor an adopted child, the Rubins did have their secrets. Charles had been married before to a woman whom the family managed to erase from its history. She was called Frances, or Fannie, Smith. And she was Harold Robbins's real mother.

Fannie Smith was born in Neshwies, then part of Russia, in 1888. At the end of the nineteenth century, when Fannie was growing up, the town, south of Minsk, was a poor and desolate place. A fellow resident remembers it as a community of between six and eight thousand inhabitants, most of whom were Jewish. With its "unpaved and unlighted streets" and "small, unventilated, and often over-crowded wooden houses, devoid of all plumbing or the simplest precautions against contagious diseases," to an outsider it appeared "unbelievably poor, dirty, criminally ignorant as to hygiene and altogether lifeless."[26] The problem was confounded by the poor supply of fresh water. Although there was a pond on the outskirts of the village, the inhabitants could not use its water without boiling it first, as a stable belonging to a cavalry regiment was located nearby. The lack of water also meant that the town was particularly vulnerable to fires that would, in the summer months, destroy many of the houses.

"About the dirt and material poverty of the town there would be no doubt," notes Fannie's contemporary. "There were no factories or large industries to sustain its economy . . . the town lived on trade with the peasants who brought to its markets their wood, potatoes, and grain and took back salt, nails, kerosene, and sometimes linen goods, shoes, and other 'luxuries.' " It had no theaters, dance halls, or other places of public amusement, yet Neshwies fostered an air of quiet devotion and intellectual curiosity from within the walls of its synagogues. Philosopher Solomon Maimon and popular novelist Shomer (N. M. Schaikewitz), who was known as "the Dumas of modern Yiddish literature," were both born in the town. The Jewish community, steeped in its rich cultural heritage, tended to look down on the "goyims"; the majority of Gentiles were, as one writer noted, "peasants or poor city dwellers, some of them former serfs, few of them literate."[27]

Presiding over the region was the Radziwill family, who lived in a rather grand château located on the outskirts of Neshwies, a building that could be reached only by crossing a causeway and a bridge. During the summer the prince (whose descendant would later go on to marry a sister of Jackie Kennedy) would condescend to tour the village in his carriage. The inhabitants of Neshwies would duly don their caps in deference to the aristocrat as he passed by.

As they watched this somewhat regal procession, Fannie's parents would perhaps have mused on the huge disparity of wealth between the Radziwills and their own family and dreamed of the possibility of forging a better life for themselves. The villagers had heard about the infinite opportunities presented by the United States, a country that at the end of the nineteenth century opened its arms to immigrants from around the world. New York was seen as a beacon of liberation compared to an increasingly repressive Russian regime. The government, commented one writer, "under Czar Nicholas I adopted the program of crushing the Jews by compelling at least a third of them to leave the country, another third to give up their religion and communal association (by adopting Christianity), and the remaining third to be crowded into a small territory where extreme poverty would gradually lead to their extermination."[28] Nicholas had introduced a policy of compulsory drafting, compelling young Jewish men to enter the army for a period of twenty-five years. In order to keep up the numbers, the government employed *khappers* (kidnappers) to swoop into villages and take away its young male population, some of which included boys of eight or nine.

After the assassination of Alexander II—who tried to introduce moderate reforms—in March 1881, Alexander III reigned over Russia, using "violence as a political instrument."[29] The so-called May laws of 1882 resulted in the further victimization, degradation, and marginalization of the Jewish population. A mass exodus ensued. Between 1871 and 1880 an estimated forty thousand Jews fled Russia (including Russian-controlled Poland) for the United States; by the following decade this figure had increased to 135,000, and by 1910 the number had swollen to 704,245.

Harold Robbins's mother was one such person. In 1896, with her parents, Harry and Sophie, the eight-year-old girl left Russia for America, most likely making her escape in much the same way as her Neshwies contemporary Morris Cohen: traveling by train from Minsk, through Vilna and Kovno, journeying on by wagon to the German border, then to Berlin and Bremen, and continuing from there by boat. "We were huddled together in the steerage, literally like cattle," Cohen says.[30]

After arriving in New York, Fannie and her family would have sought support from the Neshwieser Verin, the Brethren of Neshwies, which was designed to help immigrants overcome the difficulties of their new environment. The sense of community was perhaps even stronger in this new land than it had been in the shtetl back home; after all, "so many had come here [from Neshwies] that there could hardly be any left in the old town."[31]

At the beginning of 1915 Fannie was living in an apartment at 68 East 96th Street in Manhattan. She had fallen in love with a thirty-two-year-old druggist called Charles Rubin, one of the sons of Rose and David Rubin, who lived at 911 DeKalb Avenue. Like Fannie, Charles and his family had also fled Russia, leaving their home village of Linkuva (or Linkova in Yiddish) for America.

Linkuva, now in Lithuania, was, like Neshwies, a poor town, with "small wooden hovels" clustered around the synagogue and the bathhouse. Many of the buildings that stood in the center of the town, observed one writer who grew up in the village, were "thrown together in complete disorder . . . The walls were crooked and discoloured by rain and sun, with small, sunken windows of which many a pane was stuffed with rags or glued over with newspaper."[32]

Linkuva, which was founded in the sixteenth century, boasted around three hundred Jewish families—farmers, flax growers, and craftsmen. It had a large flour mill owned by Jews, as well as a Jewish-run bank. Its marketplace, a large cobbled square flanked by shops, attracted farmers and tradesmen twice a week. Some inhabitants were so poor that, after the market, they were reduced to sweeping up the horse dung deposited in the square; the manure was later used as a primitive flooring in some houses, or it was dried and burned as fuel.

None of the homes had any washing facilities, so the people of Linkuva were forced to make do with the bathhouse. Here the burgeoning middle class mingled with the poorest villagers. "There were small, skinny Jews withered through labour and gradual starvation," observed one inhabitant, "wealthier merchants with protruding stomachs; grandfathers with white beards and children with skinny legs. Bedlam prevailed. Men with healthy bodies rubbed against those who were deformed."[33]

Robbins's paternal grandparents, David and Rose Rubin, both born in 1855, were married in 1874 or 1875. The couple's wedding would have been a traditional affair, with David and Rose pledging their vows under a *chupah*, a canopy used in marriage ceremonies, after which a bride was supposed to cry (a sign that she would have a happy union) and the groom smash a glass at his feet. The Rubins' lives were governed by the religious rituals of the community. On the Sabbath the men in Charles Rubin's family would gather in the synagogue and crowd around the best storytellers. Upon returning home, they would find the house transformed, with "white cloths now [covering] rickety tables, and white loaves of bread . . . besides the white loaves, soup, fish and meat, there was also a plateful of chopped liver and chicken giblets."[34]

The Rubin children were brought up according to strict rules governing spiritual thought, behavior, and language. Charles Rubin would have been taught not to "allow his mind to dwell, nor his mouth to utter words on subjects of a low nature, because with the same mind he thinks of the greatness of the Almighty and the wonders of His creations . . . A Jew must endeavor to keep his mind pure and never allow it to wander from His ways."[35]

In 1888 David and Rose Rubin, together with their three children, Charles, Samuel, and Lena, made the long journey from Linkuva to America. By 1900 the couple, then living at 136 Boerum Street, Brooklyn, had had four more children—Herman, Ida, Grace, and Hannah—and two others, unnamed, who had died. According to the 1910 census, David provided for his family—who were then living at 961 DeKalb Avenue in Brooklyn—out of his own income, and his sons went on to set themselves up in business. By 1908 Charles, Samuel, and Herman had established a company called the Sal Santal Methyl Capsule Company, and five years later Charles was running a drugstore at 63 Hamilton Avenue.

How Charles met Fannie we shall probably never know, but the couple were married on 1 February 1915 at the bride's home on East 96th Street in Manhattan. In August of that year Fannie, now a housewife, conceived and on 21 May 1916 gave birth to their son by cesarean section. Complications set in, and she developed an obstruction in her intestine that led to pneumonia; on 26 May, five days after the birth, she died. The twenty-eight-year-old woman who had come to America in search of a better life was buried, in a plot paid for by the Progressive Brethren of Neshwies, in Mount Zion Cemetery, Queens, a graveyard that Robbins would later describe in his third novel, *A Stone for Danny Fisher*. In the opening chapter of *Never Love a Stranger*, the dying mother, Frances, passes on her name to her son; so too did Robbins's real mother bequeath her name to her child. Robbins's birth certificate lists his name as Harold F. Rubin, the F standing for Francis.

It did not take Charles long to get over his wife's death: the following year he was preparing for his second marriage, to Bluma or Blanche Zinnerman, a twenty-three-year-old immigrant from Lodz, which is now in Poland but was then part of Russia. The couple were married on 17 June in the bride's home at 976 DeKalb Avenue by Rabbi Israel Goldfarb. Intriguingly, on the marriage certificate, although Charles declared himself a widow, in the space designed to record the number of times the groom has been married, he initially entered "First," then crossed this out and corrected it to "2nd." This, of course, could have been a simple mistake on Charles's part, but it can also be interpreted as the Rubins' attempt to eradicate the memory of Fannie Smith from their lives.

Harold, for one, did not forget his real mother, even though he never mentioned her to any of his friends nor talked about her in any interviews. Although he was brought up by Charles and Blanche as one of their own, he often wondered what might have happened to him if Fannie had lived. She became a shadowy presence in his life, a figure who haunted his writing and a symbol of the idealized woman whom he sought out, acquired, and then subsequently rejected.

2

"I'm a Brooklyn guy, and look at me—I made it."
—Harold Robbins to Steve Shagan

T HE LITTLE BOY craned his neck and looked up at the house. It was not particularly grand—the two-story detached structure had a small front garden, a little porch, and a pitched roof—but he thought it the most beautiful building he had ever seen. As the movers continued to unload his parents' possessions from the van, he looked up and down the avenue at the other newly built houses. He felt proud that his family was the first to move onto the street. After their cramped apartment, the spacious suburban house on this tree-lined street seemed like something conjured from a dream. It represented a chance to start again, a new beginning.

Robbins wrote about the moment he first saw his new home in the opening chapters of *A Stone for Danny Fisher*. "I was so excited I could hardly speak . . . I squirmed to look at the street. This was it. I recognized the houses, each looking like the others, with a slim young tree in front of each."[1]

Today the neighborhood has a somewhat desolate air to it, but when the Rubins first moved into the house at 1184 Schenectady Avenue, East Flatbush in Brooklyn was the epitome of the newly created suburb: solid and determinedly middle class, its air reeking of fresh paint and the smell of promise. Robbins may have been born in Manhattan, but he was a Brooklynite at heart: a sentimentalist who hid his real feelings behind a tough-talking, no-bullshit exterior. Brooklyn was, by and large, the land of the immigrant, an area where the newly arrived could reinvent themselves as Americans. As it grew, Brooklyn became a symbol for the American dream, a swath of land that, in the words of one contemporary commentator, "felt the magic wand of Jewish desire for improvement."[2]

As the IRT subway snaked its way through the area and as real estate developers carved up the landscape, creating new neighborhoods at seemingly impossible speeds, ever more immigrant groups flooded in. In 1905 there were 100,000 Jews in Brooklyn; by 1930 the figure had increased to 800,000.

Robbins captures this sense of new beginnings in the opening chapters of *A Stone for Danny Fisher*. The narrator, Danny, writes of moving into his newly built house in the recently developed Hyde Park, East Flatbush area of Brooklyn. Danny's memories, although they are presented as fiction, were in fact Robbins's own. The street, as he recalled, had not yet even been paved, comprising nothing but a surface of gray-white gravel. When he ran into the house, he remembered, it smelled new: the recently laid wood on the staircase, the paint on the walls, the polish on the doors. He bolted up the stairs and opened the door to his bedroom, a small and as yet unfurnished room about fourteen feet long and ten feet wide. Initially his steps were uncertain and tentative, but as he explored, he became more confident. He walked over to the window and looked out at the house across the driveway, at the new car his father had just bought, and at the stretch of fields in the distance.

On the surface the Rubins were a typically aspirational middle-class Jewish family. Not only did Charles own the house on Schenectady Avenue, but he had made enough money from his drugstore business to employ a live-in maid and take his family on winter vacations to Florida. Ruth Narod, Harold's half-sister, remembers her parents encouraging her and her siblings to be creative. "We'd put on shows when we were kids, every Sunday, and Harold would write all the material for it," she said. "And we would all act in it, and we would make up costumes."[3]

Harold was a bright child, and photographs show his piercing dark eyes sparkling with intelligence. From the upstairs back windows of the house on Schenectady Avenue, he would have seen the vast expanses of Holy Cross cemetery, with its neatly planned graves counterpointing the surrounding suburban grid of streets. Harold often walked through the cemetery, with its gothic statuary, and was fascinated by some of the people whose lives were marked here.

He was especially drawn to the graves of local gangsters such as Antonino Cincotta, the New York mafia leader who was killed in front of 23 Union Street in Brooklyn, in 1915, and Frank "Frankie" Yale, who was shot to death by Al Capone's gang as he was driving through Brooklyn in 1928. Later, Louis Capone—one of the famous Murder, Inc. gang, the operation fictionalized in Robbins's *Never Love a Stranger*—was also buried here after his execution at Sing Sing in 1944. As a boy, Harold would have heard many stories about Murder, Inc., whose Jewish members operated out of a candy store under the elevated subway at the corner of Saratoga and Livonia Streets in nearby Brownsville. It was said that "more individual murders were planned in that store than at any other spot on earth."[4]

Although Ruth told friends that Harold started writing stories at the age of ten, from the beginning his real talent lay in numbers. He had a logical brain and a natural aptitude for playing chess, memorizing figures, and, like Danny Fisher, doing mathematics. Making money was a priority: even when he was a boy, he would insist that relatives pay twenty-five cents if they wanted to see one of the impromptu shows that he had devised.

From an early age he seems to have defined those around him by their possessions, a trait that would later find expression in *Never Love a Stranger* and *A Stone for Danny Fisher*, novels that explore the way economics can warp and brutalize an individual personality, and his more outré, glamorous tales such as *The Carpetbaggers* and *The Betsy*. Although he did not suffer, as he later claimed, from the type of deprivations described in *Never Love a Stranger*, the Depression played a central role in shaping his consciousness. In 1929, the year the American stock market collapsed, Charles Rubin nearly lost his drugstore business, and Blanche had to go out to work. The family were also forced to leave their suburban house in Brooklyn and abandon, for the moment at least, their dream of progressive self-improvement. In *A Stone for Danny Fisher* Robbins describes the impact that the resulting economic crash has on the fifteen-year-old boy when, in 1932, he is faced with the loss of his beloved house. "*Alles iss forloren*," says Danny's father, lapsing into Yiddish—"everything is lost."

"That was the night I came home and found Mamma crying at the kitchen table . . . That was the night when I stood in the darkened street at two o'clock in the morning, and my father, crying bitterly all the while, looked at the store windows and murmured: 'Twenty-five years.' . . . That was the night when, for the first time, I admitted to myself that it was not my house, that it really belonged to someone else, and there was no heart left in me for tears."[5]

In the early 1930s Harold and his family moved out of their spacious suburban house into a cramped apartment in Manhattan. By 1933 the family were living in apartment IB at 120 Convent Avenue, at the intersection with 133rd Street. Harold went on to enroll at George Washington High School. The school, on Auberon Avenue in Washington Heights, was founded in 1917; graduates include Henry Kissinger, actor and musician Harry Belafonte, and economist Alan Greenspan. This is how Robbins, in typical stripped-down prose, describes it in *Never Love a Stranger*: "It stood on the top of a hill overlooking the Heights and across to the Bronx. It was a new red brick building with a dome on it . . . When the bell rang, the halls were full of kids running back and forth to their rooms . . . I looked around me. The class seemed mixed—about twenty colored boys and girls, and twenty white."[6]

Fellow student Henderson Herod, who graduated in the same year as Harold, remembers a typical day. "We started the day at eight a.m., and everyone had to enter through the main front doors," he says. "There were student monitors on all doors, and once in the building you could not leave without a special pass, not even for lunch. George Washington was a large school of about four thousand pupils, and we graduated about five hundred students twice a year. In looking back, there is one thing that I find amazing. There was a wide diversity of students, religions, races, and nations represented, and yet I don't remember any confrontations or violent disagreements of any kind. The school had a policy that if you had a special holiday for religion or otherwise, and you had a note from home, you were excused. We were coming out of one of the worst depressions ever, and living was difficult, and so it is surprising that we had such an efficient, good school."[7]

Harold's photograph in the high school yearbook shows a serious-faced, smartly dressed youth with closely set eyes and a slight, knowing smirk playing across his thin, pale face. According to the brief biography next to his picture, Harold belonged to the chemistry club, the biology office, and Arista, which, as Henderson Herod recalls, "consisted of a group of student volunteers who aided teachers . . . in things [including] assisting backward students."[8]

Harold's home on Convent Avenue was within walking distance of City College of New York, an institution created to "provide children of the poor and new immigrants [with] the higher education that could give them access to the American dream."[9] But the young boy realized, at quite an early age, that his real talents lay outside the confines of the conventional educational system. Not only that, but he had an overwhelming urge to make money, an instinct that would never leave him. "I wanted to enjoy life," he writes in *Never Love a Stranger*, "to have things: money in my pocket, a car, a nice place to live, the things that count—the things you can hold in your hand and feel and eat."[10]

Harold's obsession with the material world—which would later find expression in his grotesquely excessive consumption of houses, boats, art, drugs, and women—can be traced back to his early life. He told interviewers that his longing for expensive objects grew out of the fact that he was born into poverty—a causal link that journalists and readers alike could understand and sympathize with—but the truth was much more complex. The real source of his psychological pre-occupation with possessions has its roots in the murky knot of emotions associated with his birth.

Throughout his life Harold chose to keep the true circumstances of his origins to himself, not revealing the identity of his real mother even to those closest to him. But various personal documents, including his marriage certificate, show that he did know her name. Although we do not know exactly when he discovered the truth about his parentage, the revelation that Blanche was not his biological mother unsettled the already precarious foundations of his world. While he was at George Washington High School, Harold started to play truant and seems to have suffered some kind of breakdown. Blanche took him to see a psychiatrist, who, according to Harold's half-sister Ruth, announced that there was "absolutely nothing wrong with him" and that he was "a genius and he's far ahead of his class and he's bored and that's why he's mischievous at school."[11]

Harold may have been known to his friends at George Washington High as "Poker Face," but behind his impassive features and inscrutable expression he may have been trying to come to terms with the fact that, to some extent, he was to blame for his mother's death. He felt guilty and responsible for the loss, and yet at the same time angry that she had deserted him. For the rest of his life he would try to prove—both to himself and to his dead mother—that he was worthy of her love, a drive that resulted in both conspicuous consumption and frequent acts of elaborate generosity. "The cars and the villas and the parties and the celebrities and the cocaine—it was all there,"[12] says Grace, Harold's second wife. The excess of riches that defined his later life—his insatiable acquisitiveness counterpointed by an instinct to overload those around him with elaborate presents and lavish entertainment—was a substitute for misdirected love. But no amount of shopping would ever bring his mother back.

Toward the end of Harold's time at George Washington High School he wrote a poem entitled "Lament of a Freshie." Published in the 1934 yearbook, the twenty-line verse articulated a world-weariness and a cynicism that belied his young years.[13] The personality that emerges from the poem is adept at manipulation and psychological camouflage, constantly shaping and reshaping his behavior according to the demands of the situation. It also indicates a character trait that can, according to interpretation, be described either as a natural raw intelligence or an underhanded ratlike cunning. "There was something quite feral about him," says Sylvia Miles, who met Robbins in the early 1950s, "both in the way he looked and in the way he behaved, especially around women. He was like an animal that eats other animals. He was totally venal."[14]

Robbins maintained that he was obsessed with sex from an early age. "When I was a kid in New York, I used to stand under the stairs and look up girls' dresses . . . So it started early with me, you see. In fact, one of my problems in school was that I talked about sex so much. But what's wrong with that? I like girls. And I was always pretty successful. My attitude is: 'If you don't ask you don't get.' "[15] In the year before he died, he told *Esquire* magazine that his favorite thing in the world was a woman's bottom. "When I was a kid and old enough to go into a Minsky burlesque show in the Star Theater on Fulton Street in Brooklyn, I caught the fever," he said. "Gypsy Rose Lee and Blaze Starr were my favorites. When they began to swish around in their gowns, I was in heaven."[16]

Later in life Harold would boast about how he was expelled from school for having sex with a girl in the bell tower. "When I was fifteen, I was f—some girl at the George Washington High School tower, and my ass hit the bell," he said. "Print that—it's the truth. Four big, burly teachers beat me up, and I was expelled from high school."[17] He told another reporter that he first learned about sex from a prostitute. "I was a kid of, hell, about twelve," he said. "I was delivering buckets of beer to the cathouses—these were the days of Prohibition. I remember one hot day when one hooker was getting no customers. So she motioned me over and gave me the treatment. When it was all over, I thought God had punished me. It was that feeling. I really thought I had done something wrong. Next day I said to myself, 'Gee, that was great,' and thought I would have another attempt with this broad when I brought the bucket of beer in. So I went in and indicated my desires. You know what that hooker said? She said, 'Only the first one is free.' Can you believe that? I've never forgotten her."[18]

These anecdotes have to be regarded as suspect. "The story about the bell tower was an [apocryphal] ongoing story that surfaced in every class,"[19] says fellow pupil Henderson Herod. The incident with the prostitute also reads like a wish-fulfillment fantasy, something that Harold imagined had happened to him rather than the reality.

Many of Robbins's novels have an underlying theme of forbidden desire, particularly incest. In *A Stone for Danny Fisher* the teenage boy is obsessed with his sister's breasts, while in *The Storyteller*, another autobiographical novel, the central character, Brooklyn-born writer Joe Crown, has a sexual relationship with, and later marries, his cousin Motty, who was brought up in his house as his sister after the death of her parents. In the opening pages of *The Carpetbaggers* Jonas has sex with his stepmother, Rina, who we later learn once had a teenage relationship with a boy she regarded as her brother; and in *The Betsy* Robbins takes great pleasure in describing in graphic detail the frenzied copulation between the elderly head of a car dynasty and his young daughter-in-law.

In truth, the adolescent boy seems to have feared women, regarding them as either pure madonnas (like the unsullied image of his dead mother) or tempting devils, symbols of lost innocence. In *A Stone for Danny Fisher* the young hero battles with his desires, dampening them down with regular cold showers. "I hated everything that was happening to me," he says, "all the things I would become, my growing manhood, and its manner of expression."[20]

For all his later boasting about erotic experimentation—soliciting strange men in grimy cinemas, losing his virginity to prostitutes—at this stage of his life Harold actually chose to go steady with the quintessential, and literal, girl next door. While he was still at George Washington High School, he started to date Lillian Machnovitch, who lived a couple of streets away at 1245 Troy Avenue. She was the daughter of Gussie Bains and Samuel Machnovitch, who had immigrated from Odessa in 1902 and later became treasurer of Universal Pictures. Lillian, the eldest of three daughters, was by all accounts a rather plain Jewish girl, a brunette with a plump face and a kind heart. "Lillian always had a lovely smile and was very generous-hearted," says her sister, Rae Exelbert, "but she was very quiet and private. She fell in love with Harold when she was a girl—they were childhood sweethearts—and he became part of our family. My parents loved him, and he spent more and more time at our house. He was a good kid, and we thought of him more as a brother than as my sister's boyfriend."[21]

If Harold separated women into two distinct types—reassuring nonsexual figures and highly desirable, dangerous temptresses—Lillian seems to have fallen firmly into the former camp. As he fell in love with her, she became the mother he had never had.

"It has long been advanced as a theory," ran the editorial in Harold's high school yearbook, "that during his high school career, every student should set a definite objective for himself—or, in other words, decide just what he intends to make out of his later existence."[22] Young people can be divided into two groups, it added; those who plan their lives like a perfectly executed game of chess and those who drift around aimlessly from one job to the next without clear direction. It is important, the editor advised, that graduates of George Washington think of their futures in a logical fashion. "While we still have the opportunity, then, of making something out of our lives, let us not . . . move our [chess] men here and there without due consideration; in other words, let's not allow the course of our lives to be led into various separate channels to suit every mere whim or fancy. At this crucial moment, just before we enter into the great, vast world that lies ahead, let us decide just what course or vocation we are going to pursue, and also, just how successful we are going to be at these various objectives."[23]

As Harold read these words, he would have been forced to acknowledge that his plans were completely without shape or purpose. He wanted to make money, that much was clear, but he had no real ambitions. Later he would brag that he had made millions without graduating from high school, claiming to have left full-time education at the age of fifteen. "I quit high school to deliver groceries full time, instead of part time," he said.[24] He also told the story about running away from home and lying about his age in order to join the navy. "When I was fifteen and a half I forged parents' consent forms and joined the navy,"[25] he said. He told another reporter that he had been stationed for two years in Pensacola, Florida, earning twenty-one dollars a month, during which time he studied for his high school diploma by correspondence course and learned about figures from Kessler's *Handbook of Accountancy*.

It wasn't only journalists he lied to. When his elder daughter Caryn was fourteen, he told her that he was a high school dropout, "during one of those great moments between father and daughter when you expect she'll throw her head back in your lap and tell you she loves you," he said. Although she didn't respond immediately, several days later she turned to him and said, "No one would ever believe you were a high school dropout, Daddy."[26] He often entertained his friends with stories about his time in the navy. "His ship was sunk and he was the only survivor and he swam to shore," television producer Bob Pollock remembers. "I would question him about it and say, 'Harold, tell me more about the details,' and he would say, 'That was it—I swam to shore, that was all.' "[27]

Robbins's friend Steve Shagan was a great deal more skeptical. "That story that he survived a submarine hit and swam to the surface—I said, 'Harold come on—there was no way you could have survived the pressure of being three hundred feet under water and coming to the surface, never mind the sharks.' He turned around, gave me a smile, and said, 'I was the only survivor.' I said, 'It's total bullshit, but if you want to tell it, then you tell it.' "[28]

In order to transform himself into the embodiment of the American dream, Robbins tapped in to the hopes and aspirations of the masses, presenting himself as an ordinary man of the people who, through various entrepreneurial means, made and lost several fortunes. While he did start work as an errand boy in various grocery stores in Brooklyn from the age of fifteen, these were just part-time, after-school positions. Records held at George Washington High School show that, far from dropping out of school, Harold graduated, along with the rest of his class, in 1934, at age eighteen. And as for his heroic spell in the navy? His death certificate shows that he never served any time in the military at all.

In the summer after graduation he got a job as a soda clerk, selling hot dogs and whipping up "fudgie-wudgies" on Coney Island beach. "I was a fair soda clerk," Robbins writes, in the guise of Frankie Kane in *Never Love a Stranger*. "After a while I became a good one."[29] In the years after graduating from high school he continued to work as a short-order cook, a counterman in a restaurant, a fruit and vegetable clerk, and a salesman for a wholesale grocer. With a bravura one has to admire, Robbins even managed to spin an elaborate series of stories out of this most banal of professions.

Three mornings a week, he said, he delivered groceries to a smart apartment building on West End Avenue in Manhattan. "Since the orders were always telephoned in, none of us at the store had ever seen the customer," he later recalled. "That was until I brought the first order. The door opened, and a blond girl peered out. I almost fell over the doorjamb as I walked in. The blond girl was naked beneath a sheer black dressing gown. I handed her the bill, trying not to stare at her body shimmering underneath her gown. She paid out the amount of the bill and placed an extra dollar in my hand. I looked at her in surprise—my usual tip was a nickel or dime. She looked back at me. 'Anything wrong?' 'That's a lot,' I said. She smiled and took the dollar back. 'What would you rather have?' "[30]

Moving on from sexual fantasy, Robbins constructed another scenario that centered on amassing enormous wealth. "I became an inventory clerk for a grocery chain, and one day I saw my chance to make a fortune," he said. "I hit on the idea of buying vegetables while they were still in the field, canning them, and selling them to small grocers in direct opposition to the big groups. I went to Morristown, New Jersey, and learned how to fly. Then I flew all around the States buying up crops. In one year I cleared a million dollars."[31]

Robbins knew that the best stories work by the constant counter-pointing of contrasts, and so according to the unwritten rules of narrative, he realized that the acquisition of a huge fortune has to be followed by its dramatic loss. He repeated the following account, in various forms, to so many friends, reporters, and family members that it became a personal myth, a story so monolithic that no one thought of questioning it.

"I began to be aware that there was a place called Europe and there might be a war," he told the broadcaster Alan Whicker. "Everybody kept saying they remembered during World War I whoever controlled the sugar market was instantly rich. So I went to a bank, and with my money and collateral I raised almost two million dollars, and I bought advances on sugar at 4.85 a hundredweight, which was then twenty-odd cents a hundredweight over the prevailing market. I was counting my money—the sugar was on the way in, I was going to set it up in bush terminal and become the biggest sugar black marketeer in the world. Then war broke out in Europe, and [the next day] President Roosevelt froze the price of sugar . . . at 4.65. I'd guaranteed to pay 4.85. All my money went, all the bank's money went, and I still owed over a million-odd dollars, and so I went through bankruptcy, but I had a problem. I wasn't of age yet—I was three months shy of twenty-one. Before they could put me through bankruptcy I had to be twenty-one."[32]

A brief perusal of the facts is enough to show the gaps in his story. First, as Robbins was born in 1916, he would have been twenty-one in 1937—two years before the start of the Second World War and four years before America entered into the conflict. Second, the Office of Price Administration and Civilian Supply fixed the price of sugar in August 1941—when Robbins was twenty-five and already working at Universal Pictures.

Throughout this time, when he pretended to be making and losing millions, Harold was actually working as a lowly clerk for Rand Tea and Coffee Stores at 158 Franklin Street in Manhattan, a company that employed him from December 1936. Rather than enjoying the high life—he claimed that he could afford a New York penthouse on Central Park South—he was in fact living with his fiancée Lillian and her parents at the Machnovitch suburban home on Troy Avenue.

As Harold arranged endless shipments of tea and coffee and added up long, monotonous columns of figures, he started to construct an alternative history for himself, a life he believed should be his. The dream merchant's imagination was beginning to stir.

3

"There was something more he wanted, something more he had to have, and what it was he didn't really know."

—*The Dream Merchants*

H E OPENED HIS EYES knowing that the day—21 May 1937, his twenty-first birthday—would be a special one. Feeling an excited flutter in his stomach, he jumped out of bed and made himself a cup of strong coffee. As he took a sip of the dark, bitter drink, he thought of Lillian over at her parents' house in Brooklyn. No longer would the couple have to spend the nights apart. No longer would he have to return alone to his small, newly rented apartment at 43 Avenue D. He and his childhood sweetheart—the girl with the laughing dark eyes and warm smile—would spend the rest of their lives together. Other women—louder, blowsier, looser women—had caught his eye, and he wasn't denying he hadn't been tempted. Gee, he'd even had a little fun with them, but they weren't the kind of broads you'd want to settle down with, the kind you'd want to bear your children.

He shaved, combed his already thinning hair, dressed in his best—and only—suit, and made his way downtown to city hall. He was met by an ecstatic Lillian, who rushed up to him and kissed him. Like two overgrown children, Harold and Lillian ran into the building and presented their marriage application to the official behind the desk. Two days later, on 23 May, the couple were married by Gustav Spund at 130 East Third Street. "It was a beautiful day, and Lillian looked gorgeous," remembers her sister, Rae Exelbert. "She was so full of hopes, and both she and Harold were looking forward to the future. They wanted to spend the rest of their lives together."[1]

Harold was still working as a grocer, but he had dreams of setting up in business for himself. In typically romantic fashion he named his company—Lillian Grocers, located at 616 Third Avenue—after his new wife, but the venture did not last long. Throughout 1940 Harold's debts mounted until on the last day of that year he felt he had no choice but to declare himself bankrupt. "I started a little business of my own . . . when I got married, but I soon went broke," he said in the 1940s. The sum he owed, $1,759, was far from the million dollars he boasted about later, but it was serious enough to warrant intervention from Lillian's father, Samuel, who was worried about his daughter's welfare. "I decided I had better get on with the big companies, rather than take the risk of little business," he said. "That's when I went in with the movie companies."[2] Samuel, treasurer of Universal Pictures, secured a job as a shipping clerk for his son-in-law at the New York warehouse of the studio.

Harold never publicly acknowledged his father-in-law's role in introducing him to the studio, but without his help he probably could not have transformed himself into a best-selling novelist. While working at Universal, Harold met many of the colorful personalities who would later populate his novels, and he had the opportunity to observe the inner workings of a company dedicated to the production of mass entertainment. "As soon as he began to work for Universal, he fell in love with the manufacture of films, not the writing of them," says his friend Steve Shagan. "He enthused about the magic of movies, not how they were written but what was behind them."[3]

The Universal story, packed as it is with ambition, intrigue, and double-dealing, reads like the narrative of one of Robbins's own novels. In fact, he would use the history of the studio as a blueprint for his second book, *The Dream Merchants*, drawing on the real-life exploits of Carl Laemmle, the Bavarian immigrant who built up the business from a small chain of nickelodeons. Laemmle formed the New York–based Independent Moving Picture Company of America (IMP) that openly defied the Motion Picture Patents Company, a monopoly that tried to control movie production and distribution by charging levies on film projectors. Laemmle was "determined to break the power of the Trust . . . I won . . . and secured the freedom of film," he said.[4] By the time Robbins came to work for the company, the studio was churning out a winning formula of Deanna Durbin musicals, Abbott and Costello comedies, high camp adventure films, westerns, and horror movies.

Although Robbins's rise through the company was rapid, his beginnings were quite lowly, and initially his weekly wage was fifteen dollars a week. "When he went to Universal, I know he worked in the post room," says Diana Jervis-Read, Harold's secretary and close friend. "I have never seen anyone pack up a box like Harold."[5] In *The Carpetbaggers* he describes how executive David Woolf, the nephew of the studio head, learns the business by working in a grimy warehouse building on West 43rd Street in Manhattan:

"It was a dirty gray factory building down near the Hudson River, which had fallen into disuse and been converted into lofts. There were two large freight elevators in the back and three small passenger elevators near the front entrance, scarcely enough to handle the crowd of workers that surged in at eight o'clock each morning and out at six o'clock at night."[6]

When he arrives for his first day at his new job, David is met by hostility; his fellow workers resent the fact that his uncle has appointed him, believing him to be nothing more than a sneak. His foreman tells him to bring up a shipment of paper, knowing that the task is impossible using only a forklift truck. But David uses his initiative and borrows a hydraulic jack from a nearby garage. He further proves himself to his colleagues by standing up to the corrupt platform boss, risking his life to fight the larger man. At the end of the scene David has not only done the right thing—saved the company money—but he has driven off a Goliathlike bully who was terrorizing the whole building, and as a result he wins the respect of his fellow workers. "When David turned toward the packaging tables, all the men were grinning at him," Robbins writes. "Suddenly, they weren't strangers anymore. They were friends."[7]

Perhaps Harold, the son-in-law of the treasurer, experienced a similar kind of resentment when he first arrived at Universal. He certainly felt the need to prove himself to his colleagues and superiors alike. "To the amazement of the executives, I found an error in freight payments which was to bring the company a refund of $37,000, and me a raise of $2.50 a week," he said. "Also, I rated the attention of the bosses—so I've climbed steadily upwards in position."[8]

The United States entered the Second World War in December 1941, after the Japanese attack on Pearl Harbor, but Harold did not enlist. Military service was not an option as, according to a document lodged with his New York literary agent, he had a "back injury of long standing."[9] The dearth of men in the employment pool—together with his shrewd intelligence and seemingly effortless ability with figures—helped to propel his rise up the company. "There was a lot of opportunity during the war because people were away," he later said. "I jumped over employees who had been there fifty years because the boss liked me. And I worked very hard."[10] From shipping clerk Harold was promoted first to statistician and then to budget analyst, estimating the cost of production and checking expenses. Later he remembered that three Universal employees had all submitted expense claims for lunch with Abe Weiler, the entertainment editor of *The New York Times*. As the slightly built man could not possibly have eaten three top-dollar lunches in one day, Robbins queried the claims. "So my advice to you fellers is to decide who's going to lie about who on any given day," he said.[11]

Bookkeeping—the tallying of profit and loss—lies at the heart of Harold Robbins's personality. When he came to write his super-successful novels, he never forgot the skills he had learned as a grocer, statistician, and budget analyst, balancing the time and effort he expended on an enterprise with the amount of money earned. Writing, for him, was not about creative expression or artistic ideals; rather, what fueled his ambition was a mercantile instinct, a desire to explore his dreams and fantasies and sell them off to the highest bidder. "He was a brilliant mathematician and a great chess player," says Diana Jervis-Read. "He could play lots of games over the telephone—he did that a lot—and he also loved baccarat. He had a real memory for numbers."[12]

During the early 1940s Harold worked behind the scenes on a number of films, calculating the budgets for a range of movies such as *The Flame of New Orleans*, *The Spoilers*, and *Follow the Boys*, all starring Marlene Dietrich; westerns like *Badlands of Dakota*, *Frontier Badmen*, and *Men of Texas*; and the "sand and sandals" epics of Maria Montez, also known as the Queen of Technicolor, the Caribbean Cyclone, or Dominican Dynamite. *Arabian Nights* (1942), starring Sabu as Ali Ben Ali and Montez as Scheherazade, was Universal's first color film and tells the story of a dancer who believes her destiny is to marry the caliph of Baghdad. The combination of a dark-eyed, generously proportioned, scantily clad beauty and exotic settings was so popular that the studio ordered the production of a series of star vehicles for Montez; these Technicolor fantasies included *White Savage*, *Ali Baba and the Forty Thieves*, *Gypsy Wildcat*, *Cobra Woman*, and *Sudan*. The glamour of movie stars like Dietrich, the true grit of westerns, and the high camp of Montez's movies would all find eventual expression in Robbins's novels.

In later life Harold liked to present himself as a fictional wunderkind, an ordinary man who one day woke up to find that he could bash out a novel. His first attempt at writing, he said, was when he sat down at a typewriter and wrote the opening pages of *Never Love a Stranger*. "From that point on it seemed as if this is what I should have been doing all my life," he said, "because when I took that first page out I said to myself, 'nobody told me it would be this easy.'"[13]

But squirreled away in the files of the Harold Robbins archive, in the Howard Gotlieb Archival Research Center at Boston University, are fragments of what appear to be one of his early fictional efforts. The incomplete novel, based on the life of the campaigning nineteenth-century British journalist William Thomas Stead, tells the true story of how the editor of the *Pall Mall Gazette* fought a battle against child prostitution. In his pioneering article "The Maiden Tribute of Modern Babylon," Stead exposed the hidden world of Victorian vice—its seedy brothels, money-grabbing madams, and insatiable upper-class rakes who enjoyed "the exclusive luxury of revelling in the cries of an immature child." In order to prove his point—and get a cracking good story—Stead bought a thirteen-year-old girl, Eliza Armstrong, and subsequently laid himself open for prosecution; he was duly sentenced to three months in prison for abduction.

The subject matter was perfect for Harold, mixing as it did some of his favorite tropes: a blend of fact and fiction with a flawed hero battling against convention; a complicated and highly controversial legal case; and the lure of illegal, illicit sex. He set out to research the novel in great detail: his bibliography runs to five pages and includes works such as Stead's essays, the *Times* law reports from 1885, a crop of biographies, and books by Josephine Butler. But the execution is poor even by Robbins's standards, packed with clichéd characters and melodramatic situations. The documentary, real-life nature of the case also seems to have been a disadvantage, as he failed to imaginatively reconstruct the personalities involved, relying instead on journalistic reportage.

Toward the end of the manuscript, writing in the author's voice, he tells a prospective editor the rest of the story—Stead's descent into depression and his death on the *Titanic* in 1912—and then adds an apology. The final chapters, written in a factual format, will have to be fleshed out, he said, while certain characters, who appear in earlier chapters, will have to be reintroduced into the narrative.[14] Although Harold spent hours at the typewriter, getting up early in the mornings before work in order to write, the manuscript never made it as far as an editor's desk.

The experience, however, was a valuable one. He came to understand the discipline necessary for writing, learned the basic techniques of popular fiction—the central importance of storytelling—and discovered his much-loved trick, one he would repeat in many of his novels, of exploiting the news value of an infamous personality. He would also remember Stead's words, of 1871: "Society . . . outwardly, indeed, appears white and glistening, but within is full of dead men's bones and rottenness."[15]

In the early 1940s Harold felt increasingly dissatisfied. Although he enjoyed certain aspects of his job at Universal—the satisfaction that came from balancing the books and the security of his position—he realized he wanted more. He became frustrated at observing the moviemaking process from the outside and aspired to become part of the action. Sylvia Miles, the actress, remembers him telling her of the moment he became aware of his ambitions:

"He was studying business at night school and working during the day at Universal. One of his jobs was delivering cans to screening rooms—New York at that time had a tremendous amount of them. One day after dropping off a can of film, just as he was walking up from a basement with another kid, he saw a limousine pull up and a little guy get out. Harold asked who it was, and he was told that the man was a producer. Harold asked, 'What's a producer?' and he learned that he was guy with the property. 'What's that?' he asks, and is told, '*Gone with the Wind*, that's a property.' 'No kidding,' he says. So that night he went home and asked Lillian, 'Did you ever read *Gone with the Wind*?' And she said, 'Of course, everyone read it.' He read ten pages and said to himself, I can do better than this, and started to write."[16]

Harold voiced his frustrations to his boss, the president of Universal, Nate Blumberg, and told him that he wanted to go to Hollywood to make movies. Blumberg, however, advised Robbins to stick to being a "fine statistician," as movie producers had to know about "story values . . . [and] the workings of a plot." Harold came up with an idea for a film, but the treatment was dismissed as clichéd, "a stock-in-trade scenario that was pitched to the studio every other week." Robbins refused to be dismissed and kept on pestering Blumberg, who finally told him that a successful producer had to be a "man of some cultural background. A man who appreciates the finer things in life, who has written, let's say, a best-selling novel. Harold, why don't you go back to your statistics?"[17]

Harold did go back to his columns of figures, but he did not forget what his boss had told him. He started to write more in his spare time, staying late in his office in Rockefeller Center while waiting to call colleagues on the West Coast. Finally, after learning that his studio had bought a novel that in his opinion was far from top quality for $300,000, he decided he had had enough and informed Raymond Crossett, the story editor, that he could do better: "I told a colleague I could write a better book myself, and he said, 'All you ever write is checks.' Then he pulled out a hundred dollars and bet me I couldn't. I was determined, by then, to prove him wrong."[18]

Diana Jervis-Read remembers hearing a slightly different form of the story from both Robbins and Crossett, with whom she worked closely at Harold Robbins International:

"When Harold was at Universal, he had an argument with Ray that forced him to write his first book," she says. "And I can quite believe it; Ray was very buttoned up, and Harold was the opposite. Some script came in that, in Harold's opinion, was absolute rubbish, and he wouldn't do a budget for it. So when Ray eventually turned up in his office to ask him what he had done with the budget for the film, Harold said, 'I'm not doing one for that piece of old rubbish.' Ray bristled and said, 'Don't tell me that—your job is to produce the budget.'"[19]

Harold was so incensed by Blumberg's and Crossett's lack of enthusiasm that he started to plot out the book that would be published as Never Love a Stranger in 1948. He started writing it in 1942, getting up at two a.m. after only a couple of hours' sleep to bash out a few pages on his typewriter. "I couldn't sleep," he said in 1949. "Something in me had to be said, and I felt relaxed, writing until five o'clock each morning."[20]

By the end of 1945 he had finished a first draft, an epic he initially entitled But One Life that sprawled across 738 manuscript pages. On 17 December 1945 he called Annie Laurie Williams, a drama and motion picture agent who worked closely with the literary agency McIntosh & Otis and who represented a range of high-profile clients including Margaret Mitchell, John Dos Passos, Kathleen Winsor, and one of Robbins's favorite writers, John Steinbeck. Harold followed up the call with a letter to Pamela Barnes, a member of Williams's staff, explaining that the manuscript he had sent over to the agency, But One Life, had not been seen by any other publisher or agent. He worked at Universal, he said, and he would be away from New York over Christmas but back at his desk on 3 January.

He later claimed that the name Harold Robbins "was given to me by Alfred Knopf, who didn't think that Rubin was literary enough," but in fact it was he who chose to submit the novel under a pseudonym, the rather odd-sounding Harrod Robbins.[21] "The nom de plume, Harrod Robbins, for a man named a good honest Jewish Harold Rubin is purely nauseating," wrote one early reader of the manuscript. "If he'd written a little simpering comedy of manners where a pretty name is necessary that might be different, but since this is almost a document, I'd suggest the more forthright name he was born with."[22] Later, of course, it would be changed to Harold Robbins.

McIntosh and Otis sent out the book to a reader, Pat Tanner—who would later find fame as Patrick Dennis, the author of the celebrated *Auntie Mame* novels. Tanner could barely contain his enthusiasm. "Settle down with a cigarette," his report begins. "This is going to take a long time. First: I want a double fee for this if you like it. Nothing if you don't . . . I think it's one of the most magnificent, most naturally written, most commercially feasible novels I've ever read . . . I believe that in the hands of a good, gutty publisher like S&S or Random House it would make a million dollars and after a good general hysterectomy it might make movie material. It's strong enough, good enough, and lusty enough to swing the trend of slums-to-Sing-Sing novels right back to where they were in the thirties. It's awfully long and I like it that way. It's sexy with an almost monotonous regularity that's well done, too. It has heaps of power—it's better than Cain, like Dos Passos. It's as episodic as Ulyses [sic] and could probably be cut under duress but I like it almost as it stands."[23]

Tanner sketched out the plot of the book—the picaresque story of an orphan, Francis Kane, who battles his way through the Depression and emerges as a gangland leader—highlighting its strengths and weaknesses. Certain elements of the narrative didn't quite add up, particularly the division of the story into "What Came Before" and "What Came After." But he thought this problem could be easily fixed, while the alternation of first- and third-person voices gave the book "a pretty U.S.A. fillip." He believed certain scenes were unconvincing, such as one sequence (later excised from the novel) in which a drunken prostitute takes off her clothes and offers to service a group of young boys swimming down by the docks of the Hudson. But others, like the section in which Francis indulges in a little light erotic play with a nun at his orphanage (again cut out from the final version), he found "perfectly delightful." He would recommend editing out the long philosophical speeches delivered by certain characters, but he stressed that it was important to keep the novel's naturalistic and, for its time, quite daring language. "The . . . dialogue is good and full of refreshing dirty words," he wrote. "In fact I think the sheer earthiness is entirely conducive to the whole strength of the book."[24]

He surmises that if Robbins has not lived through most of this story, then he has a magnificent grasp of life and of people. Not only is he tough, but his work is refreshing. "I think he may replace all the biggest names that cropped up between the wars," he prophesies, "and I hope you'll agree with me after reading it."[25]

Lois Dwight Cole, who worked at McIntosh & Otis, was not as sold on the manuscript as Tanner. The first portion of the story read as though it was most probably autobiographical, said Cole, while the rest of the narrative seemed contrived and false. It was also "unnecessarily long and vulgar."[26]

Cole offered to send the manuscript out to publishing houses such as Farrar and Rinehart or Putnam's—those "who might be interested in this type of tale"[27]—but the agency seems to have concluded that Robbins should rewrite parts of the book. Early the following year the novel was ready to submit to a publisher, and on 6 February 1947 *But One Life* was sent to William Koshland at Knopf. Koshland passed it on to editor in chief Harold Strauss, who found the book "tantalizing because it exhibits striking merits and striking faults."

On the plus side, Strauss complimented Robbins's virtuosity as a storyteller. "He has what amounts to a genius for the evocation of situations, for swift plotting," said Strauss. "He has that narrative sense which is as valuable as it is rare. His seven hundred pages move as rapidly as a [James M.] Cain novel." He also praised Robbins's ear for dialogue, especially the conversations of those on the lower rungs of society. "He knows the New York streets and their ways as well as [James T.] Farrell knows the streets of Chicago," he said. "In fact, there is so much solidity and atmosphere in the first 182 pages . . . that at first I was inclined to credit the book with some literary merit." He liked the novel's humanity and its warmth as well as the "apparent seriousness" of its treatment of issues such as race relations, gambling, racketeering, unemployment, and prostitution.

The style, however, said Strauss, was far from distinguished and somewhat commonplace. Moreover the novel was "shockingly pornographic . . . Frankie falls in and out of love and in and out of bed with more women than one would believe." One scene featuring a masochistic prostitute in Baltimore seemed particularly offensive. "The novel is shockingly obscene in its language," he added. "Four-letter words are used with inexcusable frequency. In fact, there is no reason for the use of any of them." Robbins would also need to work on the character of Ruth, who eventually marries Frankie and gives birth to his son, and completely rewrite the final section of the novel, which was hurried and executed in a careless fashion. The physical violence would also have to be toned down, as the end result was less shocking than melodramatic. And finally the issues that Strauss believed Robbins had handled with "apparent seriousness" could, on second reading, appear superficial and without substance.

In conclusion, however, Strauss thought that Knopf should accept the book, "largely on the ground that Robbins seems to be a born storyteller."[28] He then passed the novel on to Alfred "Pat" Knopf, son of Alfred and Blanche Knopf. His assessment of *But One Life* was as enthusiastic as Pat Tanner's, and while he realized that the manuscript needed a lot of work, he believed that they were on to a winner.

"Knopf has THE NOVEL for 1948, and THIS IS IT!!! These 650 pages are superheated with the pathos, the humor, the gore, the tears and the hurt, the love and the laughter that went into *A Tree Grows in Brooklyn*, *Written on the Wind*, *A Lion Is in the Streets*, *East River*— and yes, *The Yearling* and *Mister Roberts*. In short this is terrific!

"But it needs work, lots of work. It needs the type of work that *Look Homeward Angel* must have needed when Tom Wolfe first sent it into Scribners. (I don't mean to imply that this is in any remote way comparable to anything Wolfe wrote.) But if HS [Harold Strauss] can sit down with the author, and spend what may turn out to be a matter of months working over . . . this manuscript, we've got a lulu!"[29]

In addition to the problems mentioned by Strauss, all of which he agreed with, Knopf added a few points of his own. The middle section of the story, which details Frankie's life after leaving George Washington High School up until the time when he gets involved in the betting racketeering business, seemed overwritten and superfluous. The sentimentality "that works into your veins and your tearducts" at the start of the book is absent throughout the central part of the narrative, only returning for the last hundred or so pages. "If we take this, I'll get together with Harold [Strauss]," he said. "If we don't, we'll all be saved a lot of work, to be sure, and perhaps some handy income for 1948. Yours for a terrific (I can't think of any other appropriate adjective) five hours reading."[30]

On balance, Knopf believed that the book was worth publishing, and on 12 March 1947 a contract was drawn up between his firm and Robbins. They offered an advance of $1,000, half on signing the contract and half on delivery of the revised manuscript before 1 July. Knopf also confirmed the royalty rate—17.5 percent up to sales of 12,500, 21 percent to 20,000, and 25 percent thereafter—and agreed that they would have an option on Robbins's next three books over sixty thousand words in length. "I hope you will convey to Mr. Rubin," wrote Harold Strauss to Robbins's agency, "how pleased we are to become publishers of his novels, and the great things we expect of him."[31]

The signing, however, was not to everyone's liking at the upscale publishing house of Knopf, which Robbins described as rather staid. When Alfred and Blanche Knopf returned from their vacation, they were appalled to discover that their son had bought a novel they considered beneath contempt. "I think he [Alfred, his father] washed his hands of it," said Pat. "I think he said, "If you want it, you take care of it." I thought it was a terrific book."[32]

Harold Robbins told a spicier version of the same story. "My novel was purchased by Alfred Knopf Jr. while his parents were away, and when they came back and saw this novel, they almost fired him because it's not their kind of book. They said, 'Why did you buy it?' He said, 'Because I've never read a book where I cried on one page, and had a hard-on on the next.' "[33]

Over the course of the next few months Harold busied himself on the revisions, following Strauss's suggestions to the letter. By the beginning of June he had cut thirty-five pages, reducing its length to around 150,000 words. He eliminated the sequence with the masochistic prostitute, erased some scenes that featured a "hobo," cut a section that described a rape that took place in a hallway, and cleaned up the language considerably. Strauss was pleased with Robbins's rewrites but still had a number of problems with the book. First, he hated the title, *But One Life*. Could Robbins think of another one? The author wrote back, outlining an alternative title, *Give Him a Stone*—foreshadowing Robbins's third novel, *A Stone for Danny Fisher*—but Knopf did not like this either. On 19 June Strauss wrote to Robbins suggesting it should be called *Never Love a Stranger*—taken from Stella Benson's poem "To the Unborn"—a title that the

author liked and accepted. A week later Knopf formally acknowledged the acceptance of the manuscript and sent Robbins a check for
$500, the remaining balance on the $1,000 advance.

When Robbins returned from a two-week vacation at the beginning
of July, he started work on another set of revisions with Strauss,
ironing out some of the clichés and tidying up the manuscript. The
book was, Strauss believed, "in that special class of novel which
appears to have enough serious ideas about society (in this case
unemployment, race relations, racketeering, and the problem of
orphan children) to titillate the women's clubs, but actually is feather-
weight, superior slick-magazine writing with strong element of tear-
jerking sentimentality."[34]

Unknown to Robbins, the sales department had duly prepared their
predictions, of the book's sales. Classifying it as "merchandise fiction," Knopf believed that the book would sell around 25,000 in the
first six months and ordered an initial print run of 10,000 copies. And
after the first six months? "Poor," predicted the sales team. The
number crunchers at Knopf could not have been more wrong.

4

"I should prefer that my own three daughters meet the facts of life and the literature of the world in my library than behind a neighbor's barn."
—Judge Curtis Bok, quoted during
the Harold Robbins obscenity ruling

T HE TWO OFFICERS from the vice squad sat in their car and watched. The light from the red neon sign above the bookstore turned the puddle of rainwater on the sidewalk into a pool of blood. Men, with hats pulled down over their faces, lurked in the dark alleyway, occasionally entering the store to make a purchase. They reappeared with a package, sometimes two, that was invariably wrapped in brown paper, then disappeared into the darkness. The scene was the same night after night, a nocturnal parade of silhouettes and shadows.

Then one evening toward the end of March 1948 the detectives received an order from their boss, Inspector Craig Ellis, head of the Philadelphia vice squad. It was time. As the officers approached the midcity bookstore, the nervous customers who hung around the doorway melted away. "It's a raid," shouted the officers as they burst through the door, a command that cleared the shop within seconds. Almost immediately the cops started to seize the books from the shelves, forcing the store's owner to open up his stockroom. At the end of the raid the detectives congratulated themselves on unearthing a vast array of obscene material, books that were designed, according to Craig Ellis, to incite lewd and lecherous desires.

Philadelphia was in need of a serious purge, according to the authorities, and Ellis had taken it upon himself to rid the city of sleaze. Not only did he want to remove works by sensation-seeking pulp fiction authors and producers of pornography, but he also felt it important to rid the town of the novels of James T. Farrell, Erskine Caldwell, and William Faulkner. Over the course of those few days Ellis instructed his men to raid fifty-four stores and confiscate two thousand books, of which Robbins's *Never Love a Stranger* was one. Even before the novel was published, it had developed a reputation for explicitness. "By the middle of March, the country will be in a mild uproar over the daffiest, most jumbled and screwball novel of years," wrote John McNulty in January 1948. ". . . Harold Robbins wrote it and it makes *Forever Amber* look like *Pilgrim's Progress*."[1]

Two weeks after the raids Knopf launched a $200,000 lawsuit on behalf of its new author and Charles Praissman, the Philadelphia bookseller who had been selling the title. Attorney Charles E. Kenworthey charged that the Philadelphia police—in particular James H. Malone, director of public safety and vice squad detectives Craig Ellis and John McCarthy—had violated the Fourth Amendment of the American constitution. "A lot of people told me that the DA didn't like the part of my book where the main character comes out of the Philadelphia navy yard and all the whores are there," Robbins said later, "he thought it was too dirty."[2]

Publicly at least, Robbins was furious that his novel had been accused of being obscene and immoral. On 29 March he issued, via his publisher, a statement to the press in which he compared the actions of the Philadelphia vice squad to the thought-control police of Japan during the Second World War. Although Americans of his generation initially viewed the actions of the Japanese as laughable— the idea of being able to control the thoughts of a human being was ridiculous—they came to realize that citizens living under an authoritarian regime were actually terrified of the police. After all, the simple act of reading a particular book was enough to send that person to prison or possibly to an even worse fate.

Surely, Robbins argued, what the Philadelphia police were trying to do in seizing his novel was nothing less than control the thoughts of its inhabitants. He defied those who had raided the bookshops to prove that any of the novels were obscene or immoral or that they had the power to contaminate the minds of their readers. "The author who presents an irritating truth is no more to blame for the truth than a physician who must present a disturbing diagnosis," he wrote. If the Philadelphia thought-control police had been around when Harriet Beecher Stowe's *Uncle Tom's Cabin* had first been published, he claimed, they would have removed that book from stores on the grounds that it upset conventional thinking. "Social problems cannot be solved by closing the mind to ideas," he said. "Nor can they be solved by banning books which present these phenomena. The public's unrestricted right to accept or reject these books represents the intellectual freedom of America. Without such freedom there can be no other."[3]

As a result of the legal challenge—and the rather racy content of the book—the novel received blanket media coverage. "Mr. Robbins writes like a promising high school senior who's set himself the task of out Hemingwaying Hemingway, out James T. Farrelling James T. Farrell, out Ambering forever and out raising James M. Cain," Bill Leonard told his radio listeners. "The result is a book that is almost indescribable . . . a novel that bursts over with an incessant, utterly uncontrolled energy . . . a story that meanders its heroes into a wild succession of incredible incidents, almost all involving attractive ladies of various ages, creeds and colors . . . most of it . . . is not too far above the level of amateur pornography."[4]

Although the book had been heavily edited by Knopf—the four-letter words had been removed, the sex scenes had been reduced, and the overall steaminess had been cooled down—*Never Love a Stranger* still had the power to shock. Robbins remembered going down to the subway and seeing two teenage girls with a copy of the novel.

"They were pointing to a section and laughing, and I was consumed with curiosity as to what bit they were discussing," he said. "So I moved closer until I was almost leaning on one girl's shoulder. She looked at me with disgust, said something I'd hate to see repeated in print, and moved away. Embarrassed as I was, that didn't kill the thrill of seeing my book being read in public—my first encounter with fame."[5]

Contemporary readers were titillated by its overripe language—its use of phrases such as "muff diver"—as well as its frank, and quite brutal, portrayal of sex.[6] Twenty pages after first being introduced to

Francis Kane, the novel's protagonist, we witness him try to have sex with a friend's mother. The thirteen-year-old boy notices that the woman's breasts were "awful big and juicy" and, feeling aroused, he offers her two dollars for sex.[7] After the woman slips her dress over her head, Frankie pulls down his pants and lies beside her. But he is too nervous to perform.

Ten pages later, Frankie, still thirteen, loses his virginity with the housemaid of another friend. "She put her arms around me and kissed me," Robbins wrote. "I could feel her tongue flicker in and out against my lips, her hands against my body." As the woman falls back onto the bed, she asks him to be gentle with her, before changing her mind and pleading with him to "Hurt me, please hurt me."[8]

In the subsequent chapters Frankie takes a job as a heavy in a brothel in Baltimore; has sex with a fourteen-year-old black hooker; and persuades a woman who cannot afford her food bill to offer herself to him in exchange for a box of groceries. As he begins to feel aroused, he touches her but then makes the mistake of looking at her face, devoid of feeling, which he finds a turn-off. "It wasn't a woman I had there, it was an empty shell."[9]

Not surprisingly, many of the reviews centered on the novel's obsession with sex. "Mr. Robbins tells this story with a wealth of scatological terms, details of brutality and cruelty, and incident of violence,"[10] wrote a critic for the *Philadelphia Bulletin*. "It's a lurid story and in many respects a sordid one," stated a commentator in *Harper's Magazine*, "but the author tells it with a furious conviction and a story-telling gift that puts it almost in the thriller class." Francis J. Ullrich, a professor at Manhattan College, found the book to be full of "vice, vulgarity, obscenity, murder and—fornication."[11]

By the third week of March, Knopf had capitalized on the controversy, choosing to take out an advertisement in the *New York Herald Tribune* under the headline, "The novel all New York is talking about." Along with edited highlights from certain critics—"A minor Les Misérables of New York City," "Boils . . . fiercely with action and violence"[12]—the publicity executives at Knopf printed a whole paragraph from the *New York Times* review written by Isabelle Mallet.

"Here are shattering pictures of gray-faced poverty; quiet queasy corruption; cheap sordid vice; race prejudice swollen into frightening violence; unmistakable decency thriving next door to degradation; kindness born of man's direst extremity. Wherever the author has caught an echo of the tremendous adventure story of New York's jungle life, he has left a clear memorable picture. He has an easy familiarity with the sidewalks of New York which produces a solid atmosphere."[13]

But, the advertisement failed to include Mallet's more negative comments. The novel, she said, suffered from an excess of "unruly local color," too much detail at the expense of characterization. Although the book is, in part, narrated in the first person by Frankie, the motivations of the protagonist remain opaque. Fellow *New York Times* writer Orville Prescott had a similar problem with the book.

"He has tried to explain the confused motives and mysterious character of his repulsive hero, to explain why he acted as he did," Prescott wrote. "In this he has failed completely. His Frankie Kane is a vicious scoundrel all right, but he is not a comprehensible or even interesting character." Far from being a serious work of fiction, said Prescott, *Never Love a Stranger* should be viewed as nothing more than a flashy scenario for a gangster film, "juicy movie material for James Cagney or George Raft."[14]

Robbins learned from this mixed bag of comments—there were, according to Knopf, four good, four bad, and seven moderate reviews—not to take the critics too seriously. He was more interested in sales. In order to boost the novel's popularity, and in turn his royalty checks, at the beginning of May Robbins contributed $2,000 to an additional advertising campaign costing $5,000. He also wrote a letter to a number of bookstores, thanking them for their support. In the few months since the novel had been published, he had been praised and attacked, but nothing, he said, had given him more of a thrill than the experience of signing books. He flattered the booksellers into believing that the success of the novel was due entirely to their efforts rather than his own.

The combination of advertising and personal intervention worked. By 6 May sales of the novel had nearly reached the 18,000 mark. Without a doubt, the whiff of scandal brought about by the Philadelphia vice squad raid certainly helped raise the novel's profile. "I doubt very much if you'll make any money out of this," wrote Pat Knopf to Robbins about the case, "but it certainly may sell some books."[15]

Money, however, was very much on Robbins's mind. At the beginning of 1948 he had already sacked his first literary agent, believing that the $1,000 advance he had received for *Never Love a Stranger* was too low, and instead signed on with Maurice Crain, the husband of Annie Laurie Williams, who continued to represent his dramatic and motion picture rights. In a telegram he sent to Pat Knopf on publication day, he joked that *Never Love a Stranger* had not filled his pockets with dollars, unlike the enterprises of Frankie Kane, whom he described as a cross between Casanova and Superman. But he refused to be discouraged, announcing that on 21 March 1949 he would deliver another novel.

Ever since he started work at Universal, Robbins had been taking mental notes about the moviemaking business, believing that its development from the early days of the nickelodeon and the silent film to the invention of sound was the perfect theme for a novel. It had, he believed, everything—glamour, money, sex, power, ambition, corruption, and betrayal. Adding to its appeal, the industry was based on illusions, its products a construction of mass fantasies. In fact, he thought that he had amassed so much material it could easily make three books, a trilogy which he provisionally entitled *The Pictures Company*.

"When I wrote *The Dream Merchants*, I wrote about the Laemmles, and the Foxes, and the Selznicks, and how what happened to them affected them," he said later. "*The Dream Merchants* is a sentimental story; *The Carpetbaggers* is a very hard story, about people who are very greedy, and they knew what they wanted, and they were going to get it. And *The Inheritors* is about the Computer Man. They're all my world, my interpretation of movie history."[16]

He started work on the first of the novels, which he initially called *The Pioneers*, before the publication of *Never Love a Stranger*, writing during snatched moments of time at work at Universal-International's new offices on Park Avenue and on weekends and early in the morning at home in Brooklyn. Robbins was nothing if not determined and hard-working, and by the end of July 1948 he had delivered the first nine chapters to Knopf. "I think you must have heard enough about this whole project from Harold to require no more fill-in from me," Maurice Crain wrote to Harold Strauss. "He has worked out a general outline for the proposed trilogy and a detailed outline for this book . . .

"Harold has been groping for several months in an effort to find the right approach to this ambitious tale. Patience and pertinacity are among his principal virtues as an author. I have seen three starts before this, none of which seemed to me satisfactory but each a little better than the last. Now I think he has solved his main difficulties and produced some copy which is worth your attention. We'll both be awaiting your verdict with the keenest interest."[17]

Strauss was impressed by Robbins's narrative skills—"he has that miraculous sense of timing and pace which makes a story readable," he said—and by his ability to switch between characters' perspectives without losing momentum. He had a few minor quibbles—there was perhaps too much Yiddish dialogue, as well as an excess of adverbs and adjectives—but on the whole he enjoyed it. Not only that, but "Robbins achieves his effect here entirely without sex,"[18] he said.

Two months later Robbins had finished another eighty pages, bringing the story up to page 165. Crain, however, chose not to edit this section as he had the earlier submission and sent it in to Knopf in its virgin state. Harold Strauss was shocked by what he saw. On 30 September, Strauss sat down to write a report on this rough draft— "and is it *rough!*" he noted privately.

"This is the first time I have seen any of Rubin's first draft ms [manuscripts]—and I must say that the writing is mighty crude and superficial. Rubin, even for the merchandise fiction market, must probe a little deeper into Johnny's feelings, must do a little more with mood and setting, must try to ferret out more of the implications of his scenes. He relies too much on glib dialogue. What his characters say isn't nearly as interesting as what they do. He slips too often into an unpleasant sloppiness of phrase. And he will have to be very very much on his guard against using movie trade jargon. For instance, he speaks many times of 'developing a completely rounded feature' or 'editing it down to a six-reel subject.' There is a glimmer of meaning here, but it certainly is a hideous way to put it."[19]

In October, Crain sent Knopf a revision of the second segment of the novel, apologizing for the thinness of the writing. Robbins, he acknowledged, was a writer who needed a lot of polishing and a great deal of editorial guidance, but he believed the end result would be worth it. Harold worked hard on rewriting the book, submitting another draft in

March 1949. Although the novel—now renamed *The Dream Merchants*—had been vastly improved, Strauss still had difficulties with
certain aspects, particularly some of the characters' motivations and the
author's technique. He suggested that Robbins reshape certain plotlines
and flesh out some of the protagonists, and he advised him to cut back on
the amount of information in his sentences. "Sometimes this can be
cleared up by using semi-colons," he said, "(a very useful mark of
punctuation; you ought to use them more)."[20]

A month later he was surprised by what arrived in the mail. "Words
fail me to express my awe and excitement over the way Robbins has
not only improved the structural defects in the previous version," he
said, ". . . but succeeded in milking the last ounce of drama and
pathos out of the situation." Over the course of the last two edits he
had cut down the number of clichés in the writing, but many still
remained. "Robbins will never be a polished stylist," he said. "No one
can succeed in eliminating clichés and banalities from his writing."[21]

But it hardly mattered. Knopf knew that Robbins had delivered a
cracking good read, while the author realized that he had beefed up his
bargaining power. "The author's intent is to obtain a fairly substantial
sum this year," Harold Strauss told Knopf's treasurer, "so that, in the
event the book sells very well, all royalty payments will not fall into
the single calendar year of 1950."[22] After discussion with Pat, it was
decided to increase Robbins's advance from $1,000 to $2,500, plus,
on publication date, a further advance equivalent to two-thirds of
accrued royalties less the $2,500 already paid. Crain also managed to
negotiate a better royalty rate of a straight 25 percent.

Robbins's fortunes were certainly looking up. Sales of *Never Love a
Stranger* were soaring—by February it had been reprinted eight times
and had sold more than 35,000 copies, making it Knopf's best-selling
title of 1948—and at the beginning of the year the book was given some
extra publicity when a date was set for the Philadelphia obscenity trial.
Although some writers, such as Jack Woodford, author of *The Abortive
Hussy*, *Illicity*, and *Male and Female*, had chosen to withdraw their
titles from sale in Pennsylvania rather than risk prosecution, others,
including Erskine Caldwell, William Faulkner, Calder Willingham,
James T. Farrell, and Robbins, opted to battle on.

On 18 March Judge Curtis Bok, after reading all of the so-called

"dirty" books, released a twenty-thousand-word statement conclud-
ing that Section 524 of the Commonwealth Law, relating to obscene
material, could not be applied to writing unless it could be proved it
was sexually impure and pornographic. "Far from inciting to lewd or
lecherous desires, which are sensorially pleasurable," he said, "these
books leave one either with a sense of horror or of pity for the
degradation of mankind."

But would he want one of his own daughters to read such filth,
asked one of the lawyers. Surely these kinds of scurrilous novels would
corrupt an innocent mind? Judge Bok said that he would much rather
have his daughter learn about the facts of life within the confines of his
library than behind a neighboring barn.

"I suppose that by the time she is old enough to wish to read them
she will have learned the biologic facts of life and the words that go
with them," he added. "There is something seriously wrong at home if
those facts have not been met and faced and sorted by then. It is not
children so much as parents that should receive our concern about this
. . . If the young ladies are appalled by what they read, they can close
the books at the bottom of Page 1."

Society was changing, he said, and people felt a greater degree of
openness about certain matters, issues that would have been previously
censored. "The consensus of preference today is for disclosure and not
stealth, for frankness and not hypocrisy and for public and not discreet
distribution . . . It is my opinion that frank disclosure cannot legally be
censored, even as an exercise of the police power, unless it is sexually
impure and pornographic." He concluded that as the books in question
were neither sexually impure nor pornographic, they were therefore not
"obscene, lewd, lascivious, filthy, indecent or disgusting."[23]

Years later Robbins looked back on the landmark legal case.
"Because I won that suit," he said, "it opened things up so that
Henry Miller could be published, Anaïs Nin could be published, D. H.
Lawrence could be published . . . The reason I went through with it is
because I was stupid. No one ever told me that authors and publishers
don't sue the court. I couldn't understand why people just accepted
this censorship."[24]

But even fiercer sex and censorship battles lay ahead.

5

"In order to be a writer you have to stick your ass
down on the chair and write"
—Harold Robbins to his friend Archer King.

H AROLD TOOK ANOTHER drag of his cigarette and looked out
the window of his Manhattan office. He had spent the morning
scanning columns of figures in various ledger books, using the adding
machine on his desk to calculate the budget of a film, and his eyes felt
tired. Mounds of paper surrounded him—cost analyses of movies,
tallies of profit and loss, reports, memos, and schedules. He may have
written a best seller, but he was in no position to leave his job. As he
sat there, he started to fantasize about what he would do if he was rich:
how he would swap his crummy apartment in Brooklyn for a
swankier pad; how he would buy Lillian a trunkload of fur coats
and a blaze of Tiffany jewelry; how he would spend his days lounging
around the pool just like those Hollywood stars. Just then his phone
rang. It was Nate Blumberg's secretary, requesting that Robbins meet
with the president of Universal.

Harold stood up and slipped on the jacket that had been hanging over
the back of his chair. He tightened the knot of his tie, ran his hands
through his hair, and made his way up to the president's office. Waiting
outside by the secretary's desk, Harold felt more than a little nervous. How
would Blumberg feel about the way the movie industry had been por-
trayed in his latest novel, *The Dream Merchants*? What would he say if
the president took him to task for portraying the film world as populated
by a rash of power-crazed egocentrics? Was he about to lose his job?

"You can go in now, Mr. Robbins," said the secretary, giving him a knowing smile.

Harold licked his lips, took a deep breath and opened the door.

"Robbins," said Blumberg, getting up from his desk, to go and slap him on the shoulder. "How ya' doin?"

"Fine, Mr. Blumberg, just fine."

"Come over here and sit down," he said. "I don't know how best to say this, but I'm afraid you're to blame for what I can only describe as a marital dispute."

Harold felt beads of sweat begin to form on his forehead. What had he done?

"Well—I—"

"Don't look so serious, boy," said Blumberg, laughing. "I have to say that Mrs. Blumberg and I tend to agree on most things, but as far as this is concerned we are at loggerheads."

"I'm afraid I don't really—"

"This! This!" said the studio boss, picking up an early copy of *The Dream Merchants*.

So it was the book after all. Blumberg had found something he didn't like.

"I'm sorry if you find it—"

"Sorry? What's there to be sorry about? It's the best novel about Hollywood I've read in years. Couldn't put it down. In fact, Mrs. Blumberg was cussing you because I kept her awake reading it late into the night. Of course, when I'd finished it, she picked it up and did the same thing, the bedside light still shining into my goddam eyes at three in the morning. But the next day, we had this almighty argument."

"Oh, really?"

"My wife insists that the character Johnny Edge in your book is patterned after Carl Laemmle, but I don't agree. I think it's Adolph Zukor. I'm dying to settle the argument with her, tell her I'm right. So, come on Robbins, which one is it? Give me the lowdown on who's right."

"Well, you're both right," said Harold. "The characters are composites."[1]

Robbins had had to make sure of that. After all, he had already dragged the good name of Knopf into the courts once. Blanche and

Alfred certainly did not want this upstart's second novel to involve their publishing house in another costly lawsuit. Before the book was published, Harold Strauss had written a letter to Knopf's New York lawyers, Stern & Reubens (a firm that would find itself dealing with even more of Robbins's legal wrangles), asking them to take a particularly close look at *The Dream Merchants*. "I suppose because we had one Robbins case we are being ultra careful," he said, "but both Mr. and Mrs. Knopf asked me expressly to show you the changes Harold Robbins made in *The Dream Merchants* to meet your criticism."[2]

A few days later one of the company's lawyers, Arthur Farmer, had written back with a strong warning that if the novel were to be published as it stood, it would almost certainly face a libel charge. Although Robbins had successfully disguised many of the real-life models for his characters, he had failed to do so for the villain of the piece, Philippe X. Danvere, who tries to take control of Magnum Pictures. It was obvious, said Farmer, that Danvere was based on J. Arthur Rank, the film magnate who owned more than a thousand theaters in Britain and who became Universal's biggest shareholder. Although Farmer advised Robbins, in an earlier draft, to change the character's nationality and make him Swiss, he was disappointed to see that this had been ignored. "All that has been done is to change Danvers' name to Danvere and to make him of Swiss ancestry," wrote Farmer. "I must repeat what I told you and Harold Rubin when you were in my office—in order to be protected, it will be necessary to make Danvers a Swiss, not a Swiss merely by ancestry. Further, it would be wise to credit him with controlling a chain of motion picture theaters not only in England but on the Continent as well. I know perfectly well that such a chain does not exist . . .

"You must not forget that although Rank is a man of importance and ordinarily would not be likely to sue for libel, you have made him . . . such a conniving, double-dealing SOB, that he might commence an action—particularly in England, where it would hurt most."[3]

Robbins duly followed the lawyer's advice to make the movie mogul less recognizable. He informed Harold Strauss that the real personalities had been "deeply disguised and that none of the incidents related have anything to do with the people on whom the characters are modeled."[4] Nonetheless insiders such as Budd Schulberg, the son of a movie producer and author of the Hollywood novel *What Makes Sammy Run?* (1941), quickly recognized the real-life figures. In a review of *The Dream Merchants* Schulberg praised the book for its ambitious scope and its narrative sweep, tracking as it did the story of Hollywood from the days of the nickelodeon in 1908 to the Wall Street–dominated film factory of 1938. He thought that although Robbins had researched his subject thoroughly, he had failed on an imaginative level.

"Paradoxically, its verisimilitude is a source of weakness as well as strength, for while the upward climb of immigrant shopkeepers to positions of power in the industry of mass entertainment makes colorful and entertaining reading, Mr. Robbins never quite succeeds in re-creating them as vital fictional characters. With the exception of Johnny Edge, these dream merchants are seen from the outside and characterized in such broad strokes as to qualify as types rather than individuals. Since they are drawn from actuality, they are true types and therefore help to create the flavor of authenticity that assures this book of a place above the Hollywood potboilers. Yet—to underline our paradox—the characters who are most 'true to life' are the least life-like, an esthetic irony Henry James among others has called to our attention."[5]

The New Yorker dismissed the novel as formulaic—"the scenes carefully rotate melodrama, tear-jerking, and sex, with all the problems solved at the end by a banker with a heart of gold"—and *Time* magazine regarded it as a sentimental sugar-spun saga, pulp fiction that was tedious in the extreme.[6] While moviegoers went to see films, according to the novelist, "for pleasure and escape from the cares of everyday living," unfortunately that was, in the words of the *Time* critic, "rather more than author Robbins has managed to provide for readers of his book."[7]

But *The New York Times* said the novel was "ingeniously constructed and . . . excellently written"[8]; *Kirkus Reviews* stated that the book was long but "never loses its hold on the roller-coaster momentum of this business"[9]; while Lewis Gannett, in the *New York Herald Tribune*, wrote that Robbins's novel had all the merits of a perfect movie.

In order to try to generate interest within the film world, Robbins sent the book to eighty key players in the industry. Stickers proclaiming "THE DREAM MERCHANTS are coming" were plastered across letters from Knopf to booksellers; the company sent personally inscribed first editions of the book to important buyers; and Robbins was drafted to do a number of signings, including Bloomingdale's in Manhattan. It was obvious that the publisher expected sales to match, or even exceed, those of *Never Love a Stranger*, which in October stood at 40,000 copies. On 28 September Robbins wrote a letter to Alfred Knopf Sr. thanking him and his staff for all their work. Alfred and Blanche Knopf, who had rather looked down on Robbins before, condescended to invite him to lunch on publication day, 17 October, adding "You are a nice man and a pleasant author to work with. We shall always do our best for you."[10]

Robbins was flattered and amused by the invitation but reluctantly turned it down as Pat Knopf had other plans for him on that day. Alfred wrote back inviting Robbins and his wife, Lillian, to a lunch on 20 October at the Harmonie Club on East 60th Street, the elegant Jewish members-only institution designed by Stanford White. The richly decorated interior, with its atmosphere of wealth and privilege, was very different from Robbins's home (at 80 Winthrop Street in Brooklyn) in a soulless red-brick apartment building.

Harold worked long hours at the Universal offices and had written two novels; advance sales of *The Dream Merchants* stood at 32,000. But what had he got to show for it? His spirits were boosted somewhat on 24 October when he received a check for $4,684 for accrued royalties on his latest book, but then he felt disappointed when he learned of the trifling amount—£50 on signature, another £50 on publication—that had been offered for the novel by Weidenfeld and Nicholson in Britain.

"I talked to the author this morning," said Maurice Crain, "and find that he has never heard of Weidenfeld and Nicholson and is not too happy about having his book placed with a secondary publisher. They may be perfectly good publishers for all he knows or I know, but I think he would need to be reassured on the subject."

The book had already been submitted to Evans Brothers, but Robbins had heard no news from them. Ideally, he said, he would prefer to be published by Heinemann or Collins in the U.K., but Crain had to outline a series of unpalatable truths. *Never Love a Stranger* had been offered to the British literary agency Curtis Brown, but they had been unable to place it with a publisher, "probably because it is a long book and came along as a first novel during the paper shortage," Crain said. Although Robbins was "not much impressed by the size of the advance" from Weidenfeld and Nicholson, Crain "assured him that is about what he should expect."[11] He had no choice but to accept the offer.

Lord Weidenfeld had only a brief acquaintance with Robbins, but he remembers him as being "pretty tough and self-absorbed."[12] Archer King, the talent agent, who met Robbins in the early 1950s, says that his friend "was beyond cynicism, nothing would surprise him. But you never got what you saw, and he only allowed a few people to know him. I think I did get to know him, but I realized that there were so many things going on inside. He had a real facade, a great defense. He was a deep person, but a conflicted one."[13]

This aspect of Robbins found expression in a piece he wrote for *The Hollywood Reporter* entitled "Dual Personality." Written in the first person and from the perspective of a character called Harold Robbins, it opens with the author rushing into the office of his psychiatrist, Greg, and asking him whether it is possible to be two people at the same time. The psychiatrist asks him to explain, and Robbins narrates the background to the problem.

"I work in the business office of a motion picture company; occasionally I write books," he says. "People were always telling me that it was difficult for them to reconcile the two—that one was basically a job with a mathematical background, and the other, my books, basically a creative emotional thing."

He used to laugh when friends said that one day he would have to choose between the two, as he had always believed that the two jobs expressed the different sides of his personality. The logical, mathematical side had always battled for dominance with his more creative, expressive qualities, but he had thought no more of this until the day before yesterday.

He goes on to relate what happened, describing how his secretary informed him that there was a man at reception who wanted to see

him. His name was Harold Robbins. Curious, Robbins asks the
secretary to send him up, and when the strange man walks into his
office, he is disturbed because he looks exactly like him. The mysterious caller introduces himself as Harold Robbins who writes books—
as opposed to the one in the office who works for a film company—
and an argument ensues.

"I thought I was the only Harold Robbins that wrote books," says
the character behind the desk.

"I wrote two books," he said, "*Never Love a Stranger* and *The
Dream Merchants*, and I am working on a third . . ."

The Robbins behind the desk—the one who works at Universal—
springs to his feet and accuses the stranger of being an imposter,
protesting that it was he who wrote those books. But the caller turns
on him and tells him that he is fed up with being kept in some secret
corner.

"Obviously . . . we both can't be Harold Robbins, but I will tell you
this, Mr. Robbins, I am the one who will be Harold Robbins when all
this is over!" he says, then storms out of the office.

Robbins rings down to his secretary and asks her if she has any idea
of the identity of the man she has just shown up to his office. No one
has been to see him, she replies. But surely she just called with news of
a man who wanted to see him? No, she didn't, she says, and asks him
if he is feeling all right. Robbins then heads to the nearest bar and
orders his favorite drink—a Scotch Old-Fashioned, dry, with no
sugar—only to find that the barman has just served him.

Robbins relates all this to the psychiatrist, then pleads with him to
help him, to reassure him that he has been having nothing more than a
series of nonsensical dreams. As he bursts into tears, Robbins begs the
doctor to tell him that it isn't true. Of course it isn't true, the
psychiatrist says—after all, hasn't he just said that same thing to
him twenty minutes earlier during their last session?[14]

The piece, for all its contrived air and rather gimmicky ending,
articulates a very real dilemma facing Robbins: whether he should
continue to enjoy the security provided by his job at Universal-
International, where he worked as assistant to Leon Goldberg, the
treasurer and vice president, or whether he should resign to concentrate on his novels.

"Harold loved figures and numbers," says Archer King. "I remember, soon after we first met, he took me up to his office where he showed me the charts for *The Fat Man* [the 1951 film starring Julie London, Rock Hudson, and J. Scott Smart]. He would project how much money a film would generate at the box office, and from all of this information he could determine how many movies they could make the following year. And yet he wrote at the same time as doing this job. He was extraordinarily talented in those early days and very hard-working. I remember him telling me, 'in order to be a writer you have to stick your ass down on the chair and write.' And he'd do just that—he would sit down at eleven o'clock and write all the way through the night."[15]

Robbins set himself a punishing schedule. In the spring of 1950 he began writing his third novel, *A Stone for Danny Fisher*, after which, he told his agents, he would start work on the second and third volumes of his movie trilogy, planning to deliver *The Carpetbaggers*, about the "Hollywoodites who cashed in on the pioneers," in 1953 and *The Inheritors* in 1955.[16]

By the beginning of July he had written the first 150 pages of *A Stone for Danny Fisher*, "a story about 'a boy grows in Brooklyn' as it were."[17] Maurice Crain was amazed that his client had written the material easily and "with little effort," compared to "the first hundred pages of *The Dream Merchants* [which] were drawn out painfully, with about three rewrites." Early indications suggested that the book would be a long one and would need cutting, but Crain said he was "inclined to give [Robbins] rope and let him push right ahead while the story is unfolding, leaving the cutting, tightening, and patching to be done later."[18]

The draft, said Harold Strauss, showed "Robbins's usual story-telling gifts, and his usual stylistic weaknesses." The Knopf editor was pleased, however, that the author had chosen to adopt a straightforward narrative technique rather than the "tricky flashbacks" he had used in his previous novels. "The material was submitted only because Robbins wanted to know if he is on the right track," said Strauss. "He is."[19]

Robbins continued to work on the novel at his new home, another anonymous-looking red-brick apartment building at 470 Ocean

Avenue in Brooklyn. By November he had written almost half the book, but when he showed it to Maurice Crain, his agent worried that it was going to be too long. "In a time when the economics of publishing favors the 300-to-400 page book (I mean typescript), you seem naturally geared to the 600–700 pager," he said. Yet he didn't find the novel slow going at all; rather, he thought the book a real page-turner. "The things that matter most, character, relationships, motivation, flow of the story, and emotional impact on the reader, are all here," he said.[20]

Harold worked at a furious pace, completing what he believed to be a final draft at the end of January 1951. Not only was Robbins pleased with the result, he wrote to Harold Strauss suggesting Knopf send him a check as soon as possible. Knopf, however, was not as satisfied with the nine hundred manuscript pages as the author. Strauss said he enjoyed the first 473 pages of the book—"with just a little guidance, Robbins can turn it into a fast-moving hard-boiled novel about amateur boxing and the seamy side of the Lower East Side life"— but he believed there was a big problem with the remaining 427 pages. "When he tries to write about the family life of decent people, he simply produces mush—maudlin, sloppy, mush," he said. "All this must be discarded, and the story line inherent in the first half followed to a conclusion."[21] Strauss also believed that the book would work better told completely in the first person, from Danny's perspective, rather than have alternating sections in the first and third persons.

In addition, Robbins also had a tendency to overuse certain words: *strange, suddenly, unconsciously, wide-eyed, tears, almost, silently, quickly,* and *slowly* as well as phrases and actions such as *feeling pain inside, smoking a cigarette, heart pounding,* and *trembling—fingers and legs.*[22]

The editors at Knopf also felt they had to tone down some of Robbins's sex scenes, which they considered too explicit. In the published version of the novel Danny relates how he feels sexually aroused when watching one of his neighbors undress. He hates himself for the feelings this young girl provokes in him until one day she follows him into the house and kisses him, but they are forced to pull apart when Danny hears his parents returning. In the published novel the couple do no more than kiss, but in the first draft of the same scene (which Robbins originally narrated in the third person) Danny pushes hard against her until her smock falls from her shoulders; he feels her naked flesh and touches her breasts, and the girl tells him to make love to her. The whole episode is described in such terms as Robbins would later become famous for—the infliction of pain as a weapon of seduction, the prominence of erect nipples, the explosion of orgasm. But these pseudo-pornographic snapshots, these flashes of erotica, were too much for Knopf, and they were all excised from the final manuscript.

Later Robbins would develop something of a reputation as a "difficult" author, one who refused to make changes or accept editing suggestions, but in the early stages of his career he was only too happy—if not grateful—to work closely with Knopf's highly experienced manuscript doctors. He told Pat Knopf that he was not a literary author and that he did not mind being cut, reshaped, and edited. Over the course of the following few months Robbins continued to revise his material, following the suggestions of Harold Strauss.

At times Strauss lost patience with what he considered the author's rather slapdash approach to writing. "Page 299—new marks [corrections]," Strauss wrote to him. "Can't you catch things like this yourself? A tin ear for English? It shows a lazy imagination, a lack of invention, and is not just carelessness."[23]

During June and July Robbins cut back the manuscript, and on 27 August he submitted the fourth rewrite of the novel. The book was finally approaching a form where it could be published.

"There is no doubt that Robbins has done it," said Strauss. "He has produced a tear-jerker that is in some ways a tighter and better story than *Never Love a Stranger*, using the same kind of background and material. This is a book about New York Jewish life on the Lower East Side, and an individual's determination to rise above it by fair means or foul. This is the life that Robbins knows, and so there are few or none of the phoney elements that marred previous versions—versions in which his hero moved uptown, married a nice girl, etc., etc. There are now only about half the major characters that there once were; all the loose ends are gathered together; and the ending—the last 130 pages or so—is tight as a drum.

"Also, my suggestion to switch into the 1st person has worked. Robbins's inelegancies of style, which sound poorly as the author's words in a third-person narrative, fit naturally to the narrator's tongue, for Danny himself is an East Side kid, a shrewd, tough product of the streets . . . If there is any light fiction market left at all, this may do better than *Never Love a Stranger*."[24]

Strauss asked for a few additional changes—"the reason Danny tells his story must be stressed (for his son)"—and then submitted the book to Pat Knopf for reading. Knopf agreed with Strauss and, in an interoffice memo, even sounded surprised that Robbins had actually managed to turn around the manuscript. "The Robbins is *okay!*" he said. "I've reread it twice now, and he's done *everything* we asked, and then some . . . It's a better book than *The Dream Merchants*, and I think, in many ways, every bit as good as *Never Love a Stranger*. I'd look for a 25,000 sale easily."[25]

Robbins finished tidying up the manuscript on 4 September, after which the book was sent to be copyedited. Harold Strauss wrote to his colleague that, whereas in previous Robbins novels he had cut out a great deal of the sloppy phrasing and clichés, on this occasion he had not had time because there were a great many structural defects that had had to be corrected first. The copy editor, therefore, would have to be very strict in his styling.

"This is a first-person narrative, and the narrator is a tough East Side kid," he said. "Stylistically, the target is a tight, hard-boiled, corner-of-the mouth style. Robbins has a pretty good ear for colloquial speech, but often he lets an extra word or two creep into an otherwise punchy sentence and spoil it. Also, every once in a while he puts phrases that are *too elegant* into the narrator's mouth. And a third weakness is a tendency to verbal repetition. Please feel free to edit drastically. The author will not object."[26]

When the novel was published, in March 1952, it was marketed as having been written by somebody who had, according to the book's jacket, insider knowledge of Manhattan street life. "Few novelists know the seamy life of New York life as well as Harold Robbins—the terror in the streets, the way to make a shady buck by playing along with gamblers and mobsters, the unbridled lusts and passions of slum life."[27] *Kirkus Reviews* said it was "loaded with sex, nostalgia, revenge and regret,"[28] while a critic for *The New Yorker* observed that although Robbins's writing was full of sincerity and sympathy, "the spirit of self-pity that dogs this novel is its undoing."[29]

Later, Robbins would claim that his first novel, *Never Love a Stranger*, and not his third, was autobiographical, but friends who knew him from this time believe the opposite. "*A Stone for Danny Fisher* was his story, we all knew that, not *Never Love a Stranger*," says Sylvia Miles.[30] "When he became very successful Harold had the white Rolls-Royce, the yacht, the houses in Acapulco and the South of France and Beverly Hills, but the later books that made him all this money were not what he really felt inside," says Archer King. "The image that he projected was not the real Harold Robbins. The real Harold Robbins you can find in *A Stone for Danny Fisher*."[31]

Indeed you can. In the last couple of pages of the novel Danny Fisher addresses his son: once he too was just an ordinary man with a charge account at Macy's, a savings bank book, and a Social Security number, 052–09–8424. The number was real—it belonged to Robbins himself.

6

"When the unattractive Jewish boy makes it big the
first thing he looks for is the quintessential shiksa."
—Rose Tobias Shaw

H AROLD AND LILLIAN stepped out of the car and gazed at the
expanse of land before them. They had chosen this quiet corner
of Norwalk—the well-heeled Connecticut town a couple of hours'
drive from New York—as the place on which to build their perfect
home. As Harold stood there, he visualized it before him: a house built
from traditional materials in the colonial style surrounded by its own
grounds, perhaps even with a swimming pool. It would be filled with
the most modern appliances and fitted with air conditioning, central
heating, and electronically operated windows. He wanted the house to
stand as an expression of his new success, a symbol of how far he had
climbed up the ladder of self-improvement.

Harold was determined to own his little share of the American
dream. Before work could start, however, he would have to earn a
considerable sum of money—the purchase of the land and the costs of
the building work meant that would have to take out a mortgage for
$25,000, a sizable chunk of money in the 1950s. Although Knopf had
just finalized a $30,000 deal with Pocket Books to reprint *A Stone for
Danny Fisher*, under the terms of the contract Robbins would receive
only half of this amount, while his royalty would be a mere one cent
per copy on the first 150,000 sold and then 1.5 cents thereafter.

In order to raise extra cash, Robbins started to think about writing a
short novel, something that he could dash off quickly and sell to

women's magazines such as *Cosmopolitan, Redbook, McCall's,* or *Ladies' Home Journal.* Before he started, his agent Maurice Crain gave him some advice. "The only hitch is that it is a new kind of writing for you, and you'll have to be conscious of that as you go along," he said. "Actually, if you don't want to get in a rut in your writing, it would probably be good for you to experiment with another form and another kind of story. Your approach to writing is the practical one of learning by doing, and this would be better than three writing courses for discipline. You might develop a little flexibility in the process.

"First off, you'll be writing for a mass magazine market, which means you'll have to keep it clean and be conscious of taste. Mostly what you'll have to watch is over-writing . . . In books, you are accustomed to taking your time with character, scene, and dialogue. You can't do it in magazines. Economy of detail is the watchword. A little discipline of this sort won't hurt your books either."[1]

Harold sat down at his typewriter and started to write *Never Leave Me,* the story of a high-flying public relations executive, Brad Rowan, who lives with his wife in a comfortable house outside New York. Rowan—who like Robbins had worked for a movie studio and "always looked happy when he spoke about money"[2]—loves his wife, Marge, but is tempted into having an affair with a beautiful, more sophisticated woman, Elaine. Although it took him longer than anticipated, by February 1953 Robbins had finished the novella. Crain sent it off to *Cosmopolitan,* warning the editor that Robbins had "gone a little farther on the sex scenes than a popular magazine could go," suggesting that it could easily be cut, bringing the word count down to 25,000. The problem, as the editors at *Cosmopolitan* saw it, involved the central character: Brad, a philanderer who risks his marriage for an affair, does not seem to suffer, while his lover, Elaine, commits suicide, and his wife, Marge, endures his cheating before deciding to stand by him.

After *Cosmopolitan* rejected it, Maurice Crain submitted *Never Leave Me* to Knopf, telling the publishers that Robbins was considering expanding it into a short novel. Robbins's initial 1947 contract had stipulated that the publisher had options on the author's first four novels over 60,000 words in length, and so if they decided to publish this shorter book, they might not have the opportunity to buy his next, longer work. "The point is under the contract they get 50% of his reprint rights and [they] know that we will not cut them in for such a share after this contract expires," said Crain.[3]

Knopf decided to pass on *Never Leave Me*, choosing to exercise their last remaining option by waiting for his next novel. On 11 June Robbins sent off the first nine chapters of the book to Charles Byrne, the editor in chief at Avon Publishing, who subsequently snapped it up. By the end of July Harold had finished the first draft of the 60,000-word novella and was pleased to receive an initial payment of $2,500.

As an experienced statistician and budget planner, Robbins was in an ideal position to work out how best to sell the book. Although the general plans to publish *Never Leave Me* were impressive, he said, he was disheartened by the lack of advertising and publicity. Robbins wanted Avon to sell the novella for thirty-five cents; at that price, he calculated, if the publisher managed to move 250,000 copies, they would earn an extra $17,500 more than if they issued it at the more usual twenty-five cents. Robbins's share of this would total $4,200, or $1,200 more than if *Never Leave Me* sold at the lower price. This extra money, he said, would help pay for a more lavish television and radio campaign.

Avon, however, refused to sell the book for ten cents more because it thought the novella would be priced out of the market, and as a result, they could not justify a costly promotion. Robbins was so disappointed that he wrote a stern letter to Avon, reproaching them for their lack of investment. As he saw it, the company was not only turning its back on the chance to make more money for them but also reducing his own capacity to profit from the book.

At this point Robbins needed every dollar he could get, as work had started on the Connecticut house. He was happy with the way the building was progressing, but he was anxious that he would not have enough money to pay for it. In October, Maurice Crain sent his client a check for $2,500, the remaining advance on the completion and acceptance of *Never Leave Me*, plus a small amount from the German publisher of *The Dream Merchants*. "At present prices, this will about pay for one of the bathrooms in the new house, or maybe the heating system," he joked. He was delighted that the couple had decided to become Connecticut householders, but added, "Come spring, you and Lillian are both going to develop quite a few new interests in life and also discover some new problems."[4]

Crain's prophecy, although delivered in a lighthearted spirit, was about to come uncomfortably true.

"How many men have made love to their wives because of the fires started by another woman? And which betrayal is more wrong? The real or the imaginary?"[5]

The words are those of Brad Rowan in *Never Leave Me*, but they could have easily been uttered by Robbins himself. Lillian and he had been married for sixteen years, and whatever sexual spark they had once shared had evidently long since died. Whenever they did make love, an act that was becoming increasing rare, Harold performed it dutifully and perfunctorily but without passion. His books oozed sex, but the marital bed was an erotic wasteland, a sensual desert. He certainly loved Lillian—he was kind and considerate toward her, dedicated his early novels to her, and showered her with expensive presents. After her death in 1998, Lillian's will detailed an impressive list of furs and jewels that Harold had given her—a platinum and diamond ring (valued in 1998 at $20,000); a platinum pin with thirteen pear-shaped diamonds, eight marquise diamonds, eighteen round diamonds, and sixty baguette diamonds; a platinum diamond ring with a central 1.50-carat diamond surrounded by twenty-four smaller marquise diamonds; a double strand of cultured pearls set in a platinum clasp; jackets fashioned from moondust mink, Persian lamb, and white mink; a chinchilla stole; three mink hats and one fox hat; and even a leopard-skin coat.

But the very qualities that had first attracted him—her warmth, loyalty, and comeliness—left him feeling sexually disinterested. He enjoyed cuddling up to her at night—resting his head in the safety of her breasts—but her overwhelming need to nurture killed his desire. "Lillian was plain and bland, nothing like the women he normally went for," says Archer King.[6] Photographs of Lillian taken on the set of the 1954 Universal-International film *The Black Shield of Falworth* starring Tony Curtis show her to be a jolly, sweet-natured woman but quite matronly. "He never really took Lillian out, and not many people saw her," says Sylvia Miles.[7]

Although it's hard to pinpoint exactly when Harold's sexual philandering began, a previously unseen document lodged in the Knopf archive suggests it dated back to 1952. On the surface the letter—from the manager of the Carlton House, a hotel situated on Madison Avenue and East 61st Street, to the publishing house—seems innocuous enough, requesting as it does information about the writer's financial security. Robbins had inquired about establishing credit with the hotel, an odd request for someone who then had a permanent home in Brooklyn, only a quick subway or cab ride away. The implication is clear: Robbins intended to use the hotel as a seduction location or, as he might have phrased it, a fuck pad.

What drove Harold away from Lillian and into the arms of other women is more complex than it at first seems. Lillian was unable to have children; perhaps if she had had them, she would have been able to channel her mothering instinct into raising a family, fussing around her babies and seeing to their every need. As it was, she projected this compulsion, this need to nurture, onto Harold, who in turn began to find the relationship cloying and claustrophobic. He adored children, and the fact that they had not been able to conceive hit him hard. Lillian provided companionship, sure; she kept the house nice and tidy, and she was everything a man should want in a wife. But . . . he felt guilty when he thought about it, but . . . she would never be able to bear his children. And neither was she much fun in the sack. He started to fantasize about having sex—unloving, wild, dangerous sex—with women who were the total opposite of Lillian, floozies with dyed-blond hair, girls who turned tricks, sluts who talked dirty. Now, with Lillian ensconced in Connecticut, Harold felt free to explore the wilder aspects of his sexuality, staying in New York during the week and returning home to Norwalk for weekends. "He always had assignations with women, and he used to talk about sex a lot," says Archer King.[8] "He would have two or three girls at a time and he'd pay them off. They were trashy, sexy women, and he'd pay them for sex. They were prostitutes."[9]

Prostitution would be the subject of Robbins's next book, which he wanted to give the rather risqué title *69 Park Avenue*. He started working on an outline of the novel—about the prosecution of prostitute and upmarket brothel owner Maryann Flood by the New York assistant district attorney and her onetime boyfriend Mike Keyes—in early 1954. His method of working was straightforward: he plotted out the narrative in his head, then he sat down at the typewriter and blocked the story into chapters.

Reading the outline—which exists in the Harold Robbins archive at Boston University—is the literary equivalent of being hit by a series of fast-flying narrative bullets. No sentence is more than a few words long, while the pace is so souped up, it's easy to understand why the novel, in fact all his fiction, became so popular. Robbins is nothing but pure, unadulterated narrative, and his fiction reads like the novelization of a screenplay, quickly moving dialogue arranged around a series of roughly hewn stage directions. In Robbins's universe, the story reigned supreme.

Robbins said he drew his inspiration for the book from real life. Many of the details and anecdotes about New York's underworld came from a police detective named Burns, while the figure of Maryann Flood was a composite of many women he had met.

"Maryann was a whore," he said. "Perhaps she was really a feminist. But she decided she would use her own natural assets for her own kind of social security. Growing up as I did during the Depression, I came to meet real girls who came to that decision. In time I could see them rising higher into Society. Most of these girls I met were bright, interesting, and very proficient in their profession. But the one thing I had observed in common to all of them was: they were interested in money. Sex was a commodity. Love was a luxury they could not afford."[10]

By June 1954, Robbins had written the first 189 pages of the book. "We have a new partial ms [manuscript] that Pat and I think is his best book and very saleable," said Harold Strauss.[11] "This is without question Robbins's best novel. The architecture is much simpler and more direct. His remarkable storytelling gets full play. While this is still merchandise fiction, Robbins's picture of slum life in New York during the Depression has the kind of authority and vividness that cannot simply be dismissed as trash. And best of all, the ms. Needs no stylistic doctoring.

"Two years ago I cautioned Robbins that he would have to write his own books hereafter, and he has done so from the stylistic point of view. Length may still be a problem, and a good many sexy details may have to be removed, and some of the legal background is inaccurate (I propose to make this last Robbins's responsibility); but nothing here is nearly as arduous as the reorganization, the building up of character, and the rephrasing his previous novels have required.

"Within the framework of the trial and conviction of a call girl by an Assistant District Attorney who was once in love with her, Robbins tells a straight story of a beautiful girl who was pushed by poverty and her vicious step-father into making money the easy way. Put this way, the story sounds trite; but Robbins is a fertile inventor of incident; the book has a fast pace; and his details about various aspects of New York life are, as I said, remarkably rich and authoritative.

"I feel that this book is extremely saleable even in an adverse fiction market."[12]

Strauss asked Knopf's accounting department whether it would be profitable to publish a novel the length of A Stone for Danny Fisher that would sell for $3.95 and give Robbins a 25 percent wholesale royalty. He also inquired what the maximum word length would be for a $3.95 book. Knopf did the sums and told Robbins that he could not write a novel of more than 150,000 words, and that if he wanted a substantial advance, he would have to accept a lower royalty, one more in the region of 13.5 percent, terms to which he agreed.

"There would be no point publishing this unless we can make a good deal of money out of it," said Strauss. "We cannot make money out of the hard-cover edition if we pay a 25% wholesale royalty, and if the book runs to 170,000 words, as Robbins proposed, and as was the case, in both respects, with Danny Fisher. What he [Robbins] wants most, as usual, is immediate cash."[13]

On 14 July Knopf sent him, via his agent, an advance of $10,000, the largest of his career to date. "It ought to pay for at least a bathroom and hall closet in that mansion you are building, Squire," joked Maurice Crain.[14]

Robbins also asked Robert Hale—his British publisher after Weidenfeld—to send money immediately. The move into the swanky new Norwalk house was imminent, and he needed ready cash to pay for the completion of the building work, plus the fittings and furnishings. In August, after finally securing a $25,000 mortgage, Harold and Lillian took possession of their new home at 290 Chestnut Hill Road, with land that stretched on to Weatherbell Drive. "By way of a blessing on the new house," wrote Maurice Crain, "may I express the hope that the great majority of all communications I shall address there in future will be either checks or new contracts."[15]

Just as he was looking forward to settling into this suburban idyll, however, Harold met a woman who would send shock waves through his marriage and, ultimately, contribute toward its breakdown.

Yvonne Russell-Farrow was a glamorous beauty with pencil-thin, immaculately shaped eyebrows, sharp cheekbones, beautifully cut clothes, and Hollywood-inspired makeup. The young woman—described in the press as British—was everything Lillian was not: stylish, slim, graceful, and socially ambitious. "Yvonne was sophisticated and something of a beauty, very different to Lillian," says Archer King.[16] "She was a kind of exotic beauty, a brunette, very flamboyant, something of a floozy, whereas Lillian was the classic dumpy first wife," remembers Rose Tobias Shaw, a casting agent who met Robbins at this time. "I didn't much like Yvonne, and to be honest, I wasn't that crazy about Harold. He was the original bullshit artist, not my kind of person. I thought he was fairly unattractive, and yet he was so cocksure of himself. He thought he was the cock of the walk. But fame is a great aphrodisiac."[17]

When Robbins and Russell-Farrow met in 1954, it was something of a *coup de foudre*. With his receding hairline, baggy eyes, and prominent nose, thirty-eight-year-old Robbins was not the best-looking man around, but he had, according to those who knew him, a certain self-confidence and an animalistic charisma that drew women to him. Robbins also believed that in order to succeed, it was important to look, and play, the part. He dressed in smart, tailored suits—the muted tones in great contrast to the psychedelic blaze of colors he would sport later in life—and took the trouble to have his thinning hair trimmed regularly.

Yvonne was also impressed by Harold's dynamism, his unstoppable drive, and his seemingly limitless ambition. Not only could he boast about his job at Universal-International and his career as a successful novelist, but he had recently formed a movie production company, Magnum Pictures, which he named after the fictional studio in *The Dream Merchants*. "Robbins, who is a trusted employee of Universal-International in addition to being a busy author," reported *The New York Times* in November 1953, "will not only receive a cash payment from Magnum but a partnership in the company as well."[18] He envisaged that his future projects—which he planned with his codirectors John Bash, Elizabeth Dickinson, and Kurt Hirsch—would include a film starring Deborah Kerr, as well as screen versions of his own books, starting with *Never Leave Me*, which he hoped would go into production in May 1954. (Although Robbins had great hopes for the company, it proved to be a flop, like many of his ventures into the film world.)

Certainly Yvonne would have been thrilled by the $25,000 Robbins earned for a movie outline he called *Summer Flood* that he sold to Olamic Productions in June. Interestingly, the contract for the film, which was never made, shows that Robbins chose to have the advance split into two parts: one half, in dollars, was to be sent to his movie agent, Annie Laurie Williams; the rest was to be paid in British pounds sterling to a "designee appointed by Harold Rubin (Harold Robbins)," which suggests that he made over the money to his new lover.[19] "When the unattractive Jewish boy makes it big, the first thing he looks for is the quintessential shiksa," says Rose Tobias Shaw, a Jew herself. "He liked women who were flamboyant, who wore lots of makeup, lots of pancake, women like Yvonne."[20]

The couple met soon after Robbins struck a deal with writer Leonard Kantor to adapt *A Stone for Danny Fisher* for the stage. The contract was drawn up in June: the two men agreed to split ten percent of the box-office receipts and to share the advance of $1,000, half upon the completion of the treatment and the rest when the first draft was finished. By the beginning of October the play was ready, and the company started to prepare for the opening night at the Downtown National Theater, the flagship Jewish theater on Second Avenue and Houston Street, where Yvonne worked.

On the first day of rehearsals Robbins dropped by the dressing rooms to wish the cast good luck. "He was gregarious and charming and there was a nice executive ease about him," says Joseph Sargent, who played the part of Steve, a black-market crook. "He was pleasant and amiable."[21] But according to actress Viola Harris, the understudy to Sylvia Miles's part of Arlene, the production was riddled with tension. "[There was] lots of friction," she said. "Harold Robbins was not happy, nor was the writer. They may have had financial problems; you just felt things were not very secure."[22] "Leo Fuchs—a Jewish star who normally played matinee idols, counts and lovers, but was now in his fifties—was originally cast as Danny Fisher, who was supposed to be a nineteen-year-old street kid," says Joseph Sargent. "One day in the middle of a rehearsal Fuchs turned to Luther Adler, the director, and said, 'What am I doing in this role?' He walked off the stage, and we never saw him again, and his part was taken by Phillip Pine."[23]

Director Luther Adler, the brother of acting teacher Stella Adler, chose to produce the play under the pseudonym Francis Kane (the name of Robbins's central character in Never Love a Stranger) because he feared it would be a flop and would damage his career. Just before opening night, on 21 October 1954, he gathered the cast together and told them: "Look kids, I don't know anything about directing, but I'm an expert makeup man so if you have any problems in that department, I can help you."[24]

Viola Harris remembers Sylvia Miles constantly walking into Zero Mostel's dressing room unannounced. This annoyed him so much that one day "he pulled down his underpants and stark naked he started chasing her all around the backstage . . . Needless to say, she never again went into his dressing room."[25]

Joseph Sargent was so bored by the play that he took to reading books backstage and often missed his cue. "It ran for four months even though it was a pretty dismal production, a god-forsaken piece of shit," he says.[26] Nevertheless the production—which also starred Sidney Pollack as Peter and Susan Cabot as Nellie—received good reviews.

The New York Times praised Robbins's and Kantor's handling of Danny's moral disintegration. "To Mr. Kantor, and to Mr. Robbins before him, Danny is not an evil hero and the mobsters are not supermen," wrote Brooks Atkinson. "Danny is a weakling who goes beyond his depth; the gangsters are mobsters and the underworld is ugly and baleful." What distinguished the piece from most melodramas was the "author's moral point of view. Crude in many details, this is still a play about crime and punishment and a slick young Jew who runs with criminals, disgraces his family, and destroys himself." Phillip Pine made the character of Danny shifty and shallow but also likable, while the production itself was quite flamboyant and showy. "*A Stone for Danny Fisher* is composed of cheap materials. But it conveys a moral earnestness worth respecting."[27]

Robbins and Kantor were delighted with the response—and the box-office receipts. By mid-November they were taking home approximately $600 each a week. The experience of working on the play had bonded these two very different men together, and they became good friends. Kantor—author of *Dead Pigeon*, the 1953 Broadway play that was turned into the film *Tight Spot*, starring Ginger Rogers and Edward G. Robinson—thought of himself as a creative artist, while Robbins was fundamentally an entrepreneur.

"Leonard liked Harold because he loved outsider figures, people who did not quite fit in," says Joan Bragin, who, together with her husband, Ernest, was a close friend of Kantor's. "Harold liked Leonard because he was a playwright, he felt that he was being truly creative. They were total opposites—Leonard saw himself as an artist, while Harold was commercial. They both came from damaged backgrounds, they were both Jews, one from the Bronx and the other from Brooklyn, and they both wanted to escape. But they chose drastically different routes—Leonard chose art while Harold opted for money until finally money became the only weapon he had.

"Harold was not quite a gentleman, but he had great dreams. He had no manners, he was coarse, but if you strip all that away, what have you got except for sheer, unadulterated drive? And that, in itself, is a kind of work of art."[28]

7

HAROLD PUSHED OPEN the heavy door and stepped into the
smoke-filled bar. He looked around the crowded room, scanning the space for the attractive brunette. His eyes lit up when he saw
her. She was sitting at a table in the corner, sipping a dry martini, a
faint smile dancing across her face.

"Hi, baby," he said, bending down to kiss her. "How's it goin'?
Listen, I've just heard some great news."

"What?"

"But first I need a drink," he said, calling over the bartender to
order a scotch on the rocks.

He remained silent for a moment longer than necessary, his dark
eyes glinting.

"What?" shouted Yvonne, landing a mock punch on his shoulder.
"Tell me!"

"Okay, okay, calm down." He paused again for added effect. "I got
a call from Annie Laurie Williams's office today telling me Hal Wallis
has bought *Danny Fisher*."

"What! But that's amazing!"

"I know, I know," said Harold. "And he's paid twenty-five thousand bucks."

"Darling, I'm so happy for you," she said, kissing him lightly on the
cheek. "You're such a clever boy."

She leaned over and placed a hand on the top of his leg. Harold felt himself stirring.

"Hey, cut it out, will ya'? I'm trying to have a drink, not cream my pants."

Yvonne laughed, but she did not stop slowly massaging his thigh, occasionally letting her hand brush toward his crotch.

"You're a very naughty girl, do you know that?"

"Oh, yes," she said. "I've been told that many, many times."

The couple laughed.

"What do you say we get out of here?" said Yvonne. "Let's go and celebrate someplace where we can feel a little more comfortable."

"Now that—that sounds like a good idea."

He paid for the drinks, and then, outside on the cold, wintry sidewalk, he hailed a yellow cab to take them back to Yvonne's apartment at 37 East 64th Street. They had hardly stepped inside the apartment before they started to devour each other, kissing each other, groping and pulling at each other's clothes. Within a matter of seconds they were on the bed, their bodies writhing.

Harold Robbins was looking forward to 1955. He had a well-paid job at Universal-International and had published four books; he owned a comfortable house in Connecticut as well as an apartment in Brooklyn; and he could bask in his ability to flit between a devoted wife and a beautiful mistress.

His good humor was reflected in a skittish piece he wrote for *Variety* magazine published on 5 January that starts with his telephone ringing while he is trying to work. We are told, by an unnamed character who we presume is Robbins's manservant, that the caller is the writer's publisher, Pat. He would like a word with the author about one of his books being turned into a film. Robbins tells his publisher that he doesn't care what the movie executives do to his novel as all he needs is the money.

"You wouldn't always be so broke if you didn't blow all your dough," Pat said. "Then you could afford to be careful about your properties. Make sure they get the right kind of treatment."[1]

The two men then have an argument about money, and Pat accuses him of wasting his resources by employing a butler. "Suddenly I understood," said Robbins. "I looked across the room. 'Did you say you were the butler?' I asked."

Robbins is appalled and refuses to talk to his manservant for the next ten minutes. Employer and employee have an argument, and in the last paragraph, the manservant jumps up onto the chair to answer the phone once again. Finally, it is revealed that the "butler" is none other than Whiskers, the writer's wirehaired terrier.

Although the sketch is juvenile both in its tone and in its subject matter, Robbins did have a justified excuse for feeling somewhat light-headed. Not only had Paramount bought the film rights to *A Stone for Danny Fisher*, but the final draft of *69 Park Avenue* had met with an enthusiastic response. Pat Knopf said it was his "best book," while Harold Strauss congratulated Robbins on his "powerful, fast-paced story."[2] Although the writing was limited—his "vocabulary is primitive, and his figures of speech are rudimentary," said the editor—Robbins certainly knew how to construct a narrative.[3] Strauss, however, had a problem with the ending, in which the prostitute, Maryann, sacrifices her own happiness for the prosecutor, Mike Keyes, and he in turn marries a sweet-natured, respectable girl.

"For reasons I don't understand, Robbins has chosen to use a 'Hays Office' ending," said Strauss. "That is, the 'bad girl' must not be rewarded in any way ... There is no indication of Mike's emotional reaction to what Maryann has done; worse, for 420 pages we have been told that he cannot so much as look at another girl because he still loves Maryann. Therefore his decision to marry the other girl is unconvincing. The movies can write in this ending for themselves if they buy the book. We don't need it."[4] By the middle of February Robbins had rewritten the ending, so that it culminated with the revelation of Maryann's secret love child by Mike—giving the novel a final twist that impressed his editor. "It's so good and so clever that I think the added punch will really help us sell more copies," he told him.[5]

In an instance of life imitating, if not art, then at least popular fiction, a couple of months later Robbins learned that his mistress, Yvonne Russell-Farrow—who in March produced the play *Champagne Complex* at the Downtown National Theater—was pregnant and that the child was due in November. He remembered that night of passion earlier in the year when they had lost themselves in each other. Had that been the time when Yvonne had conceived? If so, how was anyone supposed to feel anything but joy? But the news, he knew, would break Lillian's heart—after all, she had so wanted to give him a child—and he thought it best to postpone telling her for the time being.

The prospect of becoming a father stirred up complex emotions within him. His own father had been somewhat cold and distant, and he had grown up knowing that his real mother had died as a result of giving birth to him. As he thought about what Frances must have gone through—all that agony, all that pain—he felt tears sting his eyes. He blinked them back, refusing to let them fall. What was he thinking? Now was a time for joy, for celebration, not a moment to dwell on the miseries of the past.

He was determined to do everything in his power to make sure Yvonne and his child were healthy and happy. He lavished his mistress with expensive gifts, took her out to New York's finest restaurants, and even decided to advance her a large sum of money. But Harold had two problems: he didn't have enough dough, and even if he did, Lillian would grow suspicious if he withdrew so much cash from their bank account. So over a couple of drinks, Harold dreamed up what he thought was an ingenious plan. He would ask his friend Maurice Coyne, the business manager of Manhattan-based MLJ Magazines, for a loan. In exchange, he would sign over to him the royalty rights to his new book, now to be called *79 Park Avenue*. By the middle of the following year Robbins had paid Coyne nearly $12,000, money that, presumably, he had already settled on Yvonne. It was, he thought, a small price to pay for a family.

Knopf hoped that *79 Park Avenue*, with its sensational theme and fast-paced storyline, would "get into the big money." As a result it took extra special care over the manuscript, especially its representation of sex. After reading the book Harry Buchman, Knopf's lawyer, said that he was worried that an obscenity charge could be brought against Robbins. He was particularly concerned about the first quarter or third of the book. Alfred Knopf agreed, and in April he ordered the author to "remove about thirty references to Maryann's breasts, thighs etc."[6] In addition, there was a strong possibility that a well-known bra manufacturer, whom Robbins had named, would sue after he had alleged that the company regularly requested "models for immoral purposes."[7] Sexual references were toned down, names were changed, and Knopf set a publication date of 25 July.

In England, meanwhile, publishers were nervous about taking on books that were seen to be too risqué. Robert Hale, Robbins's publisher in Britain, said that he would love to add *79 Park Avenue* to his list but was worried that it would be prosecuted. "The 'Blue Stockings' have been giving publishers a hard time over there [Britain]," Maurice Crain wrote to Robbins, "and have suppressed or prevented publication of a number of books, both from France and America."[8]

Reviewers were quick to pick up on the racy nature of the book, which was described on the cover as a "vivid and knowing story of the plush call-girl racket and the people who are drawn into it."[9] *Publishers Weekly* said that it was "spotted with salacious scenes, very skilfully drawn, and that will sell the book,"[10] the *Boston Herald* declared that its subject matter was "sordid,"[11] and the *Columbus Dispatch* observed that it was "topical, 'naturalistic' in its treatment of sex and morals, foul-mouthed in its dialogue."[12] *The New Yorker*, however, thought it was trash and tedious in the extreme. "His work is not subtle enough to be parody," it sniffed. "It is too soft to be regarded as case history. There are no characters in it, so it cannot be meant as a novel. Perhaps it is what it seems to be—an effort that got into print."[13]

Critics also drew parallels between the book and the recent case of Mickey Jelke, the oleomargarine millionaire who was prosecuted for procuring. "You may remember, or you may want to forget, the Mickey Jelke case earlier this year," wrote Luther Nichols in the *San Francisco Examiner*. "It took the lid off a 'call girl' business run by a pudgy New York City playboy. Some of the girls in his high-priced string were attractive models, chief among whom was Pat Ward. Many of Miss Ward's experiences are similar to those of Maryann Flood."[14]

Robbins would later employ exactly the same technique—using certain infamous, high-profile figures as inspiration for his fiction, novels that hit the bookshops with an already established frisson of sensation—in books such as *The Carpetbaggers*, *Where Love Has Gone*, *The Adventurers*, and *The Pirate*. "Mr. Robbins is obviously a careful reader of newspapers," said one commentator about *79 Park Avenue*. "The same kind of public curiosity which made that trial such a headline holiday should win a large readership for this book, especially when it reaches its inevitable paperback edition."[15]

Such a deal was already under way. On 13 July Knopf secured $100,000 for reprint rights from Pocket Books: $50,000 for *79 Park Avenue*, and $25,000 for each of Robbins's next two novels. Although it seemed an awful lot of money, Robbins, master statistician that he was, realized that not only would he have to share half of it with Knopf—they were entitled to 50 percent of money earned from reprints—but it was also based on the delivery of future manuscripts. The amount he would receive at this point, when he really needed it, would amount to only one-twentieth of the total, money that was already owed to Maurice Coyne.

"We propose to create a pool for Robbins to start in 1958, after delivery of the new manuscript, from which Robbins will be paid over a period of years, as long as the money lasts. In other words, on the basis of JCL's [Joseph Lesser, Knopf's treasurer] proposed schedule, to $20,000 in advances from AAK, Inc., on two books is added the $25,000 which is the author's share of the balance of $50,000 due from Pocket Books. The pool for Robbins is then $45,000. JCL proposes to start paying Robbins at whatever rate he wants—somewhere between $5,000 and $10,000 a year—as long as there is money in the pool. This would start in 1958, and under no circumstances would ANY OF THE MONEY in this pool be payable until delivery of acceptable manuscript."[16]

After submitting an outline for *The Carpetbaggers*, Robbins agreed with Knopf that he would deliver the book no later than 1 July 1957 and that he would hand in his next novel, which he provisionally called *The Dream Stealers*, on 1 December 1959. On 3 August Robbins signed a new contract with Knopf, and a month later he received a check for $5,000, which as an advance on *79 Park Avenue* was forwarded on to Maurice Coyne. The only money Robbins pocketed from the $100,000 deal was a paltry $1,000 that Knopf gave him after signing the *Carpetbaggers* contract. Yet Robbins managed to find it in himself to write a polite letter to Alfred Knopf Sr. thanking the publisher for his support. He promised he would do his utmost to uphold the high values expected of Knopf authors and hoped he would always produce work that would meet the publisher's exacting standards. Before the decade was out, however, the relationship would break down amid accusations of betrayal, double-dealing, and the threat of legal action.

During 1955 Robbins realized that if he wanted to make a large amount of money, he would have to get more involved in films. His own company, Magnum Pictures, had failed to develop any of its projects, and he became increasingly frustrated with his job at Universal-International, where he was employed to make money for the studio rather than for himself.

Soon after *79 Park Avenue* was published, the novel generated a great deal of interest from movie producers. Victor Orsatti, the producer who would go on to make *Flight to Hong Kong*, *The Hired Gun*, *Domino Kid*, and *Apache Territory*, wrote to Robbins via Annie Laurie Williams offering to broker a deal with United Artists.

"We are wondering if Harold would entertain the thought of coming in on a partnership with Joe [Newman, his partner] and myself, with the thought that he and Joe would prepare a treatment on the book," he wrote, "and after they feel confident that they have the censorship problems licked he could write the screenplay. In this way, he could also receive a certain amount of cash (which would be mutually agreed upon) to be paid to him during the first week of shooting on the picture.

"If we could work out a deal on this basis, we might be able to do the same on *Never Love a Stranger* which has been kicked around for a long time and which certainly would make a great picture after some objectionable facets have been eliminated."[17]

As an incentive Orsatti, who had been married to Hollywood glamour girls Marie McDonald and Pat Vaniver, offered to give Robbins an advance of $5,000, plus $20,000 during the first week of filming and a third of the profits. Although Robbins was tempted by the offer, nothing came of the project, most probably because the men were unable to come up with a treatment about "this highly censorable subject."[18]

Nevertheless, Harold had high ambitions for his book and even sent a letter to Marilyn Monroe inquiring whether she would be interested in taking the role of the blond-haired prostitute Maryann Flood. A few weeks later Milton Greene, the actress's business partner and photographer, phoned Annie Laurie Williams's office to say that unfortunately "this was not anything for Marilyn Monroe."[19]

On 7 November 1955 Yvonne Russell-Farrow gave birth to Robbin's child, whom they named Caryn Yvonne. Harold was delighted by the news, and in his 1962 novel *Where Love Has Gone* he describes his feelings on seeing his daughter for the first time. "We were in tune, we were on the same wave length, we were like locked-in to each other, and she was mine and I was hers," he wrote. ". . . And the tears came to my eyes for the tears she could not shed."[20]

The birth brought a new set of complications into Robbins's life. Harold and Yvonne had found it far from easy to keep their affair secret, but the fact that they now had a child was even harder to hide. To keep up appearances, Yvonne began to call herself Mrs. Mary Robbins, and the couple spent an increasing amount of time together at her apartment on East 64th Street.

Harold had new responsibilities, and he took his fatherly duties seriously, promising to support and provide for the child. A sentimentalist at heart, he adored the idea of a family, and while his new one may have been a little unconventional, he was determined to try and make it work. Already obsessed with earning money, he set himself new goals, agreeing to take on new projects so as to meet his rising expenses. He continued to plot *The Carpetbaggers* and in November finished two-thirds of a screen treatment for *A Stone for Danny Fisher*, which he sent off to Hal Wallis. Then in the new year he received a commission from his own studio, Universal, to write a screenplay based on the 1956 novel *Badge of Evil* by Whit Masterson, the pseudonym of William Miller and Robert Wade. The deal was a generous one—$25,000 for six weeks' work. Although Robbins's version disappeared without a trace, the resulting film, Orson Welles's *Touch of Evil*, starring Welles, Charlton Heston and Janet Leigh, became a classic of film noir.

Robbins found it impossible to hold down his job at Universal and still commit himself fully to his various writing commitments. He felt more and more exhausted. Later he said he became frustrated with his position at Universal because it necessitated an average of three West Coast trips per week. "I used to wake up midflight and not know which way I was going," he said. "I was too embarrassed to ask the hostess if we were heading to New York or California."[21] "I could have been president of Universal Pictures," Robbins boasted. "I was earning a hundred and fifty thousand dollars plus expenses when I quit—but at forty I woke up one day in a jet and didn't even know which way I was flying. I decided it was time to get off. The boss said I was cuckoo and said, 'You don't know if your next novel will sell.' I went home and told my wife, and she said I was cuckoo and said, 'You don't know if your next book will sell.' It broke up my marriage."[22]

According to those who knew him, instead of spending his working hours at Universal's New York base on Park Avenue, he set up an office in the dining room of Laurent, an upmarket Manhattan restaurant, or worked from home. "He took off work and wired his phones so that they would ring in his apartment," said Adréana, Robbins's younger daughter, "so everyone would think he was in his office, but he was at home writing."[23] Paul Gitlin, Robbins's attorney, agent, and close friend, said the reason he left Universal was that, "they terminated him . . . absenteeism."[24]

Robbins, in typical go-getting fashion, did not spend long feeling sorry for himself. "One of the things you've got to admire about Harold is his confidence in himself," says his friend Steve Shagan. "He believed he could overcome almost any obstacle."[25] In July 1956 he set up his own production company, Virgo Productions at 200 West 57th Street, with the intention of making films based on his own novels as well as adaptations of other authors' works and original screenplays. The first film Virgo intended to make was *The Street*, adapted from the 1946 pioneering novel by the African-American writer Ann Petry, but like many of Robbin's film projects, this one failed to make it on to the screen.

"He was never afraid of anything," says Archer King, who worked with Robbins at Virgo. "He was the president and the treasurer and everything else, and he found this studio up in the Bronx that he wanted to take over so we could shoot films there. He was incredibly talented at that point, he had so much energy, and I liked him an awful lot. He was laid back, but always very witty and charming, particularly about women. And he was beyond cynicism, in a way, so nothing would surprise him."[26]

As Victor Orsatti's dream to make a movie version of 79 Park Avenue had failed to materialize, word went out in the film industry that the book was available once again. Ned Brown at MCA and Seymour Nebenzal, producer of both the 1931 Fritz Lang and the 1951 Joseph Losey versions of M, inquired about the movie rights, but their requests were met by a swift rejection from Annie Laurie Williams's office. "Harold . . . wants big money for this book, and he knows Nebenzal can't pay it," wrote a member of her staff, "so tell him Virgo Productions is going to do the picture."[27]

Soon after the novel was published in paperback by Pocket Books, 79 Park Avenue was hit with an obscenity charge. In the summer of 1956 the book was seized from the stall of a New Jersey candy salesman, and although the prosecutor was unwilling to waste time on the case, a date was set for the hearing on 8 August, which was adjourned. "The Magistrate apparently does not know anything about the problem involved," William Koshland wrote in an internal memo to Alfred A. Knopf. "The Prosecutor remains completely uninterested. The Police Department still wants to try the case."[28] Before the trial, on 10 September, the judge read the novel and went through it marking certain passages he considered to be obscene. However, "off the record, it appears that the Judge was compelled to make the obscenity finding because of political pressure."

Marty Robbins, the defense lawyer acting for Pocket Books, sought to show that the novel was "in fact and law not obscene" and that when it was first published by Knopf, it was both widely reviewed and popular. "The principle will be pursued that the work is an ordinary novel reflecting life . . . and that if a line or paragraph is in itself 'dirty,' it is merely incidental to an entire panorama and is necessarily part of the plot and presentation," wrote Koshland. "The decisions in New York support the principle that the book as a whole must be obscene, dirt for dirt's sake, as distinguished from particular parts thereof being vulgar and coarse."[29]

The publicity boosted sales of the paperback, and by the end of the year Robbins had sold a million copies of the book. But, the structure of his deal with Pocket Books and Knopf, combined with Robbin's decision to forward all royalties from the novel to Maurice Coyne, meant that he could not profit from it. In December Pat Knopf wrote to the author at his home in Connecticut to tell him the news. "You'll never see any additional money, I'm sure," he said, "but you're in very select company at last."[30]

The process by which Robbins's *A Stone for Danny Fisher*, a raw novel about a Jewish boy growing up in Brooklyn and becoming a boxer, transformed itself into *King Creole*, a musical starring Elvis Presley as a hip-gyrating New Orleans nightclub singer who gets involved in organized crime, is symptomatic of Hollywood's tendency toward bastardization. Although the movie may well be one of Elvis's best films, it bears such a slim resemblance to the original book that Paramount could easily have saved itself the $25,000 it paid Robbins for using his novel as source material.

It had all started so promisingly. Hal Wallis envisaged Marlon Brando, fresh from his success in *The Wild One*, *On the Waterfront*, and *Guys and Dolls*, for the central role of Danny and enlisted the services of Michael Curtiz, the director famous for *Casablanca*, *Mildred Pierce*, and *White Christmas*. Wallis passed Robbins's treatment on to scriptwriter and actor Michael Vincente Gazzo, who earned $10,000 for the job. But Curtiz found the script, which Gazzo delivered in May 1955, disappointing. In Curtiz's opinion it was important to remain faithful to the original novel, and he suggested opening the film with the first scene of the book, in which a little boy places a stone on his father's grave. The problem, as he saw it, was that "Danny has been turned into a conventional, unreal, dead-end kid hero," he wrote to Hal Wallis, "underprivileged by his father and society . . . Thus we have an old-fashioned, unrealistic, abused hero, who does not create his own destiny."[31]

Central to both the book and the film, said Wallis, was Danny's relationship with his father, "a small professional man who has done everything possible for his son and has big plans for him, but who is trapped in an economic upheaval; and a son so eager for a place in the world and so bewildered and desperate at ill fortune that he blames his father in haste. These are two human beings we can understand and feel for, and the situation is real because one of them created it, and the other responds in a real, human way."[32]

Wallis met with his co-producer Joseph Hazen and associate producer Paul Nathan to discuss the weaknesses of the script. Hazen thought it helpful to compare the psychological dynamic at the heart of *A Stone for Danny Fisher* to the dysfunctional father-son relationship in Tennessee Williams's *Cat on a Hot Tin Roof*. "It is this impenetrable wall—this lack of communication and understanding between father and son—which is a major contributing factor to the tragedy of Danny Fisher," Hazen wrote in a memo to Nathan. "Had Danny been able to understand his father's point of view more completely and had Danny's father been more aware of and more sympathetic and understanding of Danny's problem, Danny would not have developed into a misanthrope."[33]

When Marlon Brando turned down the role, Wallis and his team were desperate to find another big star with the same kind of rebellious associations and capacity for brooding intensity. Naturally, at the top of their list was Elvis Presley, who had already made three films, *Love Me Tender*, *Loving You*, and *Jailhouse Rock*. Wallis knew the star—who was paid nearly $72,000 for eight and a half weeks' work—was guaranteed box office, but one of the consequences of hiring him was that the script would now have to incorporate some songs. After all, what was the point of casting the essence of rock 'n' roll and not taking advantage of his performing skills? A number of songs were quickly written, including one called "Sing, You Sinners," and by October 1956 Paul Nathan had persuaded the rest of the production team that they should construct the narrative of the film around the song. The source material was all but abandoned, and the project became a showcase for Elvis's talents.

The producers of the film—which now went under the title *Sing, You Sinners*—moved the action from New York to New Orleans, and Danny Fisher became the rebellious son of a minister. "We changed the leading character from a prizefighter to a singer," said Wallis.[34] Wallis then employed composer and writer Herbert Baker at a rate of $1,250 a week to polish the script. Finally, by the end of 1957 the team had something they felt they could shoot, and the screenplay was sent off to the office of the Production Code to ensure that it did not breach decency regulations.

Geoffrey Shurlock, the vice president and director of the official body, wrote to Hal Wallis with three pages of potential problems. Many of his comments were minor ones, for instance, requesting that expressions such as "Jeez" be removed from the script. Others—such an intimate scene in which Ronnie (Carolyn Jones) offers herself to Danny (Elvis Presley)—necessitated a more drastic rewriting of the script.

"This sequence is unacceptable under the Code," wrote Shurlock ". . . Such lines as, 'Do you think you could take a day out of your life and give it to me?' and 'Then love me—for today,' together with the action of both of them lying together on the sand, must be revised in such a way as to keep their relationship a moral and clean one."[35]

The shooting of the film started in New Orleans on 20 January 1958. Presley's presence in the city resulted in hysteria. "When we were on location in New Orleans, the crowds were so huge that we had to arrange for top security," said Wallis. "When we shot on the streets, police and ropes were necessary to hold back the crowds."[36]

When the film opened that July, it was met with enthusiastic reviews and became a box-office hit. But for Robbins the movie was nothing less than a travesty. Later in life he pretended to be nonchalant about it—"I got the check," he said, referring to the film—but privately he always felt frustrated that *his* Danny Fisher, a story so close to his heart, had never made it onto the silver screen.[37]

8

"All the feuding fouled up my mental machinery."
—Harold Robbins to Donald Zec

HAROLD LOVED HIS little girl. With her dark eyes and tuft of nut-brown hair, she was the most beautiful baby he had ever seen. He adored the feel of her soft skin next to his; the smell of her clean clothes; the touch of her tiny hand clutching his fingers. He took her out in her baby carriage, walking through Central Park, merging with the stream of other proud parents. He listened to her chat away in her own nonsensical language, certain that, among the incomprehensible gabble, he had discerned a "Daddy" or a "Papa." He bounced her on his lap, sometimes lifting her high into the air, not caring that occasionally she would leave some undigested milk on the lapel of one of his smart gray suits. She was his darling, and he would do anything in the world for her.

The entry of his illegitimate child into the world obviously threatened his marriage to Lillian. Normally she was a quiet, not to say passive, woman, but telling her about Caryn's existence had been hell. The sexual betrayal was nothing compared to the emotional one; the thought that another woman had carried and given birth to his daughter was what really upset her. There were tears, threats of separation, angry words, and days of silence before Lillian presented him with her decision. She did not want a divorce—the shame of it would destroy her parents, she said—and although he had seriously disappointed her, she would stand by him. She understood why he needed other women and, if she was honest to herself, why he wouldn't find her attractive anymore. But she was also wise—and pragmatic—enough to realize that dismantling their marriage would not necessarily be in her best interest. Approaching forty, slightly overweight, and unable to have children, she was hardly going to be most men's first choice. But, if she stuck with Harold, he would always provide for her; she even believed he loved her in his own way. So she would stay with him just as long as he remained discreet; after all, a public scandal was the last thing she wanted. And if she left Harold, how on earth would she support herself?

"Lillian had always helped him with his books, giving him ideas, editing his words," says Lillian's sister, Rae. "She was an avid reader—much more so than Harold—and had a library of over one thousand books. If it hadn't been for her input, I doubt he would have had the success that he had. Of course, Lillian kept this quiet—she didn't tell anybody—and only came out with it one day after she had had an argument with him. She was angry with Harold, I'd never seen her like that. But she told me that she was the one who did a lot of work behind the scenes, helping with plot, character, everything. She never spoke to me about Yvonne or Caryn, and not often about Harold really, but from this time onwards there was a private sadness that she carried with her."[1]

Harold, instead of regarding Caryn as a badge of shame, celebrated her presence on a large scale and even went so far as to name his new production company—which he formed in June 1957—after her. Robbins had no intention of letting Hollywood massacre any more of his novels. His intention was to coproduce film versions of his books, together with an adaptation of *I'd Do It Again*, the autobiography of James Michael Curley, Boston's former mayor. A deal was drawn up between Caryn Productions and Allied Artists, which promised to finance and distribute the first project, *Never Love a Stranger*, and the other movies.

He also entered into a deal with writer and producer Fred Finkelhoffe to bring *79 Park Avenue* to the screen. He started work on the screenplay with great enthusiasm, driven by the thought of a $50,000 fee and the possibility that he could co-produce. He was, he told his movie agent, "desperate" for the money.[2] Virgo Productions was in a bad way—checks he had written had started to bounce, even one due to Annie Laurie Williams; and just as he received a payment of $5,000 from Knopf as an advance on *The Carpetbaggers*, he failed to meet the payments on a $4,500 loan.

That spring of 1957 he worked, together with Peter Gettinger, on a screenplay of his first novel, *Never Love a Stranger*, finishing a first draft by 29 April. Although Robbins and director Robert Stevens succeeded in remaining faithful to the book, the end result was, in the words of one of its stars, Steve McQueen, who played Martin Cabell, a "turkey . . . the other notice I got was from one critic who said my face looked like a Botticelli angel had been crossed with a chimp."[3] "There was no pretense at range," added one commentator. "The whole thing seemed to shrink down to a stage play and then simply to have forgotten to tell the cameraman to stay home. *Stranger* was located along a narrow strip of the Hudson River, which served as a metaphor for the soggy, meandering plot."[4]

Filming in Hollywood and California meant that Robbins was away for long periods of time. In Los Angeles he was able to indulge his taste for glamorous women. The late John Drew Barrymore, who had been cast as Frankie Kane in *Never Love a Stranger*, told friends that "Harold was the horniest man in Hollywood, he was a very sexual man, the ultimate in sex. He loved hanging out with big-titted women."[5]

On set Steve McQueen, who lived with his wife Neile in Las Vegas, embarked on a relationship with costar Lita Milan, who was playing the role of Julie. "The couple signaled to each other excitedly at night with torches from their adjacent suites," wrote McQueen's biographer, "and at one point Steve climbed into an empty maid's room to eavesdrop on a call between Milan and a girlfriend immediately below, repeating the intimate conversation to her in bed. There was an abandon and fun, even frivolity, about the place."[6]

Producing *Never Love a Stranger*, together with working on other films, ate into Robbins's writing time, and on 5 July he asked Harold Strauss for a three-month extension on *The Carpetbaggers*. Although Knopf grudgingly agreed, they told him he would not receive the extra $9,000 due from Pocket Books and warned him that if the manuscript did not arrive on the agreed date, the consequences would be severe.

"In the first place, by delivery on October 1st, we mean delivery of a publishable manuscript, and not one that has to be substantially revised, as has been necessary with several of your manuscripts," said Strauss. "In the second place, any failure on your part to meet this new delivery date will put us into difficulties with Pocket Books . . .

"The spirit, if not the letter, of this agreement will have been seriously violated if you fail to deliver the manuscript by October 1st. We shall have no other course at that time but to go to Pocket Books and tell them so. I cannot tell you what action they will take, but I am certain that you will see the danger of precipitating a crisis of this kind."[7]

By October, Robbins still had not delivered the book, and he wrote to Knopf asking for another extension. "I have told Bill Koshland [at Knopf] you certainly aren't going to have time to work on a book until you are through shooting [*Never Love a Stranger*]," Maurice Crain wrote to Robbins. "I think they all understand that."[8] A date of 15 November was agreed upon, but again Robbins failed to meet it. On 6 December Harold Strauss wrote a memo to Pat Knopf outlining the situation.

"Robbins is in his usual trouble," he said, "[*Never Love a*] *Stranger* is finished. People who have seen the rushes want him to do two more pictures quickly. He plans to be through by the end of February and take the following six months off."[9] Knopf agreed upon a date of 31 October 1958 but stressed once again that Robbins would not be paid a cent until he had delivered a publishable manuscript. "He also has some legal problems involving substantial sums of money," Strauss added, "and wants to clear them by the 1st of March as well."[10]

These problems included a lawsuit that had been brought against Robbins by producer and Allied Artists stockholder Sidney Barkley for the recovery of $60,000, which he had lent the author to help finance his films. Harold paid his creditor $10,184 in November, but this sum failed to satisfy the persistent Barkley who, over the course of the next few years, plagued Robbins and Knopf for the rest of the money. Then Harold and Lillian were hit by another big tax bill, amounting to $13,295.88, dating back to 1952 and 1953. To make matters worse, the IRS, having failed to receive the money from Robbins directly, wrote to Knopf and served notice on the publishing house, which meant that, in the words of Knopf's money man Joseph

Lesser, "until such levy has been lifted we cannot make payment" to either the writer or his agents.[11] In July 1958 Robbins had royalties of $827.77 owing to him, but as he had failed to deliver *The Carpetbaggers*, Knopf decided not to forward it.

Harold called William Koshland, who later became Knopf's president and then chairman of the board, and told him that he was "straightening out" the matter, but the publisher remained nervous. "Be that as it may," wrote Koshland, "we are disturbed by the existence of our overall agreement with him for new books which provide for payments of substantial advances."[12]

Robbins, meanwhile, kept on spending money, and that July he received another summons for an unpaid debt, a sum of $213.59, due to Arthurs, a New York dress shop. This time his agent, Maurice Crain, was served a subpoena, ordering him to go before the court to testify on behalf of his client. When Crain read the official document, he must have been amazed by Robbins's lack of discretion.

"Ben Golde and Arthur Gerber, co-partners doing business under the name and style of ARTHURS against HAROLD ROBBINS and "Mary" ROBBINS, first name being fictitious, the person intended being the wife of Harold Robbins, residing at 37 East 64th St, NY."[13]

Suddenly Robbins was shaming not so much himself—friends say he seemed immune to embarrassment—as his associates, especially the august firm of Knopf. But instead of working away at *The Carpetbaggers*—his 31 October deadline was fast approaching—Robbins helped to stage a production at the Rooftop Theater of *Ulysses in Nighttown* by Padraic Colum, starring Zero Mostel, and traveled around the United States in a promotional tour for *Never Love a Stranger*. Desperate to boost the box-office takings—he did, after all, have a vested interest, as he was set to win 25 percent of the profits from the film—Robbins started to mythologize his own life.

On 15 September, in San Francisco, he told a reporter that the story was autobiographical. The journalist did not question his version of events, simply printing the "fact" that he was forty-five (actually he was forty-two) so that it would give the impression he shared a birth year with that of his protagonist, Frankie Kane. The newspaper reported that Robbins, like the character, grew up in a Catholic orphanage only to discover that he was Jewish. "It's a belt to the boy, played by John Drew Barrymore," said Robbins. "Actually I was only thirteen when my background was traced. It was a shock to me, too, although not as much of one as to a fellow in late adolescence."[14] Once he had gone into print with this lie, it was difficult to extract himself from it, and with each telling the tale became ever more elaborate.

In San Francisco Robbins also told reporters that he did not think it was unusual to combine a talent for statistics with writing—he cited Whit Burnett, Charles Dickens, and Edgar Rice Burroughs as examples. Mathematics, like language, was a matter of semantics, he added. His next novel, *The Carpetbaggers*, would be published the following spring he said, and went on to boast that he was one of three authors, along with Thomas Mann and André Gide, who had lifetime contracts with Knopf.

Back at 501 Madison Avenue, Knopf's editors were getting anxious. As Robbins's deadline passed once again, William Koshland wrote to Harry Buchman at Stern & Reubens advising that a "formal smoking-out letter should go from you as our attorney to Robbins" outlining the situation. On 14 November Buchman sent a letter to Robbins's Connecticut home asking him to explain why Knopf had not received the promised novel.

"I dislike burdening you when I know you have your own serious problems, but I have had occasion to examine the Knopf contract with you, relating to the manuscript tentatively entitled *The Carpetbaggers*, and must give advice to Knopf upon the subject of the failure by you to deliver the manuscript.

"Would you be good enough to advise me what progress, if any, has been made toward writing the manuscript, and how you contemplate handling the obligation therefor."[15]

Robbins told Koshland that he hoped to settle his dire tax situation by the end of the year. Although he had to go to the West Coast "in connection with . . . motion picture activities," he would be back in New York on 5 January. Robbins told Knopf that he would like to meet with the Knopf executives, "regarding his future plans for writing" during the week of 12 January.[16]

Although nothing was decided definitively at that meeting, Robbins had already had thoughts about trying to extract himself from his relationship with Knopf; after all, in the summer of 1958 he had taken a copy of his latest contract from the offices of Annie Laurie Williams. Robbins promised his publisher that he was working on the book and that they would have it as soon as possible. But in the spring of 1959 Knopf was served with another of Robbins's debts; "this time it's Bergdorf & Goodman [the New York store] to the tune of $672.35," said William Koshland. "As I dictate this, I'm wondering what, if anything, all the guff Harold handed me on the phone means."[17]

Robbins spent the early part of 1959 in Florida and California, trying to set up various movie projects, but on his return he was met by another tax bill for another failed venture, Russell-Farrow Productions Company at 111 East Houston Street, which he had set up with Yvonne soon after they first met. The couple had invested money in a series of three plays directed and starring Maurice Schwartz, due to be performed at the Downtown National Theater. Although Schwartz, star of films such as *Mission to Moscow*, *Salome*, and *Slaves of Babylon*, had intended to take the lead roles in *The Grass Is Always Greener* by Sholom Aleichem, together with Molière's *The Miser* and Shakespeare's *King Lear*, he only managed to work for five weeks out of the scheduled sixteen-week run. The project, together with a proposed musical version of Ethel and David Rosenberg's novel *Go Fight City Hall*, left the couple with massive debts.

Their tax bill alone for the year ending 1955 totaled $2,359.56 plus $84 interest. Yvonne assumed that Harold would pay the money, but his refusal to save, combined with years of overspending, had left him without the means to do so. The couple started to argue; Yvonne demanded more money for the support of their daughter. Harold, hemorrhaging dollars with each passing day, found himself in an impossible situation. He couldn't pay the bill, but knew that if he didn't Yvonne might stop him from seeing his daughter. And that was a prospect he could not endure.

The tax demand prompted a crisis. On 11 June 1959, the same day the notice of federal tax lien was sent out, Robbins took Caryn to stay with some friends for what he said was to be a visit of only two weeks. Yvonne consented because, according to court records, she needed to secure steady employment and the break would give her the opportunity to find a job. But when the fortnight passed, Robbins could not bear to say goodbye to his daughter, his greatest delight. Caryn had blossomed before his eyes. He told Yvonne he was going to keep her a little longer, but the days stretched into weeks. Yvonne repeatedly requested that Caryn be returned home to 405 East 54th Street, but Harold refused, and so Robbins's onetime mistress felt she had no choice but to launch a legal bid to seek the return of her child.

On 3 August Yvonne, who gave her surname as Robbins, lodged a petition with the New York Supreme Court in Manhattan to win custody of Caryn. She claimed that her daughter "should be in the care, custody and control . . . of the child's mother . . . [who is] fully capable and better able to give her the care and love which she requires." On 12 August, appearing before Justice Louis Capozzoli, she reiterated this statement, adding that Robbins, her "estranged husband," had taken her daughter away from her "and he has refused to return her." Robbins, who turned up in court with Caryn, countered that Yvonne was "not a fit person" to look after the girl and that "the health and welfare of the . . . infant would be seriously jeopardized if her custody were awarded" to her.[18]

A photographer was on hand to record the event, taking pictures of Yvonne, dressed in an open-necked blouse and sporting perfectly applied makeup, and a rather tanned-looking Robbins, who wore a slick dark suit, white shirt, and tie. The little girl, Caryn, was snapped while her father helped her drink from a water fountain in the corridor of the Supreme Court. "After a huddle of lawyers for both sides and Capozzoli, the case was resumed in the privacy of the judge's chambers," before it was adjourned to a later date.[19]

On 8 October, the couple appeared before Justice Capozzoli at the Supreme Court once again. But this time, the press had unearthed the true circumstances of the relationship between Harold and Yvonne and their illegitimate daughter. "A four-year-old secret in the life of novelist and movie producer Harold Robbins, more dramatic than any fiction he has created, was revealed yesterday in a Supreme Court decision," said the New York Daily News. ". . . The disclosure was a startling end to a custody fight between Robbins, who wrote Never Love a Stranger and A Stone for Danny Fisher, and script-writer Yvonne Robbins, who until yesterday was believed to be Robbins's estranged but legal wife.

"Yvonne's real name was not disclosed yesterday, but it was reported that she comes from the British aristocracy. During the entire custody battle, which began in August, she was identified only as Yvonne Robbins of 405 E. 54th Street, Robbins's estranged wife. Actually, it was revealed yesterday, Robbins has been married for many years to the former Lillian Machnovitch, and lives with her on a handsome estate, complete with swimming pool, on Chestnut Hill Road, Norwalk, Conn. They have no children."[20]

Although Robbins presented evidence to the court that he could bring up the child in a loving, caring home, complete with photographs of his Norwalk estate, Max Cohen, Yvonne's lawyer, argued that such documents were irrelevant. Instead the case should be based on his client's legal right to the child as an unmarried mother. "The mother of the child born out of wedlock has superior rights to the custody as against the whole world, including the putative father," he said. "Certainly in the case of a child born beyond the pale of legal wedlock, the mother who has borne it in shame and disgrace and pain, having loved not wisely but too well, and who is anxious nevertheless to keep this child close and lavish upon it all her love and devotion . . . is entitled to its custody, far more so than any other person including the putative father who invariably loves only himself." He went on to state that "the law has recognized that the unintentional translation of an unsanctified gleam in the eye of a man into a child does not vest him with the rights and privileges of a father."[21]

After weighing up the evidence, Justice Capozzoli believed that Yvonne's case was the stronger, as she had, he said, "the best interests of the child at heart" and had gone out to work to support Caryn when "told by Robbins that he was in financial straits." Summing up, Capozzoli granted custody to Yvonne and awarded Harold visiting rights so that he could see Caryn on Mondays between three-thirty and six-thirty p.m. at his former mistress's apartment; in addition, he could take the child away from the flat on condition that he returned his daughter to Yvonne by the agreed time.

Robbins was devastated by the ruling: "All the feuding fouled up my mental machinery," he said.[22] Later he would channel his sense of loss into the novel *Where Love Has Gone*, which includes a scene in which the first-person narrator, Luke Carey, describes a courtroom battle with his former wife, Nora, over the custody of their daughter, Danielle: "For the first time Nora looked at me over Danielle's head. There was a curious kind of triumph in her eyes . . . Suddenly I realized what Danielle meant to her. She wasn't a child, she was just something Nora had made."[23]

Robbins later claimed that, after losing the custody battle, he abducted Caryn. "One bitch of a cold winter's day I found myself with Caryn in a freezing hotel lobby," he said. "The manager had locked us out of our room for a lousy 500 dollars . . . The watch was about all I had left. I left Caryn on a seat in the lobby and ran out with this watch and sold it for 750 dollars. Then I paid the bill and hit the hotel manager straight in the mouth. He lost three teeth and I felt better."[24] He also maintained that he managed to take Caryn out of the country. "I took her off to South America for a few months and got charged with kidnapping," he said. "I disastered for a year. Went doping, boozing, whoring."[25]

As there is no evidence to support these stories, it seems certain they are more of Robbins's yarns, invented for the purposes of self-promotion. In reality, after losing custody, Harold returned defeated and depressed to his wife in Connecticut. Lillian had loathed the scandal—the exposé of her husband as a philanderer, the existence of his secret love child, the news that Yvonne had swanned around town as Mrs. Robbins. When Lillian went shopping in Norwalk, she felt the eyes of the local gossips on her, looking at her with pity and amusement, and heard the sibilant whispers behind her back, snatched fragments of conversation that left a stain on her heart. She knew people were wondering why she didn't leave him, why she didn't sue him for divorce. But she had promised to love, cherish, and protect him whether in good fortune or adversity, and that was just what she would do. He needed her support more than ever now, and she would not abandon him. During those summer weeks when Harold had been looking after his daughter, she had swallowed her pride and welcomed Caryn into the family house. So what if the little girl had not come from her womb? She was the flesh and blood of her husband, and that was all that mattered. And surely she had a greater chance of keeping his love if she embraced the child and treated her as if she were her own.

Lillian's self-sacrifice moved Harold to tears. He had always known that her spirit was a selfless one, but when he saw her take his little girl into her arms and kiss her, he could not control himself any longer. He had been foolish to be taken in by Yvonne's charms. She was beautiful, sexy, and good fun, but another aspect to her character was superficial and unreliable. At times he even questioned whether she had ever loved her own daughter at all. He suspected Yvonne regarded Caryn as nothing more than a plaything, a pretty doll to pick up and dispose of at will. Certainly she did not have the depth, or the strength, of Lillian. If only he could step back in time, he would do it all so differently.

As he walked through the lawned gardens, up the steps to the covered porch, and into the large hallway, he looked around him. Without Caryn—who had romped and played around the house, jumping into the swimming pool, running around the gardens—it all seemed so quiet, so empty, not like a proper home. But he was determined to win Caryn back, no matter what the cost. Of course, his finances were in an appalling state: not only did he have no money in the bank, but any royalties or advances he earned from Knopf would have to be used to pay off his debts.

On 30 October he telephoned Knopf from Norwalk, requesting a meeting that day at two-thirty p.m. with William Koshland, Harold Strauss, and Joseph Lesser. Robbins then traveled to New York for a formal appointment with the Knopf executives to discuss his future.

"He asked to be let out of his contract with us on the basis that he had heard from many quarters that we were not interested in him and that we regarded his financial and legal problems as 'messy,'" remembered Koshland. "He also stated that he had seen a letter from our attorneys stating that we regarded the contract as canceled. He was informed that to the best of our knowledge no such statement was made but that we regarded the contract as in default because of the nondelivery of the manuscript—but the contract was still in effect."[26]

Over the course of the next couple of weeks Robbins became more and more obsessed with this letter from the Knopf attorney, believing that somehow it had skewed his custody case. Koshland checked with Harry Buchman, Knopf's lawyer, and was told in no uncertain terms that the document did not exist and that it was nothing more than a figment of Robbins's imagination. In all probability, said Koshland, the author was confusing it with another piece of correspondence, "remembering the letter that Harry [Buchman] wrote him at our direction whereby we established our position financially with Robbins by telling him he was in default and that we were therefore charging monies earned against the advance of $10,000 paid him."[27]

On 16 November, at 11:05 a.m., Robbins phoned Koshland and inquired if Knopf had made a decision. "I tried to stall and said we would rather call back, but he wanted to talk," said Koshland. "He wanted to know what our position was, and thought that JCL [Joseph C. Lesser] was to have called him back after we had discussed the matter further with AAK [Alfred A. Knopf] . . . He asked directly what our position was, and I said it remained the same—that we have a contract with him and are sticking to it. He repeated if that was all I had to say, and I answered, 'Yes.' His reply was, 'Okey, dokey; okey, dokey.' "[28]

That afternoon Robbins, after speaking with his agent Maurice Crain, told Knopf that he would be willing to finish and deliver *The Carpetbaggers* if the publisher were to amend his 1955 contract so that it was a deal for one book only. "I indicated we couldn't possibly consider any such proposition until we had a final and acceptable manuscript in from Robbins," said Koshland. "Crain seems to understand our position and made passing reference to Harold's 'aginness' to writing when he knows that every penny earned must go to meeting some debt previously incurred. I shrugged my shoulders verbally over the phone."[29]

The more Robbins thought about his situation—the loss of Caryn, the mounting debts, his inability to write—the more disturbed he became. He started drinking heavily and, in the new year, phoned Koshland and requested a copy of his publishing agreement. On 21 January Robbins turned up at the Madison Avenue offices and, in the hallway of Koshland's office, repeatedly asked to be let out of the contract. "The guy has really become quite unbalanced on the whole matter," said Koshland.[30] Again, he brought up the mysterious letter detailing Knopf's cancellation of his contract that he said had been presented in court, and adversely affected his custody battle for Caryn.

"His main problem, which he repeated again and again, was the

fact of wanting to regain custody of his child and that the price put on
this is $20,000.00 and he's going to get this $20,000.00 by hook or by
crook," said Koshland. ". . . One way obviously is for him to write
potboilers for paperbacks and pocket the dough."

Robbins told Koshland that he was sure he could, with the help of
lawyers, break his contract, but obviously he would rather not do so.
Instead he presented Knopf with another alternative: a new deal by
which they would publish only his hardcover novels, leaving him free
to work out an arrangement with another company for his paperback
rights.

"Then if we insist in sticking with the contract," noted Koshland,
"what he would like us to do is to cancel out the present contract,
make a new one . . . making the necessary arrangement for a reprint
contract, give him whatever money is due on delivery, presumably
$20,000.00 and then not report the fact that said $20,000.00 had
been paid over to him until such time as he would have paid it over to,
I take it, his ex-wife's attorney in order to obtain the child, and that he
doesn't care what happens. Needless to say I pointed out over and
over again how I could not commence on behalf of the corporation
action that would hold us in contempt of the US Treasury and that
would not be normal business procedure and so on and so forth."[31]

Robbins was not happy at Knopf's decision, and through a re-
commendation from New York friends, he contacted lawyer Paul
Gitlin, who worked for Ernst, Cane & Berner. Gitlin—described by
one commentator as a "cross between Hemingway and Moses"—had
developed a reputation as a fierce negotiator.[32] "His voice was an
aggressive growl, usually sharpened with impatience and, when
opposed, a large measure of rasping, scalding contempt," says editor
Michael Korda. "Gitlin was tough and smart and made no effort to
hide it, nor was he a man to mince words or take fools lightly . . .
Gitlin's personality was more that of a street fighter than a civil
libertarian or an aesthete."[33] Korda remembers Gitlin as "short,
rotund, stocky [and he] tended to lean forward on the balls of his
feet, like a man walking into a powerful wind, and somehow gave the
impression that he was on a collision course with you, and possibly the
rest of the world as well."[34]

In early 1960 Robbins entered Gitlin's office at 25 West 43rd Street clutching the first 125 pages of *The Carpetbaggers*. After discussing the author's case, Gitlin is supposed to have exclaimed, "Anybody who can make six and a half million dollars in ten years and spend eight million needs help—consider yourself my client."[35] Although the lawyer was wildly exaggerating the amount of money Robbins had earned, the basic premise was the same. Harold was overspending at an extraordinary rate, and his tax situation was a nightmare, while his deal with Knopf, especially the 50–50 split with Pocket Books for his paperback rights, was not netting him the kind of money the lawyer thought he deserved. Something would have to be done—quickly.

On 25 February Gitlin wrote to Knopf telling them that Robbins was now looking around for a new publisher for *The Carpetbaggers*. The attorney stated that as Knopf had "elected to terminate the contract," Robbins was in a position to negotiate a new deal. But Harry Buchman, on behalf of Knopf, maintained that the contract was still valid. Over the course of the following couple of weeks the letters between the two attorneys became more heated. Gitlin threatened legal action if Knopf continued to assert its rights over Robbins.

Buchman responded in equally vigorous terms. "Times and circumstances change, apparently resulting in people changing," he wrote. "There was a time when Mr. Harold Robbins felt embarrassed because of his failure to deliver the manuscript . . .

"Mr. Robbins's problem is obvious. There is [a] reason why he does not wish to deliver the manuscript to Knopf and has therefore latterly taken the position that he has no obligation to do so. The Federal Government has filed in the Register's Office liens against all income of Harold Robbins. If Harold Robbins delivers a manuscript to Alfred A. Knopf Inc. he knows that Knopf will be unable to pay him any royalties earned over and above the advance, until the U.S. Government liens on such royalties are satisfied. What he apparently does not understand is that even if Knopf were inclined to relinquish its right to give Robbins an opportunity to make a contract with another publisher, he is no better off because the U.S. Government has a lien upon sums due from any publishing firm (even without actual notice of the lien). We had occasion to check and found that the filing and perfecting of the lien by the Government is notice to all who have property of the taxpayer.

"If the foregoing is not enough of a problem, you may be interested to know that we have had to handle at least half a dozen judgment creditors (the number escapes us) who served us with third party orders containing injunctive provisions, and the attendant nuisance. Only this morning did I receive a new one which requires attention. These creditors follow the Government lien.

"All this extra-curricular activity on our part has been very disconcerting. It does not seem to end."[36]

Meanwhile Herbert Alexander of Pocket Books had heard on the literary grapevine that two rival companies had been sent the first eighty pages of *The Carpetbaggers*, a book that Knopf still insisted it intended to publish. Alexander phoned William Koshland and asked him to try to resolve the situation. Consequently Koshland, with Harry Buchman's approval, wrote an informal letter to Robbins; he thought that, by bypassing the lawyers, he could reach some kind of compromise. "Why in God's name, if you've got a manuscript, haven't you sent it in?" he asked. "No other publisher will touch this while it's under contract to us."[37]

Just as Robbins was trying to wrestle himself free of his contract with Knopf, he found himself threatened by yet more legal action. Not only had he accrued further debts—at the beginning of 1960 he owed in the region of $17,000 in back taxes alone—he was accused of stealing another writer's ideas. Back in 1959, in order to make some quick money, he had been tempted by an offer from movie producer Barnett Glassman to write a screenplay based on the life of the notorious gangster and Mafia boss Charles "Lucky" Luciano.

The eighteen-page treatment, which Robbins finished in July 1959, opens with a police raid on a handsome country estate in upstate New York; their quarry is Lucky Luciano. The scene then flashes back to 1910 when Luciano, born Salvatore Lucania, is living in a squalid East Side tenement and sharing his bed with his three younger brothers. Robbins obviously found a great deal to admire about the self-reinvention of Luciano, and in some ways he liked to think that he had made a similar journey, becoming, in effect, a living embodiment of the American dream.

After Robbins finished the treatment, however, he and Glassman had been unable to settle on terms, and as a result the movie idea was shelved. Robbins—at this most desperate time of his life—felt loath to junk the project and thought about ways to recycle it in a slightly different form. By the end of 1959 he had completely rewritten the screenplay, renaming it *Stiletto*, after the deadly weapon carried by the movie's protagonist, Sicilian playboy and assassin Count Cesare Cardinali.

Glassman, however, was far from happy to learn that Robbins was using what he considered his material. On 28 December 1959 Glassman, who was close to Luciano, wrote a threatening letter to Robbins at his Connecticut home.

"I have now been informed that you have written a screenplay entitled *Stiletto* which is similar to the stories we had discussed. If this is so, I think it is unbecoming, unfair, and surely not in accordance with ethics among writers, especially of your category.

"I am sure you are well aware that I am quite phased in litigation. . ."[38]

Robbins wrote back defending his actions, denying charges of plagiarism, and stating that *Stiletto* had been conceived well before he started work on the project about Lucky Luciano. As Glassman had forwarded his letter of 28 December to various business associates, Robbins in turn threatened him with a lawsuit if he discovered that his reputation had been tarnished by the accusation.

The row deflated when Robbins decided to drop the screenplay, opting instead to rewrite the story as a short novel. Although he had had discussions about the project with Pat Knopf, who had left the family firm to set up Atheneum Publications, he finally placed it with Marc Jaffe, then an editor at Dell. The two men met in early January, at Dell's offices at 415 Madison Avenue, to discuss the book.

"As you said here in the office last week, this one must not be a 'stiff,'" wrote Jaffe to Robbins. "There's too much at stake here for you, aside from our own publishing interest. I don't consider this book, as I'm sure you don't consider it, merely a quickie novelization of a screenplay. And it's important to make sure that your well-established reading audience takes it likewise.

"Strength to your elbow, or whatever it is that propels the typewriter key."[39]

As Robbins worked on the book, Paul Gitlin continued negotiations with Knopf, and in May 1960, in the words of William Koshland, "the whole megillah was finally settled."[40] The publisher decided that it was best to avoid any further scandal by letting Robbins go. Alfred Knopf Sr. viewed the debacle with distaste, and in 1972 in his unpublished memoir he said of Robbins: "I had become disillusioned with the whole idea of having my name and imprint associated with his work. Through agreeable negotiations, which I knew about but in which I took no part, we met his wishes and transferred his books to another publisher."[41]

That publisher was Simon & Schuster.

Simon & Schuster seemed like a natural home for Robbins, one more attuned to his mercantile spirit than the rather loftier firm of Knopf. The company had developed a reputation for innovation and a pioneering approach to marketing, often spending five to ten times more on promotion and advertising than their competitors. They were also the first publisher to produce an "instant" book, a tribute to Franklin D. Roosevelt that was rushed into the stores just six days after the president's death. Yet when they formed the company in 1924, neither Richard L. (Dick) Simon nor M. Lincoln (Max) Schuster had had any prior experience of the industry—Simon was a piano salesman, while Schuster had worked on a car magazine. When they opened their one-room office at 37 West 57th Street, placing a sign that read, "Simon & Schuster, publishers," on the door, they came back from lunch one day to find that someone had written underneath it, "Of what?" as they had no books to their name. The two men, however, were natural entrepreneurs, and their first venture, the world's first crossword puzzle book, proved to be a best seller.

"One highly important factor in the Simon & Schuster success revolves around the personalities of the partners," wrote one commentator in 1934. "Simon, the salesman, is nervous, high-strung, with a certain suggestion of perpetual adolescence; Schuster [is] the man who has the bulk of the ideas . . . Both are Jews; one comes from a family of extremely modest circumstances. Both possess an enormous urge for self-improvement which is typically Jewish—and typical also of the heroes of all stories beginning with poor-but-honest parents."[42]

Simon & Schuster was also known for the popularity—and readability—of its books. When Michael Korda arrived at the publisher in

1958, he remembered seeing a cast bronze plaque on each of the editors' and assistants' desks that read, "Give the reader a break." According to Dick Simon an editor's job was "to make things as easy and clear for the reader as possible." Korda recalls Schuster as "scholarly" and Simon as "ebullient . . . risk-loving."[43]

In the late 1950s and early 1960s Simon & Schuster was partly owned by Leon Shimkin, the founder of Pocket Books, America's first paperback publisher. In the 1930s the industry, said Shimkin, "became aware of the fact that there was a bigger market for books that were not Literature with a capital L, but were more addressed to what we generally call the 'broader market,' provided the price was lowered and the distribution base widened." In the first decade after its launch in 1939, Pocket sold more books than the combined total of all best sellers since 1880. "The elements of mass production, of mass distribution, the raising of the standard of living by producing better goods for less money, are all wrapped up in the basic concept upon which Pocket Books was founded," said Shimkin. "The new publishing and distribution formulas pioneered by Pocket Books, Inc. and followed successfully by a number of other firms have increased book sales well over a billion copies in the past sixteen years. This has increased the revenues of authors and publishers by a sum that could reasonably be estimated to exceed $20,000,000.00."[44]

At the company's offices in Rockefeller Center, Korda remembers that Shimkin, who was of Russian-Jewish origin like Robbins, "ruled from the floor below" like "the Prince of Darkness," never venturing to Simon & Schuster's offices upstairs. The relationship between the men was far from easy. "S&S was a hotbed of thwarted ambitions and intrigue," says Korda. ". . . While Max Schuster retreated to his office to plan further volumes of philosophy and Will Durant's *The Story of Civilization*, Dick Simon chafed at having to deal with the cautious and often nay-saying Shimkin."[45]

According to Korda, Shimkin's original intention had been to publish Robbins in hardcover at Simon & Schuster, letting Pocket Books continue to serve as his paperback publisher. Shimkin duly passed the first hundred pages of *The Carpetbaggers* to Henry Simon, the high-minded brother of Dick Simon, who worked as Simon & Schuster's editor in chief. Although he thought the book to be nothing

more than "trash," he believed that the company could make a large
amount of money out of it. But as the novel also "contained, quite
frankly, a good deal of outright pornography," Henry Simon decided
to pass it on to Max Schuster for a second opinion.[46]

For all his talk about the importance of accessibility and popularity,
Schuster was shocked by what he read. He had given his wife, Ray,
who increasingly modeled herself on the classy and intellectual
Blanche Knopf, a few of the pages to look at, and she too was
disgusted. Apparently she asked her husband whether this was
"the kind of *dreck* . . . that he wanted to publish at S&S? What
would their friends think? What would people say? What was Henry
thinking of? If Leon Shimkin wanted to grovel in dirt, let him do it at
Pocket Books, where nobody would be surprised."[47]

Despite Schuster's objections, Shimkin—a master businessman—
was not ready to lose an author as potentially profitable as Robbins,
and he set about plotting to keep him within his publishing stable.
What if Pocket Books created a separate imprint to publish Robbins in
hardcover? Although it was a huge gamble, Shimkin went ahead with
the project, naming the imprint Trident Press. Not only was Robbins
flattered by the fact that Shimkin had engendered a whole new
publishing company just for him, but he realized that the deal could
make him rich, as he would receive "100 per cent of the paperback
royalties instead of sharing them with his hardcover publisher in the
usual way," says Korda. "This was unheard of, as well as an
enormous amount of money spread over several as yet unwritten
books. Thus was the 'hard/soft' multi-book contract born, ensuring
that the face of book publishing was about to be changed in a very
dramatic way. It was soon to be a case of *après nous le deluge*, as
agents sought to emulate Robbins's coup and New American Library,
Bantam, and Dell woke up to the notion that they didn't really need to
play second fiddle to the hardcover publishers or bid themselves silly
over the rights to 'major' fiction from them."[48]

The deal also had a long-term impact on the publishing industry at
large, as Shimkin's move effectively increased the number of book
publishers overnight, "with the inevitable result that the big ones
would be obliged to eat the smaller ones until there were only a few
giants left, warily eyeing each other."[49]

In the meantime, however, Trident Press set about buying up a host of authors so as to lend credibility to the imprint. Its early titles included fiction by Jack Paar and William Saroyan as well as non-fiction by John F. Kennedy, Dwight Eisenhower, and Harry Truman (a book of essays and photographs in association with the National Cultural Center) and a memoir by John Faulkner, the brother of the novelist. The imprint, however, "lost as much money on these acquisitions as was made from publishing Robbins," says Korda.[50]

A few years later, when it became obvious just how much money Robbins's novel had made, publishing insiders gossiped about how *The Carpetbaggers* had been turned down by Henry Simon. "In the end, even Max Schuster couldn't forgive Henry for letting such a hugely profitable book go," says Korda, "and Ray Schuster was heard to say that her husband was too softhearted for keeping on Dick Simon's *nebbish* brother, who had been unable to recognize a gold mine when it was right before his eyes."[51]

9

"It's all about fucking . . . I don't know anyone who doesn't like to read about that. But besides, it's a hell of a story."

—*The Inheritors*

HAROLD BENT OVER his typewriter, his two forefingers pecking away at the keyboard. As he finished a page, he whipped it out and passed it over to Lillian, who sat at a nearby table, pencil at the ready. She had already quizzed her father, once treasurer at Universal, for stories of old Hollywood, anecdotes which duly found their way first into *The Dream Merchants* and now into *The Carpetbaggers*. Although she had worked closely with Harold on his other books, suggesting ways to improve the narrative, fleshing out characters, and editing his words, she put extra effort into *The Carpetbaggers* as she realized this novel, racy both in tone and subject matter, could make a lot of money. But she knew that whatever profits were generated by the book would go to a good cause—Harold's continuing pursuit for custody of his daughter. It was love for the little girl that drove them on.

Throughout 1960 Harold and Lillian sweated away at *The Carpetbaggers*, working around the clock to finish the epic novel, which finally ran to over thirteen hundred manuscript pages. "At the height of his success Harold could write thirty to forty pages in one sitting," says his friend Steve Shagan. "He told me he did not believe in substantial rewriting, and simply said, 'You get to know when a fried egg is fried.' He didn't like talking about his writing, believing to do that would kill the magic. But when he sat at his machine it was like a smoking typewriter."[1]

According to Michael Korda, *The Carpetbaggers* is not only Robbins's greatest novel but the best work of popular fiction of the postwar era. "If you had to pick the most perfect piece of modern 'commercial' fiction it really would be a toss-up between *The Carpetbaggers*, *Peyton Place*, *Valley of the Dolls*, and *The Godfather*," he says. "Those are the four books that changed the face of world publishing and the paperback business. I would go so far as to say that *The Carpetbaggers* is a much better read than any of them. The book presented a side of America that people wanted to believe in, while its publication coincided with the huge growth of the mass market paperback."[2]

The Carpetbaggers' central character, Jonas Cord—the son of a wealthy industrialist who goes into the movie business and has a passion for aviation—was clearly modeled after billionaire Howard Hughes. In the course of the novel Cord inherits his father's explosives business, just as Hughes took over his father's tool company; he founds an airline, ICA (Hughes's airline was TWA); he has an affair with a blond bombshell, Rina Marlowe (Hughes had a relationship with platinum blond Jean Harlow); he produces films called *The Renegade* and *Devils in the Sky* (Hughes was the producer of *The Outlaw* and *Hell's Angels*); and he pilots "the biggest airplane ever built,"[3] the Centurion, to fulfill a navy contract (Hughes famously piloted the unwieldy Spruce Goose, the H-4 Hercules, which held the record as having the largest wingspan of any aircraft in the world).

"I write about the world that I see, and in a peculiar way, maybe it is my world. Maybe nobody else saw it," Robbins told Digby Diehl. "I knew Howard Hughes. I spent three months with him during some business negotiations. And I had an idea of what I thought the man was like when I wrote the character of Jonas Cord in *The Carpetbaggers* . . . Novelists can do something a biographer can't do; novelists can go inside the head, try to find the reasons for the person. Whereas a biographer is limited by the facts."[4]

According to Steve Shagan, "Harold worshipped Howard Hughes—he used to go on these wild nights with him. Harold was invited down to the Hughes electric company, and he told me that

Hughes taught him how to fly a plane."[5] "I always thought that Harold wanted to be Jonas Cord," says Carroll Baker, who starred in the 1964 film of *The Carpetbaggers* and became a close friend of Robbins. "That was his fantasy. Although he was flamboyant and wealthy, he was never quite as flamboyant or as wealthy as he wanted to be."[6]

In this way *The Carpetbaggers* can be read as an extended fantasy in which Robbins casts himself as the central character, transforming himself from a forty-five-year-old author, with a balding dome-shaped head, careworn eyes, and a hangdog expression, into a handsome, sexually virile, high-living tycoon. In the opening pages we see twenty-one-year-old Jonas flying over the Nevada desert in a plane that he has won in a crap game. As he pilots the airplane over his father's explosives factory, he feels energized, literally on top of the world, superior to the little people down below. "Their life was dull enough," he thinks. "Let them have a real thrill."[7]

Robbins constructs Jonas, his alter ego, as a Nietzschean über-mensch, shaping the world around him according to his will. Apart from the final segment of the novel, each section of Jonas's story, which stretches from 1925 until 1945, opens with him in the air, Icarus-like. "Power, power, power!" Robbins writes in the voice of Jonas in the first chapter. "Up here where the world was like a toy beneath me. Where I held the stick lovingly in my hands and there was no one, not even my father to say me no!"[8]

Although Jonas represents himself as a man with a big ego and an even more impressive id, his first-person narration reveals that he is riven by psychic conflict, much of it unconscious. Jonas plays out a classic Oedipal drama, hating his father and longing for a mother he never knew. In one particularly heated scene Jonas and his father argue, the son accusing the older man of a lack of virility. This questioning of masculinity results in the death of the father, a loss that Jonas maintains does not affect him emotionally but that is responsible for a great deal of his drive and ambition. In order to prove that he is a better, more active, more heroic, more *masculine* man than his father, Jonas pushes himself to the extreme. Only in the last paragraph of the novel, after he nearly dies in a plane crash and learns that he is the father of a child, does he come to some kind of reconciliation with his own father, who he realizes loved him all along. As he looks at a photograph of his father on the desk he asks, "Well, old man . . . did I do right?"[9]

As in Robbins's own life, however, it is the missing mother who haunts the pages of *The Carpetbaggers*. The reader knows next to nothing about Jonas's mother, who died when he was a small boy, but this mysterious figure hovers on the margins of the novel, occasionally breaking through the narrative to cast a shadow over the text. Interestingly, and no doubt unconsciously, Robbins associates the figure of the mother with sexual desire. In the opening chapter, as Jonas is in the plane, he compares the black roof of his father's explosives building and the surrounding white sands to a girl lying on the sheets of a bed, "the dark of her whispering its invitation into the dimness of the night. My breath caught in my throat. Mother. I didn't want to turn away. I wanted to go home."[10] Although Jones uses the word *mother* here as a slang term, it's no accident that a few paragraphs later he goes on to tell the reader about her death—and her replacement, the enigmatic cowboy Nevada Smith, whom old man Cord employs to look after his son. Intriguingly, Robbins gives this character his own real mother's surname. As Jonas says in the book, "There are some people who won't stay dead."[11]

Jonas recasts his lovers in the role of mother, first with Rina Marlowe, who was his girlfriend before she marries his father. "I didn't hate my mother," he says. "She wasn't my mother, anyway. I had a stepmother. And I didn't hate her. I loved her."[12] Soon after telling Rina the news of her husband's, and his father's, death, Jonas is aroused by the sight of her standing in her black negligee. He compares her flesh to the cool, soft desert breeze, and "with only my devil to guide us, together we plunged into the fiery pleasure of our own particular hell."[13]

Following Rina's death he meets Jennie Denton, whom he remodels so that she looks like his stepmother, ordering that her mousy brown hair be dyed a color that resembles sparkling champagne. After Jennie, clad only in a mink coat, is discovered by Monica, Jonas's estranged wife, with Jonas in a hotel room, she holds out her arms, lets the fur fall from her shoulders, and pulls her lover toward her. "When she spoke, there was a note in her voice as if she'd always known this was the way it was going to be. 'Come to mother, baby,' she whispered gently."[14]

Taken out of context, this interchange may sound comical, but when read as a whole, the book stands as one of the most entertaining popular novels of the twentieth century. Although Robbins always claimed his favorite novelists were John Dos Passos, James T. Farrell, and John Steinbeck, he learned the art of writing popular fiction less from reading other writers than from working within the film industry. "It's important to remember that Harold had been exposed to all these movies and scripts at a time when many of them were great, great stories," says Steve Shagan. "He was smart enough to realize that the platform was the story. His use of language was not that bad—it was good enough, shall we say—and he always used a simple sentence structure and his books were easy to read. But he had a real talent for writing stories that the world wanted to buy."[15]

The influence of film is felt throughout *The Carpetbaggers*—in fact, at times the book almost reads like a novelization of a screenplay. Description is kept to a minimum, characters are little more than sketched out, and the book is heavy on dialogue. Not only is filmmaking the subject of the novel—readers are taken behind the scenes to see how movies are really made and the kind of people who make them—but Robbins also describes and captures the appeal of the cinema, how when one walks into a movie theater, the "world seem[s] to vanish with the magic of the image on the screen."[16] He also shows how Hollywood is responsible for our changing behavior. For instance, toward the end of the book Robbins outlines, in Jonas's voice, a scene between a fourteen-year-old girl and Nevada Smith, who offers to teach her how to ride.

"Jo-Ann looked up at him worshipfully. You could tell she'd been to the movies from the way she looked at him. He was a real live hero."[17]

Robbins employs techniques stolen from classic narrative cinema—flashback and fast forward—and his fondness for interslicing first-person with third-person narration could be compared to the filmic trope of the shot/reverse angle shot, when the camera switches between two perspectives to give an impression of interiority, followed by a wider viewpoint. In *The Carpetbaggers* Robbins confines the first-person narration to Jonas, granting the reader a privileged perspective into his world. Characters we meet in Jonas's narrative are then given books of their own—Nevada Smith, Rina Marlowe, David Woolf, and Jennie Denton—stories that are told in the third person and that give us insight into Jonas's world from an outside perspective.

Another reason *The Carpetbaggers* is so successful as a piece of popular fiction is its clever mix of genres: it combines several types of novel within the framework of an epic structure. By blending action and war material, traditionally a male genre, with melodrama, usually associated with a female readership, the novel appealed to as wide a range an audience as possible.

The novel begins, with Jonas's story, as a hardboiled, action-packed pulp, then moves on, with Nevada Smith's narrative, into the territory of the western. The section that covers Rina Marlowe's history—the death of her mother, her adoption into a rich Massachusetts family, the subsequent drowning of her adopted brother and mother, her lesbian affairs, the self-castration and suicide of her husband, and finally her death from encephalitis—lie firmly within the arena of the breathy, heady melodrama. David Woolf's narrative is a testament to the self-improvement ethos—his parents were Jews who fled the pogroms to make a new life in America—of which Robbins was so fond. Jennie Woolf's story is all about sex and was steamy stuff for the early 1960s, telling as it did of her rape as a girl, her life as a top-class Hollywood hooker, her success as an actress, and her love affair with Jonas, before she renounces fleshy delights in order to become a nun.

Sex is not confined to Jennie's narrative, however—the 700 pages of *The Carpetbaggers* reek of it. Although one character says that "true sex demands a greater intellectualism than simple animal rutting," the descriptions of it in the book are far from high-minded. As sex is so often associated with violence, some critics have understandably labeled the book, and Robbins's work in general, as belonging to the realm of the pornographic. Within the first 150 pages we encounter Jonas beating his stepmother, then having sex with her—"I placed my knee across her thighs and slapped viciously at her face"[18]—violence that Robbins portrays as arousing to both parties. We are given a graphic description of a Native American marriage rite, in which a bride-to-be, Kaneha, inserts a stick inside her vagina in order to rupture her hymen so as to make intercourse easier for her husband. Ten pages later Robbins describes how Kaneha is raped and skinned, her torturers fashioning an "Injun tit" from the pocket of skin around her breast. Nevada Smith, the son who goes on to avenge her murder, has sex with a prostitute next to the body of a dead man. And Rina Marlowe takes part in an orgy that she can remember only by virtue of a series of incriminating photographs. "A sick feeling began to come up into her throat. This could not be her. Not like this. Nude. With that woman and those men."[19]

Probably the most famous sex scene in the book is the one in which Maurice Bonner, a Hollywood producer, has sex with Jennie Denton three times after which she shaves him all over, massages him with a vibrator, and gives him a bath in champagne, a few puffs of marijuana, and a blow job, followed by breakfast the following morning. "In a real sense, Robbins delivered what his readers wanted, which explains his success," says Michael Korda, describing this episode as, "for countless men of a certain age, the best-remembered sex scene in American fiction and just possibly the most popular fantasy."[20]

Although Simon & Schuster was eager to keep in as much of the erotic material as they could, even the editors thought some passages were too explicit for public consumption. In the interchange between Charles Standhurst (modeled after William Randolph Hearst), former madam Aida Schwartz, and Jennie Denton, the newspaper tycoon relates a story about getting a Southern Baptist drunk and taking him down to Aida's brothel. In the published version Robbins writes in general terms about how Mrs. Schwartz's girls show the respectable Christian man a good time. Excised from this part of the manuscript is a whole paragraph describing the intricacies of an elaborate prostate massage, in which a girl inserts a ribbon into the anal passage of one of her clients, ripping it out at the moment of climax. According to friends, this was one of Robbins's own favorite sexual peccadilloes; he said that the sensation of the ribbon being pulled out of him intensified his orgasm.

While this paragraph was censored from the text, the book still contained so many sexual allusions—it was said that there were references to either sex or sadism every seventeen pages—that, in the words of one critic, "*The Carpetbaggers* could have sent any retailer handling it to prison before 1960."[21] Robbins's genius as a writer of popular fiction was to anticipate his readers' demands, providing them with exactly the books they wanted to read. In addition, he had the good fortune to hit upon the idea for *The Carpetbaggers* at a particular point in history when a new spirit of liberality was sweeping through Western consciousness. Readers, familiar with a popularized Freudianism, had already learned about the extraordinarily varied love lives of their friends and neighbors from Alfred Kinsey's revolutionary studies in the late 1940s and 1950s, while the advent of the contraceptive pill in 1960 gave women the freedom to have sex without the fear of pregnancy.

Robbins not only tapped into this new frankness but acted as a sort of carpetbagger himself, seizing the virgin territory of postwar commercial fiction and sexualizing it. "I felt we had to get past the middle-class Victorian principles," he said. "When we got far enough from World War II, things became more open. The world changed, and I changed with it."[22]

But Robbins really owed his new freedoms of expression to a rather more upmarket author who had died thirty years previously: D. H. Lawrence, whose *Lady Chatterley's Lover* had been banned in the United States. In May 1959 the New York Post Office impounded twenty-four packages from Grove Press that contained 164 copies of an unexpurgated edition of the novel. At the end of the month a judge ruled that the book was indeed obscene and referred the decision to the Postmaster General, who, in June, banned the novel from the mail. In turn, Barney Rosset, the founder and publisher of Grove Press, sued, and in July anticensorship lawyer Charles Rembar successfully argued that the book was not obscene, a decision that was upheld in another ruling in March 1960.

Inspired by this decision, Penguin Books in the U.K. printed 200,000 copies of the novel and stored them in their warehouse, sending twelve copies to the Director of Public Prosecutions and challenging him to prosecute, which he did. In their defense, Penguin argued that the book had not been written with the intention to corrupt. Indeed Lawrence himself, in an introduction to the novel, had said that he wanted to "hygienize" our attitudes toward sex. "That ghastly crudity of seeing in sex nothing but a functional act and a certain fumbling with clothes is, in my opinion, a low degree of barbarity, savagery. As far as sex goes, our white civilization is crude, barbaric, and uglily savage: especially England and America."[23]

In the famous case, which was argued in November 1960, prosecuting attorney Mervyn Griffith-Jones asked, "Is this a book that you would have lying around in your own house? Is it a book that you would even wish your wife or your servants to read?" But the novel was acquitted. "Handcuffs dropped from the wrists of every author in England," says John Sutherland. "They could now deprave and corrupt at will . . . *Lady Chatterley's Lover* sold two million [copies] for Penguin in two years."[24] Although Robbins had already written most of *The Carpetbaggers* by this point, he realized that he could now include certain scenes and phrases that would have been swiftly cut before the *Chatterley* case.

Meanwhile in the United States Grove's Barney Rosset began another legal battle, this time for the right to publish Henry Miller's notorious first novel *Tropic of Cancer*, which had been available for sale in France since 1934 but was banned in the United States. He eventually won the fight in America in early 1961. Not surprisingly, considering their sexual content—and the concomitant publicity surrounding them—when *The Carpetbaggers* and *Tropic of Cancer* were published within a couple of weeks of each other in June 1961, they both became immediate best sellers.

Robbins would also benefit from the subsequent 1966 ruling in *Memoirs v. Massachusetts*, the case involving John Cleland's 1750 book *Memoirs of a Woman of Pleasure*, also known as *Fanny Hill*. This landmark decision ruled that "a book cannot be proscribed unless it is found to be utterly without redeeming social value. This is so even though the book is found to possess the requisite prurient appeal and to be patently offensive . . . the social values of the book can neither be weighed against nor canceled by its prurient appeal or patent offensiveness."

To Robbins the rulings on *Lady Chatterley* and *Tropic of Cancer* meant nothing more than a license to make his fortune out of sex— now he really was laughing all the way to the bank. *The Carpetbaggers* became an instant best seller. But not everybody was happy about its success. "It is not quite proper to have printed *The Carpetbaggers* between the covers of a book," wrote a *New York Times* critic in June 1961. "It should have been inscribed on the walls of a public lavatory. Ostensibly Harold Robbins's long novel is about the men and women of Hollywood, aviation, high finance. Actually it is an excuse for a collection of monotonous episodes about normal and abnormal sex— and violence ranging from simple battery to gruesome varieties of murder."[25]

Soon after its publication Robbins sent a copy of the novel to Alfred A. Knopf, and in return he received a note "saying, 'Thanks, but I don't read such trash.'"[26] Then in August the *Chicago Tribune* decided to ban *The Carpetbaggers* and *Tropic of Cancer* from its lists of best sellers. "We have come to the conclusion," ran an editorial, "that we can no longer publish this list raw. Recently and tardily, we have become aware that some of the best sellers that have appeared on our lists were sewer-written by dirty-fingered authors for dirty-minded readers. We aren't going to further this game by giving publicity to such authors and their titles."

Apparently the *Tribune*'s editor, William D. Maxwell, during a hospital stay, had taken it upon himself to read some of the titles on the newspaper's best seller list and was appalled by the sexual content of Robbins's and Miller's work. "I found language in there that you wouldn't hear in a men's locker room," he said. Some subscribers to the newspaper were pleased by the decision—"Thank you for a helpful change of policy, we should stem this dirty deluge"—but others viewed it as nothing more than nannying interference: "This new policy is something I would have expected from a country weekly, but not from one of the country's ten best newspapers."[27]

Some readers may have been shocked by the sexual content of *The Carpetbaggers*, but that did not stop the book from selling. Advance sales of the $5.95 hardback, which was published on 5 June 1961, totaled 21,199. By 8 August the figure had reached 47,771 and by the end of October Robbins had sold more than 80,000 copies of his new novel. The respected trade journal *Publishers Weekly* named *The Carpetbaggers* the fifth best-selling fiction title of 1961, with sales of 108,198 copies, after Irving Stone's *The Agony and the Ecstasy* (in first place with sales of 215,618), *Franny and Zooey* by J. D. Salinger, *To Kill a Mockingbird* by Harper Lee, and *Mila 18* by Leon Uris. Just behind Robbins, in sixth place, was Henry Miller's *Tropic of Cancer*, which sold 100,000 hardcover copies.

Inspired by his success, Robbins felt that he was in a position to make some changes to his life. In October 1960 he had sacked Annie Laurie Williams, who had looked after his film rights, and Maurice Crain, her husband and his faithful agent, believing that Paul Gitlin had the tough negotiating skills necessary to win him the kind of big-money deals he thought he deserved. But without Crain's help, Robbins's career would likely not have progressed as quickly as it did. Crain, ever the professional, never complained when Robbins told him that he no longer required his services. But in a letter Crain wrote in 1963, he hints at the heavy editing that he did on Robbins's early novels. "I have received no commission for several years on American editions of the Robbins books published by Pocket Books," he wrote, "although I did more editorial work on those early books than an editor is usually willing to do on a book."[28]

Paul Gitlin now acted both as Robbins's attorney and as his agent, simultaneously sorting out his client's back taxes and brokering his increasingly generous advances. Before *The Carpetbaggers* was published, he had sent out galleys to film producers, but studios had been wary about the novel's overtly sexual content as well as its epic scope. In June independent producer Matty Fox, who had once worked as executive vice president of Universal-International, said he would like to take an option on the book, while rumors started to circulate around Hollywood that Eddie Fisher would produce the film and that Elizabeth Taylor, his wife, would star. "Even though the Fisher-Taylor rumors seem to have rested on shaky foundations," wrote an observer in *Publishers Weekly*, "they stimulated enough interest where none had existed before to stir up brisk competition."[29] The successful bidder was Joseph E. Levine's Embassy Pictures, which in September 1961 paid a hefty $300,000 for the rights to the novel.

Harold should have been pleased, but his success left a bitter taste in his mouth. The money was rolling in, but he was unable to gain custody of Caryn, the little girl who had inspired him to work so hard. Without her he wondered what kind of future lay before him. Sure, he could bash out more books and rake in even more dough, but would that make him happy, really truly happy? When he held Caryn in his arms, he had been able to picture having a family, imagining himself, Lillian, and his daughter all living together in Connecticut. But now the courts had rejected his appeal, and Yvonne had started to poison his daughter's mind against him. What was the probability that he would be able to bring up Caryn, to raise her as his own? A snowflake's chance in hell.

He knew that Lillian still loved him, and he was enormously fond of her. In the dedication to *The Carpetbaggers* he wrote, "For My Wife, LILLIAN, without whose encouragement, support and understanding, this book would never have been written."[30] The couple continued to live together at their house in Norwalk, where in April 1961 he started to write his next novel, *Where Love Has Gone*. He finished the book—a thinly disguised take on the infamous scandal surrounding the stabbing of Johnny Stompanato, the boyfriend of movie goddess Lana Turner, by her fourteen-year-old daughter—in April 1962 and duly dedicated it once more to his wife.

In May 1963 the couple traveled to Paris for a five-day break, but on their return Harold started to reassess his life. If he stayed with Lillian, what could he look forward to? A house filled with more possessions? A new car? Expensive holidays? He was now rich enough to acquire anything he wanted, within reason, but all the money in the world couldn't buy him a child of his own. His motivation may not have been conscious, but he started to look around for a woman who was glamorous, beautiful, and most important, young enough to bear him another child.

10

"Gradually as the evening progressed these women
slowly took off their clothes until by the end of the
night they were completely naked, stripped bare. That
was so Harold."

—Carroll Baker

H AROLD ROBBINS used to like to tell a story about how he met
Grace Palermo, his second—or in some of his more fantastical
accounts his third or fourth—wife. One day in the early 1960s he was
chosen by a large liquor company as a "Man of Distinction" to
advertise a well-known brand of whiskey. "I went to Grace's office in
a suitable frame of mind—I mean I was drunk," he said. "She gave me
some coffee, and after I sobered up, I went across the street, bought her
two dozen roses, a diamond, with a note, 'What are you hanging
around here for when you could be with me?' So she left her job. Oh,
and her husband."[1]

The anecdote is, of course, another one of Robbins's tall tales, as his
friend Archer King explains. "One day Harold rang me up and asked
me if I wanted to have lunch. I said I couldn't as I had a meeting with
Grace, this casting director in an advertising agency, who was a very
attractive, smart business lady. I had broken a date with Grace once,
and I couldn't do it again. Harold told me to bring her along as he said
it was important that he talk to me, and so I did. I never imagined that
they would get married."[2]

By all accounts, Grace could have stepped from the pages of one
of Robbins's novels. Born in a poor section of Brooklyn, she was

named after her grandmother, Grazia, and raised in a Sicilian-American household, first in Bushwick and then in Queens. As her father was often unemployed, Grace's mother, a seamstress, had to provide for the family. After surviving childhood leukemia, she developed into a bright, pretty child; she worked hard at school and was rewarded with good grades. She often dreamed of growing up to be an actress, and although in the strictest sense she never achieved this ambition, later in life, as Harold Robbins's wife, she would use her talents to play the role of the consummate hostess to perfection. From a job as a receptionist she climbed the career ladder, finally winning a prestigious position at Grey, the Park Avenue advertising agency, where she worked as head of casting. Her marriage, to painter Tom Horky, was far from happy, however, and, by the time she met Robbins—in the spring of 1963—she was ready for adventure. Little did she realize that, while the relationship would satisfy many of her wildest fantasies—traveling the world, socializing with the rich and the famous, enjoying a gilded lifestyle of yachts, champagne, and caviar—the dream would turn into a depraved nightmare of orgies and drugs, and ultimately a broken marriage.

At their first meeting, at that lunch at the Americana Hotel in Manhattan, there was initially little indication that Harold and Grace would become a couple. Archer King remembers walking with Grace into Harold's suite at the hotel, to be met by the author and a bevy of female models. As Grace had just read *The Carpetbaggers*, she could talk to the writer about his novel, while Robbins, for the most part, remained silent. "It was a good job I had read a bit of the book because it gave me something to talk about," said Grace. "He didn't say a word." Harold had thinning gray hair, a sagging face, and doleful eyes, yet there was something about him that charmed Grace.[3]

"It was an instant attraction," she said. "Although it was a big lunch, all the people sort of disappeared early, and Harold and I ended up eating alone. After lunch he walked me back to the office, and on the way we passed a jeweler's shop. He pointed out a beautiful gold locket and said, 'Isn't that pretty.' I was in a hurry so I said, 'Sure, it's lovely,' and dashed back to work. Later on that day the locket and a card from Harold appeared on my desk. That's what's so wonderful about Harold, he's full of surprises."[4]

The relationship was put on hold, however, as Robbins was due in Rome, where he was to help out on the production of *Le Mépris*, Jean-Luc Godard's film of Alberto Moravia's 1954 novel *Il Disprezzo*, which the director described as a "nice, vulgar one for a train journey."[5] The partnership of Harold Robbins and Jean-Luc Godard must rank as one of the most unlikely in literary and cinematic history. But although his work on the film went uncredited, Robbins helped his new friend, producer Joseph E. Levine, with the script. *Le Mépris* tells the story of an author, Paul (Michel Piccoli), who is rewriting the screenplay of a film based on Homer's *Odyssey* for crass producer Jerry (Jack Palance), whose role is rumored to be based on Joe Levine himself. (Indeed, one can almost imagine one of Jerry's lines—"Whenever I hear the word culture I bring out my checkbook"—being spoken by Levine himself.)

It's tempting to draw parallels between the character of Paul and Robbins himself. The protagonist of *Le Mépris* not only looks like Robbins—the two men shared a penchant for sharp suits and trilbys—but he is caught in a similar dilemma: whether to pursue his literary ambitions or settle for the easy rewards of the marketplace. By this point Robbins had chosen the spoils of commercialism, and while Lillian enjoyed the comforts of her suburban life—the house in Connecticut with its swimming pool and all the modern conveniences—she realized that the large amounts of money Harold had earned from *The Carpetbaggers* was in danger of corrupting her marriage. In the film Camille (Brigitte Bardot) grows to hate her husband because of the lowering of his ideals; perhaps, as Harold became more and more successful, this was how Lillian felt too? "Why is it money is so important?" says Paul toward the end of the movie. "It determines what we do, what we are. It affects our most personal relationships."

Certainly as Harold banked his royalty checks, he felt free to reshape his destiny. If he wanted to erase Lillian from his life he knew that he had the means to do so. And now that he had found a younger replacement, the option seemed increasingly attractive. When Robbins returned from Rome, he invited Grace out to lunch at the

Four Seasons, where he no doubt enjoyed one of his favorite dishes: a chopped salad with dollops of beluga caviar mixed into the lettuce as dressing. When asked if the dish had a name, Robbins would reply, "It's called money."

Over the course of the following few months Harold courted Grace with all the decorum and panache of a gentleman, perhaps realizing that this beautiful young brunette was more wife material than the blond floozies he usually picked up for a quick conquest. He charmed her with his outlandish stories and dry sense of humor and entertained her at some of New York's best restaurants. But Grace was puzzled as to why this man, renowned for the sexual explicitness of his books, had not yet tried to seduce her. According to those who knew him, despite his image as a sex addict, Robbins was in fact a soft-hearted sentimentalist. "Harold was a huge romantic," says Diana Jervis-Read. "People assume that he was all about sex. He wasn't at all. With him it was all, 'Look at the sunset, look at the bay.' A lot of people knew only the one side to him."[6]

But during a trip to Los Angeles, where Robbins was due to meet Joseph E. Levine, the couple consummated their relationship; Harold proved himself to be an expert lover, employing many of the techniques he would describe in his books. From L.A. they flew to Hawaii and on to Kauai, where they spent the next few days in bed.

Back in New York, Robbins made it known to Grace that she was much more than a brief liaison. He wanted her to leave her husband, Tom, while he said he would divorce Lillian—a fact it seems he kept from his wife, for the time being at least. Robbins was adept at secrecy. Like a good accountant, he could massage the truth with the ease with which he balanced books. He had one life in Connecticut—safe, comfortable, but fundamentally boring—quite a different one in New York, and yet another when he was traveling the world, and he was able to move in and out of each existence without too much trouble. He knew that if he told his wife of his intentions, she would go to pieces. He had put her through too much over the years. Was it not easier, indeed kinder, to let her believe that their marriage was intact? He would tell her when it was absolutely necessary, but not until then.

After Grace left her husband, she did inform her parents about her new relationship. They were not entirely comfortable with it; later

Robbins revealed how her father had reacted to him. "He had read all the gossip items about me. He said to Grace, 'Is this the kind of man you want? Do you realize he's nothing but a lecher?!' Grace said, 'Actually, Dad, that's just the kind of man I'm looking for!' And that was that."[7]

The couple moved into a rented apartment in midtown New York, and soon afterward Grace resigned from her job at Grey. Harold, who was thinking about his next book, *The Adventurers*, realized that in order to write the novel, he would have to spend some time with the *bandoleros* of South America. The opportunity gave him the perfect excuse to get away from Lillian. She wouldn't want to come, he told her; after all, she wouldn't enjoy herself. It was dirty, not at all the kind of place for a woman like her, and above all it was dangerous. In the autumn of 1963 Harold and Grace flew to Colombia, which was still in the midst of a civil war (*la violencia*) that had raged in the country since 1946. They checked into the Tequendama Intercontinental Hotel in Bogotá, from where Robbins ventured up into the hills to talk to groups of guerrillas. Although the expedition was fraught with danger, Robbins tried to reduce the risk of being killed by giving an interview to a Colombian newspaper. He said he wanted to make contact with the rebels so as to help communicate their cause.

"I stayed in the mountains with a Father Guzman, who was priest to a killer called Sangre Negra (Black Blood)," he said. "Six months after I left him, Negra was killed and his body was exhibited in a public square. The bandit was twenty-four but looked like an old man. The *bandoleros* have no life expectancy, and it shows in their faces. I'd seen them tearing villages apart and heard stories of rape and killing. I asked him, 'Do you want your sons to live like this?' He just shrugged and said, 'I don't know. I'm just a simple murderer.'

"I lived with them and understood. To them, rape was not so much a crime as a natural spoil of war. The kids couldn't wait to grow up, not to enjoy sex, but to inflict it as a punishment. That represented success."[8]

After his return to Bogotá, the couple moved on to the coastal city of Cartagena, where in October 1963 Grace conceived their first child. "She was so relieved when I got back she became pregnant immediately," said Harold.[9] With his characteristic quick thinking Harold decided Grace should leave the country, and so in early 1964 he traveled with his new lover to the South of France. After a stay at La Réserve de Beaulieu, situated between Nice and Monaco, they moved into a rented villa in Le Cannet, just outside Cannes. On his return to America Harold still did not tell Lillian the truth. She had guessed that he was seeing another woman—she wasn't that stupid—but she had no idea that his lover was pregnant. Harold realized that if he told her, she would fall apart. It had been bad enough the first time, when he had had to confess that Yvonne was bearing his child. So he chose to keep silent, traveling between the two women and telling both only what he thought they wanted to hear.

If Harold Robbins had pursued his film career he would most likely have materialized into Joseph E. Levine, the quintessential showman of the movie world. In fact, the two men were like mirror images of each other, masters of exploitation who could tap into the tastes of the masses and, using a clever mix of self-promotion and blitzkrieg advertising, persuade millions of consumers to part with their money, with the promise that their books and films would fulfill their wildest fantasies.

Like Robbins, Levine was an archetypal American: a figment of his own imagination, a self-reinvented product. Born in a Boston slum in 1905, the child of a Russian immigrant tailor, the boy spent his early years grubbing for small change, working as a shoe shiner, a luggage carrier, and newsboy. After an unhappy childhood—he said that he did not experience "one happy day" as a boy—he left school at fourteen for a job in a dress shop. He ran a restaurant in Boston, married a singer from Rudy Vallee's band, opened a movie house in New Haven, and built up a small business distributing and exhibiting films in New England.

The term *lowest common denominator* could have been invented for Levine. One of the first films he bought was a sex hygiene documentary called *Body Beautiful*. "The picture showed the birth of a baby, guys getting tested [for VD], and lots of other stuff the army shows its soldiers," he said. "It made me sick. So I bought it."[10] Using the $20,000 he made from that film, Levine invested in distributing B-movies, westerns, and foreign imports such as the Japanese monster movie *Godzilla*, which grossed $1 million. In 1958 he bought the U.S. rights to the Italian epic *Hercules* for $120,000 and spent $1.5 million on advertising and promotion—a gamble that paid off handsomely as the movie, although panned by the critics, grossed $9 million.

Levine, at five feet four inches tall, weighed 214 pounds and was regularly described as "round," "dark-haired, moon-faced," and looking like "the 31st Sultan of Turkey." Robbins used him as a basis for the character of Sam Benjamin, the movie mogul, in his 1969 novel *The Inheritors*.[11] Robbins introduces the character at the launch of his new film *Icarus*, which the author obviously based on *Hercules*. Benjamin turns up for the event complete with a million dollars in cash, as well as giant blow-ups of half-nude actors and nearly naked actresses—exactly the kind of publicity stunt Levine would have dreamed up. Benjamin, like Levine, is a keen amateur magician who is able to make a hundred-dollar bill disappear down an actress's décolletage and who, although he is short, sees no reason why he should not act as if he were six foot two.

"He was small and seemed almost as broad as he was tall," writes Robbins. "He wore a black suit and a white shirt. He had black hair and a ruddy face that seemed to be sweating."[12] When the novel was published, much was made of the similarity between the two characters, prompting Levine to write in Robbins's guestbook on his yacht, "I am NOT Sam."[13]

Levine taught the author the value of hype and advertising and the fact that, as Robbins writes in *The Inheritors*, "promotion, publicity and exploitation even more than the picture itself would attract people to the local box office."[14]

He did not let truth stand in the way of a good story and likened his showmanship techniques of those of P. T. Barnum. "We are reminding everyone that this is a circus business," he said.[15] In addition to employing promotional gimmicks—such as four thousand rubber bombs to advertise *Hercules* and five thousand genie lamps to promote *The Wonders of Aladdin*—Levine insisted on selling by saturation, opening his films in six hundred different movie theaters around America in the first week, twice the usual number. "Since Mr. Levine has never permitted culture to get the better of him, he has never lost his Midas touch with the masses," wrote Gay Talese in a

1961 *Esquire* profile of Levine. "Mr. Levine *is* the masses. What he likes, millions of people like."[16]

His ambition, he said, was for every man, woman, and child in America to see his movies. "My audiences are people who need escape," he said. "They are the waiters, truck drivers, and little guys who work all day. When they go to the movies, they want escape. They want to see guys fighting dragons. They want action!"[17] Levine could have added sex and violence to his list. "In the last couple of years, American movie houses have been invaded by four films in which nineteen women are seduced," wrote Talese, "three hundred soldiers are slaughtered, eight tigers are strangled, four cities are burned, six chariots are flipped, and a dozen shipwrecked men are washed onto a tropical island where they are dined and wined by beautiful Amazons—and then raped."[18]

Later, when Levine was working with Jean-Luc Godard on *Le Mépris*, the producer complained that, after investing a large amount of money into the movie, it contained no nude shots of Brigitte Bardot. He subsequently ordered the director to insert one into the film. Levine knew, at the beginning of the 1960s, that sex, or at least the promise of it, was box-office gold. "He [Levine] wants sex, action, and characters who are recognizable human types," observed screenwriter John Michael Hayes, who worked with Levine on adaptations of Robbins's *The Carpetbaggers*, *Where Love Has Gone*, and *Nevada Smith*.[19]

When Levine read *The Carpetbaggers*, he realized that it was the perfect vehicle for him, a product guaranteed to make money. "It's not that many times in your life you get a shot at a movie that's so pre-sold," he said. Levine entered into a deal with Paramount Pictures, which engaged the services of John Michael Hayes, who had already written the film scripts of *The Children's Hour*, *Butterfield 8*, *Peyton Place*, *The Man Who Knew Too Much*, *The Trouble with Harry*, *To Catch a Thief*, and *Rear Window*. The challenge, of course, was to fashion a single strong storyline from Robbins's epic, multi-narrative novel.

"I do not know what Hayes has done or plans to do with this novel," wrote screenwriter Curtis Kenyon in an internal memo to Martin Rackin, head of production at Paramount, "but in my opinion there is a simple, straightforward and dramatic story line in this mass of material, and if it is dug out and the lard cut away, it would make a good commercial film that, with Joe Levine's exploitation, should ring the cash register . . .

"I think adapting this material to the screen calls more for a careful, even shrewd, job of editing than for any creative effort. The approach I am suggesting would retain the *Peyton Place* feeling that the film obviously should have, but would eliminate those narrative portions that are tedious even in the novel. As for the erotic content, I believe all of this can be handled by shading and excision without destroying the exploitation value of the book."[20]

Hayes started work on the screenplay in February 1962 and completed a first draft in January 1963, a project that earned him, after an additional five weeks of rewrites, $113,647. "*The Carpetbaggers* caused a sensation when it was first published, it was a really scandalous book full of sex, and very risqué for the time," he remembers. "Joe Levine paid a lot for it because he knew it would make money. I thought it was a book with a great deal of excitement and adventure in it, and I seem to recall that Robbins liked the adaptation."[21]

Hayes met Robbins in Hollywood and immediately liked him. "I was quite taken by him—he wasn't the opportunist that he became later," he says. "He was proud of his work, and I liked his enthusiasm. He wrote with a great sense of duty—he told me he managed to turn out twenty pages a day. And he'd do it every single day. Although his books were written for film, the irony was that none of them made good movies. But Harold was interested in money. When he discovered how to make money, he really went at it. He would do anything to get it and was very clever. Sex, of course, was very important to him also. He always needed lots of sex, and he had lots of girls. He was very gentle, but he did have lots of sexual escapades. He had new adventures all the time."[22]

In March 1963 Edward Dmytryk, director of *Murder, My Sweet*, *The Caine Mutiny*, *The End of the Affair*, and *Walk on the Wild Side*, agreed to take on the project, signing a contract for thirty-four weeks. Again, he was forced to address the problem of making a motion picture from one of the most controversial novels ever published, a book he called "this explosive tale of violence and passion." Of particular concern was the "ripe language which appears in the original Robbins novel." In this respect, he said, "we are our own censors . . . the characters and their extreme situation call for strong, forceful, and sometimes mildly shocking semantics. Our dialogue has been developed along these lines, but it is never offensive." Although he had previously directed so-called family pictures, they had been flops at the box office. "This," he said, "won't happen with *The Carpetbaggers*. This story never lets down. We have not used sex and violence for its shock appeal or to achieve sensationalism. But because some components are essentials in the story, we have made no concessions to these realistic attitudes or modes of behavior."[23]

By the end of May 1963, as the film was being cast, the novel had sold a staggering 5 million copies in hardcover and paperback. "You couldn't miss it," says Elizabeth Ashley, who plays Monica in the film. "It was hawked incessantly to the public as the most scandalous book since *Peyton Place*. I think the thing that made the book a phenomenon was the thinly disguised Howard Hughes story. Hughes was, perhaps, the most fascinating man on the planet at the time. I have a dim memory of Robbins being ferried around at Paramount. He was short and dark, wearing loud sort of clothes and some kind of cap, presumably to cover his baldness."[24]

The Carpetbaggers was Ashley's first film; she had previously made her name on Broadway, specializing in comedy, "and the girl I played [in *The Carpetbaggers*] was the only character with any funny lines," she says. "To this day, people who don't know me from anything else come up to me on the street and tell me they still remember one line I had in that movie. My fiancé says to me, 'What do you want to see on your honeymoon?' and I answer, 'Lots of lovely ceilings.' "[25]

A number of actresses were asked to screen-test for the role of movie goddess Rina Marlowe, including Katharine Ross, but Joe Levine insisted that the part be given to Carroll Baker, while he maintained that Martha Hyer play ex-call-girl Jennie Denton. "Neither of these choices thrilled," said Edward Dmytryk, "but we had no one to offer in opposition, so we gracefully acquiesced."[26]

Carroll Baker, whose last hits had been the 1956 films *Giant* and *Baby Doll*, had so impressed the producer on meeting him at a charity dinner at the Plaza Hotel in New York that, according to the actress, "he said upon meeting me, 'You're just the girl I want for my next film. It is the best part you've had since *Baby Doll*, but you have to take my word for that. Without any question, you must accept the part and shake my hand to bind the deal.'

"So that is exactly what I did. I shook Joe Levine's hand. It wasn't until months later that I discovered I had agreed to play Rina Marlowe in *The Carpetbaggers*. And it was that part in that film which shot me back up to the top of my profession. In showbiz circles it was to be hailed as a remarkable comeback."[27]

Baker, who earned $85,000 for playing the role, arrived on set in June to find herself the subject of the amorous advances of George Peppard, who had been cast as Jonas Cord and whose fee was $150,000 for ten weeks' work. The fact that Baker was a married woman did not seem to matter to Peppard. "He acquired delusions of being far more than just a talented young actor who was working his way up the ladder of success. I got the impression he felt he was God's gift to women and the cinema.

"From the moment I walked on the set of *Carpetbaggers* to play Rina Marlowe . . . George's attitude to me seemed bizarre, as though he had never met me or had any awareness of the existence of my husband. George asked me not *if* he could see me in an intimate setting, but *when*. He showed up uninvited at my house late one night and gave me a stern warning, 'If you don't have a love affair with me, I'll make love to Elizabeth Ashley.' "[28]

Peppard, who was married to actress Helen Davies, and Ashley, the wife of actor James Farentino, subsequently began a passionate affair on set, a scandal that Levine relished as it added to the illicit nature of the film. Peppard, however, was drinking heavily, and later he said of his alcoholism, "I turned into my own worst enemy." Elizabeth Ashley suspected that Carroll Baker, "like everyone else, was having problems with Peppard's drinking, which of course was never mentioned out loud as he was a big star, making lots of money for the powers that be," she says.[29]

Peppard's drinking was nothing compared to that of Alan Ladd, who was cast as Nevada Smith for a fee of $50,000. Dmytryk knew about Ladd's reputation—in November 1962 he had been discovered lying unconscious in a pool of blood with a self-inflicted bullet wound near his heart. The director was understandably anxious about his ability to perform in front of the cameras, but Martin Rackin persuaded him to hire Ladd. "I was on set a couple of times when he [Ladd] was called, and [my] only memory was of overwhelming tragedy," says Elizabeth Ashley. "A petit male creature who had drunk himself into incoherence—I literally could not understand a word that came out of his mouth. There were a couple of keepers who kept him vertical and explained what he was saying to you, very subtly and never at the expense of his dignity. He had kind, tired, seen-it-all eyes and seemed a gentle spirit."[30]

Ladd would tell visitors to the set that it was "Peppard's picture, you know," and rumors circulated in Hollywood that he had recently undergone a facelift.[31] As filming progressed, it became obvious to everyone that Ladd, his face puffy, his words slurred, was falling apart. "One day during a scene with me his drink spilled over the sides of his glass because of the trembling," remembers Carroll Baker. "Out of sheer frustration, he punched the door of the set with his hand still holding the glass and cut himself quite badly. Paramount employed a tattletale system whereby the assistant director kept a record of every spoiled take and who was to blame. Alan was desperate that his name not appear too many times on that list. Our director, Eddie Dmytryk, when he saw Alan begin to flounder, would jump in with, "Cut! It's my fault. I'd like to go again."[32]

Baker remembers that while most of the actors tried to help by covering up for Ladd's mistakes, George Peppard showed little compassion for him, as perhaps "he was too insecure about his position."[33] By the time the film was released, in April 1964, Ladd was dead from an overdose of alcohol and sedatives.

On 21 June, Baker was due to film one of the most controversial scenes in the movie, one in which she had to appear nude. Paramount issued a press release to boast that it had the "most closed set" in the history of the studio, and executives even took it upon themselves to organize a police cordon around stage fourteen where the movie was being shot. Although the scene looks tame today, it was daring for its time. "Even partial nudes were shot only in skin flicks in 1963, and most of us were embarrassed that Carroll Baker should appear nude on the set, even though we were photographing only her back," remembered Dmytryk. "The set was lit, Carroll, in a robe, seated herself at the dressing table, and a screen was placed around her. When all was in readiness, those members of the crew not absolutely necessary were excused from the stage. I started the camera, the wardrobe mistress took Carroll's robe, the screen was removed, the scene was shot, and we all breathed a little more easily. And all that eventually showed on film was a bare back which was quickly covered by a robe."[34]

The combination was irresistible: the buzz surrounding a titillating, entertaining best seller, the racy subject matter, fabulously glamorous stars, the on-set scandal, and the infamous death of one of its leading actors almost guaranteed the film would be a box-office success. Its world premiere took place on 9 April in Denver, Colorado, a city chosen by Levine because he said it was so "dynamic." A West Coast screening followed on 4 June, to which Carroll Baker wore a "slinky, jeweled net-and-chiffon transparent gown" inspired by one of Marlene Dietrich's outfits. "That dress caused a sensation when I wore it to the Hollywood premiere of *The Carpetbaggers*," she said. "I looked gorgeous—sparkling and devastatingly daring. I wore nothing underneath, and the skin-colored net and chiffon blended under the bright lights with my own flesh . . . I believe every newspaper in the world printed a photograph of me in that transparent dress, with claims that I had appeared virtually nude."[35]

A New York premiere followed, with a party for two hundred people at the Four Seasons, on 26 June. "I remember we had this wonderful party at the Four Seasons in New York and at each of the tables there was a beautiful woman whom nobody recognized," says Baker. "Gradually as the evening progressed these women slowly took off their clothes until by the end of the evening they were completely naked, stripped bare. That was so Harold."[36]

In its first week of release the movie grossed $1.5 million in New York alone. It went on to be the most profitable film of 1964, earning $36 million in box office takings in America, while in 1965 *Variety* magazine ranked it as the fourteenth highest-grossing film of all time. *Time* magazine labeled it "feisty smut,"[37] while a critic for *Variety* said it was "lusty, vulgar and gutsy, and on one notable occasion, painfully brutal. It projects with harsh, driving force—often erratically—the same two basic elements that propelled the novel into the best-seller list. One is the underlying connection of its principal characters to several real and glamorous people around whom there has always circulated a certain aura of mystery. The other is a notorious reputation—a hint of sexual wickedness."[38]

The reviewer could almost have been describing Robbins himself.

Was it kindness or cruelty that prompted Harold to invite Lillian to the premiere of *The Carpetbaggers*? Perhaps Robbins thought that he was simply doing what was right, letting her enjoy a slice of the limelight, rewarding her for all her hard work on the manuscript. She would get a chance to mingle with the stars, shake the hand of the handsome George Peppard, and chat with the divine Carroll Baker. But as he now had a mistress, safely ensconced in a rented villa in the South of France, who was only three months away from giving birth to his child, one could accuse him of being more than a little sadistic. However, in the photograph of them together at the event—he in a smart black tuxedo, his immaculate but overweight wife in an expensive rose-print dress—he does not seem to be particularly enjoying himself. Thinner, his balding hair now gray, and with black shadows under his eyes, he stood with a cigarette, his free arm not draped around his wife but hanging in front of him, redundant. Trying to look happy for the camera, all he could manage was a fixed rictus smile, the expression that of a guilty man who is about to confess.

In truth Harold was being neither altruistic nor malevolent—he was simply "being Harold," practical to the last. He would have felt there was no point causing a fuss by getting all emotional before the event. Leave that until later, he thought. And what was to be gained by walking down the red carpet with his young, heavily pregnant mistress? Lillian, ever the loyal wife, duly attended, but her instincts told her something was wrong. She didn't enjoy what was supposed to be one of the best nights of her life. She felt on edge, anxious, but could not isolate what was troubling her. When she got home and saw Harold's mask drop, she knew right away the news was going to be bad. They had to talk, he said. He had met someone, another woman, and this time it was serious.

She had endured his constant skirt-chasing, his affairs, his flirtations, before. Why was this one any different? Who was this trollop whom Harold had just picked up? Surely they could work something out? If he wanted an affair, she would turn a blind eye and wait for him to come home. What? He wasn't interested in a fling? He felt more for her than that? He thought he was in love with her? She refused to admit that the marriage could be over. It was just not possible. Then Harold decided to drop his bombshell: Grace was pregnant. The revelation made her physically sick. For a wife unable to have children to hear that her husband had impregnated two different women while still married to her was the worst kind of hell. She knew at that moment that their marriage was over.

"Lillian could not believe Harold could do that to her," says her sister Rae. "They had had a happy marriage, had worked hard on the books together, but I suppose they must have drifted apart. He had a roving eye—when men get fame and fortune, they go the way of all flesh. She was so angry with him, especially since she thought she had contributed so much to his novels. She was depressed, but she didn't want to talk about him, didn't want his name mentioned in the house. She thought he had taken advantage of her—as did my parents, who were very saddened—and she never, never forgave him. She had devoted herself to him—she loved him dearly—and she was punished for being good. It was the most dreadful betrayal."[39]

11

"He is a pyknic, bright-eyed Jew, fierce and charming
in startling terms, egotistic, energetic, generous and, as
de Gaulle said of the Israeli nation, 'sûr de lui.'"
—Anthony Blond on Harold Robbins

FOURTEEN-YEAR-OLD Cheryl grasped the nine-inch butcher's
knife in her sweaty palm as the argument raged around her.
The swarthy, dark-haired man threatened to attack her mother, to cut
up her face and leave her scarred so she would never be able to act
again. The affair between the couple—the smooth-talking gangster
Johnny Stompanato and glamorous blond movie star Lana Turner—
had been a tempestuous one. The teenager knew that the man had
intimidated her mother many times before, warning her that if she did
not do as he wanted, he would take a razor blade to her. Standing
outside the bedroom door, Cheryl pleaded with the actress to open the
door. She was scared what Stompanato would do, frightened that he
was about to follow through with his threats. When Lana finally
opened the door, Cheryl was certain that the gangster was about to
hurt her mother. As he moved toward the actress, Cheryl struck out,
plunging the knife deep into his stomach.

Stompanato sucked in his breath and looked down at the wound.
"Oh, my God, Cheryl, what have you done," he managed to say
before he collapsed onto the floor, blood beginning to seep out of his
body and over the plush carpet. Lana ran to the bathroom and tried to
stem the flow of blood with a towel. But within minutes her lover was
dead.

Press coverage of the case—a heady combination of sex, sleaze, and stardom—was sensational and dominated the tabloids for months on end. Rumors circulated in Hollywood that Turner herself had killed Stompanato, forcing her daughter to take the blame because as a minor she stood a better chance of escaping conviction. From the first day Harold followed the coverage, poring over typical newspaper headliness such as STAR'S DAUGHTER FATALLY STABS MOM'S BOY-FRIEND and studying the photographs of Lana Turner taking the stand, crying while giving evidence in a performance that many critics said was the greatest of her life.

Although Harold tweaked a few details—such as changing the profession of the mother from actress to sculptress and moving the setting from Los Angeles to San Francisco—the sensational story found its way into his 1962 novel *Where Love Has Gone*, as Turner herself realized. Although the actress tried to put the scandal behind her—Cheryl escaped with a verdict of justifiable homicide—Robbins's "exploitation had kept it alive in a distorted version he had hardly had the grace to disguise," she said. "He had turned the worst tragedy of my life into a cheap, mean, best-selling novel based on cruel fabrications."[1]

Just as Robbins had been tutored in the art of hype from Joe Levine, he learned the finer points of cooking up a corker of a melodrama from his friend and former Universal-International colleague Ross Hunter, whose influence can clearly be seen in *Where Love Has Gone*. Hunter, who began his career as an actor, started work at the studio in 1953 and went on to produce spectacularly soapy hits (all directed by Douglas Sirk), such as *All I Desire*, *Magnificent Obsession*, *All That Heaven Allows*, *There's Always Tomorrow*, and *Imitation of Life* (starring none other than Lana Turner). "It was Hunter's theory," according to one film writer, "that 'Women's Pictures' (films which deal with a woman's problem and star a beautiful woman who can wear beautiful clothes and jewelry) were the real moneymakers. According to Hunter's theory . . . women are the ones who select the films a family will see."[2]

Robbins wrote his latest novel with this readership—a gossip-obsessed, tabloid-reading, *Peyton Place*-watching audience—in mind. In October 1962, soon after the publication of *Where Love Has Gone*,

Time magazine asked the question: what makes a sleazy novel sell a million copies? Sex scenes, while often being responsible for increased sales, did not entirely explain the phenomenon, as "pop-novel sex has become fairly standard . . . Already the point has passed where even abnormal sex can shock." The answer was exploitation, and Robbins, it said, was its "new lord of the garbage heap," scanning the tabloids for racy material that he could fictionalize. "He picks a public personage who has figured in lurid headlines, changes his name and a few unimportant details, and writes the novel around him," it said, "leaving [the person] as difficult to identify as Liz Taylor in a false beard."[3]

Where Love Has Gone promised readers inside information on one of the hottest scandals in Hollywood history, and it did not disappoint, serving up helpings of lurid details and lending weight to various conspiracy theories. Robbins's use of courtroom scenes and medical procedures gives the novel a gloss of authenticity, suggesting that he had been given unique access to the case files. He even goes so far as to include the intimate medical records of Danielle (the fictional counterpart of Cheryl Crane), a document that must have made for shocking reading: "The hymeneal rupture is complete and the scar well healed and of indeterminate age. However, there are signs of irritation in the vaginal walls and a slight swelling of the clitoris, which indicates the probability of a high level of sexual activity during the period shortly preceding this examination."[4]

During the course of the book it is revealed that fourteen-year-old Danielle and her more glamorous mother, Nora, had both been sleeping with Italian gigolo Tony Riccio. At the climax to the novel, after it is suggested that Nora was the one responsible for the death, Dani finally blurts out the truth: that she was actually trying to kill her mother because she believed Nora would take Tony away from her. "The novel had such an impact that readers were convinced that it revealed the truth about Stompanato's death," said one of Lana Turner's biographers, Jane Ellen Wayne.[5] The impact on Turner's daughter, Cheryl Crane, was devastating. "The Robbins book gained a good deal of publicity, and for Cheryl, it was reliving that dreadful night all over again," says Wayne. "She was trying to make a new life for herself in Los Angeles, working as a carhop and doing other odd jobs under a different name in 1963. She began to drink heavily, became despondent, and took an overdose of sleeping pills."[6]

Although Cheryl survived, her mother never forgave Robbins for his blatant exploitation of the murder. According to Eric Root, one of Turner's lovers toward the end of her life, one night she was watching a television show about infamous Hollywood scandals when the case was mentioned. The actress told Root, a self-styled hairdresser to the stars, that she still felt angry toward Robbins. When Root pressed her further, she admitted that she had been responsible for Stompanato's death and said she resented Robbins for raking over the details of the case. "I didn't want to face the truth," she told him. "I blocked it out of my mind. You know I do that whenever I don't want to think about something that troubles me. The wall goes up and that's it. Nothing gets through. You've seen it all too many times. But now you know. I've spoken to you and said things I've never told anyone else, until tonight."[7]

On publication *Where Love Has Gone* entered the American bestseller list at number seven, and during its first two months the novel sold 52,000 copies in hardcover. The book, and in turn the original scandal, gained yet even more exposure when Joe Levine announced he was going to produce an expensive adaptation for the big screen. The total budget of the production came in at just under $3 million: in October 1962 Levine paid Robbins $275,000 for the film rights, while in February 1963 John Michael Hayes started work on the script (for a fee of $122,646). Levine hired big names such as Susan Hayward (salary of $300,000, plus a share of the profits) and Bette Davis ($125,000) for the roles of Nora (renamed Valerie in the film) and her mother, while Joey Heatherton and Michael Connors were cast as Danielle and her father Luke.

In August 1964 Levine unveiled his publicity campaign for the film, and there is no doubt whatsoever that Robbins was listening carefully to what he had to say. "There is a lot of talk today about techniques and concepts, but there is only one way to sell, and that's the hard sell," he proclaimed. "You can't be diffident, and you can't be cute. And you can't hide what you're not doing behind a lot of fancy Madison Avenue words. One man's concept can be another man's confusion. Everything begins at the grass roots and everything ends at the grass roots. New York, Chicago and Los Angeles are as much grass roots as Omaha and Des Moines. You build from the bottom up, regardless of the population or geographic location. We have a grass roots campaign for *Where Love Has Gone*. We have the kind of merchandising door-bell ringers which must create an explosive exposure that you can see and hear and feel."[8]

The statistics he presented were certainly impressive: during the course of the thirty-two-day campaign the film would feature in 14,700 commercials and be advertised on 128 different radio stations. According to Levine, this was probably the first time radio had "ever been used in such amounts in this industry or any industry to cement a campaign. To our best knowledge, this is a showmanship first. We are using local radio as it's never been used before."[9] The new Pocket Books movie edition of the novel would be available in 110,000 retail outlets, while a tie-in campaign with Kapp Records would publicize Jack Jones's album and single, both also called *Where Love Has Gone*. "Call it a concept, call it a technique, call it whatever you want," said Levine. "It's exploitation and it works."[10]

Although both Robbins and Levine hoped to re-create the success of *The Carpetbaggers*, they were disappointed by the reception of *Where Love Has Gone* when the film opened in October 1964. Of course, they didn't take much notice of the carping and sneering from the critics. "A dull and distasteful movie with little to recommend it except some star names and a lurid theme that will lend itself to exploitation," wrote James Powers of *The Hollywood Reporter*. "Joseph E. Levine, who produced, was undoubtedly thinking in terms of box-office selling when he initiated this production. That's all right. But a motion picture is not put together in the same fashion as a promotion campaign."[11] What really riled the two men was the failure of the film at the popular level: by the end of the year the movie grossed only $4.4 million, coming in at thirty-first place in the annual box-office chart. But Robbins was not one to remain downcast for too long.

Robbins arrived in London in early February 1964 to publicize the British paperback edition of *The Carpetbaggers*. Anthony Blond had snapped up the U.K. and Commonwealth rights to the novel and had published a hardcover edition the previous year, which had sold

200,000 copies. As Blond recalls, "It differed from the American edition in the suppression, by me one sunny weekend, of all the four-letter words and the softening of the more lurid or, as the code-name goes, 'explicit' passages for the benefit of the then more tender British susceptibilities in general, and for those of W. H. Smith in particular."[12]

The retailer had initially refused to stock the book, "then they agreed to supply customers' orders; then they sent for five hundred," says Blond. "In the end they sold between fifty and a hundred thousand."[13]

Blond remembers that when he first secured the U.K. rights to the book, on a trip to New York, he organized a party in the Drake Hotel on East 56th Street to celebrate. At the end of the evening, when the publisher was presented with the hefty bill, "Harold saw my face . . . and pocketed it himself without a word."[14] By this point, of course, Robbins was on his way to becoming seriously rich.

Instead of remaining with Corgi, his existing paperback publisher in the U.K., Robbins had sold the British paperback rights to Four Square, a division of New English Library, for "a record £32,000"[15]—"a huge amount in those days, as the top whack was something like four or five thousand" says Peter Haining, who worked his way up to become editorial director of the company.[16] Bringing Robbins over for a promotional blitz had been the idea of Gareth Powell, managing director of Four Square. Peter Haining recalls the excitement surrounding the paperback:

"I started work at the company as a young editor, and it was clear that The Carpetbaggers was going to be a big title," he says. "Yet I don't think anybody quite realized just how extraordinarily successful it would be. We pushed the angle that the book was about Howard Hughes, and to my knowledge, no writer of popular fiction had written this kind of book before in which a real famous person had been used as the subject of a novel.

"My first impression of Robbins was that he was quite small, and I remember he had this rather strange, square head. He was very smart, very concerned about his appearance, and came across as the archetypal American hustler. He knew he had a product that would sell and that we had gone out on a limb to buy the book.

"He came over and pressed the flesh, and he was very good at it. He was quick on his feet, full of jokes, and he knew how to put people at their ease. Most authors at this time were quite self-effacing, but Robbins was the total opposite of that. He realized that publicity was the thing, and he worked hard to create an impression.

"Robbins came out of the tradition of authors like Hank Janson, a novelist who used to be considered quite racy. He was the kind of writer schoolboys would read—the books had wonderfully sexy jackets, and they were currency at school. But whereas Janson would stop at the bedroom door, Robbins flung it open."[17]

New English Library installed their star author at the Ritz in London, but the writer found the hotel too "poky," and so after a few days he moved to the Oliver Messel suite at the Dorchester, where Anthony Blond remembers meeting him for a brunch of "smoked salmon omelette prepared by his own chef."[18] "He is a pyknic, bright-eyed Jew," says Blond, "fierce and charming in startling terms, egotistic, energetic, generous, and as de Gaulle said of the Israeli nation, "sûr de lui.' "[19]

Robbins installed Paul Gitlin, his "rottweiler of a lawyer," at the hotel, he recalls, and where the attorney interviewed European publishers for the privilege of granting them foreign rights to the book. "I saw Danish, Swedish, Finnish publishers, as well as French and German, exit the elevator, white-faced and trembling, and head for the bar to recover from his depredations, having been well and truly screwed by a man who, unlike the conventional agent, had no regard for goodwill."[20]

Meanwhile Robbins granted a number of interviews to newspaper journalists eager to ask him about the secrets of his success. He wrote, he told a reporter from the *Financial Times*, for sixteen hours a day, seven days a week, until a book was finished. "It really does seem to come by itself," said Robbins of the writing process. "Like golf, when you have your swing just right." Was it true, as one novelist had alleged, that he simply wrote to a formula, checking through a series of card indexes on which he had written the various key components of a best seller? "No, there's no truth in that at all." What sold his novels? "Reader identification," he replied. Not sex? "Let's compare *Fanny Hill*," said Robbins. "In *Fanny* the sex is not connected with the

character. The reader does not identify. He sees this sex from outside
. . . like a voyeur. But in *The Carpetbaggers* this sex is seen from the
inside, because the reader identifies."[21]

Robbins, described as "an amiable little man with a sunburned,
moon-face and a high domed forehead," told another journalist that
he believed his novels had sociological worth and claimed that nine
out of every ten universities and colleges in America included his work
on their modern literature courses. He said that he set out to "write
literature first. It just happens it's very commercial, too."[22] But
Anthony Blond believed that his instincts were purely monetary.
"Harold Robbins was the archetypal best-seller writer," he says.
"Disappointed at the reception of his early book, *A Stone for Danny
Fisher*, he decided to abandon literature and go for the money."[23]

Primed from his exposure to Joe Levine's methods of self-
promotion, Robbins elaborated on his life story, telling reporters
about his supposed time in a Roman Catholic orphanage; his tough
childhood; the "fact" that he had never met his real parents; his
running away to sea at the age of fifteen, where he was nearly killed
during a fight on the waterfront; the fortune he made out of crop-
dealing at the age of nineteen before losing the lot in a bad gamble over
sugar prices; and his four marriages, two of them to the same woman.
The journalists swallowed his stories and printed them as gospel,
reveling in the racy personal narrative.

Robbins also revealed that he had been paid a record £350,000
advance for his next novel, *The Adventurers*, money that was to come
both from his American publisher and from Joe Levine, who had
bought the film rights without seeing a word of the manuscript.

"Frankly, I think it's crazy to guarantee anything. Sure I've written
seven novels and each one has sold at least two million," he said,
vastly overestimating his sales. "But nothing in this world is guaranteed. I told Joe Levine that it would never make a film. He asked if he
could see it unfinished, but that I don't allow. He asked for first
option, but that I don't allow either. So he just went and guaranteed it.
I told him just recently what the book was about for the first 250
pages—a small boy living in South America involved in a revolution.
He went quite white, I can tell you. But I told him, 'Never mind, I'll
give you good film material in the last ten pages.'"[24]

After a round of interviews in London, Robbins did a quick tour of the country, a campaign that boosted his already healthy sales: at the beginning of April *The Carpetbaggers* stood at the top of the *Daily Mail*'s paperback best-seller list, and remained there for the whole of the year. From Britain, Robbins went on to promote the book in Hamburg, Berlin, Frankfurt, Munich, Paris, and Rome, then flew back to New York for the world premiere of *The Carpetbaggers* in Denver. Robbins did not stay away from Europe for long—within a matter of months he was back with Grace in the South of France, at his rented villa in Le Cannet. He busied himself writing *The Adventurers* and started to look for a more permanent home, finally settling on a villa situated on Avenue Victoria in Le Cannet. The new house, which he named Villa Grazia after his new lover, was ranged up the side of a hillside with a spectacular view of Cannes and the glistening Mediterranean below; Pierre Bonnard, who lived in the village from 1926 until his death in 1947, often painted the red-roofed houses, the turquoise sky, the azure sea, and the lush vegetation of the area. "The house was very simple and set up a hillside on three different levels," says Diana Jervis-Read, Harold's secretary and assistant. "It was French provençal in style, very traditional. It had lovely gardens with a vegetable patch above it and a swimming pool below. That was his favorite house."[25] He converted the attic into a writing room, blocking in a window so as to not be tempted to look out at the magnificent view and equipping it with a pull-up ladder in order to cut himself off from the world. In this sparse, cramped aerie, which he furnished with a chair and a desk, an electric typewriter, dictionaries, and foreign grammars, he worked every day from five-thirty a.m. until ten-thirty a.m. until he had finished a book. Later the couple would also buy the small property next to their garden as a place to house their servants and keep Harold's fleet of cars.

Robbins's new home was situated near the extravagant villa owned by the Begum Khan and within walking distance of Picasso's house in Mougins. One day Harold and Grace were walking toward Mougins when they came across the famous artist, who recognized Robbins instantly. Picasso introduced himself and extended his hand, before asking for an author photograph. Robbins duly sent his picture over and then, a month or so later, was surprised to receive a sketch of himself (according to one observer, looking uncannily similar to Henry Kissinger) inscribed, "A mon ami Harold." To repay the compliment, Harold arranged for a copy of one of his novels, in Spanish, to be hand-delivered to Picasso. "All he talked about was girls," said Robbins later.[26]

Grace's pregnancy had been a difficult one, and her gynecologist had told her that she might lose her baby. But after a painful labor, which lasted forty-eight hours, she gave birth to a healthy baby girl on 23 July 1964. The couple named her Adréana after the Adriatic Sea. Friends and family flocked to Villa Grazia to see her—Grace's parents, Paul Gitlin and his wife Zelda, who were chosen as the child's godparents, and fellow Gitlin clients the writers Cornelius Ryan and Irving Wallace, together with their wives Kathy and Sylvia.

Although Robbins liked to tell people that he himself had delivered the baby, with the help of Errol Flynn's doctor, these stories were nonsense; his role was limited to being present at the birth, while Grace's obstetrician had never even met the famous Hollywood actor. Robbins's fictional imagination was seeping out of the confines of his books and into the arena of real life. From now on he would become gradually more and more addicted to elaborating on reality, editing it as if it were merely strips of film to be spliced and rearranged for the best effect or words in a book that could be cut or changed at will. Wherever he went, Robbins seemed to attract people who lived exotic, superannuated lives, and perhaps he felt the need to exaggerate certain aspects of his background in order to make himself more interesting. He noticed the extra attention he received—and the additional column inches—when he told one of his tall tales, and over the years the habit grew into what can only be called a compulsion. "I knew I was talking to a 'character,' but as a character he was excellent value," says journalist Donald Zec, who interviewed him on a number of occasions. "I felt that a lot of his lines were straight out of his books. He constantly invented and reinvented himself, and as such he was good value. All I needed to do was press the play button, and he came up with lots of good quotes. He was very good at journalistic foreplay."[27]

Soon after the birth of Robbins's second child, Joe Levine announced that he had signed Steve McQueen as the lead in *Nevada Smith*, a John

Michael Hayes adaptation of a section from *The Carpetbaggers* that Dmytryk had not filmed. Robbins would not receive a separate fee for the film rights, as the project was going to be produced at Paramount, which owned the material, but the movie helped raise the writer's profile around the world. "Money rained down for *Nevada* at the box office," wrote one of McQueen's biographers, "not least in Japan, the Far East, and such virgin territory as India, Egypt and Latin America. (In Trinidad riot police were called in to quell crowds trying to break down a door to see it.)"[28]

In October, Robbins traveled from France to London for the European premiere of *The Carpetbaggers*. It was a glitzy occasion, as Carroll Baker, who had sailed over to Britain from New York on the *Queen Mary*, remembers:

"Paramount had engineered a new transparent dress for me. It was a skin-colored net foundation embroidered with strategically placed pink rhinestones in the form of roses. The stole was a mass of fluffy pink tulle roses . . . As the car approached Piccadilly Circus, I could see the searchlights above the theater and enormous crowds of people for blocks around in every direction. The traffic to the theater was hardly moving. Once I had been recognized, a huge cheer went up, and people began gathering around the car to get a closer look . . . Joe Levine insisted on being the one to be photographed with me."

As the actress's driver opened the door and helped her step from the car, the hefty Levine tried to step closer toward her so that he could take her arm. But the scrum of photographers pushed forward, and the producer was elbowed out of the way and unceremoniously fell into the gutter, where he stayed for ten minutes. Meanwhile the paparazzi shouted at the glamorous star, "One more, Carroll," "This way, beautiful," and "Turn to me, Baby Doll." It was left to director Vittorio de Sica to save the day. "Fearing riot, he stepped forward to take charge," says Carroll, who was about to star as Jean Harlow in another Levine production. "In his best director's voice, but always exuding his great charm, he ordered the press to move off and the security guards to stay put. Amazingly, everyone became silent."[29]

At the premiere at the Plaza Theatre on 21 October, Robbins presented the actors with special copies of the novel bound in long-haired sealskin. After the screening, the actors, together with

Robbins, John Michael Hayes, Joe Levine and his wife Rosalie, and George Weltner, the president of Paramount Pictures, moved on to a party at Claridge's. The *News of the World* began a serialization of the book, and by the beginning of December the film had grossed $138,000 at the Plaza alone. Robbins then flew back to New York, where he attended a black-tie premiere of *Where Love Has Gone* on 1 November, followed by a Nob Hill Ball, inspired by the San Francisco setting of the film, in the Sutton Ballroom of the Hilton. Guests included Sammy Davis Jr., Anthony Perkins, Robert Alda, Senator Jacob Javits, and Robert Shaw. Robbins, however, was far from impressed with the film. "The motivations are all wrong," he said. ". . . My novel was about a man's love for his child. The movie was a story about the struggle between two women for possession of a child—a different story."[30]

As Robbins had left his villa in Le Cannet empty—Grace and Adréana accompanied him to the United States—he was able to recommend it as a place to stay to his friend James Baldwin. In the winter of 1964 the writer had been experiencing something of a "psychosomatic crisis," manifesting itself as flu-like symptoms and a high fever, and he needed somewhere quiet where he could recover. Robbins's kind gesture proved to be the perfect solution; and, after his resident cook looked after Baldwin, "feeding me as though I were a prize hog," his convalescence was complete.[31] Later Robbins was strolling down the Croisette in Cannes when he was stopped by a young girl who asked him if he was the famous American writer. "I said, 'I don't know if I'm famous, but I'm an American writer!' She said, 'Oh, yes. May I have your autograph?' And she gave me a piece of paper, and I wrote my name, and she looked at it and said, 'You're not James Baldwin?' "[32]

From New York, Robbins and his family flew to Los Angeles, where they rented a house at 9313 Doheny Road, at the entrance to La Collina Drive, in Beverly Hills. The couple had found the house through Frankie Spitz, the exuberant widow of movie executive Leo Spitz, whom Robbins knew from his days at Universal. Diana Jervis-Read described her as "petite with dyed blond hair, very brown, [wearing] leopard-skin print and gold. She was great fun, but let's just say she didn't mince her words."[33] Frankie asked her Beverly Hills neighbor Kurt Kreuger, an actor who had branched out into the luxury real estate market, whether he knew of any properties that were suitable for her "dear friends." "They were very pleasant and charming and they liked the house," recalls Kreuger. "It was the original gatehouse to the estate, built in the 1920s. When I bought it in the Sixties, this stretch was nothing more than a sleepy little street, in great contrast to today. It was a very compact but charming house and had three bedrooms with a separate guest house that had one big studio, which Robbins used as his office."[34]

By February 1965 Robbins, who was still writing *The Adventurers*, had also managed to set up a film production company. One of its first projects was an adaptation of *The Day They Shook the Plum Tree* by Arthur Lewis, about the eccentric nineteenth-century financial genius Hetty Green, who turned a $500,000 inheritance into stock worth more than $100 million. Robbins undoubtedly admired Green, a figure who can be seen to symbolize Robbins's own ambitions, which by this time were blatantly commercial. He had no intention of producing films of his own novels, he said, because "I don't want to take the time." He simply wanted, it seemed, to make money. Hollywood bored him, and even the idea of his own movie production company failed to excite him.

In fact, he seemed wearied by, and more than a touch cynical about, the whole enterprise. "Neither Hollywood nor the movie business holds any lure for me," he told a reporter at this time. "Having watched the workings of this industry for many years, I just don't want to get sucked back in. Hollywood refuses to think of the picture itself, of making a story about people. I thought there was a good chance a few years ago that this town would start making better pictures, but they blew it."[35]

His ennui can be explained by the fact that he was finalizing the details of his protracted divorce from Lillian, a process that was reaching its inevitable ugly conclusion. His wife—who felt abandoned, rejected, and after the appearance of the glamorous Grace and the entry into the world of Adréana, publicly humiliated—was determined to seek due recompense, and her lawyers pursued an aggressive strategy to win her a decent settlement. Robbins, who at this point was earning, by his own admission, $350,000 a year, was shocked by the demands, but he knew that if he wanted to erase Lillian from his life for good, acceding to them was the only option.

By 30 April 1965 the two sets of lawyers had hammered out a deal. In legal papers it was stated that "differences have arisen between . . . husband and wife which are impossible to reconcile" and that Robbins had agreed to settle on Lillian the house in Norwalk, together with some parcels of land, which he later said "in 1965 totaled $500,000 for the house and additional land."[36]

In addition, he agreed to pay all her legal fees and give her all the jewelry, rings, brooches, necklaces, furs, and "personal ornaments" that he had bought her over the course of their twenty-eight-year marriage. He also promised to pay Lillian in monthly instalments, every year for as long as she lived, a further annual sum of $65,000. On 28 May 1965 a divorce, processed by the civil court of Tlaxcala, Mexico, was finally granted. From that moment onward Robbins would try to forget that he had ever been married to the woman who had helped him secure his first big break and was at least partly responsible for the success of his early novels. He did everything in his power to make her disappear from public view, and whenever his books were due to be reissued, he requested that his publishers remove her name from the dedication page and replace it with that of Grace.

"I remember being quite annoyed when I got a letter from Paul Gitlin asking that the dedication be changed from Lillian to Grace," says Peter Haining. "I mentioned to Gitlin that I thought this was a bit off, but he said, 'That's what Harold wants, that's what Harold gets.' So Lillian's name was duly deleted, and Grace's substituted in its place. It gave me an inkling into the kind of person—the kind of opportunist—he was about to become."[37]

12

"Lucky Strike. Coca-Cola. Harold Robbins. But what
is this product? Who is this guy?"
—Harold Robbins on himself

T HE SUNLIGHT GLISTENED on the swimming pool of the Beverly
Hills Hotel. A light breeze stirred the palm trees, and the aroma
of jasmine tinged the warm air with a heady perfume. Harold,
dressed in a vibrantly colored, striped shirt, his bald head covered by
a hat, sat in the shade of the cabana as he read through the list. He
was at the "Pink Palace," together with director Henry Hathaway,
to audition actresses for a part in his next film, *Nevada Smith*. He
was looking forward to meeting the women; after all, he might get a
chance to see them in their bathing suits. As he imagined a sexy
blonde wiggling her ass across around the poolside toward him,
bending down to test the temperature of the water, he felt a warmth
spread through his loins.

"Daddy! Daddy! Why don't you come in?" said Caryn, interrupting
his erotic reverie.

"Maybe a little later, honey," he replied. "Daddy's got to do some
work first."

He smiled as he looked at his ten-year-old daughter, who was
staying with him in Los Angeles for a few days. At one point he had
feared he would never have a chance to develop a meaningful relationship with Caryn. But Yvonne, as she bored of motherhood, came to
depend on her former lover more and more and finally agreed that
their daughter should spend more time with Harold. Initially it had

been hard for Grace, as Caryn sulked throughout their first meeting, but gradually they had learned to like each other.

"You enjoy yourself in the pool," he said, smiling down at her. "And when all the pretty ladies arrive, you come and tell me which one you like best. Okay?"

"Okay, Daddy," said Caryn.

A few minutes later the first girls arrived, a couple of leggy blondes and a handful of attractive brunettes, but then more and more women paraded down the steps of the hotel toward the cabana. He was expecting only ten women, but so many models and actresses turned up that the scene started to resemble something out of a *Playboy* shoot. Harold was, of course, in his element. "By noon the word had gone around and all the girl-watchers in Hollywood had shown up," he said. "There was standing room only. A loud roar of applause now greeted each girl as she stood at the top of the steps and walked down to the poolside as the loudspeaker blared their names."

Amid this melée one girl stood out: the writer and actress Caryn Matchinga. Later Harold would explain her appeal: "she was special," he said, "not the usual Hollywood style."[1] What drew her toward him was her spirit of independence and the fact that she shared his daughter's name, even its unusual spelling. "Look," he said to his daughter, who was still in the pool, "this is another Caryn, just like you."

Although she did not get the part—the role went to Suzanne Pleshette—Caryn became close friends with Harold, and later he would use her as the basis for the character of JeriLee Randall in his 1976 novel *The Lonely Lady*.

"I remember even after they had cast Suzanne Pleshette in the role, he kept asking me to come back and read. I realized that he liked me— I'm a mouthy, sassy kind of person, and I don't play the game like other people," she says. "Although I thought he was a bit of a phony in the beginning, the more I got to know him, the more I realized that he was doing certain things to get a rise out of people, to see how they would react. Harold was more a voyeur than a doer, and he liked to set up situations to see what would happen.

"He was a strange-looking little man; not very tall, but he had nice soft skin. He liked playing chess and talking, and my first impression of him was that he was very sad. We eventually shared an office together—I had my typewriter on one desk and he had his on another. He liked to face the wall so he didn't have anything to distract him. When he sat down to write a book, he had already written it in his head, whereas I am one of those people who constantly rewrites. He would sit down, type the page, pull it out, and put it in his bag. That was it. If there was something he didn't like, or if there was a typo, he would wrap the paper into a ball and throw it into the wastepaper basket and start again. He didn't even need to look at the original page. For me writing is hard work, but for him it was simple. It would piss me off no end, and I thought to myself, 'How can you do that?' I realized it was because he did not care if he used the same adjective three times in three consecutive sentences. When you read one of his books, you realize what a rotten writer he is—he really has only four adjectives—but he's a great storyteller."[2]

With each passing month of 1965 Robbins became richer and more successful. In March he had three novels on the British paperback best-seller list—*Where Love Has Gone*, in the number-one slot, *The Carpetbaggers* at number three, and *The Dream Merchants* in sixth position. In June, Joe Levine announced that he had bought the film rights to *The Dream Merchants*, which, in addition to *The Adventurers*, made it the fifth of Robbins's novels he had acquired. "I didn't really agree to give Joe a movie," Robbins said of *The Adventurers*. "I only agreed to give him a book. It's up to the people who do the movie to find a movie in it—if they can." Although the manuscript of the seven-hundred-page book was almost finished, he refused to hand it over to Levine until he had finished editing it.

"The novel consists of six parts or books, and when I sent the first one to my publishers, Joe heard about it," Robbins told a reporter in London in September. "We met around that time at a session of the Theater Owners of America, and he said he was told it was the best thing I had written, and [he asked] where was it so he could begin to think about casting and so on. And I said, 'No, Joe. It won't give you any ideas because the first book is about a boy 6 to 12 years old.' Joe looked a me and said, 'My God, I've just blown $185,000!'"[3]

In order to finish *The Adventurers*, Robbins worked for thirty hours without sleep—"But never again. That way you can kill yourself," he said.[4] He turned up to meet a reporter for an interview at his London hotel wearing his pyjamas and dressing gown. "He is slender, tanned . . . a powdering of gray at the temples, a faintly humorous expression around his eyes. He smiles often, but a man who can earn a million by merely announcing he is going to write a novel has the right to laugh out loud."[5]

Outside Robbins's London hotel stood a Rolls-Royce, a car that he had requested be bought for him by his British publishers, New English Library and Four Square. "We told [Paul] Gitlin how huge Harold's royalty payment was going to be," says Peter Haining, "and word came back that Harold didn't want to paid by check. Instead he wanted a Rolls-Royce."[6] Four Square publicity director Terrence Strong remembers that whenever Robbins came to Britain, "it was rumored that he would pick up suitcases of money to take back to America with him."[7]

In November Robbins traveled to New York, where he took another opportunity to see his daughter, Caryn, and meet with his editors at Simon & Schuster. For years Robbins had known the title of the third part of his Hollywood trilogy—*The Inheritors*—but he had given little thought to its actual structure. But by this point Robbins was such a huge earner for the company—and Gitlin's influence so powerful—that the publisher agreed to advance him $1 million before he had written a word. Understandably Robbins was on a high when he returned home to Los Angeles, and at the end of the month he told Grace to get ready for a trip to Las Vegas; as Paul and Zelda Gitlin were staying with the couple in Beverly Hills, they were invited too. During the Vegas trip Robbins proposed to Grace, and on 22 November 1965 the couple were married at the Eastside Church of Christ on Dora Celeste Drive. Paul and Zelda Gitlin served as witnesses, and the lawyer recorded the event for posterity on audiotape.

On their return to Los Angeles the couple moved into a larger rented house in Beverly Hills, where they hosted a swish New Year's Eve party with a guest list that included some of the city's most influential players. Robbins's new home, at 905 North Beverly Drive, was a sign that he had arrived. Built on the site of Gloria Swanson's old mansion and situated directly opposite the Beverly Hills Hotel, Robbins's house was an architectural status symbol. Yet for all its connotations of wealth and power and material success, inside the house, among his close circle of friends, Robbins continued to behave like a down-to-earth boy from Brooklyn, quaffing pints of his favorite drink, Orange Crush, and playing practical jokes.

"When Harold and Grace first had the Beverly Drive house they hired a butler who had worked at the Palace," recalls Judi Schwam Yedor, the former wife of Robbins's Hollywood publicist and close friend Gene Schwam. "I remember one dinner party one night at the house, and the butler was passing the tray of cheeses. I picked up the knife to cut the cheese—but I discovered it was rubber. That was one of Harold's practical jokes. It was his way of saying, 'If Grace wants to play at this kind of life, that's fine. But you know, I don't take this at all seriously.' He did stick up his nose at all pretension. He had no time for that kind of behavior at all.

"I first met Harold in the South of France, together with Irving Wallace and Cornelius Ryan. I was in awe of these men and had prepared for any conversation. But Harold could not have cared less. He never tried to be the big intellectual. I also remember meeting Frankie Spitz at the Carlton Hotel, and she said to me, rather grandly, about the social scene, 'the closer to the wall you are, the more "in" you are,' and things like, 'Judi dear, when in doubt of what to wear, just wear anything in black and all your white diamonds.' Harold took me to one side and said, 'Just forget all this bullshit, because if you ordered a glass of champagne, somebody else would order a bottle, and if you ordered a bottle, they would order a case.' He told me that no matter what you have, it was important to be content."[8]

But Robbins relished the money that continued to flood in. In January 1966 he signed a new deal with Joe Levine in which Harold Robbins Company, Inc., would produce films exclusively for Embassy Pictures. *Stiletto* would be his first project, followed by *Never Leave Me*, and then the adaptation of *The Day They Shook the Plum Tree*, which had been languishing in development. On 1 April he hosted a party, complete with belly dancers, at the Four Seasons Hotel in New York to celebrate the publication of *The Adventurers*, a novel described by *Variety* as a flick book because "no matter where the reader 'flicks,' supposedly some saucy situation or ribald prose will be encountered."[9]

Time magazine described the novel as "an utterly baffling story about pseudopolitical intrigues in a Latin American republic . . . in the end the book sinks of its own weight (two pounds, two ounces) and its excesses: four-letter words that are stuck everywhere like flies on flypaper and clichés that lie in clutches on practically every page." The reporter told the story of how Robbins was sitting at his typewriter bashing away at the novel when Leon Shimkin from Simon & Schuster glanced at the half-finished page and asked what happened next. Robbins did not know, he said; the typewriter had just broken, and he was waiting for someone to come and fix it. "Fixing the typewriter was Robbins's second mistake; the first was writing the book."[10]

The Adventurers is one of Robbins's worst books, a bloated, sprawling epic without the wit or brio of *The Carpetbaggers*. It is sickeningly pornographic in its violence, but ultimately it fails as a work of popular fiction because it commits the sin of being mind-numbingly boring. The novel is divided into six sections—entitled "Violence and Power," "Power and Money," "Money and Marriage," "Marriage and Fashion," "Fashion and Politics," and "Politics and Violence"—that seem to have been planned according to a preexisting formula. His characters read as if they were "projections of CinemaScope: highly colored, nine times larger than life, and relentlessly two-dimensional."[11] One reason for these flaws may have been that when Robbins envisaged the project, he thought of it as an extended television series. He had first presented the idea of a hundred-hour-long TV drama to Jim Aubrey, president of CBS Television, in 1964, but although "they liked it very much . . . it fell apart because of economics," said Robbins. "They couldn't meet the competitive bid of Paramount and Joe Levine, where I got $1,000,000. CBS thought it was too high a story cost."[12]

Although Robbins may have maintained a genial demeanor to his friends, he was beginning to present a rather more unattractive facade to the outside world. He said that Norman Mailer had lost his knack "because he ran into his belly," and he proclaimed that Truman Capote would "be all right if he took his finger out of his mouth."[13]

After spending spring in Le Cannet, in June Robbins traveled to London for the paperback launch of *The Adventurers*. Described as a "slight . . . man of fifty with receding dark hair and penetrating brown eyes, quietly spoken and quietly dressed," Robbins spent most of the interviews talking about money.[14] He boasted about earning a record £50,000 for the British paperback rights to *The Adventurers* and a further £350,000 from the film deal. What had he spent his new fortune on, asked one female journalist. "I haven't spent that one yet," he said, referring to his latest advance. "It's being paid to me over a period of twenty years. That has something to do with tax, I think."[15] He told another writer, "I have nothing in the bank. I am owed between five and seven million dollars. If I see half of it before I die, I will consider myself lucky."[16]

By the end of the year Robbins, now back in Los Angeles, was regarded as the highest-paid writer in the world, while one survey conducted by the Library of Congress concluded that he was the most widely read author of the past six years. He had well and truly established himself as an all-American brand, without perhaps understanding the consequences of his ambitions.

"I get this feeling of dissociation," he admitted. "My books sell all over the world. I see them in airports in racks. Lucky Strike. Coca-Cola. Harold Robbins. But what is this product? Who is this guy?"[17]

13

"When one looks at him, one sees, along with oneself, whatever Robbins is looking at—most frequently a passing bikini. It is rather like conversing with a television set."

—Thomas Thompson on Harold Robbins

THE AIR REEKED of cigar smoke and sweat. The men clustered around the green baize table, glasses of whiskey or bourbon at their sides. As the croupier started to deal the next hand, Harold thought he could discern a warning in the whisper of the cards, an augur of bad luck. He took another sip of his drink and picked up his hand. He had a feeling it was going to be no better than the last one. He studied his fellow players: shipping magnate Aristotle Onassis, now looking more like a wizened rhinoceros than ever; and Darryl F. Zanuck, the legendary studio head who had founded Twentieth Century Pictures and had taken over Fox. These were serious risk-takers, men who knew how to gamble, men who were rich enough to lose a fortune in one night. He stared at the sign above the table that read, "Sans limite," and swallowed nervously. But he had to retain his composure. He couldn't allow himself to lose face, not with gamblers like these, not in a casino as grand as this one in the South of France.

As the *sabot* was passed counterclockwise around the table and the game of *chemin de fer* progressed, Harold lost more and more hands until finally his friend Steve Shagan, who sat by him, shot him an anxious glance. But Harold ignored him and continued to play in the hope that he could claw back some of what he had lost. He felt his

THE MAN WHO INVENTED SEX

mouth going drier, his heart beating faster, with each game, but it was no use. His luck was not going to improve. Finally he decided to call it a night. He left the table reeling and staggered out of the casino just as dawn was breaking over the Mediterranean.

The two men walked back in silence to Harold's boat, before he turned to his friend and said, "I don't know what I'm doing, I'm just pissing it all away."

Shagan listened as Harold poured out his heart, telling him how he enjoyed the thrill that came with gambling, the allure of mixing with magnates like Onassis and Zanuck, the joy of winning and the utter misery of losing. He told him about the time he was playing in a syndicate in Monte Carlo when he dropped $180,000 in a couple of hours. The casino bosses were so angry with him that they refused to advance him enough money to pay his hotel bill. When Harold came out of the casino, he saw a Greek man admiring his car, an Eldorado Caddy, and so he asked the wealthy man whether he would like to buy it. He did, in exchange for $12,000 in cash.

"Do you want my opinion?" asked Steve.

"Yeah, sure."

"There's only one way to save you," he said. "You need to get your lawyer to write to the heads of the casinos barring you from the tables. Otherwise you will never stop. You're addicted."

Harold nodded solemnly, and although he appeared to think his friend's advice was sound, he did nothing about it.

"Harold's real entertainment was not women, it was gambling," says Shagan. "And I witnessed that, I was part of it. He could not be kept out of those casinos in the South of France. He was able to rub shoulders with the people who shape our world—and he liked that. That was his form of escape."[1]

Robbins gambled only with fellow professionals and tried not to play with his buddies in case it spoiled their friendship. On one occasion, in the course of an hour playing with friends Vince Edwards, Ernest Borgnine, and Bob Newhart, he won $19,000. "Took me darn near until dawn to lose it back to them," he said.[2]

Perhaps one reason he gambled—and indeed, spent increasingly large amounts of money—was that subconsciously he didn't believe he deserved the enormous sums he was being paid for his books. Each

time he stepped inside one of the gilded gambling palaces that graced
the South of France, he flirted with financial danger. Logically, of
course, this did not make sense, but the prospect of losing all his
money, something he had worked hard to achieve, also tapped into his
deepest desires and fears. He was a poor Brooklyn boy at heart,
somebody who really did not belong mixing with the power brokers of
the entertainment world or the superwealthy jet set. Also, if his fortune
was wiped out, that would give him the opportunity to make it all over
again; its absence would soon lead to the delicious anticipation of
repossession, the adult equivalent of Freud's classic observation of an
infant repeatedly throwing his toy out of his baby carriage, only so it
would be replaced.

This could also help explain why he loved living on different
continents, spending the winters in Los Angeles and returning to
his home in the South of France in April or May. The contrast suited
him perfectly. "It's a great way to work," he said.[3] As he jetted
between the two countries, he observed the people who clustered
around him—film directors, actors and actresses, writers, bankers,
and arms dealers—explore new ways of living. Hedonism was the
religion of the newly moneyed classes, men and women on an endless
quest for the ultimate high.

Robbins reasoned to himself that he had a duty to document the
lives of the rich and infamous—"I write about the modern scene," he
said—and so it was only fitting that he witness the excesses at close
quarters.[4] A year or so after he and Grace married, he told his wife
that he expected her to accept that he would sleep with other women.
Extramarital sex was essential for his writing, he said, and as he often
went away for long periods of time, he was simply being honest with
her. He did not mind if she slept with other men—in fact, he almost
expected it of her—but it was important that they did not keep any
secrets from each other. Grace was, understandably, rather taken
aback by the news, but as she still loved him, she did not think she had
a choice in the matter. After all, she adored the million-dollar income
that afforded her a glamorous lifestyle—the clothes, furs, jewels,
drink, and drugs and the entrée into a ritzy social scene previously
out of her reach.

From now on Robbins felt free to live out his wildest fantasies, especially when he was away from home. "Did he play around a lot? Yes, he did. Was he really discreet? No," says Judi Schwam Yedor. "He was like a ringleader. He liked making fantasies come true, in real life, for everybody. He was a hedonist—it was obvious from his novels the man was not that far from his books."[5]

Robbins's reputation as something of a sexual predator often got him into trouble with his British publisher. "We would get calls from reps from the north saying, 'That fucker Harold Robbins was all over the buyer at Smith's and she didn't like it one bit,'" recalls Peter Haining. "It was difficult to make excuses for him to some of the girls that he made quite blatant passes at. I'm sure there were a number of occasions where prostitutes were organized for him, and it was said that his great passion was for colored girls. I heard after I had left the company that he had spent a night with a black girl, and he was subsequently concerned with his physical condition. He wanted to be checked out by a doctor to make sure he hadn't got a dose of the clap."[6]

Later Robbins would enjoy orgies at his Beverly Hills home. As guests cavorted in the vast bedroom, decorated the color of champagne, the participants would be able to see their naked forms reflected in the mirrored ceilings. Friends say that Robbins's orgies were always lighthearted affairs, typical get-togethers in an age when swinging was, in some circles, as normal as a Sunday brunch party. They were popular events too—a source remembers one event was so well-attended it was limited to FRO: "fucking room only." Harold would have previously rounded up the men and women, all of whom had to be beautiful, handsome, well endowed, or famous. "I had never met any of these people before," remembered Grace of one particular orgy, "or ever would again. Harold had rounded up our 'guests' as he always did. He never told me how or where."[7] Robbins ensured that the group was comprised of an odd number of people, with, as he said, "a predominance of females . . . When the men need to rest [the women] can inspire the men for the next go-round." To get people in the mood, Harold would provide copious amounts of drink and drugs, and the evening would begin with a little gentle socializing, followed by the smoking of marijuana, the popping of a few Quaaludes, and the shaving and snorting of coke. The night was masterminded by Robbins—he was even thoughtful enough to provide terrycloth bathrobes for the men and slinky wraparounds for the women—and he laid down a number of unwritten rules. No one was allowed to move into another room, as the "reason for an orgy is to enjoy, to share," while if a participant did not find anyone in the room attractive or if no one was free at the time, it was important to "be courteous, talk, drink, light up a cigarette and wait . . . sometimes you do have to watch." When he felt the mood was right and his guests were suitably relaxed, he would begin by stroking a woman's hair or fondling her breasts. The air reeked of amyl nitrate, smoke, and desire. Naturally, people would begin to split off into pairs and some guests would indulge their taste for group sex, losing themselves in a mass of writhing bodies.

On one occasion Robbins employed a sex therapist to instruct the women on how to engage in oral sex in the manner of Linda Lovelace in the pornographic film *Deep Throat*; apparently the secret was for the woman to imagine her throat gradually opening up until it resembled a large O shape. For his part, Harold prided himself on being a master of oral sex, using a sucking technique to pleasure a woman until she experienced multiple orgasms. Lovers say that, in the midst of their climax, Harold would look up from between their legs, smile, and say, "Gotcha!" Although Harold, the ultimate sexual liberator, had freed Grace from the constraints of her Catholic upbringing, one gets the sense that she would have preferred only one man in her bed: her husband. He boasted to friends that he adored, in his words, his wife's "pussy"—he fetishized it to such an extent that he even shaved her pubic hair into the shape of a diamond, a star, and a heart. (He incorporates references to "cunt coiffeurs" into his novels *Dreams Die First* and *The Storyteller*.) Ultimately Grace came to wish that he could find happiness exclusively between her legs. But to paraphrase a line from *The Inheritors*, all the cunts in all the world weren't enough for him.

After spending the first few months of 1967 in Los Angeles, Robbins was ready to head back to the Mediterranean in the spring. On 2 April he hosted a party for 170 friends and associates at the Cocoanut Grove, the legendary Hollywood nightclub within the Ambassador

Hotel. "We're leaving for our home in France next month," he told *Variety* columnist Army Archerd. "I thought this would make a great exit."[8] The black-tie party, organized in part to celebrate the engagement of Vince Edwards and Linda Foster, cost $15,000 and culminated in entertainment that Robbins brought in from the famous Aladdin hotel and casino in Las Vegas, complete with a topless go-go show.

He told Archerd that his ambition would be to produce a movie that ran for nine hours, "like the Russians' *War and Peace*." He had had a number of meetings with executives at Paramount about the possibility of writing a script for and co-producing *The Adventurers*, alongside Joe Levine. "I want to get more of this book into the film than any of mine that have been adapted previously," he said. The deal guaranteed Robbins $1 million, plus a percentage of profits, together with an added bonus related to his book sales. After completing the screenplay, he intended to start work on his next novel, *The Inheritors*. "It will give me something to do besides looking at all the bikinis on the Riviera," he said.[9]

Back in the South of France, Robbins rented a suite in the Carlton Hotel, where he proceeded to dictate the screenplay of *The Adventurers* to a secretary who always wore a bikini under her clothes in case she had time to nip out for a quick swim. He finished the first draft, which consisted of 616 scenes, in August, but when Robbins delivered the script at the end of the year, it was rejected. Lewis Gilbert, director of the film, said, "It was too sexy, too violent, too much like the book." Robbins asked him what he meant, and Gilbert replied, "Harold, in order to write the screenplay, you mustn't look at your book."[10]

Robbins pretended not to care and boasted about how much money he had made from the project. At the end of 1967 he had earned over $2 million in royalties from *The Adventurers*—the book, published in February, had sold over 6 million copies in the United States alone. Total sales of his novels were estimated to be in the region of 40 million. And of course, Robbins had no shortage of ideas for yet more books.

He told writer Thomas Thompson, who visited him in the South of France in the summer of 1967, that after *The Inheritors* he would write a novel called *Dreams Die First*, about a character assassin who in order to secure the job of president of a company has to destroy the reputation of the man who taught him everything; that project would be followed by *The War Games*, about the battle between the sexes, and then *Memories of Another Day*, which would focus on New York in the Depression. Of these three novels Robbins would write two of them: *Dreams Die First*, published in 1977, was about a bisexual porn baron, and the 1979 book *Memories of Another Day* focused on the New York labor movement. He had also been researching the Detroit car industry, "digging into the automobile business, into the fighting that goes on when they edge for that percentage point of power," a subject which would form the basis for his 1971 novel *The Betsy*.[11]

Thompson shadowed the writer, who dressed in deep-purple slacks, a mauve V-neck shirt, and a color-coordinated cap, as he cruised around the pleasure grounds of Cannes. Robbins also sported a pair of enormous mirrored sunglasses, which had been specially made for him to protect his weak eyes from the harsh rays of the Riviera sun. "When one looks at him, one sees, along with oneself, whatever Robbins is looking at—most frequently a passing bikini," said Thompson. "It is rather like conversing with a television set." Robbins told Thompson that one of Paul Gitlin's employees was attempting to track down all of his papers, "of which there are none," he said. "He's spent about three years trying to track down the original manuscripts of my books. He says we should donate them to a library so people can read them and see how I worked and know the kind of person I am. I tell him that's crap because, very simply, anyone who wants to know a hundred years from now what I'm like, all they'll have to do is read my books. What I am is part of my world."

He went on to dismiss the critics and to mock writers like Jack Kerouac, who was acclaimed but, he declared, unpopular with the general public. "There's no question about it—I am the best there is," he said. "This is all I do. I work damn hard at it . . . I'm a novelist, purely a novelist. I tell stories, and I want people to read them. Several of us first published right after the war—me, Mailer, James Jones, Irwin Shaw—but I'm the only one whose market has continually expanded . . . James and Shaw, people like them, lost touch. They jumped to Europe, they lost touch with America, they didn't grow as human beings or as writers, they missed the all-important part of postwar growing pains."[12]

By November, Robbins was back in Los Angeles at a newly rented suite on the eighth floor of the most prestigious office building in the city, 9000 Sunset Boulevard, from where he could look down at the "delirious and almost diabolic fantasy of the Sunset Strip below."[13] Inside, the room was an expanse of brown: a teak desk, cushioned armchairs, a thick fitted tan carpet, and floor-to-ceiling mocha-colored drapes. In the center of the room stood a large round table, on which Harold placed an expensive chess set and a vase that always contained a single red rose. The look was that of the quintessential smooth operator—expensive, well traveled, and worldly wise. Ensconced in the tower and looking down at the lights of Los Angeles, Robbins was in the process of transforming himself into a corporation. His endorsement of a project was enough to guarantee financing by Hollywood's money men, while the mere addition of his name could earn the writer millions of dollars in fees.

A few years earlier Robbins, still intrigued by the idea of creating a "television novel," had been invited to lunch with Leonard Goldenson, president of ABC, and asked if he would like to write something for the network. "How about a TV series called *The Survivors*?" Robbins had said. A year later executives at ABC called him in for a meeting at their headquarters in New York and asked him to explain the story.

"I was curious myself," said Robbins. "I hadn't thought it through yet. Everybody had their eyes on me as I walked over to the glass window behind Goldenson's desk. From the . . . [office] I could see Central Park and all the way to the West 79th Street Boat Basin. There was a yacht moored in the Hudson River. I started talking the story. 'Here's your opening scene. The cameras focus on a yacht tied up off Manhattan. Then we zoom to a bed in a stateroom. It's a big bed. In a big stateroom. The bed has black silk sheets. In the bed, there's a blonde. She's a gorgeous blonde. She's naked—"

"Stop!" interrupted the executives, almost jumping out of their chairs in excitement. "We'll buy it." And what did Robbins do? "I went back to France and forgot about it."[14]

In 1967 Paul Gitlin called Robbins and told him that ABC had bought his idea, to which the writer replied, "What idea?" Gitlin got to work on the mechanics of the contract—"we structure the deal first, and then Harold worries about the writing," said the lawyer.[15] Robbins quickly roughed up a nine-page treatment that netted him an unprecedented deal: a percentage of profits, plus a guarantee of $10,000 a show for twenty-six episodes in the first year and a further twenty-six the second season, "whether it bombs or not."[16] His ambition was to reach a wider audience—the 30 million or so people who watched television but did not read books. "While I have the greatest respect for Joe Levine, who made *The Carpetbaggers*, he only used ten percent of the novel," he said. "That is a waste of talent. ABC is giving me 100 to 150 hours to tell my whole story, chapter by chapter. Something like this has never been done before."[17]

While he was in New York to sign the contract, Robbins stayed at the Regency Hotel on Park Avenue with a journalist friend. "It's a quiet hotel, but as we get off the elevator on the eighth floor, we keep hearing noise," said Robbins. "He says, 'Jesus, it's not that quiet. There must be a party going on.' I say, 'Come on, let's find it.' And in my suite I had the whole Harkness Ballet. I had all nineteen girls running around until four in the morning. Champagne, caviar, the lot. So we managed to have a bit of fun. My associate just said, 'Jesus Christ, these things don't happen!'"[18]

Meanwhile Robbins and executives at ABC and Universal, which had been commissioned to produce the show, started to think about casting the extended soap opera about the sexual and financial intrigues of a rich banking family. Harold wanted his friend Carroll Baker to play the female lead, but the television bosses wanted to cast an even bigger star—Lana Turner, the actress whose private life Robbins had exploited so shamefully in *Where Love Has Gone*. Lana and Harold had recently been introduced in Beverly Hills by Turner's latest husband, Robert P. Eaton. "One afternoon at the country club I found myself shaking his hand," said the actress about Robbins. "But when I heard the name, I snatched back my hand as though I'd touched a snake . . . Surely Bob knew I hated the man, and we fought bitterly about the introduction. But then a short time later his name up again. Bob was hired to do some minor job on a television project with

Robbins. While I didn't approve, I was even more surprised when my agent Stan Kamen approached me about the most lavish series ever concocted for television. And again, who was behind it? Harold Robbins."[19]

In April 1968 it was announced that Lana Turner was going to star in the weekly one-hour soap as Tracy Carlyle Hastings, with George Hamilton as her half-brother Duncan. The show, entitled *Harold Robbins's The Survivors*, with a budget of $250,000 per episode, was celebrated as the most expensive television series in history and was billed as "a delicious blend of sin, sex and Lana Turner."

According to Robbins's original story line—a plot that would mutate faster than Lana changed her gowns—the first year of the soap would follow the various characters as they each tried to take control of the bank. "It's also the story of how the world of banking affects our society, our ways of life, and our international relations," said Robbins in April 1968. "The American public wasn't aware of the power of money and banking. Suddenly the gold crisis brought that home to Americans—what banks can do, how it can lower your standard of living if gold is devalued, how it can affect the policies of war and peace. Freud explained there is a sexual and psychological relationship between blood and money because both are necessary for life."[20]

That was certainly the case when it came to settling the actors' salaries. At first George Hamilton was offered $10,000 a week, a sum he ran past his friend and adviser Colonel Tom Parker, Elvis Presley's manager, who told him to turn it down. The network, desperate to cast Hamilton, increased the offer several times, but the actor, on Parker's advice, rejected the money each time, believing that he could squeeze them for more. ABC sent over a Ferrari and other elaborate gifts, including a tailor-made wardrobe, and refurbished his dressing room, until finally Hamilton settled on $20,000 a week, making him the highest-paid actor on television at the time. Lana Turner, meanwhile, opted to take $12,500 a week on condition that she had top billing.

"In those days nobody wanted to do television because it was thought of as a big step down for a movie actor," says Hamilton. "But Harold was very keen for me to star in the drama. I first met him at a cocktail party at his house on Beverly Drive. I remember he was quite a flamboyant character wearing a flowered hat. The house was what I call "very sixties," there was lots of marble, a bar, and it was all very slick. But there was no tradition behind it—it was an expression of pure money.

"My first impression of him was that he was quite a strange man. One couldn't get a fix on him. I didn't know whether he was the real deal or a con man. If you didn't know he was a writer, you would think you'd better hold on to your watch. He wrote about the clubs and the old-boy system and the glamour, but I saw him as a guy much more at home in a betting shop than a casino. I didn't think I could sit down with him and have a conversation with him. I thought reading his books was as good as it got and getting to know him would not improve on that in any way. He was quite chauvinistic to women, and he had the look of somebody who had come from an all-night gang bang with two hookers. In Hollywood you are great if you are successful and nothing if you are not, and he understood those rules and lived by them."[21]

ABC was obviously trying to capitalize on the success of its twice-weekly soap opera *Peyton Place*, based on Grace Metalious's best-selling novel and starring Mia Farrow, Dorothy Malone, and Ryan O'Neal, produced by Paul Monash. But Robbins did not think much of the drama, which between 1964 and 1969 ran to over 500 episodes. "*Peyton* is well done by Paul Monash, but it's all interiors, and they talk, talk, talk about their problems," he said. "In our show, they are going to live out their problems. There will be more physical movement, reaction, and interplay between characters. I don't mean physical violence. Bankers go where the trouble is today. They go where the action is. Duncan's office will be a yacht. The staid version of banks is long since gone."[22]

And what about sex? How was the novelist famous for his racy love scenes going to deal with that on television? "I will put it in when it belongs," he said. Audiences were much more comfortable than in the past with frank discussions of sexuality on television, and if it was treated in the right manner, he saw no reason why sex should be kept off the small screen. "If I introduced sex for sex sake, I would expect them to throw it out," he said. "I don't use sex in literature promiscuously—why should I on the TV screen? Sex is used for its pertinence to life, and for its revealing insight into the character and standards of people. By today's standards *The Carpetbaggers*, which I wrote ten years ago, is not a sexy book. When it came out, it was regarded as very sexy. No matter how reluctant they feel about it, people are growing up. People in the Midwest are very hip, they know what's going on in the world. Americans have become very sophisticated, urbane, and knowledgeable of the kind of society we live in. The Victorian hangover of an earlier era is rapidly disappearing."[23]

As Robbins's involvement was limited to mapping out the story line and overseeing the scripts, once his duties were completed he was free to return to Le Cannet. In the summer of 1968 he and his friend Cornelius Ryan rented a yacht for themselves and their families, and in turn Ryan organized a cocktail party on 8 July with guests that included Pierre Salinger (journalist and former press secretary to Presidents John F. Kennedy and Lyndon B. Johnson) with his wife Nicole, and Kenneth More, the actor, and his wife. Ryan, in a letter to Robbins, described Harold as a "renowned novelist, raconteur, and bonvivante."[24] Victoria Ryan Bida, the daughter of Cornelius and Kathy, remembers meeting Harold and Grace on that holiday. "He came across like a mixture of someone from Hell's Kitchen and Tom Jones, while she was like a very beautiful Cleopatra," she says.[25]

That summer Robbins also met the lyricist Leslie Bricusse and his wife Evie, who subsequently became good friends. The British couple were introduced to Harold through the actress Natalie Wood and her future husband Richard Gregson, who also acted as Leslie's agent. "One day Natalie said that Harold Robbins had asked her to go and have lunch on his boat in Cannes to talk about a film he wanted to make of *The Adventurers*," says Bricusse. "So the four of us— Richard, Natalie, Evie, and I—went to Cannes for this lovely lunch on the yacht. I remember him as being a very expansive character—he really was larger than life. I remember, at another dinner at the house of Stirling Silliphant, the American writer, Harold arrived looking like a London pillar box, with a bright red jacket, red trousers, and black shoes. He announced himself to a group of people, 'I am to my generation what Charles Dickens was to his!' I don't think he meant it to sound arrogant. What he wanted to convey was, 'I am representing my world as I see it now in the same way as Dickens did in his day.'

"As time went on, we got to know him and Grace very well because we all lived in the same three places—the South of France, Beverly Hills, and later Acapulco—and we spent hundreds of evenings together. We had nothing but the loveliest of times together. He was incredibly generous as a host, he was great fun and very amusing. He knew how to live the good life. Below the surface I probably regarded him as brash and something of a rough diamond, but that didn't matter at all. I have nothing but the best memories of him.

"He really did believe he was the best writer around. He was totally self-confident. But he didn't care about the critics—he agreed with Alan Jay Lerner's statement about them, 'Nobody ever erected a statue to the critics.' I remember once we were having a conversation about this very subject, and he said, 'We're the ones on the boat in the South of France.' "

"Just as Kenneth Tynan was the first to say 'fuck' on television, so Harold broke down the barriers. People may question whether that was a good idea, but it had to happen. He freed other writers to do or say anything they wanted. England in the fifties was just so bleak, as rationing went on for a decade after the war. But in the early sixties, the world changed, and Harold was ahead of that. Harold really captured the essence of the times, the hedonism."[26]

That summer writer John Skow, on assignment for *Playboy* magazine, observed Robbins's sybaritic lifestyle at close quarters. Instead of working on *The Inheritors*, the novel that was due at Simon & Schuster in a matter of months, he chose to spend between six and eight hours of each day sitting with some wealthy English friends in the lobby of a Cannes hotel. "Robbins, a small, fuzzy, compact, startled-looking man . . . tastefully gotten up in a white yachting cap, mirror-surface shades, white sweater, love beads, and lavender pants, talked about whores," noted Skow. " 'She's a whore, twenty-five francs,' he would say as a woman walked through the lobby. 'That one over there, she's a whore!' " The hotel, it seemed, was nothing but a trollop trap. "At any rate, Robbins saw whores, or thought he did, and announced them as if they were trains."

Skow watched Robbins make excuses to leave a table to go look at the Rolls-Royce Silver Cloud that he had bought in London that January for £9,000 and that was parked outside the hotel. In addition Robbins had an older, maroon-colored Rolls that he intended to transport back to America, two smaller cars in the South of France, and a Jensen Interceptor in Los Angeles. He was pleased that Joe Levine's latest film was doing so well at the box office because the producer owed him $3.5 million. In the future, he added, his production company intended to adapt his novels *Stiletto* and *79 Park Avenue* so as to guarantee more sex scenes on the screen. He didn't think much of John Updike's book *Couples*, criticizing it as neither incisive nor amusing, but when he claimed for himself the title world's best novelist, Skow looked visibly shocked, prompting Robbins to admit, "It's a gag with me."

Was sex the secret of his success? Skow concluded that, although Robbins scattered a good deal of erotic content throughout his books, it wasn't sex so much as sentiment that sold, which the journalist estimated had been bought by around 70 million people. "The fact is that Robbins is the most underrated hanky dampener in modern literature," he said. "Robbins is peddling sl*sh."[27]

In October 1968 Robbins's latest soapy concoction, *The Survivors*, started filming in the South of France. The cast—which included Ralph Bellamy, Diana Muldaur, and Kevin McCarthy—together with producer William Frye, director Michael Ritchie, and costume designer Luis Estevez, all flew out to the Riviera even though the script was far from complete. Lana Turner, used to having months to learn her lines, could not cope with the fast pace of television and took to the vodka bottle for comfort. George Hamilton, who was staying with Turner in a suite at La Reserve (the rest of the cast and crew took over La Voile d'Or, in St. Jean Cap Ferrat), remembers the atmosphere of excess that ruled over the production.

"As soon as I checked in, I was told to order whatever I wanted, and so I asked for a soufflé framboises and a bottle of champagne, and that was just the beginning of the madness," he says. "Lana was having trouble learning her lines and was drinking a lot of vodka. She was a force to be reckoned with—she could square off her shoulders and, believe me, make an army flinch.

"I remember one scene in the driveway of a villa with cacti all around us. Luis Estevez had, for some reason, dressed us all in beige, except for a coral-colored tie that I wore. Lana went berserk and accused me of stealing the scene because of the vibrant color of my tie. She stormed off the set, but when I went to see her, she just laughed and told me that she had done it because she needed extra time to learn her lines. She told me to tell the producer that I thought her dress needed extra chinchilla. By the time the producer came to talk to her, Lana had had four vodkas. Luis was summoned, and I duly said I thought her dress needed a little more chinchilla fur. Luis ran off to get more chinchilla, and we had a couple more vodkas.

"Then Bill Frye realized that things were going far from swimmingly. It all came to a head one day when Luis walked up to Lana and gave her a hat to wear. But she refused to put it on. Luis told her that she had to wear it because some establishing shots had already been done with the double wearing the hat. Lana said, 'What do you mean, a double has worn the hat? Where is the other hat, my hat?' He said there wasn't one, at which point Lana said, 'Well, you obviously haven't worked in films. A star doesn't wear a hat that a double has already worn.' Luis walked off the set, got into his car, and left the production, saying that he was a bigger star than anyone. And that was the last we saw of him."[28]

William Frye was furious about Lana Turner's behavior, and later at a party in a villa overlooking the Mediterranean, the two had a heated argument. "Lana wanted to wear real jewelry and she said she was used to Van Kleef," remembers Martin Starger, who later became president of ABC's entertainment division and was a close friend of Robbins's. "But Frye said that this was a television series, not a movie, and they simply could not afford it. Harold was there, listening to it all, smiling his half-smile."[29] Finally the movie star, incandescent with rage, lashed out at Frye and slapped him across the face. The producer, equally angry, slapped Lana back.

Grant Tinker, then vice president of Universal TV (and married to Mary Tyler Moore), who was in the South of France to oversee the production, stepped in to try to resolve the situation. "Lana was stalking around her living room in La Reserve in a dramatic fashion, saying 'No one touches this face,'" he recalls. "She said that it was a choice between Frye and her. We were supposed to start filming again on Monday morning, and so it was an easy decision to make. I stayed in Frye's place for a month."

While Tinker was in the Riviera, he arranged a meeting with Robbins. "He was sort of mischievous and had this glint in his eye," he says. "He was at the top of his game at the time, and people knew better than to try and push Harold around. He liked to think of himself as a character from one of his books."[30] Tim Vignoles, then MCA Television's head of distribution in Europe and responsible for selling *The Survivors* to broadcasters, remembers meeting Robbins in Cannes at this time. "He really was living the star life in the South of France, complete with six Jensens and the villa in Le Cannet," he says. "Although he was a creature of his time and enjoyed his success, he did not take it seriously. There was something very tongue-in-cheek about his whole persona. He wore striped blazers and white polo-necks and sported a fat cigar in a holder and really looked the part—all of us at MCA were confined in our bankerlike black suits. Grace, in her bell-bottomed trouser suit and billowing sleeves, resembled a real-life Elizabeth Taylor. He was the archetypal salesman—he had an uncanny ability to remember the name of everyone he met. He was so not full of bullshit. I remember on one occasion, at this party, when he had had enough, he stood on a table, blew a whistle, and said, 'Come on Grace, we're going home now.' He was just so full of fun."[31]

George Hamilton recalls that for the most part Robbins absented himself from the production, except for one day when the shoot centered on the casino at Monte Carlo. "He turned up to give Lana a gift, I can't remember what," he says. "Although she was flattered by the attention, she didn't like him, and she didn't trust him."[32]

After the production went vastly over budget, the shoot was moved to the Universal studio lot in Los Angeles. It was obvious from the beginning that the show had problems: an ambitious storyline, temperamental stars, unsympathetic characters, and clichéd dialogue. Although Robbins had provided the narrative arc of the series, other writers were drafted to write the scripts. In August 1969 an executive from ABC told *The New York Times* that the network had junked Robbins's ideas. "The dialogue did not have the bite or strength of some of Harold's prose," says Tinker, "and I have to say we turned out a really bad piece of work. It was treacly and corny. It was not good material to begin with, and it became even worse. I think the scenery was the only good thing about it. Lana tended to act in quite an arch way anyway, and this added to the effect that we were kidding the material. The characters, all part of the international jet set, were not the kind of people ordinary Americans could identify with. We turned out a real turkey."[33]

Even before the series had its premiere on 29 September 1969, it was rumored to be a disaster. Since shooting started, the show had run through three producers, one director, a costume designer, and the executive story editor, while Robbins's original plotline had disappeared from view. "My ideas lasted no longer than it took me to get out of the country," he said.[34]

The scripts were constantly rewritten, making it even more difficult for the actors, especially Lana Turner, to learn their lines. "It was *Dallas* set in the South of France, but unfortunately before its time," says Grant Tinker.[35] By the time a director was hired to splice in action sequences lifted from outtakes of other films, everyone knew that the series was over. After broadcasting only fifteen of the proposed twenty-six episodes, the network axed the show. "If we were to film what really . . . happened behind the cameras," said Lana Turner at the time, "no one would believe it."[36]

14

"There was no point being Harold Robbins if all he
did was stay at home and write—as he might have
said, 'Fuck that shit.'"

—Michael Mewshaw

T HE YOUNG COUPLE walked up the steps of the Carlton Hotel,
through its opulent entrance, and into the bar. More than a little
intimidated as they were by the plush surroundings of Cannes's most
famous hotel, their eyes darted around the room as they searched out
the best-selling American author. The meeting had been arranged by a
mutual acquaintance, and aspiring writer Michael Mewshaw had no
idea what Harold Robbins looked like. Was he that sober-suited
executive carrying the briefcase, the red-faced drunkard propping up
the bar, or the slightly overweight bearded fellow sporting the Ha-
waiian shirt? Surely he couldn't be the tanned man sitting in the
corner, the one wearing chukka boots, a safari suit, and an Australian
bush hat decorated with a leopard-skin band? The one smoking a
cigarillo from an ivory holder and entertaining a young blonde?

A couple of moments later their search came to an end as the
eccentrically dressed man introduced himself as Harold Robbins. The
author immediately put Mewshaw and his wife, Linda, at their ease.
"He didn't stand up when I introduced myself," remembers Mewshaw, who was living in a stone cottage in nearby Auribeau sur Siagne
at the time. "He did, however, doff his bush hat as he shook Linda's
hand. Though bald, he had luxuriant sideburns, gristled with hairs as
white as dental floss . . . Conversation with some writers can be as

difficult as extracting teeth. With Robbins it was easier than lifting fruit from a Jell-O mold."[1]

After ordering drinks, Robbins launched into a (what we now know to be fictional) account of his life, presenting his story as a classic narrative of the American dream or something that could have come straight out of one of Horatio Alger's rags-to-riches tales. During the conversation Robbins discovered that it was Linda's twenty-fifth birthday, and he invited the young couple for supper. Robbins led the way in his red Jensen Interceptor up the hill toward his villa in Le Cannet, with Mewshaw following behind in his beat-up Volkswagen. The young writer, in Europe on a Fulbright scholarship, was immediately impressed by the lavishness of the property; with its rows of cypress trees, the tops of their branches shaped into Doric columns, perfectly manicured lawns, heated swimming pool, and air conditioning, the house looked as though it had been transplanted straight from Beverly Hills to the South of France. Robbins proceeded to show off his pool—"a rectangle of cobalt gleaming under the evening mist"— which he said was the first heated pool on the Côte d'Azur and his air conditioning, a system that was then new to this part of France. Then Harold turned and pointed out something in the bay below.

"That's my yacht," he said.

Michael and Linda gazed down below at the marina containing dozens of ostentatious boats.

"Nice," said Michael.

"Not that one," replied Harold. "The one next to it. The biggest one."

Linda asked how long it was, but Harold said he did not know. He used it only for parties during the Cannes Film Festival. The rest of the time, he said, his wife liked to take it out into the bay so she could skinny-dip.

"Don't you?"

"It's not that I don't like it," said Harold. "My health won't permit it."

Harold lit another cigar and then held the extinguished match up to his head.

"I've got punctured eardrums," he said.

"What a shame," replied Linda.

"Nah, I had it done by a doctor," he said in a deadpan voice, "so when I'm eating a chick, I can breathe through them."[2]

After the witticism fell flat, Harold disappeared into the kitchen to supervise the cooking, leaving Michael and Linda to be shown around the property by Robbins's blond companion, a computer programmer. "My impression was that they were certainly having some sort of relationship, and she certainly knew her way around the house," says Mewshaw.[3] The master bedroom was decorated in "high bawdy-house style," in contrast to the study in which Harold worked, an austere, windowless aerie containing only a desk, a chair, and a Dictaphone. So this was the "holy of holies," the place where Robbins made it all happen, the room in which he manufactured best seller after best seller. Earlier in the day Robbins had told Michael his secret: you'll never make a million bucks unless they print a million books, and no publisher will ever do that unless you get a million-dollar advance.

"He did talk an awful lot about money, there wasn't much about his art or his craft," says Mewshaw. "And this was at a time when it was considered impolite and impolitic for a writer to talk about book sales or advances. My first impression of him was as an amusing, monolithic vulgarian. He was exactly what you expected him to be like. Just as with Norman Mailer, Robbins inhabited the sarcophagus that he had built for himself. His whole attitude was self-created, and although it might have been natural for him, it seemed like a studied effort. But behind this vulgar, slightly buffoonish exterior, there had to be an extraordinarily keen mind, a businessman who knew exactly what he was doing. He talked about the business of publishing in a way that nobody else, certainly no writer, did then."[4]

After a delicious supper of a rack of lamb and a chocolate gateau topped with birthday candles, Robbins presented Linda with a necklace. Later that night he offered to fly them back to America if they so wished, an offer they refused. "It all contributed to the impression we had that he was creating a Harold Robbins novel for us," says Mewshaw. "There's an expression in the movie world that goes, 'The money's not showing up on the screen,' and in a way I think that applied to Harold. There was no point being Harold Robbins if all he did was stay at home and write—as he might have said, 'Fuck that shit.' If you had the money, you might as well show it and flaunt it."[5]

And boy, did Robbins have money. At this point in his life his publishers estimated that, in the course of a year, 25,000 people bought one of his novels every single day. If this statistic were not impressive enough, on 6 March 1968 Pocket Books published an extraordinary report in that day's *New York Times*. Out of the ten books featured on the list of its all-time best sellers, seven were by Harold Robbins; the only work of fiction not written by him was Margaret Mitchell's *Gone with the Wind*. His riches increased when in August 1968 Joe Levine bid for the rights to his as yet unwritten novel *The Inheritors* for a joint production between Avco Embassy and the Harold Robbins Company. Robbins boasted that the latest deal would net him a guarantee of $3.75 million. As he wrote, he thought of what he could do with the money, and by July 1969 he had finished the novel.

"This is the third and final novel of a trilogy covering a fictionalized history of an industry that has had perhaps the greatest influence on the minds and mores of man in our portion of the twentieth century—the motion picture," wrote Robbins in an afterword to the book. Robbins expressed gratitude to his editor at Simon & Schuster, Herbert M. Alexander, and to his wife, Grace, "without whose love, patience, and forbearing this would never have been written at all—turn down the sheets, lover. I'm coming home."[6]

In the summer of 1969—the summer of the moon landings, the Manson murders, and Woodstock—Robbins went shopping for a yacht, finally settling on an elegant white vessel made by Esterel that was twenty-six meters long and had three double cabins, a skipper's quarters, and two twin rooms. He named it *Gracara*, after his wife and two daughters. "She's made by the same people who make the French naval corvettes," said Robbins. "She does twenty-two knots, and each cabin has stereo, television, bath, and bidet."[7] Robbins adored spending time on the yacht, which he said was one of the three fastest vessels in the Mediterranean.

"I remember Harold would dress in clothes that had a sailor motif on them and he would take the steering wheel and sail away," says Steve Shagan. "He really would feel like he was on the top of the world. He was on a high, beyond enjoyment. Buying that yacht was an achievement of magnificent proportions. He had Chrysler engines fitted to make it even more powerful, and he would park it in the dock at Cannes, which even in those days cost a lot of money. When he was on that boat, it was like, 'My name is Harold Robbins—look at me.' It was marine proof that he had made it."[8]

That summer Robbins invited Stirling Silliphant and his wife to Villa Grazia. Harold's hospitality impressed the screenwriter, and on 22 July he wrote a thank you letter to the couple in which he congratulated the novelist on his largess. "I recognized . . . early in our relationship, yours and mine, that I was a foregone loser in any contest to out-entertain you," he said. "Christ, I can't even get to the post in the race, so the least I can do is admire your time around the track."[9]

When Silliphant—whose credits had included the television series *Naked City* and *Route 66* and the movies *In the Heat of the Night* and *Marlowe*—read an early proof of *The Inheritors*, he was eager to adapt it for the screen. He hated the book to end, he told Robbins, comparing this to "someone slamming the lid of a treasure chest on my greedy fingers." He was, he told his friend, "gassed and turned on and in perfect shape to run the three-minute mile."[10]

The Hollywood rumor mill buzzed with talk of the collaboration—it was, said Silliphant, "a secret . . . about as well kept as a two-dollar whore"[11]—and on his return to America the screenwriter started work on the script for a fee of $169,000. Both men agreed that the ideal actor for the role of Sam Benjamin—the movie mogul based, at least in part, on Joe Levine—was Rod Steiger, and Silliphant duly wrote to him.

From the South of France, Harold and Grace flew to London, where in August they met Diana Jervis-Read, who had been recommended to them as a secretary and executive assistant. Diana remembers meeting the couple for the first time at the Savoy on 5 August.

"The door to the suite was opened by Grace, who was very petite and glamorous and absolutely charming," she says. "The room was full of people, but all of a sudden this man walked straight over and said he was Harold Robbins. I liked him immediately, and he seemed to radiate friendliness. He told me that Simon & Schuster had asked him to do a book tour of America—it was a thank you gesture to the booksellers who had done such a good job of selling his novels—and he needed someone firstly to work in New York and then, later, in Los Angeles."[12]

At the end of September Harold, Grace, and Diana all arrived in New York, to be greeted by a block-long billboard advertising "The World of Harold Robbins" towering above Times Square. The enormous structure featured gigantic blow-ups of his novels, plus huge posters for *The Survivors* and two forthcoming films, *The Adventurers* and *The Inheritors*. *Stiletto*, the film starring Britt Ekland and Alex Cord, had just opened, while Pocket Books had reissued seven of his novels, with new covers designed by Bob Lockart.

On 2 October Robbins took Grace, together with Diana, Len Forman (vice president of marketing at Simon & Schuster), and Paul and Zelda Gitlin out to dinner at the Sun Luck Imperial Chinese, one of his favorite restaurants. "Harold had a very Latin quality," says Diana. "If he liked you, you were one of his family."[13] Two days later he attended a lavish party hosted by Joe Levine at the St. Regis Hotel. While all the other men were dressed in traditional black tie— photographs show a sweating Levine oozing out of his dinner suit—Harold sported a rather modish outfit comprising a black polo neck tucked into black trousers, offset by an elaborate belt. Grace too stood out from the crowd. Levine's wife, the larger than life Rosalie, glammed it up in an ensemble that looked like a length of extremely expensive curtain material; Mrs. Robbins opted for a much more fashionable look, in a sequined sleeveless dress and sheer white blouse with an enormous bow. Even five-year-old Adréana looked the epitome of style, with a white miniskirt, white tights, and ribbon sleeves.

The party organizers thought it would be fun to play with Robbins's name and transformed the Versailles room into a surreal aviary with seven artificial trees sporting hundreds of robin red breasts. As guests entered, they saw an artificial arbor, in which had been placed life-size cardboard blow-ups of all the family: there was Harold reclining in a hammock, with Grace standing by one of the trees and little Adréana on a swing. This picket-fenced area to one side of the room boasted a sign that read "Villa Grazia" while Robbins's books "grew" from the ends of sticks in the fake grass. On each of the eight tables the organizers had placed an old-fashioned typewriter spelling out the author's name in fairy lights, and on the back of each of the machines a notice had been placed saying, "Stolen from Universal."

Guests drank Dom Perignon from crystal and gold glassware and sat at tables draped in green felt. As they ate—the menu consisted of hors d'oeuvres, flaming oysters, pheasant breasts decorated with plumage, salad, cheese, and a dessert of vanilla, chocolate, and strawberry ice cream rolled into the shape of eggs, dipped into white and mocha chocolate, served in a nest of spun sugar—they would have heard the birdsong of robins emanating from a tape recorder hidden in the trees. As they staggered out at the end of the evening, Robbins's friends and associates could hardly have failed to have got the—very lame—joke.

On 10 October Harold, Grace, and Diana flew to Los Angeles where, over the course of the following few days, Robbins had meetings with Quincy Jones and Ray Brown, partners in his new venture, Symbolic Records. One of their first projects was an album entitled *Music to Read Harold Robbins By*. "One day we were having lunch, and we said, 'Let's form a record company,'" says Quincy Jones. "But we would not have formed a company had it not been for the fact that we liked hanging out with one another. One of the first records we made was the soundtrack for the film *The Adventurers*. I think Harold liked the idea of having more control over things. We also signed Jeff and Beau Bridges, but nothing came of it because Jeff went off to work on *The Last Picture Show*.

"Harold was a real man of the 1960s. He did everything. He was wild and free and not inhibited at all. He loved women and appreciated womanhood. He liked life and knew how to have a good time. He made having fun into an art. I liked his spirit, his imagination. He had a very positive energy that made you feel you could achieve your ambitions; he gave you the fuel to dream."[14]

By 1 November he was back in New York for the start of the $250,000 promotional tour. On 2 November, dressed in a shirt and tie both fashioned from the same highly patterned material and a dandyish black three-quarter-length jacket, he appeared on *The Ed Sullivan Show*. "The only thing I did not care for was some of his loud shirts," says his friend Alex Cord. "I would not have been caught dead in some of the clothes he wore. He was outlandish in everything he did. Although he lived a lavish lifestyle, I was surprised to find he was not at all pretentious. He was very down-to-earth, like a genuine working kind of guy."[15]

On 6 November he hosted a party at Nepentha, the nightclub on East 48th Street: "Join the World of Harold Robbins," read the invitation requesting guests to attend in "Mod Dress." "Nepentha was a typical stylish New York club—good subtle lighting, a great deejay, and a good-size dance floor," remembers Diana Jervis-Read. "The clothes were dressy, lots of floating chiffon panels and jewelry, and ladies had their hair put up at the beauty parlor for the occasion."[16] That weekend he saw his fourteen-year-old daughter Caryn, who was, remembers Diana, experiencing a number of emotional problems.

"She came to stay with us in a New York hotel for the weekend," she says. "She had run away from school, and Harold asked me if I would mind sleeping in the same room as her because he was afraid for her to be alone."[17] Robbins said, in an interview with a Miami-based journalist at this time, that he did not stop his daughter from reading his books. He believed there was nothing in his novels that could possibly harm a child; the important thing, he said, was to keep the lines of communication open. Caryn, he said, did not think he was particularly cool—he was just the man who paid the bills. He did not care if television executives broadcast violent or sexually explicit films, as it was up to the parent to choose whether to let a child see the material. "I don't want anyone interfering with my right to raise my child the way I please," he said.[18] Caryn, however, grew up with a huge amount of anger that she directed toward her father. Certainly she seemed to resent him for what she perceived as his initial rejection and subsequent neglect of her. She was also jealous of her father's close relationship with her half-sister, Adréana. "As she got older," says Caryn Matchinga, "Caryn seemed to really hate him."[19] Harold, of course, had tried his best to win custody of Caryn, and the knowledge that she thought him to be lacking as a father saddened him no end. If only she could see his side of the story. "Harold worried about her hugely," says Diana, "and for quite long periods of time she did not want anything to do with him. I told him that she would, most likely, come around, and eventually she did."[20]

From New York, Robbins traveled to Boston, Philadelphia, Washington, Chicago, Cincinnati, Detroit, Cleveland, Los Angeles, San Francisco, Miami, Atlanta, Houston, and Dallas, before arriving back home in Los Angeles on 5 December. One journalist who met him on the tour described him as a "slim, short man [he was five foot eight] with a quiet voice and relaxed manner,"[21] while another said he was "an old, shabby, nondescript man flaunting an Apollo hippy pendant," a gift from Joe Levine consisting of a gold chain and bauble fashioned in the shape of the moon; the spot where the Apollo 11 landed was marked by a ruby, and on its reverse one could see facsimiles of the astronauts' signatures.[22] Wherever he went, Robbins demanded the best suites, together with an additional room on either side of him, plus a supply of caviar and champagne; his wine bill alone for the tour is reported to have come to $5,000.

"His demands sounded so exotic and eccentric to me at first I couldn't believe it, but I soon learned that he asked for these things for a reason," says Diana Jervis-Read. "He needed the extra suites for people like Paul Gitlin and me, who maintained a traveling office for him. And as for the champagne and caviar, he knew in 1969 that in three-quarters of the hotels there wouldn't be so much as a coffee shop open when we arrived late at night. He said that although he could have asked for room service, coffee, and sandwiches, nobody would have made the effort. But if you asked them for caviar and champagne, the hotel staff would make sure it turned up.

"He was very fatherly and looked after everybody. I remember one day we were having lunch at the Four Seasons in New York with Len Forman and Paul Gitlin. The three men, who were all Jewish, got into a conversation about matzo brei, and the discussion about the specific ingredients became quite heated until finally Harold called over the headwaiter and asked him to bring him a trolley with the various ingredients and a stove, and he proceeded to make matzo brei for the whole restaurant. That was typical of Harold."[23]

The Inheritors, which Robbins first conceived in 1949, was published in November 1969 to lukewarm reviews. One critic labeled the novel "one of the most sloppily written books Robbins has ever published . . . it consists mainly of dialogue and action, dialogue and action, as if it were written directly for the screen . . . Few descriptive passages are present, and we rarely get below the surface of the characters."[24]

The novel was marketed, according to the blurb of an early proof copy, as the story of two very different men—Stephen Gaunt, head of a radio and television network, and Sam Benjamin, last of the old motion picture tycoons. "Their story is about their struggle to dominate the vast entertainment and communications industry that came into being after the Second World War . . . All the Robbins qualities are here, the violence and the sex, the huge cast of characters, many of whom the reader will think he can recognize, the glamour that reaches from coast to coast and from continent to continent."[25]

That was, in effect, all a prospective reader really needed to know in order to consume the book. As Marshall McLuhan, the so-called "high priest of Pop art," said, "The future of the book is the blurb"— an accurate prediction that partly explains Robbins's appeal. Readers of mass-market fiction, attuned to the medium of the televisual, did not want to be bogged down in long descriptions of landscape or the minutiae of everyday life; what they required was a story that moved along at the same furious pace as the frames of a flickering screen. *The Inheritors*, as Robbins himself acknowledged, is a quintessentially McLuhanesque text, its theme the exploration of how the media constructs and shapes the consciousness of an individual. "The little screen had a hypnosis all its own," Robbins writes in the novel. "It took your mind off your problems into another world."[26] Written in stark, brutalized prose—language that appears smashed, reduced to its bare essentials—it reads like an extended haiku to the mass media, appropriately with no more depth than a moving image.

"My new book is very modern in its telling," said Robbins. "This is the third time in my writing career that I've changed style. It's McLuhanesque . . . Descriptions and backgrounds are kept to a minimum . . . My ambition is to remove from the reader the feeling that he is holding a book in front of him."[27]

Perhaps not coincidentally, the subject of Jacqueline Susann's new novel, published in the spring of 1969, was also the television industry, and its womanizing central character, Robin Stone, was loosely modeled after James Aubrey, the president of CBS between 1959 and 1965. Susann, whose 1966 book *Valley of the Dolls* holds the record as the biggest-selling novel of all time, named the book after Aubrey's pet term for the television set: *The Love Machine*. Similarly, Robbins drew inspiration from Aubrey for the character of Stephen Gaunt in *The Inheritors*. For instance, in the novel the television executive is described as "smiling like a snake";[28] in the business Aubrey was known as "the smiling Cobra."

Throughout the 1960s Robbins and Susann played a kind of literary tag with each other, fiercely guarding their respective place on the *New York Times* best-seller list. When *The Love Machine* was published, it nudged Philip Roth's *Portnoy's Complaint* off the top of the list—"I liked the book, but I'd hate to shake his hand," quipped Susann, an expert self-promoter. When Robbins's novel *The Adventurers* hit the bookstores in 1966 and threatened to knock Susann's steamy tale off the top spot, Susann, famously described by Truman Capote as "a truck driver in drag," traveled from shop to shop rearranging displays to place copies of her book in a more prominent position—"preferably on top of the stacks of *The Adventurers*."[29] On one occasion, when Susann and her husband Irving Mansfield discovered that Harold would be staying at the Beverly Hills Hotel, they went to the pool and distributed free copies of *Valley of the Dolls*; when Robbins arrived, all he could see was people lying by the pool reading copies of the book. "I think Jackie is one of the most dynamic people in our business," said Robbins. "I think she has sold more books than I ever thought possible."[30]

According to the official list, as compiled by *Publishers Weekly*, Susann's *The Love Machine* was the third best-selling book of 1969, with Robbins's *The Inheritors* in fourth place. Beating both of them were Mario Puzo's *The Godfather* at number two and Philip Roth's *Portnoy's Complaint* in top place; standing in seventh position was a novel called *Naked Came the Stranger* by a little-known author called Penelope Ashe. When the novel—about a woman who discovers that her husband has been unfaithful and duly sets out to sleep with every man she can find—was first published in the summer of 1969 it was an immediate sensation. But by August it was revealed that Penelope Ashe did not exist and the whole project was an elaborate hoax. The novel had been penned by twenty-five *Newsday* journalists in a deliberate effort to parody the trash that was being churned out and bought in large quantities by what they saw as an increasingly gullible public. "I was really fed up with people like Harold Robbins and Jacqueline Susann," said Mike McGrady, the reporter who had the initial idea. "I saw their writing was being accepted and thought it was absurd."[31] In a memo McGrady sent to his colleagues in June 1966 he outlined the brief. "As one of *Newsday*'s truly outstanding literary talents you are hereby officially invited to become the co-author of a best-selling novel," he wrote. "There will be an unremitting emphasis on sex. Also, true excellence in writing will be quickly blue-penciled into oblivion."[32]

The book's sales seemed to suggest the ease with which one could write a formulaic best seller— the initial draft was completed during one week in 1966—and the cynicism with which it could be marketed. An alluring title, a picture of a naked woman on its cover, and the suggestion that the reader would learn all he or she needed to know about sex turned it into a sure-fire hit. The success of *Naked Came the Stranger* should have meant that, in theory, anybody with a dirty mind who could string a sentence together could write a best-selling book, and publishers, inspired by the phenomenal success of Robbins and Susann, threw money at aspiring authors in an effort to ape their success. The problem was, however, that many of these writers, such as Alvah Bessie (whose novel *The Symbol* was based on Marilyn Monroe), Morton Cooper (whose *The King* was a fictionalized account of Frank Sinatra), and Henry Sutton (the pen name of David Slavitt and author of *The Exhibitionist*) were intellectuals. They may have been better writers than Susann and Robbins, but they did not fundamentally believe in their material.

"One of the things I finally realized is that people like Jackie can write what they write because that's the smartest they are," said Slavitt. "There's an authenticity to their doing it, and people like me who condescend to write best sellers are a little fraudulent . . . She hadn't really invented anything! But why should she? She wasn't an artist. She was an anthropologist. Jackie didn't invent, because she didn't believe, or couldn't comprehend, the truth of fiction. And for America's most popular novelist to be unable to understand what fiction is—that says something about publishing, and it says something about our civilization."[33]

Similarly, Robbins acknowledged that his skills were not so much creative as journalistic, telling one reporter in 1969 that he did not have the imagination to invent, merely the ability to rearrange facts. "Given the nature of his reportage, the conclusion can hardly be avoided that the Robbins *oeuvre* constitutes a commentary on our time as bleak as Beckett's," wrote one critic.[34] Robbins, for one, accounted for his success by explaining that fundamentally he wrote from the heart.

"I guess it's because what I write is real," he said. "They're American stories, about the power game. The sex is incidental . . . I sell hundreds of thousands of copies in the Far East and the Near East—and these books are so *American* . . . And if it's so simple, how come my imitators don't do as well?"[35]

15

"This is a very juicy book. It's full of gasoline, kerosene and semen."
—Harold Robbins to Alan Whicker

AROLD PULLED OUT of his driveway and headed toward Sunset. He loved everything about his Jensen Interceptor—its sleek lines, the way it handled, the looks that it attracted as he increased the pressure on the gas and picked up speed. Next to having sex, driving a cool car was one of the greatest pleasures of his life. As he cruised past his office building and through Hollywood, the balmy night air blowing through the open windows, rock music playing on the radio, he felt a thrill pass through his body.

If Robbins's greatest love was women, then second in his affections was the automobile. His twin obsessions found perfect expression in his 1971 novel *The Betsy*, a book whose characters include a woman who orgasms to the recorded soundtrack of revving engines. *The Betsy*, like many of Robbins's novels, started life as an idea for a television series. "On this new series I will have complete control," he told a journalist in January 1970, while on a trip to London. "There will be no botch-up. I will set up my own production company."[1]

Robbins started to think about a story centering on a Detroit car manufacturing dynasty similar to the Ford clan. In addition to his fleet of Rolls-Royces, Jensens, and Maseratis, Harold added a clutch of new Fords that he had been given by the firm. "I have seven cars in the States and three . . . in France," he said. "Of course, I get pleasure out of them, but come on—who wouldn't?"[2] Robbins understood the

Harold always maintained that he had been brought up in a tough New York orphanage. "Of the sixteen boys that were in this, I guess you'd call it a dormitory, only about four of five of us are still alive," he said. "Three of them have been electrocuted [by the electric chair], four are in jail, the others are all more or less respectable citizens—except myself." In fact, this was his real boyhood home: 1184 Schenectady Avenue, Brooklyn. (Photograph by Andrew Wilson)

A portrait of the young Harold Rubin taken in 1934 at George Washington High School, New York, where he was affectionately known as "Poker Face." (Photograph courtesy of the George Washington Educational Campus)

Harold was the living embodiment of the American dream, transforming himself from an ordinary Brooklyn boy into the world's first playboy writer. "Hemingway once asked me what my literary ambitions were," Robbins said. "I told him, 'Wealth.' And I got it." (Photograph courtesy of Harry Ransom Humanities Research Center, the University of Texas at Austin)

Bookkeeping—the tallying of profit and loss—lay at the heart of Robbins's success. When he came to write his super-successful novels he never forgot the skills he learned as a budget analyst in the New York offices of Universal Studios. (Photograph courtesy of Harry Ransom Humanities Research Center, the University of Texas at Austin)

Harold believed that in order to succeed it was important to look—and play—the part. Yet his smart suits were in great contrast to the psychedelic blaze of colors he would sport later in life. (Photograph courtesy of Harry Ransom Humanities Research Center, the University of Texas at Austin. Photograph by Floyd B. Hall)

Harold signing copies of his second novel, *The Dream Merchants*, an account of the birth of the American film industry. "As soon as he began to work for Universal he fell in love with the manufacture of films, not the writing of them," says his friend Steve Shagan. "He enthused about the magic of movies, not how they were written but what was behind them." (Photograph courtesy of Harry Ransom Humanities Research Center, the University of Texas at Austin)

Harold's first wife, Lillian Machnovitch, the daughter of Universal Pictures' treasurer, Samuel Machnovitch. "Lillian always had a lovely smile and was very generous-hearted," says her sister, Rae Exelbert, "but she was very quiet and private. She fell in love with Harold when she was a girl—they were childhood sweethearts." (Photograph courtesy of Arlene Mintzer and Rae Exelbert)

Lillian with Tony Curtis, taken on the set of the 1954 Universal-International film *The Black Shield of Falworth*. By this point in his marriage, Harold had taken a number of other lovers. (Photograph courtesy of Arlene Mintzer and Rae Exelbert)

Harold's mistress Yvonne Russell-Farrow was everything Lillian was not—thin, glamorous, and sophisticated. "She was a kind of exotic beauty, a brunette, very flamboyant, something of a floozy," remembers casting agent Rose Tobias Shaw. (Photograph by Leonard Detrick, © New York Daily News L.P.)

Harold and his illegitimate daughter, Caryn, in the lobby of the New York Supreme Court, Manhattan. In 1959, Robbins and his mistress fought a bitter legal battle for custody of the child, which Harold subsequently lost. (Photograph by Leonard Detrick, © New York Daily News L.P.)

Harold and Lillian at a party to celebrate the 1964 film *The Carpetbaggers*, just before their acrimonious divorce. During their twenty-eight years of marriage Harold had fathered two children by other women while Lillian was unable to conceive, which left her feeling bitter and betrayed. (Photograph courtesy of Joseph Levine Collection, Howard Gotlieb Archival Research Center, Boston University)

In its first week *The Carpetbaggers* grossed $1.5 million in New York alone, and it went on to be the most profitable film of 1964, earning $36 million in America. (Photograph courtesy of Joseph Levine Collection, Howard Gotlieb Archival Research Center, Boston University)

The Carpetbaggers star George Peppard with actor George Hamilton, who would go on to take a lead role in Robbins's television series *The Survivors*. "I didn't know whether he [Harold] was the real deal or a con man," says Hamilton. "If you didn't know he was a writer you would think you'd better hold on to your watch." (Photograph courtesy of Joseph Levine Collection, Howard Gotlieb Archival Research Center, Boston University)

Carroll Baker, who played Rina Marlowe in *The Carpetbaggers*, at a premiere of the film. "I remember we had this wonderful party at the Four Seasons in New York and at each of the tables there was a beautiful woman whom nobody recognized," she says. "Gradually as the evening progressed these women slowly took off their clothes until by the end of the evening they were completely naked, stripped bare. That was so Harold." (Photograph courtesy of Joseph Levine Collection, Howard Gotlieb Archival Research Center, Boston University)

Harold with his second wife, Grace, at a party held in his honor in New York in October 1969. "He came across like a mixture of someone from Hell's Kitchen and Tom Jones, while she was like a very beautiful Cleopatra," says family friend Victoria Ryan Bida. (Photograph courtesy of Joseph Levine Collection, Howard Gotlieb Archival Research Center, Boston University)

Harold and Grace's daughter Adréana in 1969. (Photograph courtesy of Joseph Levine Collection, Howard Gotlieb Archival Research Center, Boston University)

Cardboard cutouts of Harold, Grace, and Adréana in a mock-up of Robbins's house, Villa Grazia, in the South of France. (Photograph courtesy of Joseph Levine Collection, Howard Gotlieb Archival Research Center, Boston University)

A sketch of the real Villa Grazia, in Le Cannet, just above Cannes. Although Robbins spent the winters in Los Angeles, he would return to this house in April or May of each year. (Photograph courtesy of Diana Jervis-Read)

Villa Grazia

Robbins with his good friend the writer Cornelius Ryan, whom Robbins supported during his battle against cancer. "The roots of his [Harold's] loyalty run deep and his generosity where friends and family are concerned is boundless," said Ryan's wife, Kathy. (Photograph courtesy of Victoria Ryan Bida and Geoff Ryan)

Harold, Grace, and Diana with talk-show host Ed Sullivan in November 1969. Robbins, an expert self-promoter, was one of the first authors to take advantage of the mass media. As author Michael Mewshaw observes, "There was no point being Harold Robbins if all he did was stay at home and write—as he might have said, 'Fuck that shit.'" (Photograph courtesy of Diana Jervis-Read)

Robbins receiving a shoulder massage from his secretary and executive assistant Diana Jervis-Read, who later became a close friend. (Photograph courtesy of Diana Jervis-Read)

Harold's yacht, the *Gracara*, named after Grace and his two daughters, Caryn and Adréana. "Buying that yacht was an achievement of magnificent proportions," says Robbins's friend Steve Shagan. "When he was on that boat it was like, 'My name is Harold Robbins—look at me.' It was marine proof that he had made it." (Photograph courtesy of Ken and Jackie Minns)

Robbins with one of his beloved Jensens—at the height of his success he owned a fleet of fourteen cars. In 1971 he published *The Betsy*, a novel that includes the character of a woman who orgasms to the sound of revving engines. (Photograph by Ini Asmann)

Harold with Ken and Jackie Minns, the captain and cook of the *Gracara*, at one of Robbins's famous New Year's Eve parties. "He certainly liked spinning stories," says Ken. "There was a Walter Mitty element to him." (Photograph courtesy of Ken and Jackie Minns)

Grace on her ninth wedding anniversary in November 1974, with Adréana. By this point Harold had told his wife of his intention to take other lovers. "If I had it to do over," said Grace later, "I would never allow an open marriage." (Photograph courtesy of Ken and Jackie Minns)

Proud parents Harold and Grace help their daughter to cut an elaborate birthday cake. Yet Adréana does not look happy. According to Jackie Minns the problem was that Harold and Grace did not spend enough "quality time" with their children; in her view the couple were more interested in entertaining. (Photograph courtesy of Ken and Jackie Minns)

Harold hard at work in the South of France. Robbins could finish a novel within three months, a speed that earned him the moniker "the man with the smoking typewriter." (Photograph by Ini Asmann)

Robbins looking bored at the prospect of signing hundreds of books during a European publicity tour. (Photograph by Ini Asmann)

Harold with members of his female staff and Paul Gitlin, Robbins's attorney, agent, and close friend. Gitlin was, according to editor Michael Korda, "tough and smart and made no effort to hide it, nor was he a man to mince words or take fools lightly." (Photograph by Ini Asmann)

Harold smoked three packs of cigarettes a day, even after he was diagnosed with emphysema in 1982. (Photograph by Ini Asmann)

Harold with a lover, the photographer Ini Asmann, at Studio 54. "When he spoke to you it was like you were the only one on the whole earth," she says. (Photograph courtesy of Ini Asmann)

Harold and Ini, in a Bo Derek, *10*-style wig. "He was very charismatic, though not particularly good-looking, and it was his personality that appealed," she says. (Photograph by Ini Asmann)

Harold with Mario Puzo, the author of *The Godfather*. Robbins claimed that Puzo had learned how to write a best seller after reading his books. Yet when Robbins tried his hand at a Mafia-themed novel—the 1991 *The Piranhas*—he was accused of cynically publishing a "nearly indecipherable mess of a knockoff" of Puzo's famous book. (Photograph by Ini Asmann)

Adréana, Grace, Harold, and Caryn, with their beloved Pekinese dogs, at their Beverly Hills home. (Photograph by Ini Asmann)

Harold with fellow best-selling writer Jackie Collins. "I always remember thinking when I read him as a teenager that when I started to write novels my women would be as strong as Harold Robbins's men," she says. (Photograph by Ini Asmann)

Robbins with good friends Judi Schwam Yedor (left) and Diana Jervis-Read (right). "He was like a ringleader," says Yedor. "He liked making fantasies come true, in real life, for everybody." (Photograph courtesy of Diana Jervis-Read)

Harold with his third wife, Jann Stapp, his former personal assistant, who cared for him after he suffered a massive cocaine-induced stroke. The couple married on Valentine's Day 1992, seven days after Robbins's divorce from Grace became final. "She [Jann] was very helpful to me and then helped herself to everything I had," said Grace. (Photograph by Ini Asmann)

Harold and Jann at their home in Palm Springs. "I walked into [the house] to see this man who had been everywhere, so active, confined to a wheelchair," says Ini Asmann, who took this photograph. "It broke my heart to see him like that. His face was swollen, he couldn't move anymore, and for a moment I was taken aback. I hope he didn't see my face." (Photograph by Ini Asmann)

Robbins's final resting place at the Palm Springs Mortuary and Mausoleum. After his death on 14 October 1997, Robbins was cremated and his ashes were placed inside an urn made in the form of one of his best-selling books. (Photograph by Andrew Wilson)

importance of the car to the national psyche, a symbol of the individualism and freedom that captured the essence of America. "Motion pictures and automobiles have had the greatest impact on this century," said Robbins. "Movies gave the imagination wings, and the automobile gave our society mobility. Both subjects are fascinating to me."[3]

The more Robbins thought about the idea, the more he realized that it would work better as a novel; although he might reach more people through the medium of television, he couldn't bear another debacle on the scale of *The Survivors*, which he described as a "disaster . . . except for the money."[4] Before writing it, however, he wanted to take some serious time off, and in early 1970 he started to lay the foundations for what he hoped would be a summer of unfettered pleasure.

From Britain, Robbins flew to Cannes, where he interviewed staff who could serve aboard his new yacht. Ken Minns, skipper of a boat harbored in the South of France, applied for the position as captain and his wife, Jackie, that of cook. After a meeting at Robbins's villa in Le Cannet and then a tour of the yacht moored in Port Canto, Robbins offered the couple the job. "He said that because he didn't have a family [parents] he liked to make the people near him, his friends and such like, into his family," says Jackie.[5] "He told me that he was an orphan and how he had been brought up in Hell's Kitchen, but I found out later from somebody that he wasn't an orphan," says Ken. "He loved to ham it up a bit, and he would try to get me to back him up on certain stories, and then they would appear in newspapers. I think Grace fell for the stories of his life as well so she never really knew the truth."[6]

At the end of January he was back in America, where on 23 February he attended the premiere of Lewis Gilbert's film of *The Adventurers*; it was shown on a cross-country flight between Los Angeles and New York. Robbins thought the $10 million movie, which starred Bekim Fehmiu, Candice Bergen, Ernest Borgnine, Anna Moffo, Charles Aznavour, and Olivia de Havilland, was "lousy," an opinion shared by the critics. *Time* magazine labeled it an "over-worked organ" . . . "breast-twisting rapes occur whenever the plot flags; sloe-eyed, heavy-breathing women chuff across the screen like freight trains . . . Masochists, lovers of camp and chroniclers of the collapse of Hollywood will sift for years *The Adventurers'* riches of embarrassment."[7]

So exasperated was Robbins by the way moviemakers reduced his already pulpy books to garbage that in 1970 he decided to do something he had never done before: commit himself to a project because he believed it had integrity and not because he thought it would make money. In 1969 he had been watching television in France when he saw Claude Vermorel's thirteen-part series *Yao*, about a young black boy growing up on the Ivory Coast of Africa. Robbins was so impressed by the program, especially its cinematography, that he wanted to rewrite and reedit it for an American audience. Although the drama—which had won the Silver Leaf award of the Cinema Congress of Human Relations in France—had originally been made in Swahili, and Vermorel had dubbed it into French, Robbins wanted it to have English dialogue. His plan was to bring the film over to America, where it could be recut, but in March he heard that the filmmakers would not allow the negative to be removed from French soil, and so the work would have to be done in Paris.

"Harold called up one of his great friends, James Baldwin, who at that time was living in Paris, and asked him to help write the dialogue for the recut of the film," says Diana Jervis-Read. "So I moved to Paris, with an American film editor who didn't speak French, and the three of us sat in a room, hunched over a moviola, for four months."[8]

Despite the anxieties surrounding *Yao*, Robbins was determined to enjoy the summer of 1970. In April he sailed to San Remo and Majorca, then returned to Cannes, where observers could easily have mistaken this "slight, balding [man] dressed very Riviera in sneakers, mauve slacks, psychedelic purple-and-gold-and-red-shirt, red peaked cap, silver-lensed dark glasses, and a charged cigar-holder" for a rich pimp.[9] Robbins enjoyed relaxing on his boat, taking in the rays of the sun, listening to the lapping of the sea around him. He let it be known that in the spring he had been offered the presidency of a movie studio—he didn't specify which one—but turned it down. "I don't wanna be a slave to any company," he said. "I'm not gonna be anyone else but me." Unlike Paul Gitlin he was not, he said, prone to procrastination; in fact, he had a real talent for enjoying himself.

"[Paul] thinks you should always be feeling a little guilty and looking over your shoulder for trouble," he said. "But I've got one great thing going for me. I'm not a worrier. I never have been. I just live my life as I like, day to day. If something goes wrong, ****'em."[10]

During the Cannes Film Festival in May Robbins indulged his taste for erotic movies, most of which disappointed, except for one, *Stille Dage I Clichy* (*Quiet Days in Clichy*), Jens Jørgen Thorsen's film based on a Henry Miller novella that was subsequently seized by authorities as pornography when distributors tried to import it into America. "This is Henry Miller the way Henry Miller was written," said Robbins, "which I hope someday happens to me."[11] Robbins loved Cannes at festival time—the topless girls on the beach, the invasion of Hollywood money men, the brash vulgarity of it all. "We'd have cocktails on the boat every afternoon," he said. "We'd take people out, and we'd go between the islands and drink from three to six. It was great."[12]

That summer Robbins invited Hormoz Sabet, chairman of Gulf Associates, and his wife on a cruise around the Mediterranean. For months Harold had been trying to lure his new friend onto the boat, but the businessman had had to turn down the invitation because he was too busy. "Harold insisted and said that he would, for once, agree to leave when I wanted and go wherever I wanted," says Hormoz. "I was honored and finally agreed. After a short while out at sea, I was alone with Harold on the rear deck. I asked, 'Harold, with the thousands of people you know, why in the world were you so insistent that I join you?' He replied, 'You are one of the few people who said that you have never read a single Harold Robbins book. You are also one of the few people who does not want to sell me anything or ask me for money.' Yet he was not modest—he told me that there were more Harold Robbins books printed than the Bible—and that although he had a great fondness for women, he did not show great respect for them."[13]

Martin Starger and his wife accompanied the Sabets on the trip, as well as on another two-week cruise to Sicily. "Harold was bigger than life and acted like someone from one of his books," says Martin. "He talked tough, like a gangster character, but he was a sweetheart of a guy. He was a tremendous dinner companion and seemed to know every restaurant in the world. He had to have the biggest table in the best restaurant with the best champagne. To him, life was a joke, and he lived as though he could lose it all tomorrow. He loved seeing people having a good time.

"His lifestyle, with his villas and boats, was so different from mine. On this cruise down from the South of France to Sicily we stopped to refuel around the boot of Italy. I remember growing up as a kid in the Bronx that if you borrowed someone's car, you returned it with a full tank of gas. So I said to Harold, 'Look, let me take care of this. I haven't spent a dime on this trip.' With a smile on his face, he asked me whether I was absolutely sure, but I insisted. What I didn't realize was that it wasn't simply a matter of filling it up with gas. They had to change the insides of the engines, and the bill came to something like $10,000. 'Holy God,' I said to myself, and my wife saw me turn absolutely white. Luckily, when I got back home, the network said that they would pay most of it, and I had to contribute only one thousand dollars or so.

"One day, while sailing around Italy, we hit some bad weather, and he was really worried that the kids, Adréana and the son of my wife, who were the same age, would get sick, and so at the next port he went into the nearest travel agency and booked a couple of first-class carriages on what he thought was a fast train to Venice. He told the captain to look after the boat, but when we turned up, this train looked like a World War I trooper. People were standing in the aisles, there was no difference between first or second class. But you know what? Harold, and the rest of us, laughed the whole way. That was what life was like with Harold—a nonstop adventure."[14]

Although Robbins did not believe in sexual fidelity, he did value and love his family. On the cruise to Sicily he delighted Grace by arranging a surprise visit to Marsala, the town where many of her relatives still lived. "We docked the boat, and this whole group of relatives rushed toward the sea," says Martin. "It seemed like the whole village was there. Later we had a dinner that Harold had arranged in advance in a place that looked like it had come straight out of *The Godfather*."[15]

Back in the South of France, Robbins organized a lavish birthday party on his yacht for six-year-old Adréana. But on this occasion he made sure that the event was covered by a visiting journalist, Donald

Zec, and photographer Doreen Spooner. An expert jazz musician named Charlie played classics such as "Ain't Misbehavin' " on a piano that had been specially installed on the teak deck, while Robbins, dressed in a frilly white shirt, violet-colored trousers, and a red jacket, posed for pictures with the glamorous young mothers and nannies of Adréana's friends, "in the manner of the sultan and his favorites."

Zec, who labeled Robbins "the Onassis of supermarket literature," observed that the author looked like a cross between the Canadian prime minister Pierre Trudeau and the actor Robert Mitchum. Robbins told the reporter that even if he didn't write another word for the next ten years, he would still earn an average of £250,000 a year. He never bothered listening to people's conversations, he said; nor did he make notes or "grope for the fancy phrase"—as was evident by Robbins's behavior. When a girl in a passing dinghy sailed by the yacht, he commented on "what a lovely pair of knockers" she had. Did he worry about how history would rate him? "Man, I don't give a shit," he said. "When I'm gone, they can grill me and throw the ashes where they please, say what they like."[16]

In the autumn of 1970 Robbins returned to Los Angeles, to discover that his good friend Cornelius Ryan was suffering from prostate cancer. As soon as he heard the news, relayed via Paul Gitlin, Robbins flew to New York and drove to Ryan's house in Ridgefield, Connecticut. He ran up the steps and embraced Kathy. Ryan, whom friends called Connie, appeared in the hallway, his face ashen white against his dark wool fishing jacket. As soon as Connie saw his friend, he began to cry, and in order to comfort him, Harold took him in his arms. Robbins spent the weekend at the house, sitting with Ryan as he slept and helping him on his occasional trips to the bathroom. "I have often wished that more people knew the private Harold instead of the public man who, I think, very often adjusts his image to what he believes his many readers of his books expect of him," said Kathy. "But the private Harold is quite different, his affections, concern, and interests unknown by his vast audience and by many associates. The roots of his loyalty run deep, and his generosity where friends and family are concerned is boundless."[17]

Both of the Ryans' children also witnessed Robbins's kindness. That weekend, on Halloween, fourteen-year-old Victoria indulged her

childish high spirits as she lathered soap all across the windows of a
nearby house. When a neighbor complained, a police officer knocked
on the door of the Ryans' house to investigate. Although the incident
was a minor one, Robbins sensed that his friend was becoming
anxious, and to lighten the atmosphere he told the policeman about
his own youthful indiscretions. "I remember feeling so dreadful
because dad had just come out of the hospital, and here I was making
trouble for him," remembers Victoria. "But Uncle Harold, as I called
him, was full of life, making jokes and trying to lighten the heaviness
that was in the air. It was difficult for me to reconcile the man who
wrote those books with the man who I knew. But I suppose I saw a
different side to him."[18]

That same weekend the Ryans' other child, Geoff, was caught
smoking marijuana, but Harold helped smooth out the situation.
"More importantly, he was a solid and good friend to my father in his
darkest days," Geoff says. During his visit Robbins realized that, in
order for his friend to survive the pain ravaging his body, he needed a
project to occupy his mind. "We've got to give him some will to get
through this," Robbins said to Kathy. Harold came up with the idea
that Ryan could write a novel based roughly on his own experiences as
a war correspondent. Geoff remembers the enthusiasm his father felt
for the project, which was provisionally entitled *The Peacemaker*.
"Harold was able to take my father's mind off his pain and the cancer,
and his enthusiasm was infectious," says Geoff.[19]

Robbins moved swiftly, insisting that Ryan produce a synopsis of
the book, about a journalist "whose fanatic devotion to the cause of
world peace leads him to the Nobel Peace Prize, but in the process
destroys his relationship with his own personal world, his wife and
children."[20] By early December it was announced that Trident would
publish the novel in 1972, while Robbins had bought the television
and motion picture rights. Although the novel was clearly Ryan's own
work, Robbins's influence was easy to spot—Harold told his friend
that it was important to stress that the character, Irish-born Michael
Essex, was a "ballsy type, [who] screwed anything in the dance halls
. . . [He was] searching for his identity."[21] Ryan also worked on an
outline for a project called *The Day They Blew Up Nelson*, written
with Julie Andrews in mind, but as he wrote to Paul Gitlin, "I would

not like him [Robbins] yakking about it and then wake up some morning and find that the idea is stolen from under our noses."[22]

During a visit to Los Angeles at the end of the year Robbins lavished Connie and Kathy with attention. Robbins picked them up at the airport, arranged a suite for them at the Beverly Hills Hotel, and spent time with them at a therapeutic spa, where he accompanied his friend to the whirlpool bath and on walks. "The public Harold would probably not be caught dead in a place that catered to the ill, the dieters, the plain people who came to be made beautiful," said Kathy.[23] In a letter Ryan wrote to his friend, he talked about how much the friendship meant to him. "I want you to know that as the years pass," he said, "even though I differ from you in many many ways—you are one of the few people I totally respect and confide in."[24]

Robbins talked to his friend in detail about what would be Ryan's last book, A Bridge Too Far—The Peacemaker never progressed beyond the early planning stages—encouraging him to believe that he could finish it. Robbins's help proved invaluable, and Ryan did go on to complete the book. But in November 1974, while on a publicity tour, he was admitted to the hospital and died.

"Both my dad and Harold came from nothing and made something of themselves," says Victoria Ryan Bida. "They also shared a mischievous sense of humor, an appetite for adventure. I imagine they often said to each other, 'Let's get into trouble together.' "[25] Both men, says Geoff, had a great capacity for loving. "They were both very warm men, and I think Harold had a big heart. He had an amazing smile that always made you feel you had something to contribute. I was just a kid when I first met him, but he never made me feel like a child; it was like he was speaking to an equal. Later I moved to Europe with no intention of ever returning to the States, and unknown to me, Harold, realizing that my mother needed me, lured me back to America with the prospect of a job on the film of The Betsy. Had it not been for that, I would never have advanced my career in the movies."[26]

At the end of December Robbins, together with Blake Edwards, Bruce Geller, and Alden Schwimmer, set up a new independent production company, Cinema Video Communications (CVC), which had its headquarters in the 9000 Sunset Boulevard building. Schwimmer remembers Robbins as something of a contradiction. "He gave out the impression that he was a flamboyant extrovert—he was a little seedy looking—but underneath he was generous to a fault, loyal and quite decent," he says. "It's almost as if he had created an image for himself that he had got stuck with."[27]

Each day Robbins would swagger out of the office and take his regular table at Scandia. There he would eat lunch with business associates or friends such as Steve Shagan, Gene Schwam, or Caryn Matchinga. "One day he invited his insurance agent with this guy who was the number-one hit man for the mob," she says. "He did it just to see whether he could unnerve the insurance agent. That was the kind of thing he loved to do."[28]

When Steve Shagan was having trouble writing his novel *Save the Tiger*, Robbins acted as a constant source of encouragement. "I was his lunch companion every Thursday when I was out of work," he says. "I think he liked people who got kicked to the floor and yet came back fighting. He had an innate respect for losers who would not stay lost. He knew I was having problems, and so he would take me to Scandia and tell me that my work was great. I showed him the first six chapters of the novel—I didn't know where it was going or how to make it stretch to 75,000 words—but he told me to look at my own experience, growing up as a kid in Brooklyn, and write about that."[29]

During the early part of 1971 Robbins busied himself with acquiring a number of future projects for CVC. The company bought options on books such as Herbert Purdum's *My Brother John*, a historical western novel; *Don't Embarrass the Bureau* by former FBI agent Bernard Conners; Kingsley Amis's *The Green Man*, which Alan Bennett was eager to adapt for the screen; Bruce Geller's script for a project entitled *Harry Never Holds* and his idea for a CBS series with the working title *Wild*. When looking for new business, CVC said that it hoped to be able to plow more money into scripts and productions, not waste it on operational bureaucracies. As Alden Schwimmer said in 1971, "We feel that in composite we represent a body of experience, accomplishment, and ability that no major studios can match, and we have been and shall continue to utilize those abilities so that ninety-five cents out of every dollar spent goes to the project as opposed to the major studio operation where seventy-five cents on every dollar goes anywhere but the project."[30]

Robbins wanted to emulate his idol Joe Levine—who had recently sold off Embassy to Avco—and inject some energy into what he regarded as a somewhat moribund industry. "There's no one left in the business who has any concept of creating excitement by selling a movie," he said. "Everything has turned into a plain merchandising, computerized operation. The reason I went into this is that I think I can put some fun back into the business. I do more trumpeting for my books than anyone does on a book today, and sales on my books reflect that. I'm going to do the same on my film and TV projects that I've been doing with my novels and promote the ass out of them."[31]

At the beginning of 1971 Robbins's novel *The Betsy*—which he realized would be one of CVC's biggest assets—remained unwritten, even though Trident hoped to publish the book in November. He knew there was only one answer: he would have to immure himself somewhere, away from the temptations of the South of France and Beverly Hills, and bash away at his typewriter until the novel was finished. At the beginning of February he locked himself in a sparsely furnished room at the Elysee Hotel in New York. He closed the blinds so he never knew whether it was day or night, tacked a chart listing the ages of his characters at various points in the narrative onto the mirror above his desk, and completed the book, sometimes at a rate of thirty-five pages a day, in just four months. "If you came in anytime during that twenty-four-hour cycle, I'd either be eating, working, or sleeping," he said. "And this went on for seventeen weeks until I finished."[32] During this time he emerged from the hotel on only three occasions: for his fifty-fifth birthday in May, to celebrate the birthday of Paul Gitlin, and to finalize the purchase of a new, single-story, three-bedroom house at 1017 North Beverly Drive in Beverly Hills. "Sometimes I think . . . it's the only time I'm functional," he said of the writing process.[33]

He wrote in his typically idiosyncratic fashion, knowing the names of the characters and the subject matter of the book but little else. Initially, Loren Hardeman I (whose name gives the reader a not-so-subtle clue as to his particular physical endowments), the founder of the car dynasty, was going to play a quite minor role in the novel, but as the work progressed, the character came to dominate the narrative. "In another case there was this one scene in the book where an automobile comes off the production line—it's the thirteenth car—and a man gets into it and drives off, and the automobile blows up," he said. "I remember looking at it after it was typed, and I said, 'My God the car blew up.' Five lines before then I didn't know it was going to happen, and yet when it did happen, it was right."[34]

In July Robbins did a deal with CVC in which he sold his own company the rights to the book for a fee of $91,000. He would also receive a further $77,500 when a final screenplay had been written and five percent of the movie's gross. Michael Wilson, whose previous credits had included *A Place in the Sun* and *Planet of the Apes*, was appointed as screenwriter, and Warner Bros. agreed to finance the film. Paul Gitlin was pleased with the arrangements but requested that, on any advertising material such as posters, Harold's name be placed in a prominent position above the title.

Relieved that he had delivered the manuscript and sorted out the deal between CVC and Warner Bros. Robbins flew to the South of France. There he hosted an evening at the restaurant Le Pirat, which he described as the most enjoyable party of his life, as he had employed a retinue of scantily clad gypsy girls to entertain his guests. "At the end of the party, we broke all the chairs in the place and ripped the clothes off all the women," he said. "It was marvelous."[35]

An addict to hedonism, Robbins went in search of even more exotic thrills with his new friend the composer Fritz Loewe, who spent the summers in Cannes. The two men had a great deal in common: they had both made huge amounts of money relatively late in life (Fritz at the age of fifty-six with *My Fair Lady* and Robbins with *The Carpetbaggers* at forty-five); they both loved gambling (Loewe quit only when he lost a million dollars); and they were both obsessed with women (they toured the sex clubs of Hamburg together).

"It was sex that drew Fritz and Harold together," says Francine Greshler Feldmann, daughter of Hollywood talent agent Abby J. Greshler and Loewe's long-time partner until his death in 1988. They would talk about it constantly. I remember sitting on one of their yachts with the two of them and a young French woman who was obviously there for Harold. Harold started talking about the intimate parts of a woman's anatomy and how some girls could do coin tricks with their vaginas. And this conversation just went on and on. Fritz had a parade of hookers that he would take on his boat, but when we got together, he got rid of them, and I got the impression that they were around Harold too.

"The first time I met Harold was in 1971 when I was invited on his yacht with my parents, who knew him from Hollywood. In fact, that was when I met Fritz for the first time too. It was obvious that Harold was looking me up and down—I was only twenty-two—and I got the impression that he was a total fiend. Fritz was a little more charming when it came to seduction, but Harold's style was to reach out and grab your ass. There was something bestial about him, something menacing and predatory. I got the sense that if you didn't do what he wanted, then he could be cruel.

"I never really saw Grace and Harold together. He would be on the yacht with his girls, and she would be off somewhere else. Looking back, the whole atmosphere was as close to a bacchanal with Caesar as possible, all food and sex and drugs."[36]

In the early 1970s Robbins's jet-setting lifestyle, flitting between Beverly Hills and the South of France, spoke of an almost impossible glamour. Each week in Le Cannet he ordered bagels, lox, and sturgeon to be flown in from Barney Greengrass in New York; he purchased a watch, advertised as the most expensive in the world, because it featured a mechanism that kept track of leap years; and he spent thousands of dollars on parties that were to become legendary. How had this man, who claimed to have been born an orphan and brought up in Hell's Kitchen, managed to transform himself into the world's highest-earning author? In August 1971 broadcaster Alan Whicker, who specialized in televisual portraits of the rich and the risqué, visited him in Cannes to find out.

Whicker, who labeled Robbins "The Thrill Peddler," estimated that the writer had sold 100 million copies of his books in thirty-two different languages. Viewers saw him sailing around the Mediterranean on the *Gracara*; lunching with Grace, Adréana, and Fritz Loewe on the terrace of a beach restaurant; and taking charge of a poolside barbecue at his home in Le Cannet. Wearing multicolored striped trousers, an open-necked shirt, a lilac hat, and enormous sunglasses that almost eclipsed his face, Robbins looked like a cross between a troubadour and a playboy.

What did he think, asked Whicker, about some critics' opinion that he was both the most expensive and the worst writer in the world? "How do they reconcile the two?" replied Robbins. None of his books had made a loss, he said; in fact every one of his novels had earned back the original advance two or three times over. "I think I'm the best writer, and because I'm the best writer, I'm the least expensive," he said. He believed that he received so much negative criticism because it was human nature to attack those at the top; and although he undeniably enjoyed his cars, his houses, and his yacht, he was not, he said, excessively materialistic. "I don't want to be rich," he maintained. "I just want to be happy."

The film also included footage of the two men in New York, walking around the area of Hell's Kitchen where Robbins said he had grown up. Whicker accepted everything Harold said as the truth, and he went on to revel in the contrast between Robbins's harsh upbringing as "a Manhattan Oliver Twist" and the extravagance of his current lifestyle.

Whicker also quizzed Grace about her husband. In a fake English accent she told the interviewer that she had adored being courted by Harold and presented her life with her husband and daughter as an idyll of ordinary domesticity. Had it ever crossed her mind, because of the sexual nature of Robbins's books, that strangers might look at her and wonder what she and Harold did in bed? No, it did not, she replied. "We have a bedroom life [but] we don't talk about it . . . He lives his own life with me and Adréana, that's really true," she said. "He's a very basic person." Now that Robbins seemed to have everything a man could possibly want—two beautiful homes, a fleet of cars, a yacht, a successful career, unlimited wealth, a glamorous wife, and an adorable daughter—what made him run? "Me," said Grace.

The interview coincided with the publication of *The Betsy*, which Whicker described as Robbins's most explicit novel to date. "There will be as much sex in this book as in my others," said Robbins, "or as much as takes place in the back of an automobile."[37] In addition to a female character who climaxes to the sound of car engines, the book also includes descriptions of sex between a young woman and her father-in-law, Loren Hardeman, and an erotically charged encounter between a French dressmaker and the founder of the car dynasty who possesses a penis like *"un vrai canon."*

The novel appeared a couple of months after the publication of Arthur Hailey's competing title, *Wheels*, also about the Detroit motor industry, which went on to become the best-selling novel of 1971, pushing Robbins's book down into fifth place. *The Betsy* received some appalling reviews. "It is no more a novel than Frankenstein's monster was a human being," wrote one commentator,[38] and Henry Ford II was reportedly so appalled by the book that he withdrew the use of Robbins's courtesy cars. "I went out and bought three Rolls and three Jensens," Robbins said. "Ford can go **** himself."[39]

16

"Sometimes when I'm tired but have some work to
finish, I might take a Dexedrine or snort some coke."
—Harold Robbins

IN THE DARKENED room the white golf-ball-size sphere seemed to
give off a strange luminescence. Harold walked over to the low-lying
glass table and picked up the razor blade. With almost surgical precision
he set to work, first slicing off slivers of the pharmaceutical-grade
cocaine, then cutting each segment into smaller pieces, and finally
chopping it into a fine powder. As he prepared the drug, he occasionally
licked his finger, dabbed it into the candy, and rubbed the coke into his
lips. When he had finished, he took a fifty-dollar note from his wallet,
rolled it up, and snorted a couple of lines. The effect was almost instant;
he felt his heart racing, his mind sharpening, his mood lifting.

In the early to mid-1970s drugs, particularly cocaine, amyl nitrate,
Quaaludes, and marijuana, became a permanent fixture in Robbins's
life. "I remember Harold had this pharmaceutical book, full of details
about different drugs, how many milligrams you should take to help you
up and down," says his friend Patrick Young. "He liked pure cocaine,
and mushrooms too. He also had this fountain pen, a Mont Blanc I think
it was, that had an adjustable top. When he turned it, it would dispense
cocaine, and he'd take a quick sniff now and again without anybody
knowing what he was doing. Yet for all this he had a mind like a trap; he
could analyze things incredibly well."[1]

Caryn Matchinga remembers lunching with him at Scandia, where
he would often whip out of his jacket pocket what looked like an

ordinary Vicks inhaler. "When coke got big out here in L.A., he would put it inside this inhaler and snort it in the restaurant," she says. "And nobody would be any the wiser."[2]

Cocaine proved to be an aid to self-definition, helping Robbins bring his own identity, or at least an imagined version of it, more clearly into focus. After a few sniffs he felt not only more confident and outgoing but better able to play at being himself. Larry Flynt recalls being invited to the author's house, where "there would be a big silver bowl, two feet wide, full of cocaine," he says. "People would just help themselves to it. Harold didn't really drink, but he did like cocaine. I don't know why he did it for as long as he did. I think he took it for twenty-five or thirty years. But he always seemed totally in control of himself and what he was doing."[3]

But his hedonistic, drug-fueled lifestyle had one casualty: his elder daughter, Caryn. She had grown up feeling rejected and unloved by her father and, at boarding school in the United States, had started to experiment with drugs, hoping that the experience would take her out of herself, if only for a few hours. Later Harold said that when she was seventeen she was "into all the drugs."[4]

Robbins's anxieties surrounding Caryn's drug abuse found expression in his novel *The Inheritors*, in which he describes a young girl's gradual descent into addiction and subsequent fatal overdose. The narrator walks into the bathroom and discovers a selection of drug paraphernalia—a teaspoon, a handful of used matches, a hypodermic syringe—and an envelope containing a fine crystalline powder.

"Suddenly it all made sense to me . . . The strange glazed look in her eyes that night in New York I went to pick her up at the party. The funny way she slurred her speech at times as if her tongue were too thick to say the words . . . But I still couldn't believe it . . . My Darling Girl was a first-class addict."[5]

Confronted by the knowledge that one's child was abusing drugs, many parents would feel the need to set an example. But Harold not only continued to feature cocaine, speed, poppers, and pills in his novels, he kept on using them in his private life as well. If he ever made the link between his debauched existence and the misery endured by Caryn, then he certainly did not articulate it, and he seems not to have suffered any guilt for his actions. Of course, Caryn's taste for durgs could have been acquired independently; one did not need a high-living father to be tempted by illegal substances. And to Harold's credit his younger daughter, Adréana, grew up to be sweet natured, well balanced, and clean living. But it seems certain that, to some extent at least, Caryn did blame her father for her unhappiness. She felt that he had not fought hard enough for her and that, fundamentally, he did not love her enough.

Harold tried to talk to her, but every conversation ended in bitter recriminations and barbed accusations of betrayal. The estrangement of his daughter was one of his life's greatest disappointments, a sadness that continued to haunt him and something he kept hidden from public view. His audience did not want to hear that side of his story. They wanted a sustained narrative of success, a slice of the dream. He had no choice but to continue playing a part.

At the beginning of 1972 Robbins jetted between New York and Los Angeles, putting the final touches to the film *Yao*. "I think Harold was very proud of the finished product—it was the same footage [as the French series], obviously cut down to feature film length and with different dialogue," says Diana Jervis-Read. "And he organized a premiere in Richmond, Virginia, which had a large black population, in order to benefit a sickle cell anemia charity."[6] The critics—and the public—were less than enthusiastic; one observer noted, "Some people say it combines some beautiful visual sequences with some of the worst dialogue the writer has ever concocted."[7]

Robbins's royalties continued to rise: at the beginning of the year Trident reissued *The Carpetbaggers* in hardcover to cash in on the recent Howard Hughes hoax. (Author Clifford Irving had tried to pass off a fake autobiography of the billionaire tycoon as the real thing.) That wheeze resulted in an extra 51,000 sales. His publisher guaranteed him an income of $1 million a year for the rest of his life. "What else is there to do?" he said of work. "You can only go to so many cocktail parties and chase so much ****."[8]

He started to think about returning to his early Depression-era novels and conceived a book along the lines of *A Stone for Danny Fisher* that he entitled *Memories of Another Day*. He told friends that he was ready to start the novel—which would be about America's labor union movement—in the summer of 1972 but was reluctant to immerse himself in the actual writing. "It's all in my head, and the story and characters develop as I go along," he said at the time.[9]

Besides, his other business interests distracted him. In June he flew from France to Los Angeles, where in addition to promoting the paperback edition of *The Betsy*, he launched his new company, Harold Robbins International, a film production and distribution enterprise, which was designed, in the words of vice president Jeff Livingston, to share its profits with producers from "the very first dollar of income . . . The way it is structured, the producers and us, the distributors, should get our investments back at precisely the same time . . . It's a direction of the future, not the present."[10] Its first release would be the film provisionally entitled *Outside In*, a movie about Vietnam draft dodgers that was released as *Red, White and Busted*.

While in the States, Robbins also had a meeting with Metromedia about a new television series, *Dynasty of Death*, based on Taylor Caldwell's novel, which he wanted to turn into a contemporary *Forsyte Saga*, and continued negotiations with Warner Bros. executives about the casting for a film version of *The Betsy*. He wanted Al Pacino for the role of Angelo Perino and thought John Wayne would be perfect as the automobile tycoon Loren Hardeman. "I think Duke Wayne is one of the greatest actors alive," he said. "Even though he won an Oscar, he's overlooked because he is so good that he makes it all look too easy. I'm going after him."[11]

From New York Robbins flew to Britain to launch the paperback edition of *The Betsy*. While he was in London, New English Library presented their star author with a gold book to celebrate 5 million paperbacks sold in the U.K. Success, he told a critic at this time, had given him the "freedom to live as I want to live. I know I've got a playboy, frivolous image, but I work, you know. I've got four companies apart from the writing."[12]

One observer, who met him in his suite at the Savoy, noted that his hair, which the previous year had been "Persil white," was now "bootbrush black." "I think it is very important not to look or feel your age and to look the best you can," said Grace. "Harold's hair would be snowy if it wasn't colored. Coloring his hair has made all the difference.

If you feel you look younger, you tend to act younger."[13] But for all his youthful accoutrements—the self-consciously flamboyant clothes, the newly dyed hair, the constant ingestion of modish drugs—Harold was beginning to feel his age. Friends noticed that he looked exhausted; the skin beneath his eyes was crinkled like crepe paper, and in August, on his return to Le Cannet, he felt so lacking in energy that he worried he was suffering from a "total fatigue illness."[14]

His low spirits were brought about, at least in part, by the decision of Warner Bros. not to proceed with a film version of *The Betsy*. In July, after completion of the final screenplay, the studio wrote to CVC to inform them that the $4 million they wanted to make the film was vastly over budget. Robbins had invested so much emotionally in the project that the news left him feeling depressed. He had assumed that, as the film would be produced by his own company, little could go wrong. Robbins was so angry that in August he told his partners in CVC that he wanted out. Schwimmer and Geller were "great guys, but we just didn't see things the same way," he told Army Archerd.[15] "Robbins was basically lazy and was interested in having fun," says Alden Schwimmer. "Yet having said that it was hard not to like him."[16]

He spent the rest of the summer trying hard to distract himself from the lingering sense of frustration left by the Warmer Bros. rejection. He enjoyed a few days with Paul Gitlin and his wife Zelda, who came to visit him and Grace in Le Cannet. He took tea with Frankie Spitz at the Carlton Hotel in Cannes. He sailed to Bandol, the Porquerolles, and Sardinia on the *Gracara* and enjoyed dinners at L'escale and Le Mechaut Loup with friends such as Count Ernesto de Stephano and screenwriters Ben and Norma Barzman, who had a house in nearby Mougins. The first time Robbins invited the Barzmans to a Sunday lunch, he served bagels, lox, and sturgeon that he had had flown over from the States. Grace showed Ben around the garden, while Harold took Norma on a tour of the house. She remembers following him through Villa Grazia, up an unsteady flight of stairs to what looked like a pigeon coop. "He climbed into this little room, that was not big enough to turn around in," says Norma. "It had no windows, but that's where he liked to work."[17]

As Norma was descending the narrow stairs she felt a "gigantic violent thrust" ripping into her back, a force that tore her dress and panties and almost knocked her over. From behind she heard Harold chuckling. "Don't be disappointed," he said holding up an enormous dildo. "Even *my* penis isn't *that* big."[18]

Harold was, says Norma, a "very generous, kind, crazy person . . . He had a very big talent—he could have been a real writer—but he made up his mind that he wanted to be a zillionaire and he did it. But there's no question that he sacrificed his talent, no question at all. Ultimately I think of him as a real showman, someone who very much enjoyed the performance."[19] She recalls inviting Harold and Grace to a barbecue at their home; at the end of the evening Harold took her to one side and told her that, while her meat was good, she could get a better cut of steak. He arranged to meet her the next morning at a boucherie in the Marché Forville. As Norma arrived, she spotted a group of men dressed in butchers' whites and was amazed to realize, as she approached, that one of them was Harold. When he saw Norma, he ordered the butcher boy to bring out a carcass, and after placing it on a marble counter, Harold proceeded to cut it up in an expert and delicate manner. "When he had finished, he wiped his hands on his bloodstained apron," recalls Norma, who was rather taken aback. " 'I toldja,' he said. 'There's nothing I haven't done. I mean it, babe. *Nothing*.' "[20]

In October, after a cruise to Porto Cervo and a trip to Rome, Harold flew back to Cannes, and at the end of the month he returned to Los Angeles. He attended a screening of *Save the Tiger*, the film made from Steve Shagan's novel, and then on 31 December he hosted another of his famous New Year's Eve parties at the house in Coldwater Canyon. Robbins did not want the evening to be a repeat performance of his previous New Year's Eve party, in which guests such as Henry Fonda and Charles Bronson surrounded themselves with their own friends in separate rooms and did not mix. He orchestrated the event so that his guests could experience what it would be like, if only for one night, to inhabit one of his novels.

"Grace and I were bored at last year's event, so this year we decided to do something different," he said. "I'm going to have scantily clad girls eating grapes out by the pool. I may even have topless waitresses."[21] Rooms were equipped with waterbeds, flowers floated on the surface of the pool, masseurs were employed to massage feet, and

Harold, that night dressed in a dark jacket and frilly open-necked shirt, even hired several little dinghies, their sides emblazoned with the name *Gracara* after his yacht, piled high with fresh fruit. At the end of the evening a rather rotund, drunk Shelley Winters launched herself into one of the miniature vessels and, surrounded by pineapples, bananas, grapes, and mangoes, and singing an Italian song at the top of her voice, paddled around the swimming pool.

Other guests included Jack L. Warner, Glenn Ford, David Jannsen, Charles Bronson and Jill Ireland, Ernest Borgnine, Irving Wallace, Joe Wambaugh, and George Hearst Jr. Catering was laid on by the Great American Food and Beverage Company—the food was described as "lavish even by the Robbins's standards"[22]—while the music was provided by the young Earl of Bradford, who had recently started work as a disk jockey on the West Coast. "Harold provided six hookers at the party including a beautiful pair of twins," he says. "I tried to become friendly with the twins, but I was told that they had not been hired for me."[23]

That night actor Laurence Harvey and model Paulene Stone were married at Robbins's house. "In fact, Harold was responsible for Larry and me getting married," says Paulene, who wore a long, apricot-colored silk dress and a matching turban with a diamond clasp and an ostrich feather. "Larry was dragging his heels, and at some point in October of that year Harold said, 'I don't know when you guys are going to get married. I know, get married at my house. Get married on New Year's Eve!' Harold was one of those old-fashioned Hollywood guys, one of those men who love great big cars and great big houses but who do not have great big taste. But he was jolly and on my side."[24]

After the wedding ceremony, conducted by candlelight and with "Strangers in the Night" playing in the background, Harvey picked up his daughter Domino, kissed her, and proclaimed, "Now you're legitimate!"[25] Richard Bradford remembers that the party went on until six o'clock the next morning, "and then at seven a.m. Harold and Grace had breakfast with everyone who had worked that night," he says. "Most of the people we worked for treated us like shit—they were new money. But not Harold and Grace. They were charming, so appreciative. Years later, when I used to run the Caviar Bar in

Knightsbridge, Harold would come by—he was always very natural and had none of the airs and graces that other people gave themselves. He called a spade a fucking shovel."[26]

The music of the orchestra was carried to shore on the gentle night breeze, its cadences rising and falling with the wind and the waves. Stepping on to the launcher, Harold breathed in the balmy, salt-tinged air. As the boat took its passengers out into the bay, he saw the lights of Cannes twinkle and glint before him, an expanse of diamonds scattered against a dark velvet sky. When he approached the two yachts—one so big it couldn't fit into the harbor, bearing the two hundred or so guests, the other carrying the orchestra—the party was already in full swing. He helped Grace out of the boat, followed by Diana Jervis-Read. All were guests of his friend Adnan Khashoggi, the Saudi-born businessman and arms dealer whose wife, Soraya, was celebrating her birthday. Harold was fascinated by the couple, especially Soraya, who could have stepped straight out of one of his books.

Born plain Sandra Daly, the illegitimate daughter of a hotel waitress from Leicester, she went on to transform herself into a jet-setting beauty—Norman Parkinson called her the most naturally beautiful woman he had ever photographed—with homes in Marbella, New York, London, and Switzerland. That night, as Harold was handed a glass of vintage champagne, he stepped back and played the role of the voyeur, watching as the rich, the famous, and the louche helped themselves to the bowlfuls of beluga caviar on the table. He'd had a few drinks, for sure, but his mind was as sharp as anything. Standing there, propping up the bar, he observed a guest stub out a cigarette in a bowl of caviar and later witnessed an argument between Soraya and Adnan that culminated in the wealthy socialite throwing a necklace given to her by Khashoggi across the deck of the ship. After a lavish dinner the yacht, a floating monument to decadence, cruised around the Mediterranean, its passengers lost in a hedonistic haze.

Almost immediately Harold realized that the event, held in June 1973, and his hosts were ripe for fictional exploration. He should have been writing *Memories of Another Day*, the novel that, back in February, had netted him $2 million, reportedly the biggest literary advance in the history of publishing. But he put the project to one side to focus on *The Pirate*, the story of Baydr Al Fay, a rich sheikh, and his American-born wife Jordana, a couple alleged to be modeled on Adnan and Soraya Khashoggi. "I remember Harold showing me a piece of paper, a three-by-five index card on which he said he had written the whole outline of a book," says Victor Lownes, the vice president of *Playboy*. "It was nothing more than a series of points, a couple of words on each line, for his book *The Pirate*, the one that is supposed to be about Khashoggi."[27]

Robbins had met the superrich couple in the early 1970s, after being introduced by Fritz Loewe. "I was flying to Nice on a very turbulent plane and grabbed the hand of an old, sweet man next to me," says Soraya. "This total stranger calmed me down and talked me through the landing. I felt I had been rude and asked what he did, and he told me he was a composer, that he was Fritz Loewe. I met Harold and Grace the next day on their yacht, and it was the beginning of a huge friendship. My first impression of Harold was that he was a tough, rough, 'what you see is what you get' sort of person, completely no bullshit, and we hit it off straightaway. He was funny, irreverent, naughty, wild and edgy; the polished side that was on show on the yacht was just a facade."[28]

Harold and Adnan shared a love of big yachts, fast living, and even faster women. The two men cruised the Mediterranean together, their boats serving as floating extensions of their egos (and quite possibly, to use a very Harold Robbins word, their "manhoods" as well). "Harold liked to go to this Moroccan restaurant in Cannes where they were belly dancers," says Khashoggi. "He had a wicked sense of humor and was entertaining in character. When you go out socially, it's important to have people around you who are funny and clever. But he was also a very sweet man, quite a gentle man. He was popular with women because he was good with charming talk. He seduced them with his ability to speak to them, which is a big asset, is it not? Yet he could lose his temper sometimes, especially with his wife, and on occasions we had to calm him down.

"He didn't talk about the past, we lived only in the present. Neither did he talk about his novels—that side of him he kept private. Even when he was writing *The Pirate*, he didn't tell me about it. Although I was a little surprised that he had taken the ambiance of my lifestyle—

the airplanes, the yachts, the fine food—I wasn't angry with him at all. I was happy to contribute to the enjoyment of his readers. Also, the main character and I do not share anything in common apart from the style of life."[29]

Soraya denies that the novel contained coded portraits of Adnan and herself. Rather, she maintains that certain aspects of Jordana were based on none other than Grace Robbins. "Grace was in love with the real 'Pirate,' Badr Al Mullah, from the time she met him until he died," says Soraya. "The real Badr was gentle, slim, soft spoken, rich and very handsome, an absolute dream. He had been married to a lovely Arabic wife in the Middle East and had had children, but he traveled constantly. I also know that many of the scenes written about Jordana were actually based on Grace, such as the one in the book describing Jordana belly dancing—Grace was an expert belly dancer and had expensive, authentic costumes made to order. I guess Harold must have been really pissed off with her at times. Harold did have a nasty streak—I always thought Grace was scared of him—and let's just say she responded to kindness from others."[30]

Robbins wrote the novel quickly, mostly at the office he rented off San Vicente Boulevard that he shared with Caryn Matchinga, completing it in May 1974. He delivered a copy of the book to his American publisher, then flew to London to hand in the manuscript to New English Library. There he also took the opportunity to buy an oatmeal-colored Jensen and do a couple of interviews. He explained to broadcaster Clive Jordan that the reason he got so much vituperative criticism was that it was human nature to attack those who were more successful.

But in countries other than Britain and America he was treated rather differently: "The Germans think I'm marvelous, the Russians think I have a view of modern society that is extraordinary in American writing, the Scandinavians think that I am a master psychologist and probably the best writer on inter-personal sexual relationships they have ever come across," he said. He had recently heard that a publisher in the Soviet Union had acquired his whole back catalog; the only other American author to receive this accolade was Robbins's hero John Steinbeck. "Everybody has their own bag about me, but none of them review my success as the American and English critics do."[31]

From London Robbins flew to the South of France, for another summer of pleasure, before jetting back to America. Warner Bros. had expressed interest in making a film of *The Pirate*, with a screenplay to be written by Robbins himself. For the first time in years the author planned to be in Europe, not Beverly Hills, for the New Year, and so in late September, with a eye for self-promotion, he organized a Middle Eastern–themed party on the Warner Bros. soundstage in Los Angeles. A camel, standing on a red carpet, greeted guests such as Adnan Khashoggi, Peter Finch, Irving Wallace, Hugh Hefner, Aaron Spelling, Ringo Starr, Zsa Zsa Gabor, Rita Hayworth, Glenn Ford, Ryan O'Neal, Doug McClure, Ernest Borgnine, and George Chakiris. "Harold always threw parties on a grand scale, but I think he really did that for Grace's benefit, who loved socializing more than him," says Chakiris. "I liked Harold—you felt you were in the presence of a real intelligence, a natural intelligence. He was kind and generous and very easy to be around. I got the feeling that Grace was in love with her husband, but I did hear that they had an arrangement, that they had orgies and the like."[32] Inside there were topless dancing girls, belly dancers, fortune tellers, and at midnight an enormous cardboard cut-out of the book descended from the ceiling. On top of the giant maquette stood a girl who proceeded to whip off her bikini. "I can even see her boobs from here," said Robbins.[33]

In October he was back in London for a launch party of *The Pirate* at Les Ambassadeurs. Guests included Victor Lownes, the Earl of Pembroke, Diana Rigg, Jane Asher, and Michael Caine, who referred to Robbins as, rather cryptically, "the Elizabeth Taylor of authors."[34] The entertainment was provided by belly dancers and eight models dressed in hot pants, wearing black eye patches and brandishing swords. At the party Robbins's publisher presented the author, whom one observer described as "nut-brown and petit," with a 22-carat-gold-nugget, diamond-studded pendant for selling more than 7.5 million copies in the U.K.[35]

Twenty-four hours before publication of the novel Robbins faced a legal challenge from a mysterious Miss X, who turned up at the High Court in London to request an injunction on the grounds that "people might think she was the person on whom one of the central characters in *The Pirate* had been based." "By a process of elimination," said

Philip Jacobsen, "it can be deduced that the person Miss X felt people might link her with was Jordana—a 'golden girl from California' who falls for and marries The Pirate of the book's title, a young Arab."[36] That woman, unidentified at the time, was Soraya Khashoggi. Adnan Khashoggi confesses that perhaps his then wife "took it [the book] too personally, but not me."[37] Caryn Matchinga remembers the day when Soraya telephoned her and asked her whether she would support her in the courts. "She wanted to sue Harold [for what he had written in *The Pirate*]," she says. "She wanted me to testify on her behalf. I said, 'To what?' and she said, 'That I'm not that way.' I told her from the little I had read of the book you are that way! And that was the end of our friendship."[38]

Soraya maintains that the reason she "took the trouble to go to court the day before U.K. publication and have some pages removed," was that she wanted to "put the record straight" and correct the "total fabrication of the tabloid press."[39] She also felt betrayed by a man she had assumed to be her friend. "He told me that he wrote *The Pirate* because he had to pay a $300,000 tax bill," she says. "Yet I felt he stabbed me in the back by using characters similar to us and making people believe that we did those things—the adultery, the drugs—when we didn't."[40]

But on 2 October Mr. Justice Roberts allowed publication to go ahead. Buoyed up by the ruling, Robbins embarked on a round of interviews to promote *The Pirate*. On 12 October he appeared on the U.K. talk show *Parkinson*, together with writer Anita Loos and comedian Harry Secombe. He told the television interviewer that he would earn approximately twenty pounds a word for *The Pirate*, adding, "Now that I know how much I'm earning, I would like to see the money." Although he was fabulously wealthy one day, the next he would be broke. He trolled out his familiar stories: how he had worked for gangsters Lucky Luciano and Frank Costello, and how he had forgotten how many times he had been married. "It took a long time to grow up," he said. "I don't think I really grew up until I was forty, when I had my first daughter." Parkinson then broached the tricky subject of sex. How did Robbins do the research for the erotic scenes in his novels? "I try to do that personally because I think that's the most fun," he said. Had he been to an orgy? Yes, he replied. Did he enjoy it? "Not as much," he replied. As when? "As when I was younger," he quipped.[41]

If critics complained that the women in his novels were little more than sex toys or mindless mannequins, then all he was doing, he said, was reflecting society. But he revealed that his next novel—which he had already entitled *The Lonely Lady*—would address this very issue, as it would focus on a "modern young woman's search for identity in this new and changing society." Rather than supporting traditional chauvinistic attitudes, Robbins claimed that he was a feminist. When he was working at Universal, he had discovered that women in the company earned 60 percent less than men for doing the same jobs. After exposing the discrepancy, Robbins ordered that the women should receive a pay raise, an action that resulted in union action. "I think he had a love-hate relationship with women," says Caryn Matchinga. "I think he adored them, needed them, wanted them. But also I think he thought that they were all out to use him. Down deep I don't think he trusted them."[42]

Diana Jervis-Read, however, disagrees. "Harold loved women, and he liked them—that's what women felt," she says. "I remember when my marriage broke up—this would be in the early seventies—and it was a very difficult time for me. I wasn't going to tell Harold, who was traveling back from L.A. to his house in France, but he asked if everything was all right, and I completely went to pieces. He sat next to me, with his arm around my shoulder, for two and a half hours. He didn't move or talk, he just sat there. After I had pulled myself together, he told me to pack a bag, and he took me back to the South of France with him for the rest of the summer. That was a side of Harold the public never saw."[43]

Although Soraya Khashoggi had felt betrayed by Harold, after her divorce she found herself drawn to him. "Only when I knew for certain that Grace was in love with another man and I was single again did I agree to meet Harold alone and we grew closer," she says. "We met for dinners and time together, often in London. He seemed to me steeped in some of the shady characters that he wrote about. For example, once I needed a private detective, the best in the world, and thought only Harold would know someone that seedy and brilliant, and indeed, he found him in one phone call. Harold was really attractive to a woman like me who had been put on a pedestal, with lots of people bowing and scraping. I always think of him similar to Byron, mad, bad, and dangerous to know."[44]

17

"While we were on the yacht we got this strange feeling that we were being spied on or that Harold had bugged our room . . . we didn't want to become characters in one of his novels."

—Steve Jaffe

THE PETITE BRUNETTE walked onto the deck of the yacht and gazed out across the shimmering azure sea. She took a deep breath and thought of her husband back in the United States. The day—22 November 1974—was their wedding anniversary, their ninth, and she felt a pang of regret that he couldn't be with her to celebrate. She thought back on their time together, the fun they had had, the romance, the high living, so many good times. There was nobody quite like Harold. He may have not been the most handsome man—he was balding, had a double chin, and had developed something of a paunch—but he was generous, romantic, funny, and adventurous in bed. She loved to listen to his stories, his mad, crazy stories, about how he had survived an attack on his submarine, how he had been taught to fly by Howard Hughes, how his first wife had died after being bitten by a parrot. She didn't particularly care whether they were true or not. They made her laugh, and that was all that mattered.

She wondered how he was occupying himself in Los Angeles. She imagined him sitting at the bar drinking an early morning coffee in their Beverly Hills home, driving his car down Sunset, taking a few calls at his office, having lunch with one of his friends at Scandia. She smiled to herself as a wave of longing surged through her. She wished she could be with him, but she knew he had to work. That's what he had told her anyway. She tried not to think what he got up to when he wasn't writing. At first it had not been easy to accept the fact he slept with other women. She told herself that at least he was being honest, unlike many of the slimeball husbands of her girlfriends who sneaked off behind their wives' backs. And she could understand that if Harold wrote about sex, it was only fair he should want to experience it with many different partners. She liked to think that she gave him what he wanted in bed. And after being initially shocked at the idea, she had even found herself enjoying hosting the odd orgy. What worried her now was the thought that one day he would meet a woman who could offer him more than she did: not only beauty, charm, and great sex but also intellectual stimulation, an equal meeting of minds, companionship, a higher social network; in short, someone who might one day replace her as his wife.

Suddenly her heart began to race as she saw Jackie, the yacht's cook, come toward her holding something behind her back. Jackie couldn't help smiling as she recalled the conversation she had had with her boss. Mr. Robbins had phoned to ask her to buy some red and white roses and arrange them in the shape of a heart, with a figure nine in the middle.

"Surprise!" said Jackie, handing over the bouquet.

"Oh, my," said Grace, for once almost lost for words.

"Aren't they beautiful."

Grace was delighted, so touched. As she posed for an informal photograph with Adréana, holding her white broad-brimmed hat to keep it from blowing off in the wind, she knew she still adored Harold. Sex was one thing, but love was quite another. Robbins maintained that he too was still crazy about his wife. Women he had known before Grace had tried to change him, but not her. "They know what sort of guy you are before they marry you, and then they want everything different . . . Grace doesn't try to own me. She's her own person. And she's beautiful."[1]

Although Harold claimed that, while he was not necessarily physically faithful, he was emotionally constant to Grace, this was not entirely true, as Caryn Matchinga discovered. "People thought that I

was this hot chick he was banging, and although I'm not going to say I
never kissed him or anything—we did go to bed a couple of times—I
wouldn't call it an affair," she says. "I don't think we could have had
any kind of [working] relationship if we had not done it. We got it out
of the way. But Grace thought I was at it with him all the time, and I
wasn't. She was always pissed with me anyway. She had a bigger
problem with me than any of the bimbos he was sleeping with. I think
she thought I was more of a threat, more wife or partner material.
Grace would want to come onto the yacht, and he would say she
couldn't because 'Caryn is here and she's got brains.'

"I remember one day we were sitting in his office, and we had just
worked out a whole bunch of problems—and he said to me, 'If I
divorced Grace, would you marry me?' I said no, he was far too old for
me. But he liked having me around because I was smart, and quick and
fast. I am very good at seeing through people, and he enjoyed having a
good conversation with me. I didn't like it when he tried to talk to me
about orgies and different sexual practices, things he thought might be
a turn-on for me. I remember him telling me how great it is when you
put beads up your ass and the girl pulls it out. I found all that
disgusting."

For all his sexual braggadocio, Robbins was, Caryn feels, a fraud.
"Harold liked people to think he was sleeping with everybody, but it
was all bluster and pose," she says. "One day I remember listening to
Harold and Paul [Gitlin] discussing their impotence. He liked people
to think there was something going on with various women, but I was
suspect of that." One image stays in her mind more than any other:
Harold sitting with his elbows on the desk in his office at 9000 Sunset
Boulevard, looking out at the sprawl of Los Angeles. "I felt so sorry
for him, even though this was at the height of his success," she says.
"He would stare out across the city and look like the last, saddest man
on earth."[2]

Harold may not have been able to persuade Caryn Matchinga to
marry him, but he nevertheless used her as his muse. Although he
insisted that his 1976 novel *The Lonely Lady* was inspired by Grace
Metalious, the author of the best-selling *Peyton Place*—while others
believed it was modeled on Jacqueline Susann—the book was born

out of his relationship with Caryn. The similarities between Robbins's fictional creation, an actress, novelist, and scriptwriter named JeriLee Randall, and her real-life counterpart, also an actress and screenwriter, are striking, as Caryn herself acknowledges.

"Although the book is not my life story, there is so much of me in there," she says. "Things like my car, my brother, my parents, and also Lee is my middle name. I remember thinking, after reading one page, 'My God, he remembered that conversation verbatim.' Harold told me he was writing a book about me, and I remember him calling me up one day [in the summer of 1975], when he was writing it in Cannes. He said, 'I've got some good news and some bad news . . . You're going to win the Oscar, but you become a lesbian!' My husband was not thrilled with the idea of people thinking it was me, especially the lesbian part, and so that's why Harold told the press it was based on Grace Metalious. But there is nothing in it that resembles her story at all."[3]

One of the central themes of the book is the sexual bargaining that takes place between aspiring actresses and screenwriters and Hollywood's elite. Robbins quizzed Caryn repeatedly about this, and she remembers telling him about a powerful Italian producer who begged for her to sleep with his wife, an internationally famous actress, in exchange for stardom. Sure enough, the anecdote found its way into the book. Producer and director Gino Paoluzzi, a short, balding man, promises JeriLee the part in a film on condition that she has sex with his wife, the Oscar-winning Italian-born actress Carla Maria. "Harold introduced me to the real-life producer and saw it all go on," she says. "He was successful at setting up scenes."[4]

During the course of the novel JeriLee experiences early success (a Tony Award, a marriage to a successful author) as well as bitter failure (her acting career stalls after she refuses to fall backwards onto the casting couch). In order to finance her writing career, she works as a nightclub dancer, but after a series of misfortunes she is forced to appear in a low-budget porn movie, becomes dependent on drugs, suffers a nervous breakdown, and is eventually confined to a psychiatric ward. Finally, writing offers her a way out of her misery—she pens a best-selling feminist book entitled *Nice Girls Go to Hell*—and Robbins's novel culminates in a televised Oscar ceremony when she wins an Academy Award for best screenplay. As she steps onstage to accept her statuette, she lets her dress fall to reveal an inverted Oscar, painted in gold, that "covered her breasts and stomach, the flat head of the figure disappeared into her pubic hair."[5] The gesture—together with her controversial speech, which names all the people she had to have sex with in order to get the movie made—should, by rights, have spelled an end to her career, but her agent calls to congratulate her on the spectacular publicity stunt. On the last page of the novel she hangs up the phone, busy with offers of work, walks onto her porch, and with tears smarting in her eyes looks out over the shimmering lights of Los Angeles.

Robbins's fiction can be seen as an extension of JeriLee's rebellious gesture: shocking, prurient, vulgar, and transgressive, but all the more compelling and popular because of it. His novels, like JeriLee's inverted Oscar, serve as a kind of a two-fingered salute to the literary establishment and the army of critics who constantly sneered at his success. "I just happen to think I've done better than anyone else in reflecting the times in which I live," he said. "My books are about today. I am never writing yesterday's story . . . If you can interest readers in life and tell them a little bit more about the world in which they live, and in a way that they can relate to, then you have a successful novel."[6]

While *The Lonely Lady* is not, by any stretch of the imagination, a piece of feminist fiction, Robbins was able to exploit the movement and, superficially at least, rework some of its issues and concerns into the book's fabric. Although his previous novels had featured strong female characters—Dulcie in *The Dream Merchants*, Maryann in *79 Park Avenue*, Rina and Jennie in *The Carpetbaggers*, and Jordana in *The Pirate*—*The Lonely Lady* contains Robbins's first attempt at first-person narration from a female point of view. In the central section of the book we see the world from JeriLee's perspective, and while it never approaches an "authentic" woman's voice, the narrative does convey a sense of the alienation, frustration, and sexual discrimination experienced by many women in the entertainment business.

Robbins said he felt a great deal of empathy for JeriLee, "because she does represent many of the young women that I do know in Hollywood." Although his heroine was talented, beautiful, intelligent, and popular, she remained lonely because "most of these people who have helped have sought other favors for the help, they have been making bargains," he said. "She . . . would be permitted to write a screenplay if she had an affair with the producer . . . She realizes that in order to achieve success, she had to bargain away her own female right, the right of being a woman, in order to achieve the success of an artist."[7]

It was a portrait Caryn recognized as taken from her own life. "The men ran the business out here [in Hollywood], and in their minds women were only good for one thing," she says. Was she taken advantage of? "Absolutely. I'm not the most gorgeous woman in the world, but apparently I was very sexy when I was young, so everyone wanted to sleep with me. When I went into a meeting, people found it very difficult—after all, there were only fifty women writers in the Screenwriters Guild at the time. I used my initials, C.L., and I remember one producer being so freaked out when I walked into the room because he thought that the script had been written by a guy."

Robbins employed Caryn to work on screenplays of his novels, which he would then pass off as his own. She maintains that Sidney Sheldon also paid her to write a television series, which the novelist then put his name to. "When you are young, everybody takes advantage of you," she says. "Paul Gitlin once said to Harold, 'She writes you better than you write you.' Other writers think I'm brilliant, but meantime they're all running to the bank and I'm getting nowhere."[8]

Harold started writing his fictionalized account of Caryn's story in the autumn of 1974, working on it in interrupted but intense bursts throughout the first part of 1975. He told journalist Alex Hamilton, during a visit to London in January, that he had taken the title of the novel from Phyllis Chesler's book *Women and Madness*, which contains the sentence: "No matter how high a price you pay, you're alone when you get anywhere—in a way that no man ever has to be." Hamilton described Robbins, who was wearing dark glasses and an outfit "sewn from equal parts denim and herringbone tweed," as a "man half way into a Jekyll-and-Hyde change," while Grace told her husband, "You know, I've never been jealous of any of your girls, but I hate Jerry Lee! [sic]."[9]

He spent the summer in the South of France working on the novel, but in late September he was forced to return to America to undergo an operation for a ruptured umbilical muscle. During his stay in the hospital, Harold became so bored, he thought of a good publicity stunt for that year's New Year's Eve party. Robbins, whose new novel flirted with feminism, betrayed his chauvinist roots when he came up with the idea of commissioning a calendar featuring twelve beautiful women in provocative poses that could be given away to guests. The event—the Harold Robbins Cover Girl Beauty Contest—was held at the Roxy Theater on Sunset Strip in early December, and although Robbins invited actors including William Shatner, Alan Alda, Lloyd Bridges, Bob Crane, Lee Majors, Sonny Bono, and James Brolin, only Marty Allen and Vince Edwards turned up, a sign perhaps that the author's own celebrity standing was on the turn.

As the models and actresses, including Erica Gavin, who starred in Russ Meyer's 1968 film *Vixen!*, trooped onto the stage, they were questioned about their hobbies and ambitions. One girl said she was interested in astronomy; when the emcee asked her which sign she was born under, she replied, "I said astronomy, not astrology," and he brought the interview to a swift conclusion. "It is possible that if a dedicated member of the women's movement had happened upon the scene," noted one commentator, "she might have been tempted to machine-gun the entire contents of the Roxy." When quizzed by a reporter about why he was holding the competition, Robbins replied, "Because it's fun, that's why. Everywhere I go it's business—business and gloom. I think we need to inject a little fun into life. And what better place than Hollywood to find twelve fresh new faces?"[10]

From Los Angeles Robbins flew first to New York and then on to London, before returning home to L.A. in time for his customary New Year's Eve party, which that year was held in the Crystal Room of the Beverly Hills Hotel. In addition to the twelve girls featured on the calendar—women who, Robbins said, might in the future grace the covers of his paperback books—Robbins also invited Glenn Ford, Tony Curtis, Cyd Charisse, Alex Cord, Lucie Arnaz, David Janssen, Charles Bronson, Mayor Tom Bradley, Steve Shagan, Sidney Sheldon, and gossip columnist Rona Barrett.

"I thought he was just a great character," says Barrett. "He was kind and generous and a wonderful host. His parties were like the parties in his books, and I got the feeling he would re-create them after the ones he had written about. Yet he had a lot of problems. It's always very sad when someone becomes involved with drugs, and the rumors were that he got very heavily involved. The personality and whole lifestyle changed dramatically, and it's always very sad when people of talent begin to destroy themselves."[11]

Keith Hodges designed Harold and Grace's outfits—a classic tuxedo with satin lapels for him, a wrapped chiffon dress with bugle-beaded belt for her—while columnist Lee Graham observed that Robbins was living the kind of life F. Scott Fitzgerald only dreamed about.

In February Harold invited Marshall Berges of the *Los Angeles Times* magazine into his Beverly Hills home to write an interiors piece. Robbins told the reporter that Grace had looked at twenty-five different houses until she found exactly the right one, a building with "space, atmosphere, charm." He trotted out the oft-repeated stories about his early life, anecdotes that, if the journalist had bothered to check, had their foundations in fantasy. Could traces of the real Harold Robbins be found in any of his novels?

"Sure," the author replied. "Every novelist takes a romantic view of himself in the mirror and puts that portrait on paper. The portrait probably isn't recognizable to others, but it's the way a novelist's mind works. My heroes are usually restless characters ready for a change of scenery, looking for something without quite knowing what it is. I'm that way. What I am looking for? . . . Whatever the object of my quest, I haven't really defined it to myself."[12]

He compared the writing process to the half-waking, half-sleeping state experienced by mediums during a séance. He preferred, he said, to do most of his writing in France but was often tempted by distractions such as sunlight or the sight of the grass outside. Nine out of every ten ideas did not work, but like baseball player Babe Ruth he was "always pressing, probing, searching, swinging . . . Most of the time I miss, but when I connect it's a big hit, and that's what the public sees."[13]

In April his seemingly insatiable fans greedily consumed another Robbins "big hit"—*The Lonely Lady*, a book that netted him one and a half million dollars in the first ten days of its paperback release. To celebrate its publication, Robbins threw yet another party, this time at his Beverly Hills house, for four hundred guests who included Vidal and Beverly Sassoon, Charles Bronson and Jill Ireland, Eva and Zsa Zsa Gabor, Alex Cord, Barbara Carrera, Tony Cointreau of the liqueur family, and Red Buttons. "If I had to use one word to describe Harold, it would be 'sharp,'" says Buttons. "He was always entertaining, very bright and what you might call nimble, not physically, but mentally."[14]

The same month Harold also had the idea to try and remake *A Stone for Danny Fisher* as a film. Robert Weston—former vice president of Avco Embassy and Joe Levine's assistant and now president of Harold Robbins International—wrote to Hal Wallis, the producer of *King Creole*, outlining the proposal. Robbins envisaged a joint venture between his company and Wallis, in which they would share both the costs of the production and the profits. But although Wallis tried various studios, such as Warner Bros., and United Artists, nobody felt enthusiastic about the project. The men then mooted adapting the novel into a miniseries and although negotiations rumbled on until 1982, nothing came of the proposal. "It's a fine book," commented Ted Ashley, chairman of Warner Bros., "but our feeling is that it's a story that's been told many times since Harold Robbins wrote it."[15]

Harold traveled to Cannes in May for the film festival, where he set up a number of meetings to finalize distribution of a film of *The Pirate* that he intended to produce through his own company. Before leaving for Cannes, Robbins had met with Just Jaeckin, director of films such as *Emmanuelle* and *The Story of O*, and he expected casting of the principal leads to be completed by the middle of the festival.

"We're doing it as a totally independent, because basically I've found that the end product of my books rarely resembles the books that I write in theme or character," he said. "They have what I call 'a surface resemblance' to my books. What I mean is, if they used the name of a character from my book that sometimes was as close as they got . . . I could have signed any one of three deals in Hollywood this past week without ever having to come to Cannes to do business. One of the reasons I'm not particularly anxious for deals is that I want the control . . . I've been offered eight million by one group and two separate groups have offered six million, but each of them wants the kind of control which I am not about to give them . . . What I will hold out for is the control necessary to make the kind of film I'd like to make—a Harold Robbins film that looks up on the screen like Harold Robbins reads."[16]

Unfortunately, Robbins's ambition was never realized, and for all his efforts, the novel was made into a 1978 television miniseries by the late Howard W. Koch for CBS. Franco Nero played Baydr Al Fay, with Anne Archer as Jordana, Olivia Hussey as Leila, Ian McShane as Rashid, and Christopher Lee as Samir Al Fay. When the drama was shown on BBC1 in September 1979 one critic complained that while the novel could be described as "Ali Baba and the forty varied positions," the transfer to television meant that after the censorship of the book's "juicy bits . . . there's not much left of Harold Robbins . . . What remained was an opulent *Peyton Place* with the occasional camel cast amid the Cadillacs, Bedouins, and belly dancers."[17]

The miniseries was directed by Ken Annakin, who had first met Robbins in the South of France in the mid-1960s. "My first impression of him was that he was a very smart character," he says. He was very interested in money—his background was in business—and he saw writing as a continuation of that. I felt that if he hadn't been determined to develop his talent, he would not have got very far; after all a businessman does not very easily become a writer. I admired the way he tackled writing stories—his brain allowed him to plot incredibly well—and the fact that he made a lot of money. He was very forthright and would not stand any nonsense. For instance, if you argued with him, he could, very quickly, come on strong, but that didn't make me dislike him. He swore like a trooper and would go straight at a subject. I knew what he was doing—instead of just chatting like an ordinary person, he got to the root of things, and I suspected that he would go home and make notes pretty quickly. Grace was not in any way a creative person. She was a sexy girl who provided him with what he wanted."[18]

While he was at the 1976 Cannes Film Festival, Robbins also organized a meeting with model and actress Susan Blakely—who had been cast as JeriLee Randall in a film of *The Lonely Lady*—and her husband Steve Jaffe. Harold invited the couple to spend a few days with him and Grace on their yacht, sailing from Cannes to St. Tropez and around the Mediterranean.

"He told us to meet him by the dock by eight a.m., but we arrived about half an hour late because of the traffic," says Steve. "I remember him standing there by his Rolls, next to his yacht, looking furious. I apologized for being late, but he was so angry, very cold. 'You're late,' he snapped. Later, I learned that he was so angry because he wanted to sail to St. Tropez and secure a prestigious place on the dock. You see there was, apparently, a hierarchy of places where the yachts would be displayed, and he wanted to set out early to make sure he got one of the best spots. By the time we got there, he had to make do with one of the less prestigious lots, sort of like the C parking lot of LAX."

Steve and Susan enjoyed the constant supply of oysters and fine champagne, but they were rather taken aback at Robbins's brashness and vulgarity: his loud trousers covered in a tomato soup print pattern, his sense of his own importance, and the constant bragging about his phenomenal book sales. But nothing quite prepared them for what happened next. On reaching St. Tropez, Steve, a public relations executive, had to go ashore to make an important call, but while he was using a pay phone, Robbins took the opportunity to sail out of harbor, taking Susan Blakely with him.

"He wanted to wait for another yacht to leave so he could sneak into its place," Steve says. "But Suzy was annoyed because she knew that it was an odd thing to do, to leave me on the boardwalk like that. Later [when I was back on board and] while we were sailing, she took her top off, and we soon realized that Harold had popped up from the deck below and was staring at her. He was ogling her. Throughout the afternoon it became obvious that he was flirting with Suzy, and he did not care what Grace thought.

"While we were on the yacht, we got this strange feeling that we were being spied on or that Harold had bugged our room. I got the feeling that he was interested in finding out what people were saying about him, just like W. C. Fields, who used to line his driveway with microphones. Susan and I would go into our cabin, and we would have to whisper. Perhaps this was his way of getting material for his books, I don't know, but we didn't want to become characters in one of his novels. Suzy did mention to Grace that Harold had come on to her—she did not want her to think that she was leading him on in any way—but Grace told her that they had an open relationship.

"By the time Harold delivered us to our point of origin, it was obvious that it was an experience we did not want to repeat; it was dangerous territory. I kept looking for things to like about him but did not find anything. If he was okay for a while, he'd open his mouth and spoil it by talking about himself; all of his stories starred himself, and he was infatuated by his own success. We thought he was a really unsavory guy."[19]

After the success of *Rich Man, Poor Man*, the television series made from Irwin Shaw's best-selling novel in which she staired, Susan had signed a three-picture, "pay or play" deal. She had been given a large bonus on signing the contract, but would lose money if she did not make one movie a year. Although she was given script and director approval, and despite the fact that she would lose a sizable chunk of money, Susan decided to turn down *The Lonely Lady*, because all the screenplays submitted to her were so poor. In the end the role went to Pia Zadora, whose husband Meshulam Riklis invested heavily in the 1983 film; it was later nominated in the 1990 Razzie Awards as the worst picture of the decade.

"I haven't seen *The Lonely Lady*," said Robbins soon after the movie was released. "I met, what's her name? Pia Zadora, yeah. She seems a nice girl, but not my idea of the main character. The motion picture industry is in such a state that it isn't a question of who's right, it's who puts up the money. And her husband put up the money. I think the film will be a bummer, and everyone will lose money. Except me. I got six hundred thousand dollars before it opened."[20]

18

"The dreams are gone now. I'm going to give them
what they really want."

—*Dreams Die First*

H E SAT DOWN at his typewriter, a feeling of resentment rising
within him. He was contracted to deliver another novel to Simon
& Schuster within the next year, but dreaded the thought of all those
hours spent alone. He took hold of a blank piece of paper and fed it
into the typewriter. He stared at the empty sheet, fingers poised, but
still nothing stirred within him. He would much rather be on his yacht
sailing around the Mediterranean or enjoying a few drinks with his
friends than confined to this small space, wracking his brain for
inspiration. Fuck. What was he going to write? He knew he would
have to come up with something. He had his taxes to pay, Grace's
ever-mounting shopping bills, Lillian's alimony, the upkeep on the
houses in France and Los Angeles, and a hundred other expenses. He
took a sip of strong black coffee, but that all-important first sentence
just wouldn't come. Then he had an idea.

With two fingers attacking the keyboard, he tapped out a three-line
poem: "SCREW YOU, I say. I am a man. You are a machine. / I am
your master. Screw you. / But she still sits there."[1]

It made him feel momentarily better, but within seconds the
frustration and anger were back again, growing inside him like a
malignant tumor. Writing had given him everything he had ever
desired—money, women, houses, yachts, drugs, sex, and fame—
but as he became ever more successful, he began to feel like he had

prostituted whatever talent he had originally possessed in the pursuit of his dreams. Sitting at his typewriter, which he had once described as the most fun you could have by yourself apart from masturbation, had now become a duty, a chore that he forced himself to perform just to maintain the trappings of his extravagant lifestyle. Although none of his books could ever be described as great literature—they are, at their best, perfect expressions of the popular, the brash, and the commercial—the novels that were published from the late 1970s onward reveal Robbins's cynicism and embitterment.

This was witnessed, at close quarters, by Michael Korda, who took over from Cynthia White as Robbins's editor at Simon & Schuster. Korda describes Robbins as a man with the kind of battered face one might see on a middleweight fighter who has seen better days. The corners of his mouth seemed permanently turned down, as if he had just sucked the juice out of a lemon, and his voice, rough and gravelly, sounded as if he had taken elocution lessons from a loan shark.

The first time Robbins met his new editor, the author growled, "I hear you pissed on my fucking invitation." Harold had invited Korda to spend a week on his yacht in the South of France, but lack of time had forced the editor to turn down the offer. "The kid is pussy-whipped!" Robbins laughed, as he accused Korda of being ruled by his wife. Although Korda had not mentioned the invitation to his wife, he was sure that she would not be pleased with the thought of him spending seven days at sea with a "yachtful of broads." He enjoyed the process of old-fashioned editing—working through a manuscript, correcting inconsistencies and errors—and realized early on that Robbins's attitude toward writing was rather different from the conventional approach. By this point in his career, Robbins associated the creation process with nothing more than the generation of large sums of money.

"According to the terms of his contract, the advance against royalties was paid out to Robbins as he delivered each chunk of the manuscript," says Korda.[2] On many an occasion Robbins would write a section of a novel, receive a large sum of money, jet off and spend it, and sit down to write the last part of the book only when he ran out of cash. Sometimes Paul Gitlin was forced to lock his client in a bungalow of the Beverly Hills Hotel, and "only after he had passed a certain number of manuscript pages under the door would Gitlin allow room service to send a meal in," says Korda. Robbins had also been known to jump out of various rooms in Las Vegas or Palm Springs, necessitating Gitlin to watch the author, trapped in his gilded prison, like a jailer.[3]

By the time Korda started to edit Robbins, he believes, the writer had long since lost his touch. "I don't think Harold was putting in a third of the time or thought that he used to put into a novel," he says. "By the end of this period, which was drawn out and went on for a number of years, I think Harold was sloughing off pages in exchange for a check and couldn't give a shit. I also think he had lost that capacity, either the working or mental capacity, to stop and change even if he wanted to. He was caught up on a never-ending roller-coaster of his own needs, which were very considerable.

"Although people talked about Harold's generosity and kindness to his friends, I must say that in the years when I knew him I never saw that side of his personality. I saw an abrasive, disagreeable, aggressive, challenging man who was someone you'd run a mile to avoid. He was as disagreeable and odious in the days of his success as the days of his failure. He had every reason to be generous and good-natured and happy, but he was a mighty unpleasant fellow. There was a sort of growling, sneering, aggressive bitterness to him. He was doubly difficult to be around when he was with Paul [Gitlin], especially when they'd both had a few drinks. It was like defending yourself against an army of enemies.

"I'm a very structured editor—I take a manuscript and hand it back with what needs doing. I would send him a letter [of suggested corrections], and he would say he wouldn't have time for this shit, these fucking changes. And so I would change what I wanted to change. I don't think it made any difference. When Harold was really writing, he didn't need any editing, that's the truth of the matter. But when he gave up on writing, all the editing in the world wouldn't have made those books one percent better because they were just a piece of shit to begin with."[4]

Korda remembers one instance when Robbins submitted a manuscript in which the characters in the second half of the book did not resemble those in the first half. After receiving the advance for the first couple of hundred pages, Robbins had taken off to enjoy himself, picking up the book only when he needed another injection of cash. The problem was, as Korda recalls, the author had not bothered to look over what he had written, and so the two halves read as if they belonged in two separate novels—neither the events nor the characters were consistent. During a lunch meeting to discuss the problem—at which Robbins ordered pastrami sandwiches and plates of salad with beluga malossol caviar, which he proceeded to spoon onto his lettuce leaves—Korda raised the subject. He told Robbins that he could straighten out the problem, but he just needed an indication of whether the author preferred to use the events and characters of the first half or the second. So he wouldn't have to do a thing? Robbins asked. Korda would do it all? Yes, the editor replied, his star author would not have to lift a finger or tap out one word on his typewriter.

When Robbins replied that he wanted the manuscript to stay as it was, Korda was rather taken aback. People would assume the author had made some terrible mistake, Korda said, and readers would write in the thousands to complain. Robbins remained unmoved. "Fuck 'em," he said. "Let the readers do some work for a change." Although Korda tried to persuade him, Paul Gitlin injected "You heard the man." But what about the letters of complaint? "Who gives a fuck?" said Robbins. With that the meeting was over. Korda picked up his briefcase and left. True to his word, Korda published the book as it was, and Simon & Schuster did not receive one letter of complaint. Was this because Robbins's readers "skipped over the parts between the sex scenes, or did they simply have faith in Robbins as a storyteller?" wonders Korda.[5]

After finishing *The Lonely Lady*—arguably his last "good" book— Robbins started work on a novel about the porn industry, which he entitled, rather tellingly, *Dreams Die First*. In May 1976 he told a British journalist that Universal Pictures had paid him £700,000 for the rights to the book, even though he had not yet written a word; not surprisingly, when studio executives finally saw the manuscript, they rejected it because of its hardcore content. The novel is narrated by Gareth Brendan, Robbins's first bisexual hero and founder of *Macho*, a porn magazine with a fold-out centerfold featuring a life-size "supercunt of the month."[6]

Although Robbins was neither a stylist nor a master of character, he did once have the ability to spin a good yarn. Not so in *Dreams Die First*, a book that reads like the mere notes for a novel. During the course of the narrative Gareth ingests huge amounts of drugs, particularly pure rock crystal cocaine, and the book seems to have been created under similar conditions. In fact, *Dreams Die First* could be interpreted as a self-conscious lament to extinguished hopes and long-lost talent. As Gareth says, "There was a time I used to believe in a lot of things. Honesty, decency, goodness." Now, he only wants to be rich. "When you're superrich, you've got the world by the balls. Money buys everything—society, politicians, property, power. All you have to do is have the money to pay for it."[7]

Robbins certainly had the wealth, but at this point of his career he became aware that he had lost whatever dignity and self-esteem he had ever possessed. Like Gareth Brendan, he "hit people where they live. In the balls,"[8] but by catering to the lowest common denominator, Robbins sacrificed his integrity. Ultimately, success—the achievement of the American dream—corrupted him.

"I think of his story as a dreadful warning of what happens to people who become suddenly successful," says Michael Korda. "Saying that he sold out is putting it both crudely and mistakenly, as I don't think Harold made that decision. I think it was built into Harold from the very beginning. If his schemes to co-produce movies had ever worked out, I think he would have been perfectly happy never to have set finger to typewriter again, just as long as the checks rolled in from the studio. Writing for him, [at this stage], was a chore, something he didn't want to do."[9]

His friend Steve Shagan agrees. "Harold destroyed himself not with booze, drugs, or women. He destroyed himself with success."[10]

The beginning of 1977 was taken up by the trial of Larry Flynt, the founder of *Hustler* magazine and the man Robbins had chosen as the inspiration for Gareth Brendan, the hero of *Dreams Die First*. Robbins traveled to Cincinnati to attend the final part of the five-week hearing, in which Flynt was accused of obscenity. The case was brought by Hamilton County prosecutor Simon Leis Jr., who had taken it upon himself to rid Cincinnati of sex shops, massage parlors, and magazines that he considered immoral. In February Flynt was sentenced to between seven and twenty-five years in prison and ordered to pay a fine of $11,000—a ruling that reignited the debate surrounding obscenity and free speech. The jury had to balance the undeniably distasteful content of *Hustler* magazine—which had run a series of explicit photographs, including ones of a naked pregnant woman posing with a snake; close-ups of various genital mutations; and a gallery of intimate pictures featuring readers' wives—with the right to freedom of expression. "We are genuine entertainment with no pretensions," protested Flynt, in a line that could have been spoken by Robbins himself. "We have proved that barnyard humor has a market appeal."

Certainly Flynt—like his fictional offspring, Gareth Brendan—made a fortune from filth: in 1977 he had netted somewhere in the region of $20 million from *Hustler* and from an offshoot business selling sex aids. Like Robbins, Flynt was a master of the common touch. "When I see a long word that I don't know," he said of the editing process, "I take it out."

Robbins, for one, was outraged by the verdict and in February wrote an open letter expressing his disgust. Entitled "A New McCarthyism?" the five-hundred-word piece drew parallels between the suppression of pornography and prosecution of its producers and the Communist witch-hunts of the early fifties. Although President Jimmy Carter sought the freedom of dissident writers in the Soviet Union, the basic right of expression was being denied in an American court. He went on to allege that the civil rights of the defendants were being jeopardized by the actions of the court; he accused four police officers from the Indianapolis vice squad of taking photographs of witnesses and tape-recording their remarks for possible future use. He also said that the phone in his hotel room was being bugged, an allegation he said he had had verified by an electronics expert. Surely it was no coincidence, he said, that Larry Flynt and his defense team were staying on the floor below his in the same hotel. Robbins said he was worried that certain freedoms guaranteed by the First Amendment were now about to disappear.

"Obscenity is like the concept of sin—it defies definition," said Flynt at the time. "If we start restricting adult reading habits by what's fit for children, we could be left with only Little Red Riding Hood." The view was shared by William Shawn of *The New Yorker*. "This is a very serious threat," said Shawn. "In this instance it has to do with taste, but ultimately it has to do with what our attitudes are. In a free society nobody should be the judge."[11]

Flynt, for one, was pleased to have Robbins's support, and the two men became close friends. Rather than be offended by the portrait the author painted of him in *Dreams Die First*—Gareth is a bisexual drug fiend—Flynt was amused and also slightly flattered.

"Don't forget Harold was a celebrity," he says. "He was as much a celebrity as Tom Cruise is today. There were always lots of people trying to get Harold to write a fictionalized book about them. Although *Dreams Die First* was totally fictional, there was a lot of real stuff in there. What he got from me was lots of detail such as things like how much does it cost to make a magazine, how much is the paper, how much is the color separation, the photography.

"I first met him at the Beverly Hills Hotel, and I remember coming down the steps and seeing this guy leaning up against a Rolls-Royce. I said, 'Are you Harold Robbins or the driver?' He was a very unassuming kind of guy, and if people saw him walking down the street, they might have thought he was a truck driver. When a lot of people become successful, they tend to become rather pretentious. Harold didn't have a pretentious bone in his body. He had a great sense of humor and was always pulling jokes on people. When the book came out, I said to him, 'Harold, I'm not gay,' but he just laughed. 'But you are in my book,' he said."

Did he ever go to any of Robbins's orgies? "I went to a couple," he says. "In the sixties and seventies we used to all get naked and lay in a pile. Harold always enjoyed himself—he lived every day as if it was his last one. He was a man who lived life to the full, and he played it out through the characters in his books. In the future Harold will be remembered as a liberator."[12]

Robbins continued to work on *Dreams Die First* during the spring of 1977, finishing the manuscript in April. On the seventh of that month he organized a surprise birthday party for his wife at My Place disco in Beverly Hills. Invitations read, "Bring your best mood, wear your wildest" and guests—such as Phyllis Diller, in an outfit that consisted of hot pants and boots, Jaclyn Smith, Tony Bennett, Henry Mancini, Polly Bergen, and Princess Marusia Toumanoff—had what one commentator described as a "swinging" time.[13] Waitresses wore T-shirts emblazoned with Grace's face, while the room was ablaze with yellow roses, her favorite flower. At midnight Robbins asked the question, "What does a man give a wife who has everything?"—at which point one drunken reveler yelled out, "A divorce!" Instead, four muscle-

bound men, "wearing smiles and little else," jumped out of an enormous
cake, scooped the petite Grace out of her seat, and then carried her
around the dance floor, "Cleopatra-style in a palanquin."[14] According
to friends, at the end of the night Harold offered his wife the choice of
one—or all—of the hunks as a birthday present, but Grace was
apparently too drunk to take him up on the offer. "It was high, it
was dynamite, it was fairyland" was how Harold described the party.[15]

From Los Angeles Harold flew to London for the paperback launch
of *The Lonely Lady*. He did a number of book signings, including
Selfridges in London and W. H. Smith in Manchester; appeared on
Melvyn Bragg's BBC show *Read All About It* along with Jack Higgins,
who described the narrative of Nevada Smith in *The Carpetbaggers* as
one of the finest westerns ever written; and agreed to an in-depth
interview with Jean Rook of the *Daily Express*. "Well, I've tried it
all, and some I've liked and some I haven't," he replied when "the first
lady of Fleet Street" asked him about sex, drugs, and drink. "If you live
long enough, and your health holds out, you can enjoy all life's
experiences." Had he tried homosexuality? Yes, he had, he replied,
but he found it too narcissistic for his liking. "It's like kissing yourself in
the mirror because you're afraid you won't perform well with a girl," he
said. "Homosexuality's on the increase because that's the way a lot of
young men feel now that we've acknowledged women's sexual suprem-
acy . . . Women are capable of doing wonders with sex. Men have to
repair themselves." Was he in love with Grace? Yes, he said, he was.
Was he faithful? "No. What's faithful got to do with love?"[16]

After dashing off *Dreams Die First*, Robbins decided he needed a
vacation, and he spent the summer of 1977 in Europe. On 2 June he and
Grace arrived in Athens, where they stayed at the Hotel Caravelle,
joining Ken Minns on the *Gracara* the day after. "Family all came on
after lunch," the captain of the ship wrote in his diary. "We now sit very
low in water with all the extra luggage we have here. I've never seen so
much clothing for a cruise."[17] Conspicuous consumption was the order
of the day, especially when it came to Grace, who had recently taken to
sporting a set of fourteen-carat gold fingernails bought for her by
Harold; friends say that the effect of the sun reflecting off them was
enough to nearly blind you. "She had so many jewels that if she fell off
the boat she would drown," adds Caryn Matchinga.[18]

It should have been an idyllic holiday, but Harold did not care for swimming or sightseeing. After they reached the top of the Acropolis, a reluctant Robbins asked a guide how long it would take to be shown around. When he was told that it would take at least two hours, Harold asked for a condensed version in forty-five minutes. And even then he appeared bored and unmoved. Grace, of course, did not even bother to feign interest, choosing to stay aboard the yacht. "I remember she didn't go because she wouldn't have been able to wear her high heels," says Ken.

Although Robbins had had far from an easy relationship with his elder daughter, he invited Caryn to accompany him, Grace, and Adréana on the cruise around Hydra, Milos, Santorini, Crete, and Rhodes. She accepted, but it was far from a smooth sail. Ken Minns wrote in his diary that he overheard Harold having an argument with Caryn, symptomatic of only one thing—boredom was setting in.[19] According to Jackie Minns, the problem was that Harold and Grace did not spend enough "quality time" with their children; in her view the couple were more interested in entertaining.[20]

At the end of June Harold and Grace flew from Athens to Israel, then set out on another cruise around the Mediterranean at the beginning of August, together with guests Paul and Zelda Gitlin. That summer he also invited journalist Donald Zec aboard the *Gracara* to write a two-part feature about his jet-setting life for the *Sunday Mirror*.

"The yacht on which he stood," wrote Zec, "relishing the topless beauties, bronzed and nipple-proud to starboard, has been called a 'floating aphrodisiac.' Mr. Harold Robbins, the celebrated millionaire author who owns it and who, with his floral shirt, medallions and wide straw hat resembled a Mexican bandit imitating Robert Mitchum, will dispute this description. Yet there he was, staring at the defiantly unfurled nymphs of the French Riviera and declaring, 'I can't think of anything more delicious than a horizon of naked bosoms!' "[21]

Zec was given a tour around the boat, noting the full-length mirror at the foot of the master bed; the calendar featuring women in full-frontal poses that hung alongside Lloyd's Register of Shipping; and the long line of Robbins's paperbacks next to the nautical charts. "Most of the people I meet are all sexual people," Robbins said, "so

I'm in pretty good company." The author also let it be known that when he died, he would like to be cremated, his ashes ground into a fine powder and secreted away inside a locket worn by his wife, Grace. "Then, if another guy gets into the act I can always sit on her shoulder and watch!" he said.[22]

In November Robbins traveled to London for the launch of *Dreams Die First*, a book described by Peter Lewis of the *Daily Mail* as setting a new low, "in the use of lavatory wall expletives passed off as English prose . . . As it is I regard him as one of the chief threats to public decency—not of morals—for who would take such unconvincing stuff seriously?—but of prose style."[23] He flew on to New York, where he had a launch party at Regine's. At the event, which was held mostly for the benefit of booksellers and journalists, one reporter from *The New York Times* asked him whether he really had experienced, as he had previously claimed, everything in the book, including the gay sex. Robbins related the story of how one television interviewer quizzed him about the same subject and how he had offered to kiss his male host and drop his trousers on television. "Try and remember something," he said. "I'm sixty-one. I grew up in the Depression. A lot of these experiences I had before today. There's homosexuality in orphanages . . . and these things are part of growing up."[24]

From New York he flew to L.A., where at noon on 14 December he attended the unveiling of a star named after him on Hollywood Boulevard. To celebrate, interior designer Phyllis Morris, who had decorated Robbins's house in Beverly Hills, hosted a party for her friends at her L.A. showroom, complete with two dance floors shaped like stars. For the first time in thirteen years Harold and Grace decided not to have a New Year's Eve party—the event was simply too exhausting, they said—and decided to see in 1978 in a more sedate fashion, opting for a quite dinner with Caryn and Adréana instead. On 1 January the couple went for lunch at the Polo Lounge of the Beverly Hills Hotel, where they met a man—Mexican playboy Oscar Obregon—who would subsequently introduce them to the delights of Acapulco. Robbins was about to experience a whole new range of pleasures.

19

"We could forget the political forces, Socialism, Communism, Fascism, whatever. Hedonism is the only remaining hope of mankind."

Harold Robbins

THE SCENE RESEMBLED something from one of his own books. Gorgeous women dressed in the skimpiest of bikinis mingled around the enormous swimming pool, occasionally glancing up from their reflections in the water to gaze across the enormous semicircular sweep of bay. Men—rich, dripping in gold, and with skin the color of burnt sienna—stood by the bar, knocking back their club sodas. Servants glided around the pool area, catering to the guests' every need, while the host, Oscar Obregon, dressed in what looked like a one-piece white cape and wearing a medallion around his neck and a headband to keep his curly hair in place, wandered around chatting with his friends and acquaintances. Obregon, a descendant of one of the presidents of Mexico, opened the doors of his lavish mansion—Villa Nirvana, which featured an Olympic-size swimming pool surrounded by Ionic columns on which sat torches that burned so bright that at night they seemed to light up the whole of Acapulco—to the crème of Mexican society and a few American friends. There was Warren Avis, the car rental tycoon, whose own villa, La Barranca in the exclusive Las Brisas area, was so enormous he claimed it took guests three days to explore it. Sitting by the pool was Teddy Stauffer, who with Errol Flynn "discovered" Acapulco, which had then been nothing more than a handful of buildings surrounded by the jungle, in the 1940s; he was so enamored of what he called this "beautiful, tropical paradise" that he opened a hotel for the stars, the legendary Villa Vera, where Elizabeth Taylor and Mike Todd spent their honeymoon. And standing nearby were oil baron Ricky di Portanova and his wife Sandra, friends of the Robbinses whom they had met in Monte Carlo; their Acapulco house, the forty-thousand-square-foot oceanfront Villa Arabesque, cost $3 million in the late 1970s. (Recently the "fantasy destination . . . created with royalty and celebrity in mind" came onto the market for $22 million.) Grace was in her element—she adored the di Portanovas, who were among the richest of their superrich friends. In Monte Carlo the couple invited acquaintances to eat in the bar of the Hotel du Paris, where guests were served a constant stream of pink Dom Perignon and so much caviar that waiters took to dispensing it with ladles.

Harold, however, was a little more subdued that day, preferring to enjoy a few drinks at the bar and make a few wisecracks with the staff. He got to talking to a visiting blond magazine journalist, who, with a photographer, had been commissioned to cover the party as part of a feature on the jet set of Acapulco for an American magazine. The attraction between the two was instant, and unknown to Grace, within a matter of months Harold took her as his mistress. Subsequently Robbins would buy his new lover an expensive apartment in New York and a glamorous new wardrobe from Paris; whenever Grace was in America, he would invite his mistress to stay on the yacht and in their house in Le Cannet. Harold had started to break the rules that he had set down regarding their open marriage, rules that stated that although they could both enjoy multiple sexual partners, neither of them should become seriously emotionally attached to another person nor embark on an affair; in addition, they were to be open and honest with each other.

Yet that day Grace had little to worry about. In fact, she had such a fabulous time staying at their new friend's house that she begged Harold to buy a home in Acapulco. After all, she argued, it was only a quick plane ride from Beverly Hills, much nearer than the South of France. Finally Harold relented. In fact, the so-called "pearl of the Pacific"—with its perfect climate, its glitzy discos, and its reputation for sexual experimentation—was the perfect expression of Harold and Grace: brash, vulgar, loud, and ostentatious but undeniably great fun.

Harold's worldwide sales in the late 1970s, which topped the 200 million mark, let him easily afford a villa in Las Brisas, but instead he settled on a house in the less prestigious district of Hornos Insurgentes. "He did not want to live in Las Brisas," says his friend Tony Rullan. "Once he told me, 'I came here to get away from those kind of people.'"[1] "He wanted to be away from that scene, that was so Harold," says his friend Patrick Young. "Although he loved Acapulco, one of the reasons he bought a house there was that he did not want to pay state tax in California. In order to get away with this, he had to be out of the country for six months a year. If he traveled between Acapulco and his place in the South of France, he could easily do that. I liked being with him, and he always engaged you. He made you feel like you were the most important person in a conversation. He also had a great sense of humor. He once said to me, 'I did not know I was straight until I went to a gay bar.' He was not a particularly attractive man in the physical sense—he was small, balding, with a small paunch—but the minute you talked to him, he captured you."[2]

Harold purchased the four-story, seven-bedroom house in the rather run-down area for next to nothing. "He bought it because it was eighty thousand dollars and he loved a deal," says Leslie Bricusse, who had a house in Las Brisas. "It was the most awful, broken-down, terrible thing I've ever seen. It looked like a converted parrot cage, with all these wrought iron bars. It was hideous."[3] Steve Shagan maintains, "Harold employed a man armed with a machine gun to watch the house, it was so unsafe. I asked him why on earth had he bought the place, and he replied, 'I got it cheap.'"[4]

Grace called in interior decorator friends Phyllis Morris and Eileen Kreiss, who proceeded to work "wonders" on the house. But according to friends, the result was far from spectacular. "It had palm trees made out of clay," says Nicholas Dominguez. "And it was painted in colors such as lime green, all very showy."[5] Boutique owner Esteban Matison remembers it as "the ugliest house in the whole of Acapulco . . . they put a lot of money into renovation, but it just got uglier and uglier, and the bedroom had a mirrored ceiling in the shape of an inverted pyramid."[6]

Although Acapulco was, at this time, frequented by a mix of

Hollywood royalty (Merle Oberon, Kirk Douglas, Robert Evans, Frank Sinatra), American business tycoons, and the idle rich, Robbins preferred to spend time at his modest home on the wrong side of town. "He loved having dinners in his house, he liked engaging and stimulating people," says Patrick Young.[7] Mary Wells Lawrence, the first female president of an American advertising agency and occasional resident of Acapulco, remembers one of his parties. Lawrence was wary of attending as she had heard that Robbins often used these events as a way of drumming up publicity for himself, and whereas most of the women were wearing what she describes as the local uniform of a minuscule bikini and handkerchief, she turned up for the buffet brunch dressed like a girl guide. Harold was plastered in gold jewelry and little else, while Grace "was wearing a thong bathing suit that made a point of revealing her masses of black curls—not the ones on her head."[8]

Robbins's friend Tony Rullan maintains that Harold enjoyed life's simple pleasures. "He would import hot dogs from America and then invite a few friends over," says Rullan. "He was a very basic man, a bon viveur, with a great sense of humor. I remember one day asking him why he looked so young, and he replied, 'It's because I eat a lot of pussy.'"[9]

Of course, Harold was not entirely joking. In the late 1970s and early 1980s, he enjoyed a number of long-running extramarital affairs: not only with the blond magazine journalist, but also with a young Australian former heroin addict, whom strangers took to be his daughter, and a tall and striking-looking black woman. Grace also enjoyed her fair share of dalliances. "The most important thing in my life is that I have a man who is creative," said Grace. "It's most stimulating. We never have a dull moment . . . He allows me to do what I want; he has complete trust and confidence in me. I cherish this relationship and thrive on it. It's what keeps me going."[10]

The couple, however, began to spend increasingly large chunks of time apart. If Harold was in New York—where he bought a three-bedroom apartment in the Sherry-Netherland Hotel—then Grace would be in Le Cannet. If he was in Acapulco, entertaining his latest girlfriend, then she would seek out new lovers in Beverly Hills.

Harold and Grace liked to think that having an open relationship injected extra sizzle into their marriage. The truth was that while it was sexual nirvana for Harold, Grace could not forgive him for what she thought was a betrayal. He had laid down a rule forbidding long-running affairs, and here he was breaking it. The poison of resentment ate away at the foundations of their marriage, despite the fact that, to the outside world, their world seemed solid. In 1978 Robbins bought a new house, formerly owned by Steve Crane, restaurateur, former husband of Lana Turner, and father of Cheryl Crane, at 1501 Tower Grove Drive. The seven-and-a-half-acre Beverly Hills property, over-looking Los Angeles, needed complete remodeling and refurbishing. Over the next couple of years the house was transformed into a vast high-tech living space, complete with floor-to-ceiling windows and a $30,000 computerized telephone system.

While work progressed on his new house, Harold made an effort to finish his labor movement epic, *Memories of Another Day*, the book that he had started to research six years previously. By May 1978 he had written three hundred pages, and in August of the following year he finally handed the manuscript to his publisher. "It involves my theory of genetic memory, which is what I think our inherited memories are all about," he said. "It is the story of one of our great American labor leaders, someone similar to John L. Lewis."[11] But reviewers warned readers not to look to the novel for a history of the American labor movement; rather it was the familiar Robbins story of "upward mobility tinged with sentimen-tality and violence."[12]

After completing the book—which was published only three months after its submission—Robbins escaped onto the *Gracara* for a cruise around the Greek islands with Grace and Adréana. In the autumn he traveled to Munich, Brussels, and Antwerp, then arrived in London in November for his usual spate of promotional interviews. Sue Arnold, who wrote about the encounter for the *Observer*, remembers him wearing "a crimson shirt, a white silk tie with a very fat knot that seemed to be propping up his head, and a tight black waistcoat—so tight that he looked curiously trussed-up like an oven-ready chicken."[13] She recalls him as "a short, unattrac-tive man . . . if there is proof that money gets you pretty girls he was it."[14]

By late 1979 Harold had embarked on yet another passionate love affair, this time with the photographer and journalist Ini Asmann, whom he had met the previous year at the Cannes Film Festival. Ini, a Munich-born former actress, was married with two daughters at that time, and although Harold pursued her relentlessly—sending her flowers, inviting her to the South of France, paying for her and her mother to stay at the Carlton Hotel in Cannes—she refused his advances until after she divorced her husband in July 1979. Soon after Ini traveled from Munich to see Harold in New York, the two became lovers. A photograph taken at the time shows Ini, wearing a canary yellow catsuit, and Harold, in a matching yellow silk shirt, at Studio 54. In another picture, snapped in St. Tropez, the couple—she sporting a Bo Derek 10-style wig, and he, his bald head topped by a baseball hat—look like a pair of lovestruck teenagers.

"When he spoke to you, it was like you were the only one on the whole earth," she says. "I couldn't speak very good English at the time, and I always had a dictionary with me and had to look up words. He loved that. Sometimes I would choose the wrong word, and he had a ball about that. He was very charming, fabulous with my children and my mother, and I cannot say anything bad about him. He was very charismatic, though not particularly good-looking, and it was his personality that appealed. He had other affairs, of course, but ours was really down to earth. He certainly knew how to make me feel good. He was a great lover, and I had a magnificent time, I can tell you.

"One day I was in Cannes, and he gave me his credit card and told me to go shopping for whatever I wanted. I found one pair of jeans, which cost something like one hundred dollars. When I told him, he just shook his head, because he expected me to buy a lot more.

"Although Harold and Grace had an open relationship—most of the time they did not live together—at times it would get uncomfortable. She would say that he was spending too much time with me. But the truth was, he was in love with me. He wanted me to move out to Los Angeles. He said, 'I have a very nice home behind the Beverly Hills Hotel, and I'm buying a bigger one. Why don't you move into the house?' I said, 'As a kept woman? No way!' He said he would write the house into my name, but I told him I was not someone he could buy."

The relationship lasted three years until Ini, still based in Munich, met another man. "I called him and told him it was better if we didn't see one another," she says. "But you don't leave a Harold Robbins. That almost broke his heart.

"He didn't want to get a divorce from Grace because of the financial impact. I heard from one of his very good friends who told me that Harold would have got a divorce and married me. Although I would have married him had I not had my daughters, who were four and six at the time of my divorce, I didn't want my children to grow up in that circle, that set. I had a wonderful time [with Harold], I loved him dearly, but with children I had other responsibilities."[15]

At the end of 1979 Robbins started to plot his sixteenth novel, *Goodbye, Janette*, which he said would be an exposé of the international fashion set. He started writing the book in 1980, and by June, after isolating himself in Le Cannet, where he subsisted on a diet of spaghetti and cold chicken, he had dashed off 117 pages. He claimed he did extensive research into the heady world of Paris haute couture, interviewing Pierre Cardin, Marc Bohan, and Emanuel Ungaro and attending the Paris collections (where he nodded off during an Yves Saint Laurent show). But the novel fails to capture the glamour of the fashion industry. Although the book has a plot of sorts—"Three women, sensual, exciting—and dangerous," reads the tagline of the novel, which explores the lives of a mother, Tanya, and her two daughters, Janette and Lauren—Robbins simply used it as a framework on which to hang a series of increasingly explicit sex scenes.

After only eight pages Tanya, a Polish prisoner of war, offers herself to a German general, an act which saves both her life and that of her daughter, Janette. Twenty-five pages later Robbins describes a sadomasochistic act involving Tanya, her new husband, the aristocratic Maurice—who happens to be both homosexual and equipped with the largest penis in Paris—and a cat-o'-nine-tails. After Tanya outmaneuvers Maurice, now her business partner in a fashion house, he proceeds to wreak revenge on her by luring Janette to his apartment, where he and his boyfriend—whom Robbins can't decide whether to call Jerry or Jimmy—make her their sex slave. Perhaps the most obnoxious aspect of it all is the suggestion that a victim of serial sexual abuse could actually enjoy it. "She began to await the times they would come for her," Robbins writes. "Even to look forward to the pain because always with it came the exquisite agony of release."[16]

The more Robbins investigated the world of haute couture, the more he despised it. "I hate clothes that make men look like women and women look like men," he said. "I find designers make clothes that make girls look more like themselves than like women. The result is that the average woman can't wear them. They cannot all be six-foot, long-legged . . . with no tits, no ass. No way."[17] Robbins finished the book in the autumn of 1980, returning to Los Angeles for a Thanksgiving dinner at his recently completed hilltop home on Tower Grove Drive. Friends and associates were staggered by the size of the writer's new house; one commentator remarked that its parking lot was as big as Chasen's, while Robbins himself said, "I have the biggest acreage here, but no one can find my house because it is so well hidden from view."[18]

Critics, never kind to Robbins, attacked the book with a renewed frenzy. Deborah Moggach, in the *Daily Mail*, said that *Goodbye, Janette* was "peopled by over-sexed clones with permanent suntans that pass for characters." The book, she said, was neither outrageous nor scandalous; rather it was "just depressing and deeply boring."[19] Peter Andrews, reviewing *Goodbye, Janette* and *Sirens* by Eric Van Lustbader in *The New York Times*, reached the conclusion that if these two novels were anything to go by, the heavily marketed sex novel was in desperate trouble. Although Simon & Schuster would like Robbins's book to be seen as erotic and shocking—*Cosmopolitan* carried what it called "a blushing excerpt"[20]—it was nothing of the sort. "It is, quite simply, a dirty book written with the demands of the form . . . The setting, of course, is merely a backdrop for the author's sex scenes in which various characters work themselves into a froth and actually do things I wouldn't even talk about when I was in the Army." The problem was that Robbins's book was tedious and his dialogue mind-numbingly boring. "When you are reading a novel in which characters talk like that for hundreds and hundreds of pages, a bit of bondage begins to seem like a blessed relief."[21]

According to David Thomson, whose review appeared in *Playgirl*, the novel indicated that Robbins was bored both by his material and by the actual writing process. He classified the book as stuffed with "silk, semen and suet prose" and corrected the author on a number of minor details: two teenage girls swoon over a poster of James Dean in *Rebel Without a Cause* without seeming to realize that the star is dead, while Robbins also spells Lord Snowdon's name incorrectly. These are minor issues compared with the novel's main fault: "the claustrophobia of sleazy intent without talent has set in, as sullen and sticky as July humidity."[22]

Robbins, of course, did not care. At the end of May he traveled from Acapulco—and Grace from the South of France—to host a $100,000 launch party at L'Orangerie in Los Angeles. After hors d'oeuvres and drinks the guests—who included Vincente and Lee Minnelli, Sidney Sheldon, Eileen Kreiss, Lady Sarah Churchill, Tony Martin, Mrs. Clark Gable, and Princess Marusia Toumanoff—took their seats for a fashion show, the re-creation of a scene from *Goodbye, Janette*. "The traditional French fashion show finale—the bride—was a little different this time," wrote one observer. "Out came The Devil in skin-clinging tights. He carried off the blushing bride, who by this time had shed the upper half of her red wedding dress and veil."[23]

Despite its faults, the dirtiest of Harold's dirty books was an instant success. In the U.K. it sold 77,000 in ten days, while *Goodbye, Janette* had the largest advance first printing of any novel in the world: a total of 3.75 million copies in the United States, Canada, England, Australia, and Germany. "Call it pornographic," said Robbins of the book, "because the people it deals with in the fashion world live pornographic lives—they exist to accentuate sex, that's what fashion is all about: the body . . . They do things to heighten physical and sensual sensitivity, push themselves to the limits with flagellation, bondage and domination, mind-expanding dope, drugs that speed you up and slow you down, cocaine, acid."[24]

That spring Robbins was named the world's best-selling living author, with total sales of 200 million, beating Barbara Cartland (150 million); Irving Wallace (130 million); the writer of westerns Louis L'Amour (110 million); and the author of contemporary gothics Janet Dailey (80 million). While the *New York Times* best-seller list was compiled using statistics from *Publishers Weekly* and from bookstores and wholesalers with more than forty thousand outlets across America, genre fiction was often absent from its chart because romances, thrillers, and Robbins's novels were sold in establishments like truck stops that did not report their sales to the *Times*. All these authors, said Scott Haller in *The Saturday Review*, "satisfy—and, at the same time, reflect—the fantasies and desires of vast segments of the book-buying public." Robbins's books were both "an exposé and a masquerade" as they "inundate us with gossipy inside information, and at the same time, they invite us to solve a mystery. Who is that masked celebrity climbing into the king-size bed?"

What all these authors have in common, besides enormous wealth, is a clear understanding of the importance of story. Their books have an easily demarcated beginning, middle, and end. Narrative closure is essential—"these novels seldom conclude with a question mark or a questionable move," said Haller. Aspiration is also a key ingredient— the writers create "worlds that are beyond the reach of most read- ers"—as is possession of the common touch. They all share a "sincere mass-audience mentality," while their real lives tend to reflect, at least to some degree, the fictional worlds of their novels. Finally, the writers all explore the age-old battle between good and evil, rewarding the virtuous, punishing the wicked, and reminding us that "the rich are more miserable than you and me."[25]

Harold Robbins may have been rich, but he was far from happy. By this point in his career he realized that he had started to plagiarize himself—many of the tropes of his novels were well worn, while the majority of his characters could wander into his other books without too much difficulty—and that the fictional image he had created for himself, the holograph that he had designed for the purpose of attracting money, sex, fame, and freedom, was in danger of imprison- ing him. In order to maintain his playboy lifestyle—the yachts (he now had another one, harbored in Marina del Rey), the houses, Grace's increasingly large credit card bills, and the properties he bought his mistresses—Robbins churned out a series of substandard novels that seemed to lack the spark of his earlier work. He had never been a great writer, but at least he could claim to have spun a good story; now, however, even that ability was beyond him.

The things that once had given him pleasure had lost their luster, and he turned to taking increasingly large quantities of drugs to keep up the charade that he was having a good time. If friends did not want to take part, then they sometimes found themselves banished from his circle. "I remember Harold invited us to a party at his house in Acapulco," says Caryn Matchinga. "There were two Mexican policemen with submachine guns guarding the door, and inside was the crème de la crème of Mexico. On the tables were huge, huge bowls filled with cocaine. Harold said, "Take a line," but we refused. And all of a sudden we didn't hear from him for years, we were just cut off because we didn't do the lines of coke."[26]

To the outside world Robbins seemed to be the embodiment of the American dream. But in the summer of 1981, as he cruised the Mediterranean—where, said Ken Minns, one could smell the Ambre Solaire two miles out at sea—few of his readers would have been able to guess at his state of mind. "He seemed really bored by cruising," says Ken, who kept a diary of the trip. "And he had got to the stage where he didn't enjoy writing anymore. In fact, he hated doing it."[27]

From Cannes, Harold, Grace, and Adréana sailed to Minorca and planned to continue to Barcelona, but midway through the trip he cut short the sail. "I'm glad we're getting out of there," said Harold of Minorca. "I've had it with that place." Ken tried to persuade his employer to explore the various ports of call, but from the 9th to the 28th of July Robbins set foot on land only once.[28] Back in Cannes, Robbins ordered Moët & Chandon champagne in jeroboams, but as he drank, he found that the fizz lacked its usual sparkle. As he sat on his yacht in the harbor, people gaped at him and his family—"They're looking at us as if we're animals in the zoo," he said.[29]

Robbins had promised Paul Gitlin that in 1982 he would deliver another manuscript. He had settled on a juicy subject, the world of a money-mad television evangelist, but the thought of actually writing it left him feeling depressed. In October he embarked on a tour of the American South, traveling from Louisville to Charlotte and then on to Lynchburg. A researcher drew up a list of televangelists—including Jim Bakker in Charlotte, Jerry Falwell in Lynchburg, and Oral Roberts in Tulsa—and also compiled a file of newspaper and magazine reports on the subject. He visited each of the ministries without informing them of his identity or purpose, and although the evangelists openly attacked Robbins on their television shows, none of them recognized him.

"Here were all these preachers who have been telling people to take my books out of libraries for years, and not one of them knew my name," he said. "To them, I was just another guy from the audience, another sucker to be fleeced. When I began to get a look on the inside, I was not surprised by the corruption. But I didn't expect the business sophistication, the computerization of the operation. These people are tougher than Las Vegas, and they cash more Social Security checks too. I'm an atheist, but I respect genuinely religious people. People who really believe and practice their beliefs are entitled to those beliefs. I am after the hypocrites in this book, the people who think they are the ayatollahs of America."[30]

Robbins wrote *Spellbinder* quickly, finishing it in thirty-one days. In order to meet his deadline—and to make sure he banked the hefty check from Simon & Schuster—he knocked back a homemade cocktail of Coca-Cola, into which he heaped spoonfuls of instant coffee, no doubt accompanied by frequent snorts of cocaine. By February he completed the book, relieved that he had done so before the wedding of his daughter, Caryn, to her boyfriend, Michael Press. Little did he know, however, that 25 April 1982 would mark the beginning of his descent. Robbins, the ultimate dream merchant, was about to experience his worst nightmare.

20

"My lawyer claims God is punishing me for having a terrific life. Even the doctor said, 'You're paying for all those women, drink and good times.'"

—Harold Robbins

A T FIRST HAROLD did not realize anything was wrong. He went through the day as if nothing had happened: greeting guests as they arrived at his house, chatting to friends, family, and old acquaintances, and directing the staff so that the wedding celebrations went smoothly. Then toward the end of the day, just as he was enjoying another scotch on the rocks, a friend asked him a question: who was the woman in the picture in the living room? He did not know. Grace, whose portrait it was, rushed over to her husband. She knew something was desperately wrong and, without a moment's hesitation, phoned for an ambulance.

After a series of tests, doctors discovered that Harold had had a minor stroke. Although the cause of the embolism was not known, it was likely exacerbated by stress. Not only had Robbins pushed himself to the extreme to finish *Spellbinder*, abusing his body with excessive levels of cocaine and caffeine, but he also felt anxious about the forthcoming wedding. After all, he had not had an easy relationship with Caryn, and the thought of hosting the reception at his house only added to his anxiety. He also learned that his good friends Ben and Norma Barzman had written a novel, *Rich Dreams*, about a bestselling author who bore an uncanny resemblance to himself.

The book was born after Norma spent a night chatting with Harold about his past, which she was unaware was fictional. "I didn't sleep all night, *une nuit blanche*, a white night, as the French call it," says Norma. "The *entire* plot of a novel came at me. An antihero like Harold, a zillionaire writer of steamy best sellers who lives like the characters in his books and whose values boomerang. His life is threatened. By morning, I had the story completely worked out."[1]

As Harold read the book, he could not have failed to notice the similarities between himself and the Barzmans' fictional creation, Arnold Elton, who boasts, "More people read me than the yellow pages of the phone book." Born into a Jewish family, he does not know the identity of his real mother but is adopted by his father and stepmother and later admits, "I guess you can say I only half know who I am." He works for a Hollywood studio, then tries his hand at writing a novel, which becomes an immediate best seller. After hitting on a winning formula, a "combination of fucking and a special background or institution," he churns out book after book. He writes in a small enclosed space, with the drapes drawn, just like Robbins, and lives in a mansion in Los Angeles and a villa in the South of France. Elton, again like Robbins, transforms himself into a corporation, and with the help of his heavy-drinking attorney and agent, Oscar Brenner (who is clearly modeled on Paul Gitlin), Elton becomes the richest author in the world. "I'm the most successful writer and one of the greatest of all time, the biggest moneymaker ever made money out of words."[2]

Key to his success is his depiction of sex—he is the first author of popular postwar literature to use the word *fuck* in a book. As a writer he proves that "the penis is mightier than the sword."[3] Even little details, such as the guestbook that Elton keeps on his yacht—a book into which he asks visiting celebrities to sign their names, which he then submits to the tax authorities as proof of business expenses—were lifted straight from Robbins's own life.

"Harold was so angry with me when he found out about the book," says Norma. "It was a novel about someone like Harold, and he recognized himself as that character. He was so furious, he did not want our daughters [Adréana and Suzo] to be friends, and he banned them from seeing one another."[4]

The confrontation with a fictionalized version of himself was, perhaps, too much to bear. After all, he had spent half a lifetime constructing—and indeed living—a fantasy. As his identity was threatened, it fragmented and then split apart, a process that, exacerbated by his excessive lifestyle, finally culminated in a stroke that, in turn, left him with aphasia. Robbins frequently forgot words, and when he tried to write, his sentences were garbled and often written back to front.

Robbins was desperate to keep the news secret. Although he should have attended that year's Cannes Film Festival, where it was announced that Meshulam Riklis had bought the rights to *The Lonely Lady*, Harold was too ill to travel. Grace stood in as his ambassador, excusing her husband's absence because of the pressure of work. "You see, my mission in life is to make sure the world knows that even when Harold hides himself, he's still there," she said at the time.[5]

In Grace's absence, Harold took it upon himself to hire a new personal assistant, Jann Stapp, a former advertising executive from Oklahoma who was in her late twenties. "The secretary took me upstairs, she opens these big double doors, and there's this huge bedroom with mirrored ceilings and a white satin sofa," she says. "He's sitting in the middle of this huge bed, smoking a cigarette, having a cup of coffee and wearing his red jockey shorts."[6] The writer introduced himself by his full name and proceeded to conduct a formal interview, at the end of which he offered her the job. Later, Jann said, "I think we fell in love the first time we met each other. I felt he was the most wonderful thing."[7]

Harold, now sixty-six, was immediately attracted to the young woman and, at some point, made a move on her. "Yeah, that's what they call sexual harassment today," he said. "All that talk about harassment is bull——. If I hadn't harassed her, we'd never have married. She was a virgin. All girls from Oklahoma are virgins . . . Adultery doesn't mean anything because everybody does it. Through my whole life, I don't know one married person who hasn't fooled around."[8] Later, when asked by *Esquire* magazine to describe his favorite thing, Robbins responded, "a beautiful woman's derriere . . . She [Jann] came from Oklahoma and gave my life more happiness than the biggest oil gusher. Her derriere made all my dreams come true."[9]

Although Robbins was in no condition to write, he knew that if he wanted to maintain his lifestyle, he would have to deliver another manuscript to Simon & Schuster. The stroke had left him with a lingering sense of his own mortality, and he started to think about a man who searches for the secret to everlasting life. He began work on *Descent from Xanadu* that autumn, finding himself increasingly dependent on Jann, who helped restructure his sentences, fill in gaps in the text, and tidy up his scrambled words.

In October he traveled to London to promote *Spellbinder*. Frank Delaney, who interviewed him at the Savoy for his radio program *Bookshelf*, described Robbins as a "small, nut-brown, tired-looking man whose speech was slow, probably because of the medication for a badly sprained back." Delaney asked him what was the best compliment anybody had ever paid him. "You're a great fuck," said Robbins, laughing. And the worst thing? "You're a lousy fuck." Why, if he was such a rich man, did he continue writing? "Because I am not a very wealthy man," he said. "I enjoy all my money—I spend it all. And I write because that's what I do. I will not live long enough to write all the stories I have to tell." Robbins tried to maintain his easygoing demeanor—"If I could get the stiffness out of my back and into another part of the anatomy it wouldn't be so bad," he joked to one journalist.[10] But Delaney remembers him as "rather like a character in one of his own books, but much sadder and, as he said himself, tired."[11] He was dependent on an oxygen bottle, which in London he hid under the covers of his bed, and his voice was accompanied by a constant wheeze, a symptom of emphysema. Nonetheless Robbins continued to smoke three packs of cigarettes a day.

He returned to America to more bad news: his new son-in-law, Michael Press, had been killed during a car accident in Los Angeles on 1 December. Caryn, a widow at twenty-seven after only seven months' marriage, was understandably devastated. Karen Russell, Michael's first wife and one of Caryn's closest friends, recalls attending the wake at Robbins's house on Tower Grove Drive. "I remember it was the longest driveway in the world," she says. "When I arrived, I was put off because it seemed to me more of a party than a wake, and he [Harold] could not get in touch with Caryn's feelings. They had a stormy relationship, very much on and off, and from what Caryn told me he was not particularly pleasant. I left feeling this is one cold guy."[12]

Throughout 1983 he continued to work on *Descent from Xanadu*, which Paul Gitlin claimed would earn him $2 million, or two hundred dollars a word. By the end of the year he had nearly finished the book, writing on average four pages a day, a rate of production that he said was "good going, but whether or not it's good writing I don't know. I'm a little tired, and surprised I'm here."[13] The novel, which centers on a billionaire's quest for immortality, contains some of Robbins's worst writing. Jann maintained that even though his stroke and the aphasia turned his words into gobbledygook, Harold always enjoyed working on the sex scenes—"I can tell when he's on the sex part . . . He's typing like crazy."[14] But even these seem lackluster. The novel went on to be attacked in the House of Commons for what Tory MP David Harris believed to be its glamorization of cocaine use. "Without asking Mr. Fowler to read such trash, may I draw it to his attention," said Harris.[15] Social Services secretary Norman Fowler replied, during the debate on 16 July 1985, that he "would deplore, as would the rest of the House, any book or publication which seeks to glamorize drug taking."[16]

In November Robbins traveled from the South of France to Los Angeles, where he agreed to meet journalist Steven Young. Wearing a pair of black sunglasses and a broad black-brimmed hat throughout the interview, he tried to recapture something of his playboy image, flirting with a black woman whom he spotted across the room. "My God, I'm in love, get her address," he said to Young. "Sex got me into trouble from the age of fifteen. I'm hoping that by the time I'm seventy I'll straighten out . . . I've been hooked on everything—doping, drinking, loving."[17]

He complained that Simon & Schuster seemed to have lost interest in him; as long as they made money out of his name, that was all they cared about. Michael Korda remembers it rather differently. "Harold's sales began to plummet," he says.[18] "In interviews he always sounded cocky and quick to defend his books against the critics, but the truth was that he despised his readers and despised himself for catering to them."[19]

His unique selling point of being able to churn out erotically charged, fast-paced epics was now being threatened by a whole new generation of mostly female novelists such as Judith Krantz, Shirley Conran, Celia Brayfield, Jackie Collins, and a host of imitators. These writers invested Robbins's tired formula with a new energy, an emotional intensity that had been long absent from his novels. In addition, they challenged Robbins's male perspective, shifting the presentation of the female from passive object to active subject. "I always remember thinking when I read him as a teenager that when I started to write novels my women would be as strong as Harold Robbins's men," says Jackie Collins.[20] They were better at writing sex scenes too, more descriptive, more sensuous, more daring. Robbins may have invented the "sex and shopping" novel, but his female counterparts adapted the genre and in the process kidnapped a large share of his core readership.

In order to boost his morale Robbins snorted even larger quantities of cocaine. On 23 February 1984, after a night out with Jann and a couple of friends, he took one toot too many and, while in the shower at his house, suffered a drug-induced seizure. Jann, who was downstairs at the time, noticed water seeping through the ceiling, and after getting no answer from the bathroom phone, she rushed upstairs to find Harold unconscious on the floor. "They tell me I slid unconscious across the bathroom floor with such force that I hit the toilet bowl, knocking it off its pipes," he said. "The water began pouring out. My legs wound up on either side of the bowl."[21]

Grace returned from Acapulco to find her husband in the hospital with a broken pubic bone and a shattered hip. Although the couple managed to keep the cause of the fall out of the press, there were certain things they could not control. Over the couse of the next eight months Robbins underwent three operations, but none was totally successful. Confined to a wheelchair, he was now in constant pain, and although he had a certain level of health insurance, he had to pay out a million dollars to cover additional medical expenses. The recreational drugs that he had enjoyed over the years were now replaced by ones issued by the pharmacy; more than thirty different tablets a day. Suddenly his jet-set life—the international travel, his luxury houses and yachts, the parade of celebrity friends, and the endless supply of girls—shrank before his eyes as he was now confined to the reality of four walls. It was far from an attractive perspective.

But with Jann's help Harold managed to keep on working. In April 1984 he concentrated on an autobiographical novel, which he entitled *Lifestyle* and would be published in 1985 as *The Storyteller.* "It's sort of Henry Miller revisited," he said. "The things he did forty or fifty years ago, I'm going to do in our times. That kind of story."[22]

In July he began negotiations with several studios for rights both to his unproduced works and to future projects, finally closing a deal with Twentieth Century Fox. By November he had plotted out character sketches and a pilot for a television series for ABC, which he called *Empire* and which centered on the machinations of media tycoon Richard Blakeslee. However, from reading the screenplay it's obvious that whatever talent Robbins had once possessed had now deserted him, and unsurprisingly the show was never commissioned.

Robbins, ever a fighter, continued to battle the effects of his fall, but finally he had to concur that he was no longer fit to travel. In early January 1985 the decision to sell the house in Acapulco was made for him when three men, intent on kidnapping Grace, burst into the property and raped the female servants; fortunately for her, Grace was by chance in Los Angeles at the time of the attack. The sale also prompted the couple to take stock of their financial situation. With dwindling royalty payments, high medical expenses, and a raft of unpaid taxes, Robbins realized that it would be foolish to continue running properties he could not use. Grace traveled over to France, where she organized the sale of the fleet of cars and the villa in Le Cannet and the yacht and office in Cannes. Although the sale netted him more than a million dollars, most of the money was eaten away by back taxes. Harold and Grace also realized that a house perched atop a hill, with an elaborate spiral staircase, was not the best home for a man in a wheelchair, and so they put the property on Tower Grove Drive on the market too. As each month progressed, the status symbols that Harold had used to prop up his fantasy world were being stripped away from him. What, he was forced to ask himself, was his worth now?

Confined to a wheelchair, Harold gazed up at the faded photograph of his yacht on the wall. God he had loved that boat, taking it out of the harbor and cruising around the islands off Cannes. He remembered the feel of the breeze and the spray of the sea on his skin as he sailed the blue waters of the Mediterranean, the smell of barbecuing meat, the pop of champagne corks, the taste of salt as he ran his tongue over a blonde's beautiful body. Looking down at his immobile legs, he cursed to himself. Wasn't life a bitch, he murmured.

From a mansion overlooking the lights of Los Angeles, Harold, Grace, and Jann moved to a single-story rented house in the desert. Robbins was attracted to Palm Springs because of its aura of decadence, its association with Hollywood (it was one of the original party grounds for stars who wanted to escape the controlling influence of the studios), its proximity to Los Angeles, and the relatively cheap property prices. But Robbins must also have felt that he was retreating from the limelight. Palm Springs, for all its recent reinvention as a hip destination, was in the mid-1980s something of an elephant's graveyard, a place where old Hollywood went to die; indeed, Robbins himself had once described it, in his novel *The Inheritors*, as "too dull."[23]

Grace tried to establish a social life, mixing with Kirk Douglas and Sidney Sheldon and their wives, but Harold became more and more reclusive, preferring to spend time at home with Jann, who worked closely with him on *The Storyteller*, which they completed by the autumn of 1985. After Robbins handed the manuscript to Michael Korda, he heard that his editor was disappointed with it. "Michael is a good editor, but he's a little too structured for me," he said at the time. "He likes everything to go into a slot. Also, he's nervous. He says he's never read anything like this new one since Henry Miller. He says, 'Are you sure you're writing this with a typewriter or your prick?' He says, 'This is the dirtiest book I've ever read.' 'Don't take it so seriously,' I told him. 'Enjoy it.'"

Robbins told Dick Lochte that the novel was "the most autobiographical of all my books."[24] There are a number of superficial resemblances between Robbins and his fictional alter ego, best-selling novelist Joe Crown. Like Robbins, Crown is born in Brooklyn and changes his surname so that it sounds less Jewish; he gets taken in by the New York agency that represents John Steinbeck; he works with Ray Crossett, the story editor at Universal; he enjoys sex, consumes copious quantities of coke, and understands the value of publicity. ("This is a bullshit business," says one character.[25]) He is represented by lawyer Paul Gitlin and a PR man called Gene; and later in life, he suffers a hip fracture before developing emphysema.

These details that Robbins plucked from his own life served as a smokescreen to obscure the truth of the matter. He created Joe Crown as a way of buoying up his self-image, a fantasy that by now was in danger of slipping away. For instance, although Robbins frequently told friends and journalists that he had once delivered cocaine to Cole Porter—as Joe Crown does in the book—this was nothing more than a fiction. As a result, Crown functions as a substitute for the kind of man Harold had always wanted to be, enjoying the kind of life he always wanted to live.

Robbins, ever since he first learned the importance of publicity, had deliberately marketed his novels as though they were an extension of his life, luring readers by the promise that, if they bought his books, they could taste a slice of his sexed-up world. Now that he had had a stroke and was confined to a wheelchair, he needed even more than ever to make them believe in the authenticity of his fictional image. But ironically Robbins, who had over the years spun so many versions of himself, no longer knew who he was anymore. Like the potted biography Joe Crown gives to his agency in the appropriately titled *The Storyteller*, he was now made up of nothing but "Lies, all lies."[26]

21

"Jann did not marry a wealthy man—she married a notorious reputation."

—Yolande Guest

A S HE TURNED to adjust his position in his wheelchair, a wave of
pain consumed him. His skin felt as though it were being peeled
back, his nerves like they were being flayed. Biting his lip so hard he
almost drew blood, he swore to himself, silently. He took a couple of
deep breaths and attempted to move again; then the pain threatened to
overwhelm him once more. He felt the beads of sweat break out on his
forehead and the familiar nausea in his stomach, but he did not
complain; instead, when Jann appeared from the kitchen, he tried to
smile and started to chat. He wasn't going to be beaten, no goddam
way. He was going to fight this son of a bitch until the very end.

After *The Storyteller* Harold Robbins did not write another book
for five years. He was so plagued by ill health that it was rumored that
he had developed throat cancer. "It doesn't look good," said one
friend at the time. "We are very concerned for him."[1] Robbins may
not have had cancer, but the aftereffects of the fall had left him in
agony.

In April 1987 he underwent surgery to have a remote-controlled
electric implant inserted into his spine. Although the device was
designed to mask the pain—whenever he felt it become too much
for him to endure, he was supposed to give himself an electric shock—
it only caused more problems. "I can't stand the buzzing from the
implant," he said. "It drives me crazy when I work, so I don't use it."

He also risked giving himself a massive electric shock. "If you pour on too much juice, it can knock you on your ass," he said. As a result he relied on increasingly large amounts of Tylenol to kill the pain, and although he managed, for small amounts of time at least, to clamber out of his wheelchair and onto crutches, he was left feeling frustrated and angry. "The pain will always be there, but you can take it if you can move around," he said. "The main thing is I *believe* I'm going to walk. I *believe* I'm going to move. I *believe* I'm going to get around."[2]

Robbins's stoicism has to be admired, believes his friend Carroll Baker. "He was in enormous pain toward the end, but he was very brave," she says. "He always had a twinkle in his eye, a sparkle, and he always tried to make you laugh."[3] Bob Pollock, a friend and fellow resident of Palm Springs, remembers one time when Robbins was scheduled to be admitted to the Eisenhower hospital in Palm Desert. "Harold stipulated that he did not want a general anesthetic, as he was afraid he might not wake up," says Pollock, who with his wife created the long-running TV soap opera *Dynasty*. "The doctors agreed that they would operate using a spinal injection, but when he arrived at the hospital, he learned that as the surgery was going to take longer than expected, the surgeons needed to use a general. 'I'm not going to do this,' he said, within sight of the operating room, and got himself wheeled right out of there. Later, he had a set of T-shirts printed on which was written the slogan 'Cowards Live Longer.' "[4]

He hoped that he was still improving as a writer: "what keeps me going is something called creative conceit," he said. "I always think I can do it better next time."[5] But the five-year gap did nothing to enrich his style or deepen his characterization. In fact, *The Piranhas*—about the double dealings of a Mafia family—is so shoddy that it is amazing that Simon & Schuster agreed to publish it. Years earlier Robbins had claimed that Mario Puzo, author of *The Godfather*, had learned how to write best-selling commercial fiction from reading his books; now, sneered the critics, Robbins was cynically publishing a "nearly indecipherable mess of a knockoff" of Puzo's own novel.[6]

Robbins said that the book was about "the spoilers of the American dream . . . they are the corporate raiders and bottom-liners who will stop at nothing to make a dollar," without realizing the irony of the comment. After all, many believed that Robbins himself was at least

partly responsible for introducing crass commercialism into the publishing world. Ed Weiner of *The New York Times* said that there was
"something sad and musty about the novel." With books like *A Stone
for Danny Fisher* and *The Carpetbaggers*, Robbins had been, for his
time, genuinely shocking; the problem was that now other authors
were not only able to "outsex, outviolence and outgross him," but
"these newcomers can outwrite him, too."[7] Val Hennessy of the *Daily
Mail* objected to Robbins's portrayal of women—"his bimbo female
characters still have scrambled eggs for brains, they still say the sort of
disgusting, whore-like things that are only ever said by women in
Harold Robbins's books"—and felt rather dismayed by the fact that
his fiction was read by such a wide audience. Surely, she suggested,
future Americans would look back and wonder how Robbins got
away with making his fortune from trash such as this.[8]

In the offices of Simon & Schuster Michael Korda and his
colleagues asked themselves the very same question. In 1987 a story
appeared in the press alleging that the publisher had told Robbins they
no longer wanted his books. Although the report was not true, Simon
& Schuster was far from happy with his work. So, it seems, was Paul
Gitlin, who realized that his star client was no longer physically or
mentally capable of producing readable, and more important, salable
novels. Robbins's fans may not have bought his books for his elegant
sentences or realistic characterisation, but they were far from stupid,
and his last few books—*Dreams Die First*, *Goodbye, Janette*, *Descent
From Xanadu*, and now *The Piranhas*—were simply insults to their
intelligence. Drastic action was now called for: the employment of a
ghostwriter.

"[Gitlin] invented the final downward step, which was to have other
people write Harold's books," says Michael Korda. "*The Piranhas*
was the last book Harold wrote. All the others, such as *The Raiders* [a
sequel to *The Carpetbaggers*] and *Tycoon*, were not by Harold. Part
of the deal was that he would shut up and not interfere. I think Harold
felt, to a degree, ashamed and even angered by this and probably even
more angered by the fact that there was nothing he could do about it.
He needed the money."[9]

Gitlin felt particularly defensive about the fading talent of his star
client, and perhaps for this reason he acted overzealously when he

heard, through a news item in the British press, that experimental writer Kathy Acker had lifted a section of *The Pirate* for use in her short novel *The Adult Life of Toulouse Lautrec*. The novella was first published in 1975, but only when the story was collected in *Young Lust* in 1989 did journalists note similarities between a passage of Robbins's novel describing Jordana's wild sex with a well-endowed black man and a similar section in the Acker anthology. Thinking he was acting in Robbins's best interests, Gitlin fired off an angry letter to Acker's publisher, Pandora, accusing the author of plagiarism and threatening legal action. Instead of fighting the case—after all, the manipulation of existing texts was central to Acker's technique—Pandora felt it had no choice but to order Acker to issue a public apology, and to pulp all remaining copies of *Young Lust*. "As Kathy told me (and others), it seems Robbins did not know this was happening and that the lawyer was just proceeding in a standard way to protect his client's intellectual property," says Acker's literary executor, Matias Viegener.[10] Fellow author William Burroughs tried to intervene, and Robbins himself stated that she had his "entire permission to use his work" and that he was "shocked [that] anyone would be so ill-informed as to accuse her of plagiarism," but it was too late—Pandora had already ordered the pulping of the book. According to Acker's friend Roz Kaveney, "She was devastated by the experience, felt utterly misunderstood by the U.K. literary community as well as betrayed by her publisher, and it led to her leaving London."[11]

The incident, together with Gitlin's suggestion that Robbins hand over his books to a ghostwriter, cannot have helped the relationship between the two men. The agent and the author who used to pop open a bottle of Dom Perignon to mark the completion of a new blockbuster—Gitlin placed the corks under glass and displayed them on a wall in his office—now had little to celebrate. Both Robbins's reputation and his royalties were on the way down.

The tension simmered beneath the surface of the conversation all night. Whenever Grace opened her mouth to utter a witticism or flirt with the young man sitting next to her, Harold shot her a look of pure hatred. Similarly, when Harold threw a conversational gambit across the dinner table, or made a simple observation, Grace fired off a quick but devastating putdown. Finally Robbins could bear no more, and at the end of the evening he turned to his wife and said, "The only reason we're still together is money, you gold-digging bitch!"

Grace tried to laugh off this gratuitous insult, but increasingly there seemed to be little of substance keeping them together. Ever since moving to Palm Springs they had spent less and less time together: He seemed to be wrapped up with Jann, and she was always visiting friends in Los Angeles. The rare occasions when they did see each other always seemed to culminate in an argument.

By the end of 1989—the year in which his elder daughter Caryn gave birth to his first grandchild, Alyxandra Jacqueline Press, and Adréana married her boyfriend Jeffrey Greenberg—Robbins realized that his own marriage was over in all but name. Grace couldn't abide the way Jann had taken over her role, rising from mere secretary to her husband's invaluable assistant and constant companion. "Social secretaries get to know everything about you," she said later. "You shouldn't let that happen. You shouldn't give her any of your clothes, and you shouldn't tell her the name of your plastic surgeon. What you'll have is an *All About Eve* situation . . . She was very helpful to me and then helped herself to *everything* I had."[12] Robbins, in turn, felt neglected by Grace, who seemed more interested in socializing than in looking after him. Harold had fast developed into an ailing, aged man, while Grace still felt young, the center of the party. The gulf between them widened, until finally, after one confrontation too many, Harold asked Grace to leave the house.

She returned to Los Angeles, where she bumped into Ini Asmann, Harold's former lover. "Grace came over and asked to speak to me," says Ini. "She told me that I had always had such a big influence on Harold and explained that he wanted to leave her. She said, 'Can't you call him, can't you intervene?' I told her, 'You've had your chances, but I think you blew it.' "[13]

Over the next couple of years the couple played a waiting game, each hoping that the other would sue for divorce. Although Grace was advised against it she finally started divorce proceedings in June 1991, prompted by an article in an American newspaper in which Jann was quoted as saying of Harold, "He is very romantic. He knows how to make a woman feel like a woman."[14]

The couple cited "irreconcilable differences" as the reason for the split, but Grace believed her marriage had started to fester long before, as a consequence of Harold taking other lovers. "If I had it to do over," she says, "I would never allow an open marriage."[15] Finally, after a prolonged battle between the couple—"We'll work out the property settlement amicably," said Harold, "with guns and knives!"[16]—their lawyers thrashed out a deal. Although Grace claimed she received $250,000 plus half the royalties from the books Harold had written during their marriage, others believe the sum to be much more. "All the money went to Grace. Even though she says she didn't get that much, all of it went to her," says Ini Asmann.[17] Nicholas Dominguez alleges, "Before the divorce Grace started to stash away a lot of money. I also heard that she arranged to have their fantastic art collection [which comprised Buffet, Chagall, Léger] copied. She made off with the real thing, while Harold was left with the fakes."[18] Later Robbins himself said, "I haven't any money. First of all, my medical bills were unbelievable. Then I got divorced. Cleaned out, really cleaned out."[19]

After Harold ordered Grace out of the house, he made up his mind to leave Palm Springs. "It's wonderful for the gay nineties if you're gay or ninety," he said of it.[20] The high temperatures of summer were too much for him, and he was bored. "You go to one party, and that's okay, but when you go to ten parties, all you see are the same people, so I'm getting the hell out," he said. He hoped to relocate to San Juan Capistrano in California—"That's where the swallows are and I hope they don't crap on my eyeballs," he said[21]—but nothing came of the plan. Instead, he and Jann decided to make a new life for themselves in the desert.

On Valentine's Day 1992—seven days after Robbins's divorce from Grace became final—Harold and Jann were married at the house in Palm Springs. During the wedding ceremony, when Harold was asked whether he would forsake all others, he looked up at her from his wheelchair and rolled his eyes as if to say, "Are you kidding?" He played the role of the dirty old man to the last and reveled in telling friends that his pet Pekinese, the appropriately named Kinky, had to be tranquilized because of "chronic masturbation." Judi Schwam Yedor remembers on one occasion, when she was shopping with

Adréana, running into Harold and Jann in Victoria's Secret. "From across the shop Harold shouted, 'You two CUNTS get over here. Let's see what we can do to cover up your CUNTS.' And that was his daughter he was talking to," says Judi. "He did it to get a reaction, to live up to an image he had built. If you understood his sense of humor, it was hilarious, but if you didn't, I can imagine you would be appalled."[22]

Val Guest, the film director, says that whenever he and his wife Yolande asked Harold and Jann over to dinner, "you had to be very careful whom you invited because you never knew what Harold would get up to." "He was feeling his wife up the whole time at dinner," adds Yolande, "and so we had to invite people who were shock-proof."[23]

Yolande, who had starred in the film version of *The Adventurers*, believes Robbins was far from a happy man. "A happy person wouldn't have been as caustic as he was," she says. "I remember one time I rushed into a restaurant to meet him and Jann and told them that I had just passed my exams—I had gone back to college to do a liberal arts course. Harold said, 'I don't give a damn.' Later he did phone to apologize, but it is the first response that is the telling one. He wasn't a raconteur, and neither was he an observer; in fact half the time I got the impression that he wasn't even listening.

"People thought he was a rich, famous man and Jann was a younger woman and that was that. Although he had a white Rolls-Royce, Harold did not have any money. Jann did not marry a wealthy man—she married a notorious reputation."[24]

Harold had earned a fortune—some put the figure as high as $50 million—but over the years he had frittered it away. Now for the first time since *The Carpetbaggers* had catapulted him into the superstar league, the playboy author had serious money worries.

"I wasn't supposed to worry about money," he said. "I hired accountants and lawyers to deal with that. The funny thing is, I never saw most of it. I don't know where it went . . . I like money. I've had so many things because of it. Now, all of a sudden I'm just living in just one house, in just one small town."[25]

Robbins wanted to carry on living a jet-set lifestyle, even though he couldn't pay his bills. The couple moved into an Alexander house at

601 Camino Sur, on the corner of Via Monte Vista. They financed the purchase by taking out two mortgages totaling $315,000, a figure that was higher than the property's market value ($235,000 in early 1997). The discrepancy between his earnings and his debts was ever widening—his monthly disposable income totaled $4,700 after deductions, while his monthly expenses came to $16,650.

Year by year the situation worsened. In 1994 Robbins's gross earnings were $300,000, a figure that dropped to $196,000 in 1995 and $166,800 in 1996, while his debts added up to $1,144,000 in November 1994 and rose to $1,414,000 in early 1997. Robbins attempted to explain his actual, financial, and metaphorical fall in documents lodged with the Riverside Superior Court, California.

"Prior to 1994, I suffered fractures of both legs and both of my hips. A femur bone replacement and hip replacement on both hips were performed. Since 1994, the 'prosthesis' holding the hip replacement together has loosened, causing unmanageable pain, so that instead of being able to sit at the typewriter for 17 to 19 hours per day, as I did when I was writing in 1965, I can now sit at the typewriter only an hour or less a day. I find myself irritable, and it is far more difficult to focus because of the heavy sedatives and painkiller[s] I must take. To an author, this medication, although it does not completely mask the pain, in itself reduces one's ability to remain focused on details. Details are an essential element to a novelist. The inability to remain focused inhibits my ability to write, develop characters or create.

"I cannot undergo the surgical procedure necessary to replace the 'prosthesis' in my hips because, since after 1982, I became a victim of emphysema. My emphysema requires constant wearing of blow-by oxygen canula, limits my breathing, and requires that I take medications and bronchial breathing treatments which tend to inhabit my speech beyond the power to dictate, rather than typewrite, when I am writing.

"My speech is also impaired by the stroke which I suffered prior to 1994, but the effects of which have since considerably worsened. Since 1994, I have lost about 20 pounds of weight, reducing strength, muscle mass and endurance. This change has required that I receive respite nursing care 24 hours per day. The net effect of my various infirmities is to almost completely reduce my capacity to work at my regular occupation or at any other occupation and precludes any future improvement in my income."[26]

Early in 1994 Robbins stopped paying the $5,416 monthly allowance to his first wife, Lillian. By November of that year Robbins owed her $43,333.33, and subsequently Lillian filed an official complaint for breach of contract. Robbins tried to argue his case, presenting the court with the evidence that, since the couple were divorced in 1965, he had paid his ex-wife a total $1.8 million. Lillian, however, would not relent and proceeded to win more than $100,000 from Simon & Schuster and an order that allowed her to raid her ex-husband's Social Security benefits. In November 1996 Robbins was forced to pay her a partial settlement of $125,324—almost two years' alimony—and in early 1997 the court agreed that, as the author was now in rather more straitened circumstances, he could pay his former wife $2,000 a month, not $5,000. The $3,000 saving, however, had hardly any effect on his mushrooming debts. He owed a total of $60,000 on various credit cards; $545,085 in federal and state taxes; $153,160.70 in promissory note and legal professional services; $97,753.25 in outstanding accountants' fees; $340,000 for his mortgage; and $174,600 to miscellaneous creditors.

The man who had been the world's richest writer was now in financial meltdown.

As Harold got poorer, so he got sicker. In early 1995 he was admitted to hospital suffering from pneumonia. Although he beat that infection, his immune system was nearing the point of collapse, he needed around-the-clock nursing care, and he was increasingly dependent on painkillers. Ini Asmann, who had not seen her former lover for a couple of years, remembers her shock on meeting him again. "I walked into 601 Camino Sur to see this man who had been everywhere, so active, confined to a wheelchair," she says. "It broke my heart to see him like that. His face was swollen, he couldn't move anymore, and for a moment I was taken aback. I hope he didn't see my face."[27]

In March he agreed to be interviewed by the *Los Angeles Times* to publicize *The Raiders*, the first of his secretly ghostwritten books. He told the reporter that he had just finished another book, a sequel to *The Betsy* (again choosing not to reveal its true authorship), and that he was about to start work on "the greatest story ever told"—his autobiography, which he later provisionally entitled *Who the Fuck Knows Anything?* Although it was difficult for him to concentrate, by the end of the year he had written the first few chapters, opting to open the book with an account of his stroke at Caryn's wedding in 1982. But since he had fictionalized so much of his life—and transformed himself into one of his characters along the way—separating fantasy from reality must have been difficult for him.

Certainly when he came to be interviewed by Ian Parker for *The New Yorker*, in December 1995, he was still intent on spinning the same old stories about his past. Robbins had told these tales so many times that they had become ingrained on his consciousness, so that even he seemed to believe them.

"He looked small and a little fragile," says Parker. "Jann was taking care of him, and had something of the role of a nurse. He seemed out of place in the desert, and he had brought some urban manners with him; when Jann drove us to dinner—down fairly quiet, empty streets—he was shouting obscenities at other drivers, as if he were trying to force our way through Manhattan in the rush hour."[28]

From the passenger seat, Robbins repeatedly swore at drivers, barking out "Cocksucker!" at one and "You fucking son of a bitch!" at another. He often referred to friends as "bitches" or "cunts." Parker remembers going out to dinner with Harold and Jann and their friends the Pollocks. When conversation shifted away from Robbins, he tended to "growl amiably or do something strange with his food or sing, loudly, a line of his own composition: 'I love cannoli in the springtime.'" At one point the Pollocks started talking about sexually transmitted diseases, and Bob admitted that he had once contracted scabies. Harold did not quite catch what his friend had said and leaned across the table. What was that? "Scabies, Harold," said Jann, to help her husband. "Rabies? Bob got *rabies*?" he replied. When he wanted to leave the restaurant to go home, he held out a tip by his shoulder and said, "Assholes!" soon followed by "Get me out of here!"[29]

For the piece Robbins was photographed by Helmut Newton. He is
pictured, sitting in his wheelchair, his face swollen and bloated, the
skin around his neck sagging, looking up at Jann, who is plastered in
thick foundation, wearing caterpillar-like false eyelashes, a glitzy
necklace, and a low-cut gown. In Harold's eyes there is an expression,
if not of love, then at least of gratitude.

Despite the insufferable pain, Harold kept entertaining to the last.
Wizened and shrunken, he spewed out profanities like a court jester
with Tourette's syndrome. Since he broke his hip, he said, not only
had he lost height from his frame, but he had lost a couple of inches
from his cock. He continually buried his head in Jann's generous
cleavage and told friends that a painting hanging on his wall of a
naked figure in front of a fire showed a woman warming her "pussy."
He had met Steinbeck a couple of times. What did the two writers talk
about? "Cunt," he would reply. "That's all."

"This lovely little guy was totally wild," remembers Colin
Webster-Watson, who met Robbins in Palm Springs toward the
end of his life. "He was totally outrageous, telling women what
beautiful breasts they had—he loved breasts, he was always admir-
ing them. He was outrageous and outspoken, which I found quite
marvelous. There was nothing hypocritical about him, which is
saying something considering he lived in Palm Springs, where there
is lot of hypocrisy around. He was also a great appreciator of good
cooking and of art."

To add to his collection, Robbins bought a piece by Webster-
Watson, a sculpture of an Indian leopard cat made from black Belgian
marble, which he displayed on a pedestal in his sitting room, near his
enormous aquarium of brightly colored tropical fish. "Although the
house did feature some art it was discreetly placed and not overwhelming," says Webster-Watson. "In a way you could say that
Harold was the centerpiece, you walked in, and there he would be,
sitting in his wheelchair, larger than life."

On 14 April 1996, still in great pain, he managed to attend Colin's
seventieth birthday party in Palm Springs. To celebrate the occasion he
wrote a sixteen-line prose poem, praising his friend for his culinary
skills, his poetry, and his sculpture. "I was very moved as it really

showed Harold's sensitive side," he says. "I admired him on so many levels, not least because in those last couple of years he never showed how much pain he was in. He kept it all to himself, something I think shows great dignity of spirit."[30]

At the end of the summer of 1997 Robbins was admitted to the hospital for yet another operation on his hips. The doctors performed the surgery, which went well, and Harold seemed to respond to the treatment. He regained some strength and was looking forward to returning home. Then on the morning of 14 October—the day before he was due to start walking again—he suffered a respiratory arrest, brought on by chronic obstructive pulmonary disease. Doctors did all they could to save him, but at 11:35 a.m., in Desert Hospital in Palm Springs, he died with Jann by his side. He was eighty-one.

Jann was devastated by his death, as that October she had watched his health improve and had been told to expect him home the next day. But she looked back at their time together with fondness. "I always say it was like fifty years of marriage, we went through so many things together," she says. "There was never a dull moment."[31] Jann arranged for her husband to be cremated in Palm Springs Mortuary and Mausoleum and for his ashes to be placed inside an urn made in the form of one of his best-selling books; on its spine are the words "Beloved Husband and Father" and etched into the glass front of the niche is the phrase "To live in hearts we leave behind is not to die," the last line of his novel *A Stone for Danny Fisher*. Robbins had managed to be kitsch even in death.

The service, organized by Jann, a practicing Christian Scientist, was conducted by a minister from her church, a fact that displeased some of the guests such as Buddy Hackett, who was so incensed he walked out of the chapel and stood outside until it was his turn to speak. The number of people who had chosen to attend was small: Jann, Adréana—but neither Grace nor Caryn—and friends such as Steve Shagan, Bob Pollock and his wife, and Judi Schwam Yedor. "What struck me was how the very famous who were always around him were nowhere to be seen," Yedor says.[32] But Colin Webster-Watson's poem, which he read at the service, captured the sense in which Robbins had enriched his friends' lives:

Harold with the twinkle
the wrinkle
the knowing look,
ever so, ever so
filling a book.
Puckishly playful
entertaining with glee
nodding and prodding
anxious to see
if you followed his pleasure
in articulate measure.
Loving, laughing
living with fun
we love you Harold
our hearts you've won.
So thanks for it all,
through your love
we've had a ball.[33]

The news of Robbins's demise was reported around the world. *The New York Times* said that Robbins's novels "were always gossipy, always offered a mystery of sorts and always seemed to be interminable, much to the delight of readers."[34] The *Daily Telegraph* defined him as the "ultimate airport novelist . . . His success was more far-fetched than the plot of his novels."[35] The *Independent* credited him with inventing the 'bedroom and boardroom" genre—which was subsequently exploited by a host of imitators—as well as inspiring the producers of long-running television soap operas such as *Dallas* and *Dynasty*.[36] Neil Norman of the *Evening Standard* remarked, "The rarefied world of American letters is a poorer place having lost one of its most successful players . . . Robbins mastered the art of publishing alchemy, turning trash into dollars."[37] John Sutherland, writing in the *Guardian*, claimed that Robbins, whose estimated sales topped 750 million copies, "pushed forward the boundaries of the sexually permissible for Anglo-American fiction in the 1960s (thus clearing ground for writers of quality) and, early in his career, he wrote a couple of good novels."[38]

The London *Times* agreed, stating that Robbins's early fiction showed that he had talent. The newspaper picked out *A Stone for Danny Fisher* as perhaps his best work: "It actually smelt of the sweat of the prize ring, and captured a sense of a talented individual, striving to better himself, becoming submerged in a culture of bribes." But Robbins chose to swap prestige for profit: "He took his subject matter upmarket and his prose style down."[39]

Jackie Collins, writing in *Time* magazine, stated that Robbins was her inspiration: "He created such an exciting, glamorous, visual trip that, from the first chapter of *A Stone for Danny Fisher*, I was totally hooked." She remembered how she had first met him in 1972, soon after the publication of her novel *Sinners*. He signed a copy of *The Betsy* with the inscription, "For Jackie Collins. Beautiful authors have an advantage for openers—but when they can really write, it's positively unfair."[40] Karren Brady, the managing director of Birmingham City football club and a columnist, congratulated Robbins on his anti-snobbishness and his services to education. "Harold succeeded where hordes of teachers failed," she said. "He inspired youngsters to get stuck into a damn good read. Many went on to enjoy a whole range of books they would never have discovered without the thrill of being hooked by a riveting Robbins."[41]

Later Wayne Koestenbaum would write in *The New York Times*, "Robbins's material is smutty but his prose is clean. Simple, speedy and efficient, his sentences demonstrate, in a parodic fashion, what Roland Barthes called "writing degree zero." They seem transparent but in fact are opaque bonbons, coldly functional fetishes, absurdly themselves . . . Such bland utterances are so fake, they're real. They have a quiet, mercenary dignity. Their refusal of insight makes them as modern as neon, or Niagara Falls."[42]

On 16 October, perhaps in a spirit of postmodern irony, the Mayor Gallery on Cork Street in London marked his passing by displaying a lily in its front window, together with a copy of one of his novels and a book of condolences. "We're a gallery specializing in Dada, surrealism and pop art," commented a spokesman. "So this is a Dada statement about his death."[43]

It was Robbins, however, who had the last laugh. Every one of the obituaries trotted out the elaborate mythology that he had invented, the well-worn stories that he had told about his past, and faithfully printed them as fact. The ultimate storyteller had succeeded in creating his best fiction—himself.

In Robbins's final will, drawn up on 26 October 1994, he bequeathed everything to his wife. But as he had left many debts—$15,259 owed to the Desert Valley professional nurses' registry; a claim of $90,000 by Lillian for unpaid alimony; $439,437 in federal taxes and $219,362 in state taxes; $32,000 to Hanson & Schwam the public relations company owned by his good friend Gene Schwam; and many more—Jann was far from rich. Realizing perhaps that she had better get as much money from Robbins's account as possible before the creditors started calling, she began taking out money. In the period from 6 November 1997 to 1 September 1998 she withdrew nearly $110,000 from the bank. With the help of a clever lawyer and accountant, the estate managed to balance the books perfectly, matching the $196,967.96 in charges to the very same amount in credits, a trick that, had he still been alive, would have pleased Harold. In reality, however, Robbins died over a million dollars in debt, leaving his two daughters practically nothing. Robbins had paid into a trust fund for Adréana, who had assumed that she would never have to work. But during the last few years of his life Harold had raided the fund until it was virtually worthless. This is, perhaps, one of the reasons Adréana chose not to be interviewed for this book; she says her memories are all she has left, and as an author herself—in 1999 she penned the Robbins-like novel *Paris Never Leaves You*—one day she may decide to write about her father. She still lives in Los Angeles and, in the last couple of years, has been working for Larry Flynt.

Of Robbins's other daughter, Caryn, there is little trace. While living in Los Angeles she gave birth to two daughters, Alyxandra in 1989 and Nycolette Marielle in April 1993. Before he died, Robbins told a reporter he did not like the thought of being a grandfather—he was too young for that sort of thing. How old had one to be? "Dead!" was Harold's reply. "I'll see the kid [Alyxandra] in another year when maybe it will seem human. Now she looks like a monkey." Both Caryn's children were conceived with the use of a sperm donor, again something that did not please her father. "I told her to get married if she wanted a baby, but she said, 'I don't have to.' I don't think that's such a great idea."[44]

These comments can hardly have helped bring a father and daughter, who had spent nearly four decades at war, closer together. Understandably Caryn did not want people to know how her daughters had been conceived—it was a sensitive private matter that she thought best kept within the family—but it was typical of her father to shoot his mouth off in public. And why did he have to go and compare her baby to a monkey? Although Caryn settled her differences with her father before he died, since the funeral, which she chose not to attend, she has not wanted to be associated with his legacy and turned down the opportunity to appear in a *Biography* tribute on American television. Instead, she decided to get on with her life, setting up a couple of short-lived business ventures such as a baby clothes shop on Beverly Boulevard. Friends say that she was always something of a loner, an enigma. She would wear dark glasses even when she was inside or at night, often invented fictional stories about herself, repeatedly disguised her voice on the answering machine, and never invited any of her friends inside her home. Then in 1995, telling no one where she was going, she packed her two children into her car and disappeared. She seems to have wanted to break free from her infamous father once and for all, to erase him from her consciousness. She had admired his success, his ability to make money out of stories, but fundamentally she felt that life had dealt her a raw deal.

Lillian—Robbins's childhood sweetheart whom he repeatedly betrayed and ultimately rejected—outlived her fast-living former husband by seven months. When she died in May 1998, she left $1,124,189 in assets, amassed from money that Harold had given her over the years. The house in Norwalk was valued at $350,693, and the additional land surrounding it at $280,000. Her furs were worth over $2,000; she left $65,000 worth of jewelry, books to the value of $6,000, which she bequeathed to the local library, and over $400,000 in stocks, shares, and savings. Ironically, if Harold—who always said it was his life's ambition to make a lot of money—had stayed with his first wife, he would undoubtedly have died a richer man.

Grace, too, did not fare too badly and is still playing the part of a Robbins heroine to perfection. After her divorce from Harold she pursued a career as a torch singer; dictated her memoirs to a ghost-writer (the resulting book, *Stranger Than Fiction: My Wild Life with Harold Robbins*, failed to find a publisher); and met Paul Barnes, a wealthy businessman. On 18 December 2005 Grace, wearing a platinum- and champagne-colored dress and a fitted long-sleeve bodice-length jacket emblazoned with shimmering beads, and carrying a lily and white nosegay, walked down the aisle of the chapel aboard a cruise ship bound for Acapulco; after exchanging vows, the couple celebrated the marriage by hosting a champagne reception and banquet.

By contrast, Jann survives on modest resources. After her husband's death friends say she left Palm Springs without leaving a forwarding address. "She was left behind with so much debt that she disappeared overnight," says Ini Asmann. "Her friends and myself tried to find her because we wanted to help her, but no success."[45] Today she lives in an apartment in Valencia, outside Los Angeles. "I'm not penniless, I'm not destitute," she said in 1998, "but I do have to work. There's not scads and scads of money."[46] Recently Jann has turned to writing, helping Major General Sidney Shachnow, a concentration camp survivor who went on to win senior positions in the American army, to complete his memoirs. As inheritor of his estate, she has gone on to take advantage of the once-lucrative brand. She has written a book about her marriage to Harold, and has worked with Matt Cimber and Julius Podrug to produce a series of novels bearing Robbins's name. But these books lack the spark and energy of Robbins's best fiction.

Unfortunately, the stress of being Robbins's ghostwriter was too much for one author. In early November 2000 sixty-eight-year-old William G. Harrington sat down at his desk in his spacious home in Greenwich, Connecticut, and wrote his own obituary. He set out when and where he was born—on 21 November 1931 in Marietta, Ohio—and went on to describe his qualifications, a master's degree from Duke University and a law degree from Ohio State University. For almost twenty years, he explained, he practiced as an attorney, supplementing his income by writing novels such as *Jupiter Crisis*, *The Search for Elizabeth Brandt*, and *Trial*. From 1980 he worked full time as a writer, specializing in thrillers such as *The English Lady*, a Second World War adventure story about a glamorous heroine who spies for Winston Churchill. Although he wrote twenty-five novels under his name—including six featuring Columbo, the television detective—he failed to build up a readership and decided to hire out his services to other authors, such as mystery writers Margaret Truman and Elliott Roosevelt, both children of former U.S. presidents. After detailing his career and personal life—he was married twice and went on to adopt the son of his second wife—he put the finishing touches to the obituary and proceeded to kill himself. At the time of his death Harrington was in the process of working on a manuscript with Jann; perhaps he reasoned that it was better to take one's life than end up like Robbins, with whom he said he had collaborated on four books. As novelist Stephen King said in 2002, "I don't want to finish up like Harold Robbins—that's my nightmare."

In 1975, when the idea of having other people write his novels for him was nothing but a joke, Harold liked to tell a story about his lawyer, Paul Gitlin. The powerful attorney had panicked after realizing that one day Robbins would no longer be around to bash out his best sellers. Why, asked Gitlin, didn't he just jot down a one-page synopsis for three or four books; then if Robbins died, at least he could get another author to write them. "I love the whole thing," said Harold at the time. "It's purely ghoulish. There I am, gone to my grave, telling stories like crazy."[47]

NOTES

Introduction

1. Ian Parker, "Making Advances," *New Yorker*, 1 April 1996.
2. Roger Berthoud, "From 'Hell's Kitchen' to Affluence," *The Times* (London), 14 April 1977.
3. John Robbins, "100 Million Reasons Why I'm Happy," *Evening News*, 6 July 1972.
4. "Things Go Better With Sex!" *Daily Express*, 12 June 1981.
5. Steven Young, *News of the World Sunday Magazine, 11 December 1983.*
6. Barbara Isenberg, "The Word Factory," *Wall Street Journal*, 5 June 1972.
7. Ibid.
8. "Harold Robbins: Fact, Fiction and Fantasy," *Biography*, ABC and A&E Television, 1999.
9. *Sunday Express*, 24 February 1974.
10. *Sunday Express*, 3 April 1977.
11. Lewis Gannett, "Books and Things," *New York Herald Tribune*, 2 November 1949.
12. Interview with Michael Korda, 11 May 2004.
13. Parker, "Making Advances."
14. Ibid.
15. Ibid.
16. HR, *The Inheritors*, p. 373.

Chapter 1

Chapter opening: HR, *Never Love a Stranger*, p. 268.
1. "Harold Robbins—I'm the World's Best Writer," *Whicker's World*, ITV, 13 December 1971.
2. "Olivier and the Maid," *Evening Standard*, 10 March 1978.
3. *Never Love a Stranger*, p. 13.
4. "World's Best Writer," *Whicker's World*.
5. Donald Zec, "As He Writes Hollywood Is Trembling," *Sunday Mirror*, 11 September 1977.
6. Denise Abbott, *Beverly Hills [213] Magazine*, 15 January 1986.
7. Philip Oakes, "See It, Feel It, Smell It, Write It," *Sunday Times Magazine*, 13 November 1966.
8. Steven Young, *News of the World Sunday Magazine*, 11 December 1983.
9. Gerry Kroll, "Master Harold," *Advocate*, 22 August 1995.

10. Ian Parker, "Making Advances," *New Yorker*, 1 April 1996.
11. Kroll, "Master Harold."
12. George Christy, "The Great Life," *Hollywood Reporter*, 16 July 1991.
13. *Never Love a Stranger*, p. 283.
14. Marshall Berge, "Home Q & A—Grace and Harold Robbins," *Los Angeles Times Home Magazine*, 22 February 1976.
15. Interview with Diana Jervis-Read, 3 March 2005.
16. Interview with Sylvia Miles, 6 May 2004.
17. Interview with Ini Asmann, 16 May 2005.
18. Interview with Caryn Matchinga, 12 July 2005.
19. Interview with Michael Korda, 11 May 2004.
20. Interview with Steve Shagan, 23 May 2005.
21. Interview with Ken Minns, 21 February 2005.
22. Interview with Father John Lynch, 15 February 2005.
23. Parker, "Making Advances."
24. Interviews with Diana Jervis-Read, 3 March 2005, 8 April 2005.
25. "Harold Robbins: Fact, Fiction & Fantasy," *Biography*, ABC and A&E Television, 1999.
26. Morris Cohen, *A Dreamer's Journey: The Autobiography of Morris Raphael Cohen* (Boston: Beacon Press, 1949), p. 25.
27. Ibid., pp. 25, 27.
28. Ibid., p. 5.
29. Masha Greenbaum, *The Jews of Lithuania: A History of a Remarkable Community, 1316–1945* (Jerusalem: Geffen Publishing, 1995).
30. Cohen, *Dreamer's Journey*, p. 61.
31. Ibid., p. 69.
32. Leslie Goldblatt, *It Was But Yesterday: The Story of a Lithuanian Village* (Johannesburg: Kayon Publishing House, 1951), p. 10.
33. Ibid., p. 13.
34. Ibid., p. 18.
35. Ibid., p. 14.

Chapter 2

Chapter opening: Interview with Steve Shagan, 23 May 2005.
1. HR, *A Stone for Danny Fisher*, p. 12.
2. Samuel Abelown, *History of Brooklyn Jewry* (New York: Scheba Publishers, 1937), p. 12, quoted in Ilana Abramovitch and Sean Galvin, eds., *Jews of Brooklyn* (Hanover, N.H.: University Press of New England, 2002), p. 5.
3. "Harold Robbins: Fact, Fiction and Fantasy," *Biography*: ABC and A&E Television, 1999.
4. Robert A. Rockaway, "Bad Jews: Jewish Criminals from Brooklyn," in Ilana Abramovitch and Sean Galvin, eds., *Jews of Brooklyn* (Hanover, N.H.: University Press of New England, 2002), p. 196.
5. HR, *A Stone for Danny Fisher*, pp. 86–87.
6. HR, *Never Love Stranger*, p. 72.
7. Henderson Herod to author, 22 February 2005.
8. Ibid.
9. Mission statement, City College of New York.
10. HR, *Never Love a Stranger*, p. 339.

11. "Harold Robbins: Fact, Fiction and Fantasy."
12. Ibid.
13. George Washington High School Yearbook, 1934, p. 107.
14. Interview with Sylvia Miles, 6 May 2004.
15. Michael Sheldon, "Life Was Great, Lots of Cash, Cars—and Sex," *Daily Telegraph*, 16 October 1997.
16. "My Favorite Thing," *Esquire*, June 1996.
17. Denise Abbott, *Beverly Hills [213] Magazine*, 15 January 1986.
18. Paul Callan, "£336. That's What Harold Robbins Would Be Paid for Writing This Headline," *Daily Mirror*, 24 October 1980.
19. Herod to author, 22 February 2005.
20. HR, *A Stone for Danny Fisher*, p. 55.
21. Interview with Rae Exelbert, 24 July 2006.
22. George Washington High School Yearbook, 1934, p. 8.
23. Ibid.
24. *New York Post*, 29 November 1949.
25. Philip Oakes, "See It, Feel It, Smell It, Write It," *Sunday Times Magazine*, 13 November 1966.
26. Elizabeth Weiner, "Sex and the Super-Writer," *Coronet*, February 1970.
27. "Harold Robbins: Fact, Fiction and Fantasy."
28. Interview with Steve Shagan, 23 May 2005.
29. HR, *Never Love a Stranger*, p. 241.
30. Harold Robbins, "How All My Dreams Came True," *Mail on Sunday*, 20 May 1984.
31. Oakes, "See It, Feel It."
32. "Harold Robbins—I'm the World's Best Writer," *Whicker's World*, ITV, 13 December 1971.

Chapter 3

Chapter opening: HR, *The Dream Merchants*, p. 94.
1. Interview with Rae Exelbert, 24 July 2006.
2. Interview with HR by Mark Barron, unsourced, 1949.
3. Interview with Steve Shagan, 23 May 2005.
4. Bernard F. Dick, *City of Dreams: The Making and Remaking of Universal Pictures* (Lexington: University Press of Kentucky, 1997), p. 26.
5. Interview with Diana Jervis-Read, 3 March 2005.
6. HR, *The Carpetbaggers*, p. 438.
7. Ibid., p. 453.
8. Knopf publicity sheet bio, 1947, Knopf Archive, Box 1257.9, Harry Ransom Humanities Research Center, University of Texas at Austin (hereinafter HRC).
9. Annie Laurie Williams Collection, Box 109, Rare Book & Manuscript Library, Columbia University, New York. (hereinafter RBML-CU).
10. Denise Abbott, *Beverly Hills Magazine*, 15 January 1988.
11. Alex Hamilton, "Harold Robbins," *Guardian*, 3 January 1975.
12. Interview with Diana Jervis-Read, 3 March 2005.
13. HR, BBC Radio Interview by Clive Jordan, 1 June 1974.
14. Harold Robbins Collection, Box 30, Howard Gotlieb Archival Research Center, Boston University.
15. W.T. Stead, *Echo*, 27 October 1871.

16. Interview with Sylvia Miles, 6 May 2004.
17. "This Is New York, Bill Leonard Reporting," WCBS, 1948, Knopf Archive, Box 1257.12, HRC.
18. Linda Hawkins, "My Simple Life," *Daily Star*, 20 October 1982.
19. Interview with Diana Jervis-Read, 3 March 2005.
20. *New York Post*, 29 November 1949.
21. Martin L. Gross, *Book Digest*, April 1978.
22. Pat Tanner, reader report on *But One Life*, 28 December 1945, Box 20, Maurice Crain Collection, RBML-CU.
23. Ibid.
24. Ibid.
25. Ibid.
26. Lois Dwight Cole, Memo to Pamela Barnes, 28 January 1946, Box 20, Maurice Crain Collection, RBML-CU.
27. Ibid.
28. Harold Strauss, report on *But One Life*, Knopf Archive, Box 1258.2, HRC.
29. Alfred A. Knopf Jr., report on *But One Life*, Knopf Archive, Box 1258.2, HRC.
30. Ibid.
31. Harold Strauss, letter to Mary Squire Abbott, 14 March 1947, Knopf Archive, Box 56.14, HRC.
32. Ian Parker, "Making Advances," *New Yorker*, 1 April 1996.
33. Digby Diehl, *Supertalk* (New York: Doubleday, 1974), pp. 193ff.
34. Harold Strauss, report on *Never Love a Stranger*, 25 June 1947, Knopf Archive, Box 1258.2, HRC.

Chapter 4

Chapter opening: William G. Weart, "9 Novels Cleared, Held Not Obscene," *New York Times*, 19 March 1949.
1. John McNulty, *PM*, 26 January 1948, p. 2.
2. Gerry Kroll, "Master Harold," *Advocate*, 22 August 1995.
3. Harold Robbins public statement, 29 March 1948, Knopf Archive, HRC.
4. "This Is New York, Bill Leonard Reporting," WCBS, undated, Knopf Archive, HRC.
5. *Cosmopolitan*, undated.
6. HR, *Never Love Stranger*, p. 25.
7. Ibid., p. 23.
8. Ibid., p. 33.
9. Ibid., p. 209.
10. Richard O'Connor, "Malefactions and Betrayals," *Philadelphia Bulletin*, 14 March 1948.
11. Francis J. Ullrich, *Publishers Weekly*, 15 May 1948.
12. *Never Love a Stranger* advertisment, *New York Herald Tribune*, 19 March 1948.
13. Isabelle Mallet, "Unruly Local Color," *New York Times Book Review*, 7 March 1948.
14. Orville Prescott, "Books of the Times" *New York Times*, 1 March 1948.
15. Alfred Knopf, letter to Harold Rubin, 6 April 1948, Knopf Archive, Box 56.14, HRC.
16. Digby Diehl, *Supertalk* (New York: Doubleday, 1974), p. 193ff.

17. Maurice Crain, letter to Harold Strauss, 22 July 1948, Knopf Archive, Box 56.14, HRC.
18. Harold Strauss, report on first 81 pages of *The Pioneers*, July 1948, Knopf Archive, Box 962.3, HRC.
19. Harold Strauss, report on *The Pioneers*, 30 September 1948, Knopf Archive, Box 962.2, HRC.
20. Harold Strauss, report on *The Dream Merchants*, 28 March 1949, Knopf Archive, Box 56.14, HRC.
21. Harold Strauss, report on *The Dream Merchants*, 29 April 1949, Knopf Archive, Box 962.2, HRC.
22. Harold Strauss, memo to Joseph Lesser, 19 May 49, Knopf Archive, Box 56.14, HRC.
23. Weart, "9 Novels Cleared."
24. Robert Palm, *Los Angeles Herald-Examiner*, 18 April 1984.

Chapter 5

Chapter opening: Interview with Archer King, 30 April 2004.
1. *New York Post*, 29 November 1949.
2. Harold Strauss letter, to Arthur Farmer, 17 June 1949, Knopf Archive, Box 56.14, HRC.
3. Arthur Farmer, letter to Harold Strauss, 24 June 1949, Knopf Archive, Box 56.14, HRC.
4. Harold Strauss, report on *The Dream Merchants*, 29 April 1949, Knopf Archive, Box 962.2, HRC.
5. Budd Schulberg, "Review of *The Dream Merchants*," *Saturday Review of Literature*, 29 October 1949.
6. *New Yorker*, 29 October 1949.
7. "Hollywood Pulp," *Time*, 24 October 1949.
8. Frank S. Nugent, "Movie-Makers, Without Caricature," *New York Times*, 16 October 1949.
9. *Virginia Kirkus' Bookshop Service Bulletin*, 15 August 1949.
10. Alfred A. Knopf, letter to Harold Rubin, 30 September 1949, Knopf Archive, Box 56.14, HRC.
11. Maurice Crain, letter to John Green at Bodley Head, London, 28 October 1949, Maurice Crain Collection, Box 20, RBML-CU.
12. Interview with Lord Weidenfeld, 11 February 2005.
13. Interview with Archer King, 30 April 2004.
14. Harold Robbins, "Dual Personality," *Hollywood Reporter*, 30 October 1950.
15. Interview with Archer King, 30 April 2004.
16. *Variety*, 22 November 1950.
17. Harold Strauss, report on *A Stone for Danny Fisher*, 7 August 1950, Knopf Archive, Box 1258.2, HRC.
18. Maurice Crain, letter to Harold Strauss, 7 July 1950, Knopf Archive, Box 76.8, HRC.
19. Harold Strauss, report on *A Stone for Danny Fisher*, 7 August 1950, Knopf Archive, Box 1258.2, HRC.
20. Maurice Crain, letter to Harold Robbins, 18 November 1950, Maurice Crain Collection, Box 20, RBML-CU.

21. Harold Strauss, Report on *A Stone for Danny Fisher*, 5 February 1951, Knopf Archive, Box 1258.2, HRC.
22. Ibid.
23. Harold Strauss, notes to Harold Robbins on second draft of *A Stone for Danny Fisher*, Knopf Archive, Box 1258.2, HRC.
24. Harold Strauss, report on fourth version of *A Stone for Danny Fisher*, 27 August 1951, Knopf Archive, Box 1258.2, HRC.
25. Alfred "Pat" Knopf, report on *A Stone for Danny Fisher*, 29 August 1951, Knopf Archive, Box 1258.2, HRC.
26. Harold Strauss, letter to Mr. Preston, 28 August 1951, Knopf Archive, Box 94.2, HRC.
27. HR, *A Stone for Danny Fisher* (New York: Alfred A. Knopf, 1952), front flap.
28. Virginia Kirkus Review, quoted in *New York Times* advertisement for *A Stone for Danny Fisher*, 9 March 1952.
29. *New Yorker*, 15 March 1952.
30. Interview with Sylvia Miles, 6 May 2004.
31. Interview with Archer King, 30 April 2004.

Chapter 6

Chapter opening: Interview with Rose Tobias Shaw, 25 April 2005.
1. Maurice Crain, letter to HR, 18 March 1952, Maurice Crain Collection, Box 20, RBML-CU.
2. HR, *Never Leave Me*, p. 26.
3. Maurice Crain, letter to John Green at Hughes Massie, London, 21 May 1953, Maurice Crain Collection, Box 20, RBML-CU.
4. Maurice Crain, letter to HR, 9 October 1953, Maurice Crain Collection, Box 20, RBML-CU.
5. HR, *Never Leave Me*, p. 62.
6. Interview with Archer King, 5 August 2005.
7. Interview with Sylvia Miles, 6 May 2004.
8. Interview with Archer King, 30 April 2004.
9. Interview with Archer King, 5 August 2005.
10. Harold Robbins, "How All My Dreams Came True," *Mail on Sunday*," 20 May 1984.
11. Harold Strauss, letter to Mrs. Jacobs, 15 June 1954, Knopf Archive, Box 217.12, HRC.
12. Harold Strauss, report on *69 Park Avenue*, 15 June 1954, Knopf Archive, Box 962.2, HRC.
13. Harold Strauss, report on *69 Park Avenue*, 1 July 1954, Knopf Archive, Box 962.2, HRC.
14. Maurice Crain, letter to HR, 15 July 1954, Maurice Crain Collection, Box 20, RBML-CU.
15. Letter from Maurice Crain to HR, 29 July 1954, Maurice Crain Collection, Box 20, RBML-CU.
16. Interview with Archer King, 5 August 2005.
17. Interviews with Rose Tobias Shaw, 18 November 2004, 25 April 2005.
18. *New York Times*, 15 November 1953.
19. Contract, Summer Flood, 2 June 1954, Annie Laurie Williams Collection, Box 109, RBML-CU.

20. Interview with Rose Tobias Shaw, 25 April 2005.
21. Interview with Joseph Sargent, 14 May 2005.
22. Arthur Sainer, *Zero Dances: A Biography of Zero Mostel* (New York: Limelight Editions, 1998), pp. 165ff.
23. Interview with Joseph Sargent, 14 May 2005.
24. Interview with Joseph Sargent, 14 May 2005.
25. Sainer, *Zero Dances* p. 165ff.
26. Interview with Joseph Sargent, 14 May 2005.
27. Brooks Atkinson, "Theater: Crime Play," *New York Times*, 22 October 1954.
28. Interview with Joan Bragin, 12 July 2005.

Chapter 7

Chapter opening: HR, "Wire Service," *Variety*, 5 January 1955.
1. Ibid.
2. Alfred A. Knopf Jr., memo, 2 February 1955, Knopf Archive, Box 962.2, HRC.
3. Harold Strauss, report on *69 Park Avenue*, 31 January 1955, Knopf Archive, Box 962.2, HRC.
4. Ibid.
5. Harold Strauss, letter to HR, 16 February 1955, Knopf Archive, Box 217.12, HRC.
6. Harold Strauss, letter to HR, 12 April 1955, Knopf Archive, Box 217.12, HRC.
7. Harry Buchman, letter to Harold Strauss, 21 February 1955, Knopf Archive, Box 217.12, HRC.
8. Maurice Crain, letter to HR, 17 June 1955, Maurice Crain Collection, Box 20, RBML-CU.
9. HR: *79 Park Avenue* (New York: Knopf, 1955), cover copy.
10. Dom Bruno McAndrew, *Publishers Weekly*, 1 August 1955.
11. *Boston Herald*, 24 July 1955.
12. *Columbus Dispatch*, 31 July 1955.
13. *New Yorker*, 24 September 1955.
14. Luther Nichols, "Story of a 'Party Girl,'" *San Francisco Examiner*, 26 July 1955.
15. *Toledo Blade* (Ohio), 24 July 1955.
16. Alfred A. Knopf, memo to Alfred A. Knopf Jr., 13 July 1955, Knopf Archive, Box 726.1, HRC.
17. Victor M. Orsatti, Sabre Productions, letter to Annie Laurie Williams, 12 October 1955, Anne Laurie Williams Collection, Box 179, RBML-CU.
18. Victor M. Orsatti, letter to Annie Laurie Williams, 22 August 1955, Annie Laurie Williams Collection, Box 179, RBML-CU.
19. Annie Laurie Williams, memo, 13 September 1955, Maurice Crain Collection, Box 20, RBML-CU.
20. HR, *Where Love Has Gone*, p. 34.
21. Elizabeth Weiner, "Sex and the Super-Writer," *Coronet*, February 1970.
22. John Robbins, "100 Million Reasons Why I'm Happy," *Evening News*, 6 July 1972.
23. "Harold Robbins: Fact, Fiction and Fantasy," *Biography*, ABC and A&E Television, 1999.
24. Ian Parker, "Making Advances," *New Yorker*, 1 April 1996.
25. Interview with Steve Shagan, 25 May 2005.
26. Interview with Archer King, 30 April 2005.
27. Annie Laurie Williams, letter to Seymour Nebenzal, with added note from

Pamela Barnes, 26 December 1956, Annie Laurie Williams Collection, Box 109, RBML-CU.

28. William A. Koshland, memo to Alfred A. Knopf, 8 August 1956, Knopf Archive, Box 195.19, HRC.

29. William A. Koshland, memo to Alfred A. Knopf, 11 September 1956, Knopf Archive, Box 195.19, HRC.

30. Pat Knopf, letter to HR, 4 December 1956, Knopf Archive, Box 195.19, HRC.

31. Michael Curtiz, letter to Hal Wallis, 3 May 1955, Hal Wallis Collection, Box 30, Paul Nathan File, Margaret Herrick Library, Academy of Motion Picture Arts and Sciences, Los Angeles. (hereinafter MHL-AMPAS).

32. Ibid.

33. Joseph Hazen, memo to Paul Nathan, 29 April 55, Hal Wallis Collection, Box 30 MHL-AMPAS.

34. Hal Wallis and Charles Higham, *Starmaker: The Autobiography of Hal Wallis* (New York: Macmillan, 1980), p. 150.

35. Geoffrey M. Shurlock, letter to Hal Wallis, 8 November 1957, Hal Wallis Collection, Box 30, Paul Nathan File, MHL-AMPAS.

36. Wallis and Higham, *Starmaker*, p. 150.

37. Barbara Isenberg, "The Word Factory—Author Harold Robbins Churns Out the 'Crud' and Rakes in the Loot," *Wall Street Journal*, 5 June 1972.

Chapter 8

Chapter opening: Donald Zec, " 'Lecher' in Love: How Our Hero Found the One Woman Who Made Peace, Not War," *Sunday Mirror*, 18 September 1977.

1. Interview with Rae Exelbert, 24 July 2006.

2. Pamela Barnes, memo to Jo Feilner, undated, Annie Laurie Williams Collection, Box 109, RBML-CU.

3. William F. Nolan, *McQueen* (New York: Congdon & Weed, 1984), p. 28.

4. Christopher Sandford, *McQueen: The Biography* (New York: Taylor Trade Publishing, 2001), p. 74.

5. Interview with Judy Altman, 7 May 2004.

6. Sandford, *McQueen*, p. 74.

7. Harold Strauss, letter to HR, 12 July 1957, Knopf Archive, Box 217.12, HRC.

8. Maurice Crain, letter to HR, 9 October 1957, Maurice Crain Collection, Box 20, RBML-CU.

9. Harold Strauss, memo to Alfred Knopf Jr., 6 December 1957, Knopf Archive, Box 726.1, HRC.

10. Harold Strauss, memo to Alfred Knopf Jr., 6 December 1957, Knopf Archive, Box 726.1, HRC.

11. Joseph Lesser, memo, 23 July 1958, Knopf Archive, Box 726.1, HRC.

12. William A. Koshland, letter to Harry Buchman, 22 July 1958, Knopf Archive, Box 726.1, HRC.

13. Subpoena, 1 July 1958, Maurice Crain Collection, Box 20, RBML-CU.

14. Emilia Hodel, *San Francisco News*, 16 September 1958.

15. Harold Buchman, letter to HR, 14 November 1958, Knopf Archive, Box 726.1, HRC.

16. William A. Koshland, memo to Harold Strauss, Alfred Knopf, and Joseph Lesser, 17 December 1958, Knopf Archive, Box 726.1, HRC.

17. William A. Koshland, letter to Annie Laurie Williams and Maurice Crain, 11 May 1959, Knopf Archive, Box 268.7, HRC.
18. *Yvonne Robbins v Harold Robbins*, Index 10413/1959, County Clerk and Clerk of the Supreme Court, New York County Court House, New York.
19. Alfred Albelli, "It Was Children's Day in Court—4 Custody Suits Before Justice Capozzoli," *Daily News*, 13 August 1959.
20. Alfred Albelli, "Mom Wins Child of the 'Love Not' Author Who Did," *New York Daily News*, 9 October 1959.
21. Ibid.
22. Zec, " 'Lecher' In Love."
23. HR, *Where Love Has Gone*, p. 22.
24. Zec, " 'Lecher' In Love."
25. "Olivier and the Maid," *Evening Standard*, 10 March 1978.
26. William A. Koshland, memo, 10 November 1959, Knopf Archive, Box 726.1, HRC.
27. William A. Koshland, memo of conversation with Harry Buchman, 4 November 1959, Knopf Archive, Box 726.1, HRC.
28. Ibid.
29. William A. Koshland, memo, 16 November 1959, Knopf Archive, Box 726.1, HRC.
30. Harry Buchman, letter to William A. Koshland, 8 February 1960, Knopf Archive, Box 726.1, HRC.
31. William A. Koshland, memo, 25 January 1960, Knopf Archive, Box 726.1, HRC.
32. Zec, " 'Lecher' in Love."
33. Michael Korda, *Another Life: A Memoir of Other People* (New York: Random House, 1999), p. 107.
34. Ibid.
35. Zec, " 'Lecher' in Love."
36. Harry Buchman, letter to Paul Gitlin, 2 March 1960, Knopf Archive, Box 726.1, HRC.
37. William Koshland, letter to HR, 4 March 1960, Knopf Archive, Box 726.1, HRC.
38. Barnett Glassman, letter to HR, 28 December 1959, Box 39, Harold Robbins Collection, Howard Gotlieb Archival Research Center, Boston University. (hereinafter HGARC-BU).
39. Marc Jaffe, letter to HR, 14 January 1960, Box 39, HR Collection, HGARC-BU.
40. William A. Koshland, memo to Alfred A. Knopf, 1 November 1972, Knopf Archive, Box 889.6, HRC.
41. Alfred A. Knopf, unpublished memoir, p. 1110, Knopf Archive-Box 611.4, HRC.
42. "20,000 Per Cent Increase," *Fortune*, January 1934, p. 51.
43. Korda, *Another Life*, pp. 41, 43.
44. Shimkin, 28 December 1955, quoted in "Reminiscences of Freeman Lewis and Leon Shimkin," Oral History Collection, Columbia University.
45. Korda, *Another Life*, p. 44, 43.
46. Ibid., p. 49.
47. Ibid., p. 50.
48. Ibid.
49. Ibid.
50. Ibid., p. 51.
51. Ibid.

Chapter 9

Chapter opening: HR, *The Inheritors*, p. 189.
1. Interview with Steve Shagan, 23 May 2005.
2. Interview with Michael Korda, 11 May 2004.
3. HR, *The Carpetbaggers*, p. 682.
4. Digby Diehl, *Supertalk* (New York: Doubleday, 1974), pp. 193ff.
5. Interview with Steve Shagan, 23 May 2005.
6. Interview with Carroll Baker, 4 May 2005.
7. HR, *The Carpetbaggers*, p. 13.
8. Ibid., p. 14.
9. Ibid., p. 717.
10. Ibid., p. 14.
11. Ibid., p. 368.
12. Ibid., p. 31.
13. Ibid., p. 57.
14. Ibid., p. 569.
15. Interview with Steve Shagan, 23 May 2005.
16. HR, *The Carpetbaggers*, p. 152.
17. Ibid., p. 712.
18. Ibid., p. 41.
19. Ibid., p. 156.
20. Michael Korda, *Another Life: A Memoir of Other People* (New York: Random House, 1999), p. 125.
21. John Sutherland quoted in Ian Parker, "Making Advances," *New Yorker*, 1 April 1996.
22. Gerry Kroll, "Master Harold," *Advocate*, 22 August 1995.
23. D. H. Lawrence, *A Propos of Lady Chatterley's Lover and Other Essays* (London: Penguin, 1961), p. 99.
24. John Sutherland, *Reading the Decades: Fifty Years of the Nation's Bestselling Books* (London: BBC Worldwide, 2002), p. 51.
25. Murray Schumach, "The Gaudy Career of Jonas Cord Jr.," *New York Times*, 25 June 1961.
26. George Christy, "The Great Life," *Hollywood Reporter*, 16 July 1991.
27. "See No Evil," *Time*, 25 August 1961.
28. Letter from Maurice Crain to Hughes Massie & Co., 13 May 1963, Maurice Crain Collection, Box 20, RBML-CU.
29. Paul Nathan, "Rights and Permissions," *Publishers Weekly*, 2 October 1961.
30. HR, *The Carpetbaggers*, dedication.

Chapter 10

Chapter opening: Interview with Carroll Baker, 4 May 2005.
1. Donald Zec, " 'Lecher' in Love," *Sunday Mirror*, 18 September 1977.
2. Interview with Archer King, 30 April 2004.
3. Margaret Pride, "I Don't Write Dirty Books," RW, 22 July 1972.
4. Trudi Pacter, "Woman with the Solid Gold Fingernails," *Sunday Mirror*, 25 July 1982.
5. Jean Narboni and Tom Milne, eds. *Godard on Godard* (New York: Viking Press, 1972), p. 200; originally published in *Cahiers du Cinema*, 146, August 1963.

6. Interview with Diana Jervis-Read, 8 April 2005.
7. Zec, " 'Lecher' in Love."
8. Ibid.
9. Ibid.
10. "Gay Talese, "Joe Levine Unchained: A Candid Portrait of a Spectacular Showman," *Esquire*, January 1961.
11. Paul O'Neil, "The Super Salesman," *Life*, 27 July 1962.
12. HR, *The Inheritors*, p. 100.
13. Linda Elfman, "Harold Robbins: The Understated Super-Author," *Reporter*, 4 December 1969.
14. HR, *The Inheritors*, p. 158.
15. "Joe Unchained," *Time*, 24 February 1961.
16. Talese, "Joe Levine Unchained."
17. Ibid.
18. Ibid.
19. Stanley Penn, "Show Biz Success: Energetic Joe Levine Climbs Quickly to Top Ranks of Film Makers," *Wall Street Journal*, 22 January 1965.
20. Curtis Kenyon, memo to Martin Rackin, 4 October 1962, Folder 2, *The Carpetbaggers*, Paramount Pictures Corporation Collection, MHL-AMPAS.
21. Interview with John Michael Hayes, 15 July 2004.
22. Ibid.
23. Edward Dmytryk, Paramount press release, 23 August 1963, Folder 9, Paramount Pictures Corporation Collection, MHL-AMPAS.
24. Elizabeth Ashley, letter to author, 9 May 2005.
25. Elizabeth Ashley with Ross Firestone, *Actress: Postcards from the Road* (New York: M. Evans, 1978), p. 33.
26. Edward Dmytryk, *It's a Hell of a Life but Not a Bad Living* (New York: Times Books), 1978.
27. Carroll Baker, *Baby Doll: An Autobiography* (New York: Arbor House, 1983), pp. 218ff.
28. Ibid.
29. Elizabeth Ashley, letter to author, 9 May 2005.
30. Ibid.
31. Beverly Linet, *Ladd: The Life, the Legend, the Legacy of Alan Ladd* (New York: Arbor House, 1979), p. 254.
32. Baker, *Baby Doll*, pp. 218ff.
33. Ibid.
34. Dmytryk, *It's a Hell of a Life*.
35. Baker, *Baby Doll*, pp. 223ff.
36. Interview with Carroll Baker, 4 May 2005.
37. "Low & Inside," *Time*, 3 July 1964.
38. *Daily Variety*, 10 April 1964.
39. Interview with Rae Exelbert, 24 July 2006.

Chapter 11

Chapter opening: Anthony Blond, *The Book Book* (London: Jonathan Cape, 1985), p. 13.
1. Lana Turner, *Lana: The Lady, the Legend, the Truth* (New York: Pocket Books, 1983), p. 240.

2. Michael G. Fitzgerald, *Universal Pictures: A Panoramic History in Words, Pictures and Filmographies* (New Rochelle, N.Y.: Arlington House, 1977), p. 15.
3. "The Garbagepickers," *Time*, 26 October 1962.
4. HR, *Where Love Has Gone*, p. 235.
5. Jane Ellen Wayne, *Lana: The Lives and Loves of Lana Turner* (New York: St. Martin's Press, 1995), p. 137.
6. Ibid.
7. Eric Root with Dale Crawford and Raymond Strait, *The Private Diary of My Life With Lana* (Los Angeles: Dove Books, 1996), pp. 185ff.
8. Folder 9, Press Releases, *Where Love Has Gone*, Paramount Pictures Corporation Collection, MHL-AMPAS.
9. Ibid.
10. Ibid.
11. James Powers, "*Where Love Has Gone* Aims for the Sensation Seekers," *Hollywood Reporter*, 9 October 1964.
12. Blond, *The Book Book*, p. 13.
13. Anthony Blond, *Jew Made in England* (London: Timewell Press, 2004), p. 161.
14. Ibid.
15. "He's Back Making Millions," *Evening News*, 5 February 1964.
16. Interview with Peter Haining, 27 September 2005.
17. Ibid.
18. Blond, *The Book Book*, p. 13.
19. Ibid.
20. Blond, *Jew Made in England*, p. 162.
21. "How to Write One of Those Sexy Novels," *Daily Mail*, 6 February 1964.
22. Peter Grosvenor, "A Fortune in the Bag for the World's Top-Paid Novelist," *Daily Express*, 6 February 1964.
23. Blond, *Jew Made in England*, p. 162.
24. "The Man Who Only Writes Successes," *Daily Sketch*, 6 February 1964.
25. Interview with Diana Jervis-Read, 8 April 2005.
26. Ian Parker, "Making Advances," *New Yorker*, 1 April 1996.
27. Interview with Donald Zec, 26 November 2004.
28. Christopher Sandford, *McQueen: The Biography* (New York: Taylor Trade Publishing, 2001), p. 179.
29. Carroll Baker, *Baby Doll, An Autobiography* (New York: Arbor House, 1983), pp. 223ff.
30. Peter Bart, "One for the Books," *New York Times*, 28 February 1965.
31. David Leeming, *James Baldwin; A Biography* (New York: Knopf, 1994), p. 242.
32. Parker, "Making Advances."
33. Interview with Diana Jervis-Read, 8 April 2005.
34. Interview with Kurt Kreuger, 10 May 2005.
35. Bart, "One for the Books."
36. Declaration of Harold Robbins, 20 February 1997, Court Records, Superior Court of the State of California, County of Riverside.
37. Interview with Peter Haining, 27 September 2005.

Chapter 12

Chapter opening: Philip Oakes, "See It, Feel It, Smell It, Write It," *Sunday Times Magazine*, 13 November 1966.
1. Harold Robbins, "How All My Dreams Came True," *Mail on Sunday*, 20 May 1984.
2. Interview with Caryn Matchinga, 15 July 2005.
3. Robert Musel, "Levine Stuck with $1 Million Novel," *Los Angeles Times*, 4 September 1965.
4. Oakes, "See It, Feel It."
5. Musel, "Levine Stuck."
6. Interview with Peter Haining, 27 September 2005.
7. Interview with Terrence Strong, 31 May 2005.
8. Interview with Judi Schwam Yedor, 11 May 2005.
9. Abel Green, "A Best-Seller King Acts That Way at Party Time," *Variety*, 6 April 1966.
10. "The Adventurers," *Time*, 15 April 1966.
11. Ibid.
12. Dave Kaufman, "*Survivors* Budget 250G Per Episode, TV Record," *Variety*, 20 April 1968.
13. "The Adventurers," *Time*, 15 April 1966.
14. *Evening News*, 1 June 1966.
15. "Mr Robbins on Money," *Daily Mail*, 2 June 1966.
16. *Daily Mirror*, 2 June 1966.
17. Oakes. "See It, Feel It."

Chapter 13

Chapter opening: Thomas Thompson, "The World's Best-Paid Writer," *Life*, 8 December 1967.
1. Interview with Steve Shagan, 23 May 2005.
2. Thompson, "World's Best-Paid Writer."
3. Philip Oakes, "See It, Feel It, Smell It, Write It," *Sunday Times Magazine*, 13 November 1966.
4. *Evening News*, 1 June 1966.
5. Interview with Judi Schwam Yedor, 11 May 2005.
6. Interview with Peter Haining, 27 September 2005.
7. "Harold Robbins's Real-Life Orgies," *New York Post*, 13 April 1999.
8. Army Archerd, "Just for Variety" *Variety*, 4 April 1967.
9. Ibid.
10. Digby Diehl, *Supertalk* (New York: Doubleday, 1974), pp. 193ff.
11. Thompson, "World's Best-Paid Writer."
12. Ibid.
13. Ray Loynd, "A Smart Typewriter," *Los Angeles Herald-Examiner*, 26 November 1967.
14. Marvin Kitman, "Harold Robbins? Sounds like a Million Bucks," *New York Times*, 17 August 1969.
15. Ibid.
16. "Rescuing the Survivors," *Time*, 1 August 1969.

17. Kitman, "Million Bucks."
18. Diehl, *Supertalk*, pp. 193ff.
19. Lana Turner, *Lana: The Lady, the Legend, the Truth* (New York: Pocket Books, 1983), pp. 240–41.
20. Dave Kaufman, "*Survivors* Budget 250G Per Episode," *Variety*, 30 April 1968.
21. Interview with George Hamilton, 5 June 2005.
22. Kaufman, "*Survivors* Budget."
23. Ibid.
24. Cornelius Ryan, Letter to HR, 26 June 1968, Box 8:3, Cornelius Ryan Collection, Mahn Center, Alden Library, Ohio University Athens, OH.
25. Interview with Victoria Ryan Bida, 13 January 2005.
26. Interview with Leslie Bricusse, 14 April 2005.
27. John Skow, "The Harold Robbins Co.," *Playboy*, December 1969.
28. Interview with George Hamilton, 5 June 2005.
29. Interview with Martin Starger, 30 March 2005.
30. Interview with Grant Tinker, 13 May 2005.
31. Interview with Tim Vignoles, 16 October 2006.
32. Interview with George Hamilton, 5 June 2005.
33. Interview with Grant Tinker, 13 May 2005.
34. Jeanne Miller, "How He Met His Wife—Like a Robbins Novel," *San Francisco Examiner*, 26 November 1969.
35. Interview with Grant Tinker, 13 May 2005.
36. "Rescuing the Survivors," *Time*, 1 August 1969.

Chapter 14

Chapter opening: Interview with Michael Mewshaw, 21 July 2005.
1. Michael Mewshaw, *Do I Owe You Something? A Memoir of Literary Life* (Baton Rouge: Louisiana State University Press, 2003), p. 69.
2. Ibid., p. 73.
3. Interview with Michael Mewshaw, 21 July 2005.
4. Ibid.
5. Ibid.
6. HR, *The Inheritors*, pp. 381–82.
7. *Daily Express*, 20 January 1970.
8. Interview with Steve Shagan, 23 May 2005.
9. Stirling Silliphant, letter to HR, 22 July 1969, Stirling Silliphant Papers, Collection 134, Box 49, Folder 2, UCLA Arts Library Special Collections.
10. Stirling Silliphant, telegram to HR, undated, Stirling Silliphant Papers, Box 49, Folder 2, UCLA.
11. Stirling Silliphant, letter to HR, 22 July 1969, Stirling Silliphant Papers, Box 49, Folder 2, UCLA.
12. Interview with Diana Jervis-Read, 3 March 2005.
13. Interview with Diana Jervis-Read, 8 April 2005.
14. Interview with Quincy Jones, 24 May 2005.
15. Interview with Alex Cord, 11 April 2005.
16. Diana Jervis-Read, letter to author, 29 August 2006.
17. Interview with Diana Jervis-Read, 3 March 2005.
18. Linda Elfman, "The Understated Super-Author," *Reporter*, 4 December 1969.
19. Interview with Caryn Matchinga, 15 July 2005.

20. Interview with Diana Jervis-Read, 27 July 2006.
21. Ivan Sandof, *Worcester Gazette*, 12 November 1969.
22. Benn Friedman, "From My Point of View," *Philadelphia Jewish Times*, 20 November 1969.
23. Interview with Diana Jervis-Read, 3 March 2005.
24. Deac Rossell, "Robbins: Where the Bread's At," *Boston After Dark*, 3 December 1969.
25. *The Inheritors*, uncorrected proof copy, Stirling Silliphant Papers, Collection 134, Box 49, Folder 1, UCLA Arts Library Special Collections.
26. HR, *The Inheritors*, p. 165.
27. Ivan Sandof, *Worcester Gazette*, 12 November 1969.
28. HR, *The Inheritors*, p. 281.
29. Barbara Seaman, *Lovely Me: The Life of Jacqueline Susann* (London: Sedgwick & Jackson, 1988), p. 318.
30. Ivan Sandof, *Worcester Gazette*, 12 November 1969.
31. "Writing a Novel in 25 Awful Stages," *Daily Express*, 7 August 1969.
32. *New York Times*, August 7, 1969.
33. Seaman, *Lovely Me*, pp. 334–35.
34. Paul Nathan, "Rights and Permissions," *Publishers Weekly*, 17 November 1969.
35. Herb Green, "The Magic Money Machine," *San Francisco Chronicle*, 28 November 1969.

Chapter 15

Chapter opening: "Harold Robbins—I'm the World's Best Writer," *Whicker's World*, ITV, 13 December 1971.
1. "Surviving the Survivors," *Daily Mirror*, 15 January 1970.
2. Graham Lord, "I'm the Best Writer Around, says Harold Robbins," *Sunday Express*, 26 April 1970.
3. Vernon Scott, United Press International, 1971.
4. "Surviving the Survivors," *Daily Mirror*.
5. Interview with Jackie Minns, 28 July 2005.
6. Interview with Ken Minns, 21 February 2005.
7. "Overworked Organ," *Time*, 30 March 1970.
8. Interview with Diana Jervis-Read, 3 March 2005.
9. Lord, "I'm the Best Writer Around," *Sunday Express*.
10. Ibid.
11. Joyce Haber, "Writes One Style, But Lives Another," *Los Angeles Times*, 2 June 1970.
12. Cari Beauchamp and Henri Behar, *Hollywood on the Riviera: The Inside Story of the Cannes Film Festival* (New York: William Morrow, 1992), p. 146.
13. Hormoz Sabet, letters to author, 29 September 2005, 14 October 2005.
14. Interview with Martin Starger, 30 March 2005.
15. Ibid.
16. Donald Zec, "Mr Robbins Has It All in the Bag," *Daily Mirror*, 30 July 1970.
17. Cornelius Ryan and Kathryn Morgan Ryan, *A Private Battle* (London: New English Library, 1980), p. 232.
18. Interview with Victoria Ryan Bida, 13 January 2005.
19. Interview with Geoff Ryan, 7 January 2005.
20. Press release, *The Peacemaker*, Cornelius Ryan Collection, Box 5:2. Mahn Center, Alden Library, Ohio University.

21. Cornelius Ryan, Synopsis of *The Peacemaker*, Cornelius Ryan Collection, ibid., reproduced courtesy of Geoff Ryan and Victoria Ryan Bida.

22. Letter from Cornelius Ryan to Paul Gitlin, 16 February 1971, Cornelius Ryan Collection, ibid., reproduced courtesy of Geoff Ryan and Victoria Ryan Bida.

23. Ryan and Ryan, *Private Battle*, p. 232.

24. Cornelius Ryan, letter to HR, 5 January 1972, Cornelius Ryan Collection, Box 5:2, reproduced courtesy of Geoff Ryan and Victoria Ryan Bida.

25. Interview with Victoria Ryan Bida, 13 January 2005.

26. Interview with Geoff Ryan, 7 January 2005.

27. Interview with Alden Schwimmer, 2 March 2005.

28. Interview with Caryn Matchinga, 15 July 2005.

29. Interview with Steve Shagan, 23 May 2005.

30. Alden Schwimmer, letter to Edwin Appel, 5 October 1971, Business Projections, Bruce Geller Collection, Box 1, Folder 1, UCLA Arts Library Special Collections.

31. Bill Orstein, "Harold Robbins Expands Interests in Film and TV," *Hollywood Reporter*, 28 December 1971.

32. Digby Diehl, *Supertalk* (New York: Doubleday, 1974), pp. 193ff.

33. "Harold Robbins—I'm the World's Best Writer," *Whicker's World*, ITV, 13 December 1971.

34. Interview by Clive Jordan, BBC Radio, 1 June 1974.

35. Barbara Isenberg, "Author Harold Robbins Churns out the 'Crud' and Rakes in the Loot," *Wall Street Journal*, 5 June 1972.

36. Interview with Francine Greshler Feldmann, 8 May 2005.

37. Vernon Scott, United Press International, 1971.

38. Harlan Ellison, "*The Betsy* Tests the Devotion of Robbins Fans," *Los Angeles Times*, 28 November 1971.

39. "Olivier and the Maid," *Evening Standard*, 10 March 1978.

Chapter 16

Chapter opening: Doris Klein Bacon, "Happy: France Has the Mitterrand Jitters, but Harold Robbins Is Making Out like a Pirate," *People*, 24 August 1981.

1. Interview with Patrick Young, 28 March 2006.

2. Interview with Caryn Matchinga, 15 July 2005.

3. Interview with Larry Flynt, 17 May 2005.

4. Steven Young, *News of the World Sunday Magazine*, 11 December 1983.

5. HR, *The Inheritors*, p. 342.

6. Interview with Diana Jervis-Read, 3 March 2005.

7. Barbara Isenberg, "The Word Factory: Author Harold Robbins Churns Out the 'Crud' and Rakes in the Loot, *Wall Street Journal*, 5 June 1972.

8. "Harold Robbins: An Industry," *Variety*, 28 June 1972.

9. Margaret Pride, "I Don't Write Dirty Books," *RW*, 22 July 1972.

10. Will Tusher, "Robbins Distribution Deal: Better Deal for Producers?," *Hollywood Reporter*, 3 June 1972.

11. James Bacon, "Harold Robbins: No Struggling Author Is He," *Los Angeles Herald-Examiner*, 12 November 1972.

12. John Robbins, "100 Million Reasons Why I'm Happy," *Evening News*, 6 July 1972.

13. "Dark Side of Mr Robbins," *Daily Mail*, 6 July 1972.
14. Cornelius Ryan, telegram, to HR, 8 August 1972, Cornelius Ryan Collection, Mahn Center, Alden Library, Ohio University.
15. Army Archerd, "Just for Variety," *Variety*, 13 April 1973.
16. Interview with Alden Schwimmer, 2 March 2005.
17. Interview with Norma Barzman, 17 March 2005.
18. Norma Barzman, *The Red and the Blacklist: The Intimate Memoir of a Hollywood Expatriate* (New York: Nation Books, 2003), p. 367.
19. Interview with Norma Barzman, 17 March 2005.
20. Barzman, *Red and Blacklist*, p. 368.
21. Bacon, "No Struggling Author."
22. James Bacon, "Robbins Starts the New Year Write," *Los Angeles Herald-Examiner*, 2 January 1973.
23. Interview with Richard Bradford, 23 March 2005.
24. Interview with Paulene Stone, 25 April 2005.
25. Paulene Stone with Peter Evans, *One Tear Is Enough* (London: Michael Joseph, 1975), p. 163.
26. Interview with Richard Bradford, 23 March 2005.
27. Interview with Victor Lownes, 6 May 2005.
28. Soraya Khashoggi, letter to author, 21 September 2006.
29. Interview with Adnan Khashoggi, 14 August 2006.
30. Soraya Khashoggi, letters to author, 28 October 2006, 1 December 2006.
31. HR, Interview by Clive Jordan, BBC Radio, 1 June 1974.
32. Interview with George Chakiris, 12 May 2005.
33. Martin Walker, "Walking Planks," *Guardian*, 10 October 1974.
34. Ibid.
35. "Big and Brash," *Evening Standard*, 8 October 1974.
36. Philip Jacobsen, "The Pirate and Miss X," *Sunday Times*, 6 October 1974.
37. Interview with Adnan Khashoggi, 14 August 2006.
38. Interview with Caryn Matchinga, 15 July 2005.
39. Soraya Khashoggi, letter to author, 25 September 2006.
40. Soraya Khashoggi, letter to author, 25 November 2006.
41. Parkinson, BBC1, 12 October 1974.
42. Interview with Caryn Matchinga, 15 July 2005.
43. Interview with Diana Jervis-Read, 8 April 2005.
44. Soraya Khashoggi, letters to author, 25 November, 1 December 2006.

Chapter 17

Chapter opening: Interview with Steve Jaffe, 8 May 2005.
1. *Sun*, 26 October 1974.
2. Interview with Caryn Matchinga, 15 July 2005.
3. Ibid.
4. Ibid.
5. HR, *The Lonely Lady*, p. 399.
6. Donald Zec, " 'Lecher' in Love: How Our Hero Found the One Woman Who Made Peace, Not War," *Sunday Mirror*, 18 September 1977.
7. *Read All About It*, BBC TV, 10 April 1977.
8. Interview with Caryn Matchinga, 15 July 2005.
9. Alex Hamilton, "Harold Robbins," *Guardian*, 3 January 1975.

10. Dave Smith, "Calendar for the Man Who Has Everything," *Los Angeles Times*, 3 December 1975.
11. Interview with Rona Barrett, 11 May 2005.
12. Marshall Berges, "Home Q & A—Grace and Harold Robbins," *Los Angeles Times Magazine*, 22 February 1976.
13. Ibid.
14. Interview with Red Buttons, 12 May 2005.
15. Ted Ashley, letter to Hal Wallis, 27 May 1976, Box 31, *A Stone for Danny Fisher*, Hal Wallis Collection, MHL-AMPAS.
16. "Robbins's *Pirate* Goes Independent," *Hollywood Reporter*, 11 May 1976.
17. "Sheiking the Bottom of the Barrel," *Daily Mail*, 4 September 1979.
18. Interview with Ken Annakin, 17 March 2005.
19. Interview with Steve Jaffe, 8 May 2005.
20. "Here Soon. Harold Robbins's Latest (and Shortest) Novel," *Daily Mirror*, 1 June 1983

Chapter 18

Chapter opening: HR, *Dreams Die First*, p. 216.

1. Sandra Hochman, "Harold Robbins Never Met a Celebrity He Couldn't Turn Into a Best-Seller," *People*, 19 July 1976.
2. Michael Korda, *Another Life: A Memoir of Other People* (New York: Random House, 1999), p. 127.
3. Ibid., p. 111.
4. Interview with Michael Korda, 11 May 2004.
5. Korda, *Another Life*, p. 129.
6. HR, *Dreams Die First*, p. 194.
7. Ibid., p. 70.
8. Ibid., p. 36.
9. Interview with Michael Korda, 11 May 2004.
10. Interview with Steve Shagan, 23 May 2005.
11. "A Bad Case Makes Worse Law," *Time*, 21 February 1977.
12. Interviews with Larry Flynt, 30 March 2005, 17 May 2005.
13. *Los Angeles Times*, 11 April 1977.
14. *Canyon Crier*, 18 April 1977.
15. Jean Rook, "At £28 a Word, He's the Man with the Golden Typewriter," *Daily Express*, 15 April 1977.
16. Rook, "At £28 a Word."
17. Ken Minns, diary, entry for 3 June 1977.
18. Interview with Caryn Matchinga, 15 July 2005.
19. Ken Minns, diary, entry for 13 June 1977.
20. Interview with Jackie Minns, 28 July 2005.
21. Donald Zec, "As He Writes Hollywood Is Trembling," *Sunday Mirror*, 11 September 1977.
22. Ibid.
23. Peter Lewis, "Enough to Make Fanny Hill Blush," *Daily Mail*, 17 November 1977.
24. Jane Perlez, "Dirty Harold's Dream Market," *New York Times*, 9 December 1977.

Chapter 19

Chapter opening: William Hall, "The Christian Martyr with a Message of Sex and Sin," *Evening News*, 19 May 1978.

1. Interview with Tony Rullan, 27 March 2006.
2. Interview with Patrick Young, 28 March 2006.
3. Interview with Leslie Bricusse, 14 April 2005.
4. Interview with Steve Shagan, 23 May 2005.
5. Interview with Nicholas Dominguez, 28 March 2006.
6. Interview with Esteban Matison, 28 March 2006.
7. Interview with Patrick Young, 28 March 2006.
8. Mary Wells Lawrence, *A Big Life* (New York: Simon & Schuster, 2002), p. 98.
9. Interview with Tony Rullan, 27 March 2006.
10. Martha Moody, "Beverly Hills Seasons: Around Town with Mrs. Harold Robbins," *Los Angeles Times*, 5 November 1978.
11. Martin L. Gross, *Book Digest*, April 1978.
12. Martin Levin, "More of the Same," *New York Times*, 18 November 1979.
13. Sue Arnold, "Muscling In on Harold," *Observer*, 11 November 1979.
14. Interview with Sue Arnold, 22 March 2005.
15. Interview with Ini Asmann, 16 May 2005.
16. HR, *Goodbye, Janette*, p. 99.
17. Paul Callan, "£336. That's What Harold Robbins Would Be Paid for Writing This Headline," *Daily Mirror*, 24 October 1980.
18. Steven Young, *News of the World* Sunday Magazine, 11 December 1983.
19. Deborah Moggach "The Clones That Feather Robbins's Nest," *Daily Mail*, 30 April 1981.
20. "Coverline," *Cosmopolitan*, August 1981.
21. Peter Andrews, "Bad Smut," *New York Times*, 7 June 1981.
22. David Thomson, "Harold Robbins Goes Bob, Bob, Bobbin' Along," *Playgirl*, October 1981.
23. Lee A. Salem, "Devil of a Time at Novelist's Party," *Los Angeles Times*, 22 May 1981.
24. George Christy, "The Great Life," *Hollywood Reporter*, 12 June 1981.
25. Scott Haller, "The World's Five Best-Selling Authors," *Saturday Review*, March 1981.
26. Interview with Caryn Matchinga, 15 July 2005.
27. Interview with Ken Minns, 21 February 2005.
28. Ken Minns, diary, Summer 1981.
29. Doris Klein Bacon, "Happy: France Has the Mitterrand Jitters, But Harold Robbins Is Making Out like a Pirate," *People*, 24 August 1981.
30. Digby Diehl, "Harold Robbins Spits in Eye of Moral Majority," *Los Angeles Herald-Examiner*, 29 December 1982.

Chapter 20

Chapter opening: "Out to Lunch," *Sunday Express Magazine*, 21 January 1990.

1. Norma Barzman, *The Red and the Blacklist: The Intimate Memoir of a Hollywood Expatriate* (New York: Nation Books, 2004), p. 427.
2. Ben and Norma Barzman, *Rich Dreams* (New York: Warner Books, 1982), pp. 36, 39.

3. Ibid. p. 38

4. Interview with Norma Barzman, 17 March 2005.

5. Trudi Packer, "Woman with the Solid Gold Fingernails," *Sunday Mirror*, 25 July 1982.

6. Ann Oldenburg, "A New Chapter for Robbins's Widow," *USA Today*, 21 August 1998.

7. Ian Parker, "Making Advances," *New Yorker*, 1 April 1996.

8. Michael Sheldon, "Life Was Great, Lots of Cash, Cars—and Sex," *Daily Telegraph*, 16 October 1997.

9. "My Favorite Thing," *Esquire*, June 1996.

10. "Gotta Lotta Oxygen Bottle," *Observer*, 16 October 1982.

11. *Bookshelf*, BBC Radio Four, 24 October 1982.

12. Interview with Karen Russell, 23 May 2005.

13. Steven Young, *News of the World Sunday Magazine*, 11 December 1983.

14. Ian Parker, "Making Advances," *New Yorker*, 1 April 1996.

15. "Robbins Novel Attacked by Tory MP," *Times*, 17 July 1985.

16. "Robbins Book 'Trash,'" *Daily Mail*, 17 July 1985.

17. Young, *News of the World Sunday Magazine*.

18. Interview with Michael Korda, 11 May 2004.

19. Michael Korda, *Another Life: A Memoir of Other People* (New York: Random House), p. 125.

20. Parker, "Making Advances."

21. Michelle Green and Doris Klein Bacon, "Sequel: Paperback King Harold Robbins Writes an Almost Happy Ending to a Battle with Excruciating Pain," *People*, 31 October 1988.

22. Robert Palm, *Los Angeles Herald-Examiner*, 18 April 1984.

23. HR, *The Inheritors*, p. 334.

24. Dick Lochte, "Remembering Harold Robbins," *Salon*, 16 October 1997.

25. HR, *The Storyteller*, p. 180.

26. Ibid., p. 67.

Chapter 21

Chapter opening: Interview with Yolande Guest, 3 May 2005.

1. "Cancer Fear for Robbins," *Evening News*, 30 October 1986.

2. Michelle Green and Doris Klein Bacon, "Sequel: Paperback King Harold Robbins Writes an Almost Happy Ending to a Battle with Excruciating Pain," *People*, 31 October 1988.

3. Interview with Carroll Baker, 4 May 2005.

4. Interview with Bob Pollock, 9 May 2005.

5. Green and Bacon, "Sequel."

6. Ed Weiner, "Nibbled to Death in the Amazon," *New York Times*, 7 July 1991.

7. Ibid.

8. Val Hennessy, "A Dislikeable Fish Called Wanton," *Daily Mail*, 20 June 1991.

9. Interview with Michael Korda, 11 May 2004.

10. Matias Viegener, letter to author, 21 June 2006.

11. Roz Kaveney, letter to author, 9 July 2006.

12. Monique P. Yazigi, "Alter Egos Who Put the 'R' In RSVP," *New York Times*, 5 December 1999.

13. Interview with Ini Asmann, 16 May 2005.

14. Elizabeth Venant, "One for the Books: Harold Robbins, the Icon of Sleaze, Is Back—and He's as Nasty as Ever," *Los Angeles Times*, 31 May 1991.
15. "Harold Robbins's Real-Life Orgies," *New York Post*, 13 April 1999.
16. *Evening Standard*, 14 June 1991.
17. Interview with Ini Asmann, 16 May 2005.
18. Interview with Nicholas Dominguez, 28 March 2006.
19. Ian Parker, "Making Advances," *New Yorker*, 1 April 1996.
20. *Newsweek*, 1 July 1991.
21. George Christy, "The Great Life," *Hollywood Reporter*, 16 July 1991.
22. Interview with Judi Schwam Yedor, 11 May 2005.
23. Interviews with Val and Yolande Guest, 3 May 2005.
24. Interview with Yolande Guest, 3 May 2005.
25. Bettijane Levine, "Older and Wiser," *Los Angeles Times*, 15 March 1995.
26. Declaration of Harold Robbins, *Lillian Rubin v Harold Robbins*, case number 250934, Superior Court of the State of California, County of Riverside.
27. Interview with Ini Asmann, 16 May 2005.
28. Interview with Ian Parker, 5 May 2004.
29. Parker, "Making Advances."
30. Interview with Colin Webster-Watson, 26 July 2006.
31. Ann Oldenburg, "A New Chapter for Robbins's Widow," *USA Today*, 21 August 1998.
32. Judi Schwam Yedor, letter to author, 30 July 2006.
33. Poem about Harold Robbins, reproduced by kind permission of Colin Webster-Watson.
34. Obituary of HR, *New York Times*, 15 October 1997.
35. Obituary of HR, *Daily Telegraph*, 15 October 1997.
36. *Independent*, 16 October 1997.
37. Neil Norman, "Exit the Godfather," *Evening Standard*, 15 October 1997.
38. John Sutherland, "Sex, Schlock and Spectacular Sales," *Guardian*, 16 October 1997.
39. Obituary of HR, *Times* (London), 16 October 1997.
40. Jackie Collins, "Eulogy," *Time*, 27 October 1997.
41. Karren Brady, "Bonkbuster Harold Really Was a Class Act!," *Sunday Mirror*, 19 October 1997.
42. Wayne Koestenbaum, "Harold Robbins," *New York Times*, 4 January 1998.
43. "But Is It Art?," *Evening Standard*, 16 October 1997.
44. Steven Young, "Out to Lunch," *Sunday Express Magazine*, 21 January 1990.
45. Ini Asmann, letter to author, 4 March 2003.
46. Ann Oldenburg, "A New Chapter for Robbins's Widow," *USA Today*, 21 August 1998.
47. Alex Hamilton, "Harold Robbins," *Guardian*, 3 January 1975.

ACKNOWLEDGMENTS

My interest in Harold Robbins began when I was in my early teens. With my parents' approval I would borrow his novels from the local library or use my pocket money to buy one of his racy best sellers. So the first—and biggest—thank you has to go to my mother and father, who let me devour his risqué novels even when they probably knew it was hardly "improving" literature.

I owe a great deal to Clare Alexander, my agent at Gillon Alexander Associates in London, who helped me at the onset and at innumerable stages along the way, as well as everyone at the agency, in particular Lesley Thorne and Sally Riley. A huge thank you is also due to Liz Calder at Bloomsbury UK and Colin Dickerman and Karen Rinaldi at Bloomsbury USA, who commissioned the book. At Bloomsbury I would also like to thank the wonderful Jenny Parrott, Erica Jarnes, Kate Bland, Colin Midson, Ruth Logan, Victoria Millar, Miles Doyle, Alan J. Kaufman, Greg Villepique, and the brilliant teams on both sides of the Atlantic.

Although Robbins did not leave what could be called a substantial archive, what does exist—mainly the manuscript copies of his novels—is expertly preserved at the Howard Gotlieb Archival Research Center, Boston University. I would like to thank the late Dr. Howard Gotlieb, archivist J. C. Johnson, and associate director Sean Noel for allowing me access to the Robbins and Joseph E. Levine collections.

The first part of this book could not have been written without consulting the vast Alfred A. Knopf archive held at the Harry Ransom Humanities Research Center, University of Texas, Austin. For access and help I would like to thank Tara Wenger and Richard Workman, and for reproduction of the material I must acknowledge the Harry

Ransom Humanities Research Center itself, which holds the copyright of the Knopf files.

Equal in measure is the help I received from the Rare Book & Manuscript Library at Columbia University, which holds the collections of Maurice Crain, Robbins's literary agent, and of Annie Laurie Williams, the writer's drama and motion picture rights agent; and the archives of Simon & Schuster. These resources proved invaluable. Thank you to Tara C. Craig, Jennifer B. Lee, and Tanya Chebotarev for their help with my research and for permission to reproduce the material.

I would also like to thank Julie Graham and Lauren Buisson at the Arts Library Special Collections of UCLA for access and use of material from the archives of Bruce Geller and Stirling Silliphant as well as the scripts of the television series *The Survivors*. I also consulted and quoted material—such as the impressive Hal Wallis archive and the Paramount Pictures Corporation Collection—held in the special collections department of the Margaret Herrick Library, Academy of Motion Picture Arts and Sciences, Beverly Hills. Thanks to Barbara Hall and Jenny Romero.

For the reproduction of previously unpublished copyright material of Cornelius and Kathy Ryan I would like to thank their two children, Victoria Ryan Bida and Geoff Ryan. Thank you too to George Bain and Doug McCabe at the Robert E. and Jean R. Mahn Center for Archives & Special Collections, Ohio University Libraries, Athens, for sending me the correspondence between Robbins and Ryan.

Use of Patrick Dennis's unpublished report on Robbins's first novel, *Never Love a Stranger* (or *But One Life*, as it was originally called), is reproduced by kind permission of New York literary agent Ray Power. The poem cited at the end of the book is reproduced by the kind permission of Colin Webster-Watson.

Other libraries, organizations, and archives that provided information and help include the Archive of American Television, Los Angeles; the BBC Written Archives Centre, Berkshire (Erin O'Neill); BBC Information & Archives, London (Helen Turner); the British Library, London; the British Library National Sound Archive, London; the Brooklyn Historical Society Library; the Brooklyn Public Library; school records of George Washington High School, New York; the National Film & Television Archive, London (Sue Woods); the New

York Public Library; the New York County Supreme Court, Manhattan; the New-York Historical Society; the New York Genealogical & Biographical Society; the New York Foundling Hospital; the Museum of Television and Radio, New York (Shu-Lin Lee); the Norwalk Public Library (Luis Ayala); the records of the Superior Court of the State of California, county of Riverside; the Los Angeles Public Library; and the records of Mount Zion Cemetery, Maspeth, New York.

The mystery surrounding Robbins's origins could not have been solved had it not been for information provided by New York–based genealogical expert Jordan Auslander. I must also thank my close friend the Mexico-based writer Barbara Kastelein, who helped me research Acapulco's glittering social scene and put me in touch with many of Robbins's friends from the "pearl of the Pacific."

Oral testimonies form a central part of this book, and I would like to thank each of my interviewees for their memories. In particular I owe a great deal to Diana Jervis-Read, Robbins's secretary, executive assistant, and good friend, who gave up many hours of her time to talk to me and put me in contact with Robbins's network of close friends.

Some of the following granted interviews; others wrote letters or e-mails, or helped secure important pieces of information (certain individuals not named here expressed a wish for anonymity, which was granted): Judi Altman, Ken Annakin, Sue Arnold, Elizabeth Ashley, Ini Asmann, Carroll Baker, Rona Barrett, Norma Barzman, Victoria Ryan Bida, Lisa Bishop, Susan Blakely, Anthony Blond, Richard Bradford, Joan Bragin, Leslie Bricusse, Red Buttons, George Chakiris, Ann Coates, Alex Cord, Dick Delson, Steven DeRosa, Nicholas Dominguez, Dominick Dunne, Father Michael Eveden, Rae Exelbert, Francine Feldmann, Larry Flynt, Jonathan Gitlin, Yolande and Val Guest, Gene Gutowski, John Michael Hayes, Peter Haining, George Hamilton, Henderson Herod, Dolores Hicks, Evan Hunter, Steve Jaffe, Quincy Jones, Roz Kaveney, Adnan Khashoggi, Soraya Khashoggi, Archer King, Michael Korda, Kurt Kreuger, Mary Wells Lawrence, Ruth League, Joseph Lisbona, Dick Lochte, Victor Lownes and Marilyn Cole Lownes, Caryn Matchinga, Robin McGibbon, Esteban Matison, Michael Mewshaw, Lita Milan, Sylvia Miles, Jackie and Ken Minns, Arlene Mintzer, Eric Myers, Ian Parker, Marci Press, Bob Pollock, Diana Jervis-Read, Tony Rullan, Karen Russell, Geoff Ryan, Samir Saab, Hormoz Sabet,

Frank Sanello, Joseph Sargent, Alden Schwimmer, Barbara Seaman, Steve Shagan, Rose Tobias Shaw, Sidney Sheldon, Rochelle Skala, Michael Silberkleit, Martin Starger, Paulene Stone, Terrence Strong, Bob Tanner, Grant Tinker, Matias Viegener, Tim Vignoles, Colin Webster-Watson, Lord Weidenfeld, Robert Whalen, Alan Whicker, Judi Schwam Yedor, Patrick Young, and Donald Zec.

I used a wide number of books, journals, and newspaper and magazine articles, all of which have been referenced in the endnotes. However, I would like to highlight the following: Thomas Thompson, "The World's Best-Paid Writer," *Life*, 8 December 1967; Donald Zec, "As He Writes Hollywood Is Trembling," *Sunday Mirror*, 11 September 1977, and " 'Lecher' in Love: How Our Hero Found the One Woman Who Made Peace, Not War," *Sunday Mirror*, 18 September 1977; and Ian Parker, "Making Advances," *The New Yorker*, 1 April 1996.

Acknowledgment is also due to a number of broadcast sources, including: *Parkinson*, BBC1, 12 October 1974; interview with Clive Jordan, BBC Radio, 1 June 1974; *Read All About It*, BBC, 10 April 1977; *Bookshelf*, BBC Radio Four, 24 October 1982; "Harold Robbins: Fact, Fiction and Fantasy," *Biography*, ABC and A&E Television, 1999.

For use of the photographs in the book I am grateful to George Washington High School; Harry Ransom Humanities Research Center, University of Texas at Austin; Arlene Mintzer and Rae Exelbert; Leonard Detrick, *New York Daily News*; Howard Gotlieb Archival Research Center, Boston University; Diana Jervis-Read; Victoria Ryan Bida and Geoff Ryan; Ken and Jackie Minns; and Ini Asmann, whose collection of unpublished photographs form a central part of the book's illustrations.

Finally I would like to thank the following for their friendship and hospitality. In New York: Christopher Fletcher and Susan Shaw, Tanith Carey, Susan Hobson and William Stingone, Kate Kingsley Skattebol, Fred Bernstein. In Mexico: Barbara Kastelein, Miguel A. Muñoz (Boca Chica hotel, Acapulco), Ron Lavender, Tony Rullan, Manuel Diaz at the Mexico Tourism Board, London, and Andy Pietrasik of the *Guardian*. In the South of France: Jackie and Ken Minns. In Los Angeles: Sarah McBride, Catherine Elsworth, Rachel Himbury, Philippa Bender, Marc Lavine. In London and Spain, all my friends, and one in particular: Marcus Field.

INDEX

A NOTE ON THE AUTHOR

Andrew Wilson is the author of *Beautiful Shadow: A Life of Patricia Highsmith*, which won the Mystery Writers of America Edgar Allan Poe Award for Best Critical Biography, and the novel *The Lying Tongue*. He lives in London and Spain.

A NOTE ON THE TYPE

The text of this book is set in Linotype Sabon, named after
the type founder Jacques Sabon. It was designed by Jan Tschichold
and jointly developed by Linotype, Monotype, and Stempel
in response to a need for a typeface to be available in identical
form for mechanical hot metal composition and hand
composition using foundry type.

Tschichold based his design for Sabon roman on a font engraved
by Garamond, and Sabon italic on a font by Granjon. It was
first used in 1966 and has proved an enduring modern classic.